The Gospel of Kindness

The Gospel of Kindness

Animal Welfare and the Making of Modern America

JANET M. DAVIS

OXFORD
UNIVERSITY PRESS

OXFORD
UNIVERSITY PRESS

Oxford University Press is a department of the University of Oxford. It furthers the University's objective of excellence in research, scholarship, and education by publishing worldwide. Oxford is a registered trade mark of Oxford University Press in the UK and certain other countries.

Published in the United States of America by Oxford University Press
198 Madison Avenue, New York, NY 10016, United States of America.

© Oxford University Press 2016

First issued as an Oxford University Press paperback, 2020

All rights reserved. No part of this publication may be reproduced, stored in a retrieval system, or transmitted, in any form or by any means, without the prior permission in writing of Oxford University Press, or as expressly permitted by law, by license, or under terms agreed with the appropriate reproduction rights organization. Inquiries concerning reproduction outside the scope of the above should be sent to the Rights Department, Oxford University Press, at the address above.

You must not circulate this work in any other form
and you must impose this same condition on any acquirer.

Library of Congress Cataloging-in-Publication Data
Names: Davis, Janet M., author.
Title: The gospel of kindness : animal welfare and the making of modern America / Janet M. Davis.
Description: Oxford ; New York : Oxford University Press, [2016] | Includes index.
Identifiers: LCCN 2015043336 (print) | LCCN 2016002418 (ebook) |
ISBN 978-0-19-973315-6 (hardback) | ISBN 978-0-19-009244-3 (paperback) |
ISBN 978-0-19-991132-5 (Epub) | ISBN 978-0-19-990888-2 (Updf)
Subjects: LCSH: Animal welfare—United States—History. | Animal rights—United States—History. | Social values—United States—History. | United States—Social conditions. | United States—History. | BISAC: HISTORY / United States / General. | NATURE / Animal Rights.
Classification: LCC HV4764 .D38 2016 (print) | LCC HV4764 (ebook) |
DDC 179/.30973—dc23
LC record available at http://lccn.loc.gov/2015043336

To Zachary, Andrea, and Jeff
Duke and Lincoln
and in loving memory of my mother,
Jean B. Davis
(1931–2002)

Contents

Acknowledgments — ix

Introduction — 1

1. "A Righteous Man Regards the Life of His Beast": The Roots of the Gospel of Kindness in the Second Great Awakening and Antebellum Reform — 26

2. "A World of Kindness Is a Copy of Heaven": Animals, Moral Uplift, and the Woman's Christian Temperance Union — 50

3. From Dog Eaters to Mule Beaters: Representing the Accused as Alien Other — 84

4. An Empire of Kindness: American Animal Welfare Policy and Moral Expansionism Overseas — 116

5. "A Country Rich in Cattle": Gospels of Kindness in Colonial South Asia — 151

6. "So Thoroughly Un-American": Making Historical Sense of the Bullfight — 179

Conclusion — 209

Notes — 227

Index — 291

Acknowledgments

ON JULY 23, 2006, I was slowly biking up a steep, short hill. I was only minutes from home. The temperature was 97°F and the humidity was thick. Suddenly, on the right side of the street, I spotted two stray dogs sniffing around a neighbor's house. I greeted them. They wagged their tails and followed me home. They were thin, hungry, and covered in sores, fleas, dirt, and—as we soon found out—they were not housebroken. But they were exceedingly friendly. My family and I took them to the Town Lake Animal Center to see if they were microchipped. They were not. Shelter employees entered the dogs' photographs and our contact information into their database. I plastered the neighborhood with "FOUND—TWO DOGS" posters. No one claimed them. We decided to keep them, reconciled to the fact that the larger dog, a Boxer/Labrador mix, might not be with us for very long. His teeth were brown and worn down. He had heartworm. Our vet estimated his age at "nine or ten." The other dog, a small, slender, buff-colored mystery mix, was little more than a puppy.

Nearly ten years later, Duke and Lincoln are still with us. They have been my constant companions in the stillness of night and early morning while I've researched and written this book, and they've helped clear my mind during our daily walks and runs. When I took them to our local shelter on that memorable July day in 2006, I turned to a local institution whose existence is a testament to the remarkable historical movement that is the subject of this book.

My heartfelt thanks to everyone who has helped me—a lot—in making this book a reality. I've been researching and writing for so long that "the book" has seemed more of an abstraction than something solid. But here it is. I couldn't have done it alone.

I would like to thank the University of Texas at Austin for providing generous research support at key stages of this project. I am deeply grateful to the College of Liberal Arts for funding a research assistantship while I served as chair of the American Studies department. A huge shout-out of thanks to each of the fantastic graduate students who worked for me in this capacity: Erin McClelland, Phil Tiemeyer, Audrey Russek, and Rebecca Onion. The University of Texas also awarded me a Special Research Assignment, a Faculty Research Assignment, and a College Research Fellowship, which gave me the invaluable gift of time to explore far-flung archives in the United States and abroad. A University of Texas Research Grant provided generous financial support for my research travel. An earlier University of Texas Research Grant funded a summer assistantship during the initial exploratory stage of this project: my sincere thanks to Allison Perlman for her exemplary work as my research assistant. In 2008, the College of Liberal Arts funded my participation in a semester of generative dialogue and spirited exchange at UT's Humanities Institute, where key ideas in this book germinated.

Librarians and archivists gave me invaluable research guidance. My heartfelt thanks to the staff at the National Archives and Records Administration in College Park, Maryland; the Minnesota Historical Society in St. Paul; the Social Welfare History Archives at the University of Minnesota in Minneapolis; the British Library in London; the American Historical Collection at Ateneo de Manila University in Quezon City, Luzon, Philippines; the Massachusetts SPCA's Archives Project in Boston; the Catholic Archives of Texas in Austin; the Dolph Briscoe Center for American History at the University of Texas at Austin; the Harry Ransom Center at the University of Texas at Austin; the Texas State Library and Archives Commission in Austin; the Perry-Castañeda Library at the University of Texas at Austin; the Robert L. Parkinson Library and Research Center at Circus World Museum in Baraboo, Wisconsin; and the Ringling Museum of Art in Sarasota, Florida. I would like to offer special thanks to Jan Holmquist, head of the MSPCA Angell's Archive Project. Jan was incredibly helpful, kind, and generous with her time during my research visit. Additionally, I would like to thank Maureen Heath at the British Library for double-checking key references via email long after my visit to London. I am so grateful to Dave Klaasen at the Social Welfare History Archives; Dave kindly alerted me to the Minnesota Woman's Christian Temperance Union records, which became the genesis for an entire chapter. At the Briscoe Center, Catherine Best and Anne Serrano generously offered their expertise as I navigated materials related to the Texas Centennial collections. I owe a great debt to Andrew Wilbur at the Perry-Castañeda Library Media Lab for his superb guidance in helping me scan my illustrations. Thanks also to Andres Ramirez at the Perry-Castañeda Library for his assistance in locating an elusive image. I am deeply grateful to Georgia Harper at the Perry-Castañeda Library for her expert advice regarding copyright and public domain questions. My sincere thanks to David M. Hardy at the US Department of Justice, for fielding my Freedom of Information Act query so quickly. Thanks to Erin Foley and Peter Shrake at the Robert L. Parkinson Library and Research Center at Circus World Museum for generously answering my questions over the years. Further, I offer my sincere thanks to Deborah Walk, Fred Dahlinger, and Jennifer Lemmer Posey of the Ringling Museum for their expertise and unfailing generosity of spirit.

I owe an enormous debt to Susan Ferber and her colleagues at Oxford University Press. Susan took an early interest in this project and she has been a superb editor and a wellspring of generosity, patience, clarity, and wisdom throughout the process. I would like to thank Patterson Lamb for expert copyediting and Maya Bringe for wonderful guidance during production. A huge shout-out of thanks to Alana Podolsky for her tremendous help in marketing this book. Alana, Maya, and Susan have pulled out all the stops to publish an anniversary book. I am incredibly grateful to Brett Mizelle for his very thorough and helpful reader's report. Brett's incisive observations have clarified my thinking and have deepened my insights into the material. I would also like to thank the anonymous reader at Oxford University Press for her/his excellent comments and suggestions. Throughout this project, I have had to steel my heart in order to jettison beloved sources for the sake of narrative cohesion. Thanks to all for helping me make tough decisions.

Thanks to the American Studies Association for permission to publish portions of the following article in Chapter 4: "Cockfight Nationalism: Blood Sport and the Moral Politics of American Empire and Nation Building," which first appeared in *American Quarterly* 65, no. 3 (September 2013): 549–574. Thanks also to Oxford University Press for permission to publish portions of the following book chapters, which now appear in Chapters 4 and 5: "Bird Day: Promoting the Gospel of Kindness in the Philippines during the American Occupation," in *The Nation-State and the Transnational Environment*, ed. Mark Lawrence, Erika Bsumek, and David Kinkella (New York: Oxford University Press, 2013): 181–206; and "Propagating the Gospel of Animal Kindness: Sacred Cows, Christians, and American Animal Welfare Activism with Reference to India at the Turn of the Twentieth Century," in *Speaking Truth to Power: Religion, Caste, and the Subaltern Question in India*, ed. Manu Bhagavan and Anne Feldhaus (New Delhi: Oxford University Press, 2008): 47–61.

Colleagues, friends, and graduate students, past and present, at the University of Texas and elsewhere, have given me invaluable feedback at various stages of this project—listening to presentations, reading sections of the manuscript, and/or offering sources. It is a great pleasure to thank Bob Abzug, Rick

Baldoz, Laura Beausire, Ali Berlow, Doug Biow, Bill Brands, Paul Breese, Erika Bsumek, Jerome Bump, Amon Burton, Charlotte Canning, John Cline, Judy Coffin, Francesca Consagra, Cary Cordova, Fred Dahlinger, Diana Davis, Kathleen Donegan, Rebecca D'Orsogna, Robin Doughty, Monica Drane, Carolyn Eastman, Ed Emery, Elizabeth Engelhardt, Linda Ferreira-Buckley, Tom Ferraro, Shelley Fisher Fishkin, Carla Freccero, Caroline Frick, Andrew Friedenthal, Irene Garza, Danny Gerling, Adam Golub, John Morán González, Sam Gosling, Laurie Green, Katherine Grier, John Gronbeck-Tedesco, Nicole Guidotti-Hernández, Andrew Hamsher, Tony Harkins, John Hartigan, Matt Hedstrom, Benita Heiskanen, Linda Henderson, Pamela Henson, Vicky Hill, Steve Hoelscher, Vicki Howard, Jeff Hyson, Ken Kawata, Liam Kennedy, Alison Kibler, Claire Jean Kim, Ivan Krielkamp, Ellen Cunningham Kruppa, Mark Lawrence, Brian Levack, Randy Lewis, Nhi Lieu, Stephen Marshall, Elaine Tyler May, Carol MacKay, Sue McKean, John McKiernan-González, Clay McShane, Jeff Meikle, Jason Mellard, Julia Mickenberg, Karl Miller, Gail Minault, Tatsuya Mitsuda, Narisara Murray, Franny Nudelman, Rebecca Onion, Naomi Paik, Allison Perlman, Jennifer Price, Paul Raushenbush, Nigel Rothfels, Sharmila Rudrappa, Audrey Russek, Kim Simpson, Aaron Herald Skabelund, Mark Smith, Denise Spellberg, Clint Starr, T. J. Stiles, Cynthia Talbot, Shirley Thompson, Anna Thompson-Hajdik, Phil Tiemeyer, Tom Tweed, Jeannette Vaught, Amy Nathan Wright, Tracy Wuster, Estelle Young, and Leslie Zemeckis. I'd also like to offer my collective thanks to all of my fantastic undergraduates who have explored the history of animal/human relationships over the years with me.

I am so grateful to Julia Mickenberg for reading the entire manuscript and giving me peace of mind with her excellent feedback. My sincere thanks to Denise Spellberg for reading several chapters and offering great suggestions and support. Many thanks to John Morán González for alerting me to key sources related to the Centennial bullfighting controversy. A big thanks to Amon Burton and his colleague Randy Turner for helping me navigate Texas bullfighting laws. I would like to give a special shout-out to Stephanie Kaufman for her administrative expertise over the years, for her great generosity of spirit, and for being such a wonderful colleague. I'd also like to extend my heartfelt thanks to all of my colleagues in the Department of American Studies for providing such a congenial and creative work environment.

Thanks to my teachers who continue to inspire me: Bob Bonner, Paul Boyer, Linda Gordon, Tom McCormick, Kirin Narayan, Diethelm Prowe, Emily Rosenberg, and Eleanor Zelliot. Diet, who passed away in March 2015, enthusiastically mentored generations of Carleton history majors. My fellow

Carls and I miss him greatly. Paul offered constant support for this project from the get-go and kept the faith that I would finish. I will always be grateful to him for his historical insights, wisdom, irreverent sense of humor, and generous mentorship, and, along with his wife, Ann Boyer, for serving as a model of how to live. Paul passed away in March 2012. My graduate school classmates and I miss him very much.

Finally, my family has sustained me with their unconditional love. A giant thanks to my mother-in-law, Karen Leveque Osborne. I would also like to thank Karen Teske Osborne and to my late father-in-law, Jim Osborne. I am profoundly grateful to my siblings: Steve Davis, Kathy Davis Messerich, and Betsy Davis Moran, and to my siblings-in-law, Dan Osborne and Ellyn Mohs. Thanks for always being there for me. A special shout-out to Kathy and her husband Jeff for their wonderful hospitality during my research trips to the Twin Cities. Another special shout-out goes to Betsy for her great hospitality during my archival journeys. My father, Hugh L. Davis, has patiently awaited the publication of this book for a long, long time. Thanks, Dad, and to Heidi Harkins, for always believing in me. And here's to my late mother, Jean B. Davis, for her compassionate view of animals, humanity, and the world, and for love that even death cannot conquer. She is with me always.

My children, Andrea and Zachary, grew up alongside this book. They were in elementary school when it all started. They are now taller than I am and thriving in college. We have raised many animal companions together and we enjoy the myriad creatures living around us, including the red-eared sliders at Town Lake; the peach-stealing fox squirrels in our yard; the squadrons of lime-green parrots patrolling our neighborhood; the Gulf Coast toads chorusing after a drenching rain; and the raucous flocks of great-tailed grackles in our trees at dusk. Even though we live apart, our hearts are forever near. They sustain me with their love. My husband Jeff read this manuscript twice, including one time aloud, so that I could "hear" my words as someone else would. Jeff gently urged me onward throughout this journey. Whether I was traveling to the archives or staying up late to meet a deadline, Jeff stepped in and took care of our growing children, dogs, guinea pigs, and box turtle, in addition to his own fulltime teaching duties. Words cannot fully express my gratitude and love.

The Gospel of Kindness

Introduction

IN 1926, MISS Bessie Dean Cooper of New York City traveled across Europe on her Grand Tour, a long-standing rite of passage for wealthy young Americans. Like many other tourists, Cooper and her friends ventured into North Africa, an increasingly popular exotic addition to the traditional Mediterranean excursion. The experience transformed her. In letters home, she and her traveling companions chronicled the "distressing condition of the animals" laboring in this preindustrial, muscle-powered world.[1] Miss Cooper wrote in graphic detail:

> I have recently returned from a trip across North Africa—Tunisia, Algeria, and Morocco. Though no animal there can be called happy, and dogs especially are treated with hideous cruelty, the draft animals—horses, mules, camels, and, above all, donkeys—are perhaps the most wretched.... I have seen many a sore full of maggots.[2]

Cooper and her friends were moved to action over "teas in Paris, discussions in Monte Carlo, and lengthy transatlantic correspondence."[3] In 1927, these American travelers joined with the Massachusetts Society for the Prevention of Cruelty to Animals (MSPCA) to create an animal hospital and shelter in Fez, Morocco, that would operate entirely on private charitable donations, the vast majority of which would come from the United States. They named the facility the American Fondouk (funduq), meaning "merchant's inn" or "hotel" in Arabic. Mrs. Amy Bend Bishop donated $8,000.00 to build the hospital in memory of her mother, who loved animals.[4] Bessie Dean Cooper became the first secretary treasurer, and Reverend Francis Rowley, president of the MSPCA, served as the Fondouk's first president when it became fully operational in 1929.

The American Fondouk, or "Fondouk Americain" in French, offered free medical care, sustenance, and shelter for the city's injured, sick, laboring animals and strays.[5] Initially, however, many Moroccans feared that the facility was trying to ruin them. MSPCA officials recalled, "Natives saw the hospital as a threat to their livelihood—while an animal was a patient there, it could not be out on the streets working."[6] Such suspicions were seemingly confirmed in 1933 when the local pasha and the French colonial government mandated new anticruelty laws, which ordered city police to take any sick or suffering animal to the American Fondouk for treatment.[7] Yet as local residents gradually began to trust the Fondouk's intentions and purpose, they brought their ailing animals voluntarily.

Animal welfare advocates and US leaders alike proudly noted that the American Fondouk was the only animal hospital or shelter flying the American flag in a foreign country.[8] Moreover, they saw the Fondouk as a living testament to the nation's benevolent mission abroad. The United States did not have an embassy in Fez; thus, the American Fondouk represented an informal, but highly visible US presence in the everyday life of the city.[9] Additionally, the MSPCA's decision to establish the American Fondouk in Morocco, instead of Tunisia or Algeria, was historically meaningful. The United States had had a special relationship with Morocco since the Revolutionary era. Morocco was the first country to recognize American independence in December 1777. The two countries signed a fifty-year peace treaty in 1787, the Treaty of Friendship and Amity, which was renewed indefinitely in 1836, along with favorable trade relations.[10] In this historical context, the MSPCA's establishment of the American Fondouk in Morocco made sound political sense, even if its founders were not explicitly thinking about diplomacy. The Fondouk endured during the Cold War. Its political significance grew in the immediate aftermath of Morocco's independence from France in 1956 when the United States and Soviet Union were wooing African nations into their respective political orbits. The American ambassador to Morocco, Cavendish W. Cannon, recognized the Fondouk's importance as a demonstration of American benevolence to North Africa and to the world:

> We all are proud to see our flag flying at that fine outpost, and we rejoice in the excellent reputation of the institution and the affection in which it is held by the people of the region.... I consider this to be a very important contribution to the work of the American Government and people in promoting the interests of the United States in Morocco.[11]

FIGURE I.1. In 1927 American philanthropists and the MSPCA founded the American Fondouk in Fez, Morocco. Supported entirely by private donations, the animal hospital provided free veterinary care to local animals. American animal advocates and policymakers alike viewed the Fondouk as an embodiment of the nation's benevolent mission abroad. The American Fondouk is still fully operational today. "What's New in Morocco?" *National Humane Review*, July 1943, 10.

Why were discussions of an American animal hospital in Morocco consistently connected to questions of patriotism, uplift, and American benevolence? Why did a group of wealthy Americans define their own moral purpose—as well as that of their nation—through the status of animals in a foreign country? How did their concern for animals clash with the economic needs of Fez residents and others whose livelihood was dependent on animal labor? How and why did a movement dedicated to protecting animals throw questions of human equality and cultural difference into sharp relief? For that matter, how did an organized movement, which began in cities across the United States, become a vanguard for the nation's aspirations abroad? These questions are hardly unique to the MSPCA's activities in Morocco. Instead, they are historically germane to the evolution of American animal advocacy as a whole.

This book explores the cultural, social, and political meanings of the American animal welfare movement at home and overseas from the antebellum Second Great Awakening to the eve of the Second World War. Animal protection, it argues, defined kindness to "our silent friends" as a signature American value. Expanding their vision of the nation to include humanity's "fellow creatures," animal welfare leaders enthusiastically embraced what they called the "gospel of kindness" to build a harmonious union, which could transcend the potentially divisive particularities of culture, region, race, religion, and class.[12] This "gospel" was at once spiritual and broadly secular. Although the majority of animal protectionists in this period were mainline Protestants, their interpretation of this gospel extended beyond the first four books of the New Testament regarding the life, death, and resurrection of Jesus Christ.[13] They preached kindness as an infallible secular and spiritual truth, a mark of human potential and perfectibility, and a guiding moral principle that would uplift the world. The MSPCA's popular monthly magazine, *Our Dumb Animals*, had little patience for religious leaders who were disinterested in animal welfare: "The Gospel that ignores the weak and helpless, whether man or bird, or beast, is not worth preaching."[14]

Animal advocates characterized their gospel of kindness in teleological language. They envisioned their activism as a patriotic, progressive historical march away from "barbarism"—a favorite term—to a higher plane of civilization. The etymology of "barbarism" had its own racial history, which shaped how animal protectionists represented the accused. The term "barbarian" and its cognates "barbarism" and "Barbary" were rooted in a derogatory Greco-Latin term for an unintelligible foreign outsider, which also came to represent an entire geographic region in northern Africa, the so-called Barbary States, which included Morocco. The Arabic verb, "barbara," also meant unintelligible speech, as well as an unflattering synonym for the indigenous Berber. According to historian Denise Spellberg, "Like 'Barbary' it denoted otherness (at best) and absence of civilization (at worst)."[15] During the early nineteenth-century Barbary Wars, a series of trade and piracy skirmishes in North Africa, American political leaders described the pirates of the region as "barbarians."[16] Over time, the term lost its geographical specificity.

Brewing in the anxious promise of human perfectibility during the Protestant Second Great Awakening of the early nineteenth century, animal kindness became a barometer of free moral agency and the boundaries of proper, civilized comportment and citizenship. As a movement dedicated to the biblically evocative "least among us" (Matthew 25:31–46), animal protection promised the all-inclusive assurance of kindness as a universal moral balm to unite and heal a violent world. And yet, given the enormous diversity of the United States and its empire, definitions of kindness and cruelty were culturally contingent and therefore contentious: those accused of animal cruelty invoked their own culturally specific ideas regarding their rights of self-determination to defend culturally situated animal practices others judged repugnant.

Animal welfare advocates worked tirelessly to prevent animal pain and suffering, yet in this era, few leaders confronted broader, more slippery questions of animal subjectivity, ethics, and rights. Because animal protectionists primarily treated animal suffering as an expression of human depravity, they trained their moral sights on drunkenness, greed, gambling, family violence, and other human sins. Consequently, actual animals periodically drop out of this book. Animals disappeared in other ways, too. For those animal advocates who were denied the full rights of American citizenship, such as people of color and women, the suffering animal body was a blank cultural canvas on which to project their own potentially radical ideas about human equality. In short, animal activism was a way for marginalized people to claim the rights of citizenship, just as law enforcement and other mainstream groups used charges of animal cruelty to validate exclusion. Animal kindness became a flashpoint for cohesion, citizenship, and conflict, demonstrating the conundrum of universalized ideals of civilization in a modern, culturally pluralistic society.

THE GRADUAL TRANSFIGURATION of American society from animal muscle to motor power from the nineteenth to the mid-twentieth century was a form of technological nation building. This animal-to-machine metamorphosis involved a sensory reckoning of time and speed—from the sensation of clip-clopping twenty miles per day on horseback to the exhilarating and bewildering sense of speed at twenty miles per hour on an "iron horse" railroad or a "horseless carriage" automobile. This process was a transformation of smell, sight, touch, and sound as well. Animals shaped the sensory experience of industrial modernity in ways that made human and animal relationships more intimate and paradoxically more abstract: the growth of a pet-keeping consumer culture and a wildlife conservation movement heightened animal-human bonds, while the gradual disappearance of laboring and food animals from urban spaces segregated human and animal interactions. Historian Richard Bulliet refers to the contemporary predicament of intimacy, sentimentality, and distance as "postdomesticity": people are at once more deeply connected to companion animals and to wildlife, and spatially disconnected from those creatures that become food, leather, and the subjects of scientific research.[17]

It is important to remember, however, that the nation's transformation from muscle power to motorization was uneven. While the urban laboring horse population plummeted from 1910 to 1930 with the rise of the automobile, rural farming (with few exceptions) was not fully mechanized until after World War II. Historian Susan Jones notes that the hardy horse was ideal for short haulage and an excellent cultivator for small corn crops because its nimble hooves prevented damaging soil compression. Less than a third of all midwestern farmers owned a motor truck in 1930, even when they owned a tractor.[18] Yet with the introduction of the gasoline automobile engine in the 1890s, urban journalists swiftly placed the horse "in company with the pterodactyl and the megatherium" in declarations of impending equine extinction, which occluded the continued participation of muscle power in the nation's economy and cultural life.[19]

The US animal protection movement was born in a muscle-powered urban world, which strongly resembled what Miss Bessie Dean Cooper and her friends encountered in the cities of North Africa. In the middle of the nineteenth century, animals were everywhere in the urban United States. Animal muscle—in the form of horses, oxen, mules, donkeys, and dogs—powered city transportation and commerce. Armies of hogs rooted through mounds of garbage, while stray dogs and cats skulked in alleyways and chickens scratched for bits of food. In an age before refrigeration, American stockyards, dairies, slaughterhouses, and butcher shops spawned fetid olfactory clouds. Whale bodies were a primary source of nightlight, with the rendering of blubber into lamp oil and highly prized (sperm whale) spermaceti into smokeless candles. Parts of baleen whales adorned the fashionable human female body as corset stays and parasol ribs. Animals—living and dead—were omnipresent features of the urban landscape.

Introduction 7

GOING TO THEIR LAST HOME.

FIGURE I.2. In a nation where muscle power still dominated, nineteenth-century American cities were packed with livestock and laboring animals, similar to these cattle walking to the Union Stock Yards in Chicago. "Going to Their Last Home," in W. Joseph Grand, *Illustrated History of the Union Stockyards: Sketch-Book of Familiar Faces and Places at the Yards* (1896; reprint, Chicago: Thos. Knapp, 1901), 40.

Attempts to control urban animals were a major preoccupation for local authorities across the country. In the nation's largest city, police officers tried to improve the sorry state of local sanitation by routing some 5,000–6,000 pigs out of people's cellars and garrets during a cholera epidemic in 1849. The police also rounded up approximately 20,000 pigs in Lower Manhattan and drove them to the city's upper wards. Roving bands of boys clubbed some 3,520 stray dogs for municipal bounties.[20] In 1868, the New York State Court of Appeals upheld rules created by the Metropolitan Board of Health for driving livestock through designated streets in New York City and Brooklyn. The resolutions, passed over the strong objection of local butchers, stipulated that "cattle, swine, pigs, or calves" only could be driven through designated streets between 8:00 PM and two hours past sunrise the next day. Sheep were not allowed from noon until 8:00 PM. During permissible driving hours, the narrow streets were often clogged with livestock, as evidenced by the following rules: "nor shall more than 20 cattle, or more than 100 hogs, or more than 150 sheep, be driven together."[21] Five years later, however, handlers still drove livestock through the streets with impunity.²² Livestock were also important to preserving the pastoral vision of Frederick Law Olmsted and Calvert Vaux at Central Park. When New York divisions of the Union Army lobbied to use the park for drills during the Civil War, park officials tried unsuccessfully to thwart the military by dedicating fifteen acres of pastureland for grazing sheep. The area subsequently became known as Sheep Meadow, home to approximately 200 sheep until 1934.²³

Clashes between impoverished New Yorkers and the police were often centered on animals. Because meat was expensive and land scarce, poor New Yorkers, like deprived urban dwellers everywhere, kept swine and fowl and let them forage in the streets for food.²⁴ Local officials periodically ordered the confiscation of wandering pigs, citing sanitation concerns and the unsightly scenes of noisy porcine copulation, but working-class Irish and African American women fought the police to reclaim their animals during the regular hog riots of the 1820s and early 1830s.²⁵ The area around 125th Street was so thick with hogs that people called it "Pig's Alley." Moreover, Irish American immigrant men were dependent on the city's animal-powered economy for their livelihood, representing 84 percent of the city's immigrant hostlers (grooms).²⁶ The grim, rough-and-tumble lives of hostlers, drivers, and carters mirrored that of their horses. Cajoled and often beaten into pulling nearly impossible loads of freight and people, workhorses frequently died from overwork. In New York City alone, some 15,000 dead horses were removed from the streets per year in the 1880s.²⁷

New York City—mucky, simultaneously rural, urban, and animal-powered—was the birthplace of the nation's first officially incorporated animal protection organization on April 10, 1866, a year and a day after the Civil War ended. Henry Bergh, a shipping scion, forged a powerful coalition of New York elites to create the American Society for the Prevention of Cruelty to Animals (ASPCA). In launching the organization, Bergh and his colleagues sponsored revised and fortified anticruelty legislation. A solemn, lanky, fifty-three-year-old Columbia University dropout, Bergh had been professionally adrift much of his adult life. He had no interest in his father's vast shipping business or in studying law. He tried his hand unsuccessfully as a playwright, occasionally worked for the US government, and traveled through Europe and East Asia for twelve years with his wife, Katherine Matilda Taylor Bergh, the daughter of a wealthy Englishman.²⁸ As evidence of his family's status, Bergh served as President Lincoln's Secretary of Legation in St. Petersburg, Russia, from 1862 to 1864. Chronic health problems in the severe climate, however, forced his resignation.

Bergh's time in St. Petersburg was revelatory. There he found his calling in a country long characterized as a bastion of brutality in the American imagination.[29] Bergh regularly witnessed animal beatings, but when he tried to intervene, Russian drivers ignored him, as did gendarmes nearby. Bystanders openly taunted and threatened him. Finally, clad in full formal court dress and colorful Legation ribbons, Bergh confronted a particularly violent driver. This time, the driver, gendarmes, and crowds were respectful and fully cooperative.[30] According to Bergh, "At last I've found a way to utilize my gold lace and about the best use I can make of it."[31] During his journey back to the United States, Bergh stopped in England for a recuperative visit, where he met with animal welfare leaders at the Royal Society for the Prevention of Cruelty to Animals, founded in 1824.[32] Bergh's careful planning and lobbying over the next year culminated with a passionate lecture delivered to a crowded house at Clinton Hall in New York City on February 8, 1866. Bergh characterized animal kindness as a universal moral cause:

> This is a matter purely of conscience. It has no perplexing side issues. Politics have no more to do with it than astronomy, or the use of the globe. No, it is a moral question in all its aspects; it addresses itself to that quality of our nature that can not be disregarded by any people with safety to their dearest interests; it is a solemn recognition of that greatest attribute of the Almighty Ruler of the Universe, mercy, which if suspended in our own case but for a single instant, would overwhelm and destroy us.[33]

Bergh's speech made a sweeping moral case for animal protection, but it was also a political call to arms, which kicked off a vigorous legislative campaign. Supporters flocked to sign his "Declaration of the Rights of Animals." John Jacob Astor Jr., George Bancroft, and other powerful allies eagerly embraced Bergh's urgent appeal for animal mercy.[34] Bergh found an especially effective ally in Ezra Cornell, university founder, philanthropist, businessman, and state senator. Cornell and fellow state senator Charles Folger helped Bergh acquire a state charter.[35] On April 10, 1866, the New York Legislature voted to incorporate the ASPCA. This law of incorporation stipulated that the ASPCA's officers could legally arrest anyone on the streets beating or neglecting an animal under the state's extant (but rarely enforced) anticruelty statute passed in 1829.[36] Because this new organization was "invested with power to bring the cruelest to justice," its officers possessed unprecedented policing authority and, in turn, wore police-like badges and uniforms.³⁷ Bergh's epiphanic moment in St. Petersburg had stuck. Uniforms were a critical symbol of authority for the fledgling ASPCA.

On April 11, 1866, an unnamed ASPCA officer exercised the freshly incorporated organization's new powers by arresting a German butcher named Manz for animal cruelty under the tenets of the 1829 statute. Manz was driving a cart loaded with live calves "piled up like wood . . . and one of them so disposed of as to bring his eye in contact with a sharp stick, thereby destroying his sight."³⁸ Eight days later, Bergh and his allies successfully

FIGURE 1.3. ASPCA founder and president Henry Bergh believed in the "power of the uniform" as a visible sign of his organization's policing authority in the streets of New York City. "Henry Bergh, Founder and President of the American Society for the Prevention of Cruelty to Animals, 1866 to 1888," in Sydney H. Coleman, *Humane Society Leaders in America* (Albany: American Humane Association, 1924), plate facing 33.

introduced a new animal welfare bill to the New York Legislature. One year later, Bergh drafted an even more comprehensive state anticruelty statute, "An Act for the More Effectual Prevention of Cruelty to Animals," which applied to "any living creature" and prosecuted additional forms of cruelty, such as blood sports, abandonment, and impoundment without food and water, set out in ten detailed sections.[39] Until his death in 1888, the uniformed Bergh—wearing a top hat that made him look even taller than his six-foot-plus height—was a ubiquitous presence on the streets of New York City. While Bergh advocated for diverse animals, including turtles, pigeons, and rabbits, he was chiefly devoted to the interests of the city's domestic laboring animals. He flashed his badge, physically placed his body between angry drivers and their animals, and arrested thousands of people over twenty-two years. In 1879, *Scribner's Monthly* claimed, "Since Horace Greeley's death, no figure more familiar to the public has walked the streets of the metropolis."[40]

TORTURE.

FIGURE I.4. Although post–Civil War animal welfare laws addressed a range of abuses, the majority of prosecutions targeted cruelty to laboring animals. Not only are these horses being whipped but they are also wearing blinders and the suffocating checkrein. "Torture," *Our Dumb Animals*, September 1888, 48.

Bergh's presence was matched by the visibility of new animal welfare laws across the country. In 1879, thirty-three out of thirty-eight states in the Union had passed anticruelty legislation. By 1900, every state in the Union had passed animal welfare laws, the majority of which were modeled after Bergh's legislation in New York State.[41] Animal protection societies tackled a wide spectrum of animal abuse, paying special attention to domestic animals. They mandated the humane treatment of laboring horses, oxen, and dogs; they built urban watering troughs for thirsty animal workers; they condemned the fashionable checkrein (which kept a horse's head painfully arched or extended); they abolished cockfighting, dog fighting, coursing, and live pigeon shoots; they combated the practice of vivisection; they prohibited the sale of adulterated milk; they successfully lobbied the US Congress for guaranteed food and water stops for animals bound for the stockyards during railroad transport; they denounced drunkenness; and they pioneered "noiseless" and painless methods of euthanasia for strays. Animal advocates also helped establish the movement to prevent child abuse in the 1870s, creating consolidated new "humane societies" to protect animals and children. Confusingly, however, some SPCAs engaged in child protection work and some humane leaders worked exclusively in the field of animal advocacy. Thus, these terms often were used interchangeably, despite their specific historical origins.

The early movement's scope was expansive, but one prominent domestic animal was conspicuously absent as a subject of sustained programmatic concern—the cat. To be sure, animal protectionists prosecuted individual cases of cruelty to cats. Yet most municipal pounds and SPCA shelters rarely collected stray cats en masse, while ownerless dogs were routinely seized. Unlike dogs, cats were not subjected to local licensing, leash, and muzzling ordinances. Humane groups feared that cats would strangle themselves in mandated collars while climbing, leaping, and slipping through small spaces. Muzzling and leashing were likewise impractical for a creature that straddled the divide between wild and tame. Some urban residents disliked cats: in an age before effective reproductive control, fecund cats proliferated wildly, piercing the night with their caterwauling. A docile but promiscuous outdoor housecat could produce abundant feral offspring. Superstitious associations between cats and the occult were still prevalent, as were cultural assumptions about cats as carriers of disease.[42]

Perhaps most damningly of all, cats preyed on beloved songbirds. Hostility to outdoor cats ran so high among bird protectionist members of the Pasadena

Humane Society that they proposed a feline extermination program in 1903. Mrs. Fordyce Grinnell led the charge against cats: "Of course, I do not mean that people should not be allowed to have cats in their own houses, but those which run wild should be put out of the way."[43] Grinnell and her colleagues reserved special loathing for the unmarried women who reportedly hoarded cats. This disgust was ultimately a form of misogyny, a rejection of human beings and animals who defied normative categorization. Grinnell believed that her extermination plan would force "cat ladies" to embrace their proper place in society: "There is but one substitute, and that is marriage. I really believe that cats stand in the way of many marriages, and I have no use for either the old maids or the cats they keep."[44] Although the proposal failed, bird lovers still readily killed stray cats.

While local issues, such as Pasadena's abundant stray cat population, remained central to animal protectionism at the turn of the twentieth century, the movement's influence expanded overseas as the United States became a fledgling world power. Animal advocates proselytized the gospel of

FIGURE I.5. Many early animal protectionists had an ambivalent relationship with the cat, who was often condemned for killing cherished songbirds. "Don't Let Your Cat Kill Birds," *Our Dumb Animals*, March 1887, 147.

kindness in new overseas territories and in countries such as India, Morocco, Syria, and Turkey, where the United States had little direct political control. Further, the movement's scope expanded to include slaughterhouse reform, feather fashions, and animal entertainments, such as film and the rodeo. Humane leaders were also more attentive to the welfare of wild animals, especially furbearing mammals caught in agonizing steel traps, in conjunction with a new conservation movement at the turn of the century. The gospel of kindness increasingly emphasized human rights, as well as animal welfare, which illuminated its historical roots in abolitionism. Denunciations of lynching, domestic violence, and American militarism abroad appeared in movement periodicals alongside long-standing appeals against the checkrein and cockfighting.

Ultimately, animal advocates saw the gospel of kindness as the foundation of a humane new world rising phoenix-like out of the ashes of the Civil War—a moral rampart to defend, strengthen, elevate, and unify a fractured country. Many journalists agreed. Like the movement's leaders, journalists cast the success of animal advocacy as a stamp of human progress. Reflecting on nearly four decades of social change in 1902, actress and journalist Clara Morris proclaimed, "This Society, in constituting itself in defense of the defenseless, truly served man as well as beast, in teaching to control if not conquer his savage instincts—his senseless furies."[45] During these years, the alchemy of faith and war forged a new crucible of kindness whose architects made animal protection a defining American value.

In a symbolic coupling of American nationhood and animal advocacy, Henry Bergh was especially pleased that the passage of New York's new animal welfare law on April 19, 1866, was the anniversary of the Battle of Lexington and Concord. The new law, a fellow animal welfare leader later observed, "was to be equally as significant in the cause of animal protection as was that famous skirmish of American patriots in their struggle for human liberty."[46] This evocation of battle was especially powerful in 1866, just a year after the Civil War ended. Even though the moral and ideological foundations of animal protectionism lay in the evangelical revivalism and secular reform of the Second Great Awakening, the Civil War helped catalyze the formation of an organized secular movement. Through the medium of photography, even those Americans far from the battlefields of Antietam, Shiloh, Gettysburg, and others, experienced intimate and graphic visual evidence of agony and destruction. Dead horses and soldiers lay side by side.[47]

Reportage and letters from the battlefield described unrelenting animal suffering. The Christian Commission, a Union-wide voluntary charitable organization, pleaded for animal kindness as essential to "the lessons of humanity" in the Army: "Men should be taught the worth of all that God has created . . . the average endurance of the horses in the army is only about three months. This is owing not to legitimate service, but to abuse of every kind. . . . Let there be moral appeals and legal regulations that shall put an end to this cruelty and shame."[48] In recognition of pervasive equine hardship, Union Army officers hired internationally famed horse tamer John Solomon Rarey to teach his gentling methods to Union cavalry in 1862.[49] Rarey, whose childhood commitment to singing "the gospel of kindness with patience and firmness in dealing with the brute creation," published *The Modern Art of Taming Wild Horses* (1855), which explained his methods of gentling fearful, incorrigible horses with trust and building equine confidence through calm repetition.[50]

Despite attempts to adopt Rarey's gentling methods in the Union Army, warhorse suffering persisted in a mobilization of unprecedented scale and geographical range. In letters to his mother, Charles Francis Adams wrote of his quandary as a cavalry officer to nurse his exhausted, sore-ridden horses, while pushing them to their limits to win the war: "You have no idea of their sufferings. . . . Imagine a horse with his withers swollen to three times the natural size, and with a volcanic, running sore pouring matter down each side, and you have a case with which every cavalry officer is daily called upon to deal, and you imagine a horse which has still to be ridden until he lays down in sheer suffering under the saddle. . . . The air of Virginia is literally burdened today with the stench of dead horses, federal and confederate. You pass them on every road and find them in every field, while from their carrions you can follow the march of every army that moves."[51] The experience of total war also meant the wholesale slaughter of millions of livestock animals, predominantly in the Confederate States. South Carolina, for example, contained roughly 965,000 hogs in 1860, but in 1865 those numbers had plummeted to approximately 150,000.[52] In 1880, the South bred 2.6 million fewer hogs than in 1860.[53]

Embracing the "power of the uniform," Henry Bergh adopted a martial aesthetic and a language of national healing that evoked the immediate memory of a war that he and many other elite animal welfare leaders did not fight.[54] SPCA officers continued to summon the public's indelible memory of the Civil War in prosecuting animal cruelty cases decades later. In 1895, for example, crowds of farmers and other spectators filled a rural Los Angeles County courthouse to hear expert testimony from a veteran named Mr. Hodgman, a survivor from Georgia's Andersonville Prison, who took the stand in a starvation case involving a heifer left to die in a barren field that neighbors dubbed "the Dead Cow Pasture." The *Los Angeles Times* explained that he was "therefore well qualified to judge as to what starvation is. Mr. Hodgman was present at the so-called autopsy on the body of the heifer and was satisfied that it was a clear case of starvation. . . . He said his prison experience taught him that after a certain point the victim lost all desire to feed."[55] The jury agreed with Hodgman and found the defendant guilty of cruelty and neglect.[56]

Decades after the Civil War, many northern animal advocates viewed the South as a vast field for reconstruction—a call for the gospel of kindness to heal the wounds of war through Yankee uplift. The American Missionary Association (AMA) made these connections explicit. Founded in Albany, New York, in 1846, by mainline Protestant abolitionists, the AMA provided refuge for runaway slaves, established foreign missions, and created new schools for freedmen and women during the Civil War and Reconstruction. In the late nineteenth century, the AMA instituted animal kindness curricula in its southern schools to combat neglect, violent forms of animal discipline, and blood sports in which rats, for example, "are torn to pieces": "The children among whom we are working in the South are being taught cruelty and brutality in a more direct way. . . . [W]e are trying to 'speak for those who cannot speak for themselves' and instill in the minds of our boys and girls the thought that gentleness and mercy are not signs of weakness, but are traits of character that belong to the great and noble."[57]

The transformative political climate of Reconstruction profoundly reconsidered the meaning of American citizenship and property. It also generated new thinking about the moral status of animals as living property in American society. A historical precedent for this link between human bondage and animals existed in Great Britain during the early nineteenth century, when organized animal protectionism grew out of the abolition movement. Such formative connections were forged in antebellum America as well. In the midst of Reconstruction, New York's new anticruelty statute in 1866 marked a departure in American legal thought, historian Susan Pearson observes, because it simultaneously recognized animals as property and as sentient beings with a right to protection from suffering and neglect. Before 1866, the handful of existing American anticruelty laws defined animals solely as property. Accordingly, the crime of cruelty was a crime against the animal's owner, or the public peace, but the animal's status as a crime victim was wholly unrecognized.[58]

THE MYTHOLOGY OF American exceptionalism—that is to say, a belief in the uniqueness and benevolence of America's republican political institutions, free market capitalism, and "melting pot" cultural pluralism—shared a long history with animal welfare concerns.[59] During the early days in their settlement of New England, Puritan lawmakers viewed animal mercy as an outward sign of inward grace. In 1641, the General Court in the Massachusetts Bay Colony included anticruelty measures in its legal code, the Massachusetts Body of Liberties, which were designed to dictate upright moral conduct as the bedrock law of Puritan society:

> 92. No man shall exercise any Tirranny or Crueltie towards any bruite Creature which are usuallie kept for man's use. 93. If any man shall have occasion to leade or drive Cattel from place to place that is far of, so that they be weary, or hungry, or fall sick, or lambe, It shall be lawful to rest or refresh them, for competent time, in any open place that is not Corne, meadow, or inclosed for some peculiar use.[60]

The status of animals in the Body of Liberties must be understood in its broader historical context. For one, its anticruelty provisions articulated the ostensible divide between upright Puritan civilization and American Indian "savagery." Moreover, the Body of Liberties should be considered in relation to political turmoil in England. English Puritans vehemently opposed violent blood sports and their attendant cultures of drunkenness and gambling. In response, the Stuarts issued the King's Declaration of Sports (1618, 1633), which proclaimed that blood sports and other animal entertainments were beyond the reach of Puritan reform. During the English Civil War, the Puritans established the Protectorate's ordinance of 1654, which banned cockfighting and cock-throwing (i.e. throwing clubs at a tethered rooster until he died). Historian Kathleen Kete notes that the treatment of animals remained a major source of political friction between the Royalists and Puritans. During the Restoration, the Protectorate's ordinance was terminated.[61] Seen from this transatlantic perspective, the Massachusetts Body of Liberties fused animal kindness with broader declarations of Puritan identity and political authority.

The humane treatment of animals in America became a marker of assimilability and potential readiness for citizenship. After the Civil War, federal and church-based Indian boarding schools stressed the importance of animal kindness in building a productive, harmonious society of assimilated

American Indian yeoman farmers. For example, in 1893 members of the American Missionary Association—who also included Native Americans and Appalachian whites in their educational work—gathered at Fort Berthold, North Dakota, to prioritize their educational goals at mission schools. "Humane Education for Indians" was a featured topic.[62] As part of preparing Native American children for an occupational future in private enterprise and family farming, teachers stressed the relationship between gentle stewardship and financial independence. In addition to specific instructions for proper care, a government-sponsored *Course of Study* (1901) advised teachers, "Teach the boys to handle and treat the cows gently. They must not be abused or frightened, as this injures their milking qualities."[63] The presence of kindness curricula in mission and government schools demonstrates the wide influence of the gospel of kindness, even among those who were not directly affiliated with the movement. The bond between an assimilated empire of liberty and animal kindness was globalized at the turn of the twentieth century with American-sponsored animal welfare legislation and the growth of humane education programs in America's new overseas empire.

Animal protectionists saw the practical, day-to-day activities of patrolling the streets, rounding up strays, and providing water to beleaguered livestock in railway cars as essential to their larger civilizing gospel of kindness. Their ideals complemented concurrent exceptionalist ideologies of manifest destiny and uplift, which applied nineteenth-century continental expansionist mandates internationally. Political leaders (especially President Woodrow Wilson) and writers alike embraced the notion that America's manifest destiny was a "providentially assigned role" for the United States to lead the world by benevolent example.[64] Animal protectionists shared this sense of moral mission. Generally opposed to American militarism, they believed in the peaceful expansion of American ideals. The Student Volunteer Movement for Foreign Missions (1886) and surging numbers of missionary organizations expressed a similar sense of mission to propagate Christianity as an American value at home and abroad through private international organizations. Clergyman, author, and Social Gospel activist Josiah Strong explicitly linked missionary work to manifest destiny and the progressive promise of American expansion and racial uplift in popular works such as *Our Country* (1885) and *Expansion* (1900).[65] In this spirit of moral elevation and nation building abroad, numerous missionaries actively participated in animal welfare work.

Animal advocates were important participants in complementary programs of American compassion and humanitarianism. Indeed, they often referred to themselves as "animal humanitarians." Yet their work has generally been overlooked in relation to better-known examples of private American aid organizations and formal state humanitarian programs, such as the American Red Cross (1881); the American Relief Administration after World War I; and the Berlin Airlift and the Marshall Plan following World War II.[66] Animal welfare activists possessed little direct, formal power in making American foreign policy, but in words and deed, they contributed to the formation of modern American exceptionalist values, convinced that the United States could peaceably transform a violent world through a humanitarian empire of kindness. Fusing mainline Protestant legacies of revivalism and reform with universal moral standards, a vision of global justice founded upon kindness to animals, and a commitment to racial equality alongside paternalistic notions of the white man's burden, members of the humane movement helped broadcast the contradictory ideological contours of the modern nation and its place in the world.

Despite the wide historical influence of the early phase of the American animal welfare movement, it is little known today, especially among animal rights authors. They either overlook historical animal advocacy or briefly mention it as a short footnote in the history of the contemporary animal rights movement.[67] A possible reason for this omission is that early animal welfare activism often took place at Protestant churches, whereas contemporary animal advocacy generally occurs in secular spaces.[68] Similarly, the kinship that nineteenth-century activists felt with animals was often rooted in biblical concepts of stewardship rather than biological evolution. In the early twentieth century, growing numbers of humane leaders amplified this human-animal kinship with biological, evolutionary evidence, but the early moral impetus for animal activism excluded biological explanations for humanity's kinship with animals.

Early animal advocates, by and large, ate meat, whereas vegetarianism is a virtual litmus test of one's commitment to the movement today. As a stark contrast to the contemporary no-kill shelter movement, earlier generations of activists viewed euthanasia as the only compassionate solution to overpopulation and terminal suffering on the streets. Humane publications such as *Our Dumb Animals* and the *Starry Cross* contained articles that would seem anathema today, such as "How to Mercifully Shoot Horses, Dogs, and Other Animals" and frank advice for cat population control: drowning all of one's kittens, "except one" to suckle and relieve its painfully engorged mother. Mainstream newspapers like the *New York Times* told of well-dressed ladies quietly etherizing colonies of stray cats.[69] In an age before safe surgical

TO MERCIFULLY KILL HORSES, DOGS, AND OTHER ANIMALS.

THE HORSE.

Shooting. — Place the pistol muzzle within a few inches of the head, and shoot at the dot, aiming toward the centre of the head. *Be careful not to shoot too low.*

THE DOG.

Shooting. — Place the pistol muzzle near the head, aiming a little one side of the centre of the top of the skull, and shoot downward at the dot, so that the bullet shall go through the brain into or toward the neck. *Do not shoot too low, or directly in the middle, because of thick bones.*

After much consultation with veterinary surgeons and experts, no better or more merciful method of killing cats has been found than to put with a long-handled wooden spoon, about half a teaspoonful of *pure* cyanide of potassium on the cat's tongue, *as near the throat as possible.* The suffering is only for a few seconds. Great care must be used to get *pure* cyanide of potassium, and to keep it tightly corked.

FIGURE I.6. In the nineteenth and early twentieth centuries, American animal advocates generally viewed euthanasia as a compassionate end to suffering. "To Mercifully Kill Horses, Dogs, and Other Animals," *Our Dumb Animals*, July 1887, 24.

sterilization, people took pet population control into their own hands. Until the 1910s, SPCA advocates were generally unconcerned about the ethics of animal performances at zoos, circuses, and vaudeville, although they quickly denounced specific stunts that might cause physical pain. In a world still powered largely by animal muscle, animal entertainers simply represented another form of animal labor. In short, a flesh-eating, deeply religious constituency that supported euthanasia and tolerated the presence of animals in entertainment would likely seem unfamiliar to animal activists today.

Though animal protectionism has recently been a wellspring of scholarly interest, historians have generally paid less attention to the global dimensions of the American animal welfare movement.[70] Historians of the British and Japanese empires have examined the connection between imperialism and animal humanitarianism, but the American example has not similarly been placed in a transnational context of empire and nation building.[71] *The Gospel of Kindness* considers the wider global setting of the American animal welfare movement to understand the movement's relationship to the nation's changing place in the world. Put another way, it explores the historical meanings of nation and empire building with the American animal welfare movement as its lens. Paying special attention to the historical nuances of gender, race, and class, this book's focus extends beyond formal institutions and animal protection leaders to consider the activities of missionaries, purity reformers, rabbis, ministers, and other people not readily associated or formally affiliated with the movement. This includes individuals whose attention to animals was secondary to other human-centered objectives, but whose activities intersected with those of animal welfare advocates. As a result, this book is not an institutional history; rather it is an exploration of the movement's variegated meanings in unexpected places: the street, classroom, baseball field, laboratory, church, fighting pit, mission field, bullring, and saloon.

This book is chronologically bounded but does not have a strictly linear organization. While the Civil War helped trigger the movement's founding and explosive growth in 1866, animal protection's moral and tactical cores coalesced during the antebellum era. The Second Great Awakening (1790–1840) and its fusion of evangelicalism, social reform, and a growing theology of human perfectibility helped shape the identity of the postbellum animal protection movement and its link to cultural pluralism, assimilative values, citizenship, and American civilization. The eve of World War II provides a logical end point to this story. By 1941, the nation's transformation from animal power to motor power was almost complete. For a social movement whose original focus centered on kindness to laboring animals, this shift had important implications for the future. In the context of the "rights revolution" of World War II and the postwar civil rights and transnational anticolonial movements, animal welfare advocates expanded the scope of their activism to include the rights of animals.[72] Although the prevention of suffering and neglect remained at the heart of the movement, a growing ethical emphasis on animal subjectivity signaled a new ideological and tactical frontier for animal advocacy.

Chapters 1 through 3 of this book focus on animal welfare activities within the United States. Chapter 1 explores the era of Protestant revivalism and social reform that generated a movement theology and a language of kindness and cruelty, which circulated nationally in a burgeoning mass print culture. Abolition and antebellum temperance activism were significant ideological and tactical antecedents to the postbellum animal welfare movement. It is important, however, to remember that the revivalist underpinnings of animal protection were not rigidly denominational nor even literally spiritual. Henry Bergh, for one, was a decidedly non-evangelical Unitarian. Yet his faith in the unbounded power of moral uplift and potential human perfectibility were enmeshed in the secular and spiritual reformist imperatives of the Second Great Awakening. Chapter 2 analyzes the Woman's Christian Temperance Union (WCTU) and its Department of Mercy, an organization usually examined for its fight against alcohol. The WCTU defined animal cruelty as a form of intemperance—both involved a loss of free moral agency. Using kindness to animals as a springboard for all reform, WCTU activists made their own claims to citizenship with moral suasion in an era before women possessed the right to vote. Their attention to the "least among us" eventually addressed child labor, prisoners, and racism. Chapter 3 explores the public dynamics of animal protection. Reportage of animal cruelty in the press, culturally specific animal practices, and popular representations of cruelty collectively translated acts of animal kindness and cruelty into a benchmark of American belonging, exclusion, and fitness for citizenship in a culturally pluralistic society.

Chapters 4, 5, and 6 place animal advocacy in conversation with America's place in the wider world. While animal protectionists were often directly involved in overseas activities, these chapters also consider the role of formal state actors, such as government authorities and military officials, in addition to informal movement critics and advocates. Chapter 4 explores US animal welfare policy in the new empire—specifically, the US Occupied Philippines, Cuba, and Puerto Rico—after the Spanish-American War (1898). Although animal advocates were highly critical of

American militarism and formal empire building, they still believed in the universal promise of American benevolence and were strongly supportive of US programs of moral uplift in building potentially assimilable subjects of empire. Chapter 5 examines animal advocacy in colonial India, where American humane leaders maintained regular contact with Indian reformers and animal welfare activists. SPCAs also funded humane education programs taught by American missionaries.[73] Reflecting the hybrid character of nineteenth-century American Protestantism, many animal advocates valorized South Asian religious traditions of animal kindness and vegetarianism—more so than any other religious or cultural field, while still other Americans used the status of Indian animals to discredit Indian culture. Chapter 6 explores bullfighting as an American crucible for ideologies of exceptionalism and merciful expansionism. Influenced by Protestant mythologies of the "Black Legend" and Spain as the "Sick Man of Europe," American animal protectionists, writers, tourists, and policymakers alike treated the bullfight as a symbol of Spanish cruelty, decadence, and national decline in locations as diverse as the *Plaza de Toros* in Madrid, Mexican bullrings, and the Texas Centennial in Dallas (1936). As the victorious claimant to Spain's crumbling empire in 1898, American leaders trumpeted bullfighting bans in the nation's new overseas territories as a distinctly American form of rule that distinguished progressive empire building from "barbarous" Spanish imperialism.

Animal advocates believed that the world was suffering—wounded by war, strong liquor, military domination, and scientific experimentation. Unlike their predestinarian ancestors, they believed that the gospel of kindness, as an evangelical mission expressed in secular terms, gave them the power to improve, even perfect, their world. Mercy toward animals, they reasoned, would invariably spark a chain reaction of sustained compassion around the globe. However, in placing animals at the center of their considerations of welfare and mercy, they often unwittingly reinforced other forms of human inequality. Laws in defense of the laboring horse did not contain a corresponding guarantee of higher wages for the laboring hostler. In addition, it was the struggling driver who was most commonly fined for animal cruelty rather than his boss, the stable owner, who relentlessly demanded that the driver increase his passenger load. Similarly, American animal welfare activists abroad frequently deployed a universal standard of suffering and kindness, often without regard to culturally specific social practices and attitudes toward animals, a stance that often unintentionally reinforced normative ideologies regarding race, gender, class, and civilization.

The movement's potential to reify and individualize rather than challenge extant forms of inequality echoed European critiques of animal welfare activism. Karl Marx and Friedrich Engels included the humane movement on their list of "Conservative or Bourgeois Socialism" in *The Communist Manifesto* (1848). They contended that animal welfare and other areas of reform ultimately preserved bourgeois, or middle-class, dominance: "A part of the bourgeoisie is desirous of redressing social grievances, in order to secure the continued existence of bourgeois society. To this section belong economists, philanthropists, humanitarians, improvers of the condition of the working class, organizers of charity, members of societies for the prevention of cruelty to animals, temperance fanatics, hole-and-corner reformers of every imaginable kind. This form of socialism has, moreover, been worked out into complete systems."[74]

Still, it would be a mistake to dismiss the animal welfare movement wholesale as simply an anxious group of elite Euroamerican hypocrites who were hell-bent on a project of social control. For one, they sincerely cared about animals, they believed passionately in their broader mission to aid humanity, and they readily prosecuted the rich, often with little success. They worked hard to deflect charges that they were insensitive to the poor. Although they relied on diverse sources of surveillance (e.g., police, SPCA officers, and volunteers) to help achieve their goals, over time they made education rather than prosecution their main end. This point was noted in the ASPCA's annual report for 1923: "Corrective and educational means, rather than punitive measures, are to-day accomplishing greater good for the humane cause, though prosecutions are still necessary in extreme cases."[75] While the towering, uniformed policing presence of Henry Bergh visually embodied the social control ethos of the new organized animal protection movement, SPCAs and humane societies increasingly devoted their resources to promoting moral change. The Massachusetts SPCA, in particular, became the vanguard of humane education in America. For that matter, any modern assumption regarding the early movement's WASPY homogeneity would be a misleading presentist projection onto a movement history that contains a surprising degree of racial and ethnic diversity.[76]

In the end, it is more productive to treat this movement as both reflective and constitutive of its time. A critical historical approach, instead of unreflective hagiography or wholesale condemnation, reveals the movement's remarkable significance in shaping the ideological contours of our modern world. By placing animals at the center of their project of social and cultural reform, humane advocates compellingly demonstrated the interconnectedness of animal welfare with virtually all facets of American life at home and abroad: food, religion, sanitation, entertainment, alcohol consumption, literature, labor, art and photography as a tool of reform, education, gambling, domesticity, science, and transportation. Most of these categories—both the quotidian and the expansive—addressed broader human rights issues, such as child welfare, civil rights, women's rights, militarism, and domestic violence. As such, a movement in defense of animals helped recast the rights of human beings. Nonetheless, by putting animal welfare into dialogue with human welfare, humane activists created a potentially difficult ethical balancing act: could one consider the welfare of people and animals in a way that avoided privileging one to the detriment of the other? This tension is exposed in the pages that follow.

I

"*A Righteous Man Regards the Life of His Beast*"

THE ROOTS OF THE GOSPEL OF KINDNESS IN THE SECOND GREAT AWAKENING AND ANTEBELLUM REFORM

ON FEBRUARY 24, 1868, a self-made Boston attorney named George Angell had an epiphany as he read his morning newspaper. Two fine horses had been driven to death over the weekend during a forty-mile race from Brighton to Worcester. The news of this senseless tragedy compelled Angell to change his life's work: "When I saw . . . the record of this cruel race, my determination was at once taken. I had heard that Mr. Bergh had started a society in New York. I said to myself, 'Somebody must take hold of this business, and I might as well as any body.'"[1] Angell quickly penned an editorial for the *Boston Daily Advertiser* announcing that he was "ready to contribute both time and money." He invited other readers to join him.

The editorial attracted instant attention. Mrs. Emily Appleton offered full support, noting that she had previously submitted articles of incorporation for a new SPCA to the Massachusetts legislature, which promptly lost her papers. With the assistance of Appleton and other powerful Bostonians, Angell drafted new articles of incorporation, which were quickly approved by the state legislature on March 23, thus making the Massachusetts SPCA (MSPCA) the second official state SPCA in the nation. (Animal advocates in other states and major cities were simultaneously working with their legislators: the Pennsylvania SPCA was granted a charter on April 4, and the San Francisco SPCA was incorporated on April 18.) George Angell was elected the MSPCA's first president, a position he held until his death in 1909.

In a move that Angell called "almost a providential interposition," he successfully enlisted Boston police officers to canvass the entire city to mobilize support for the new MSPCA. In June 1868, police officers delivered over 30,000 gratis copies of the organization's brand-new monthly magazine, *Our Dumb Animals*, to households across Boston. As proof of his expansive vision, Angell believed that his mission for the new MSPCA should extend far beyond its geographical namesake, so he published and distributed an additional 170,000 free copies of the magazine to groups that could most effectively propagate his message: law enforcement, missionaries, politicians, educators, and reformers across the United States and overseas.[2] Angell was so exhausted after the MSPCA's exceptionally busy first year that he traveled to Europe for a vacation in 1869, which proved to be short-lived: while in England, he guided the creation of new humane education programs for the Royal Society for the Prevention of Cruelty to Animals (RSPCA). Further, *Our Dumb Animals* had already proven so successful that it inspired the RSPCA to begin publication of its own new magazine, *The Animal World*.[3]

The birth of state SPCAs occurred at a critical historical juncture when urgent questions of rights, suffering, and property had moved to the center of the nation's consciousness. The moral imperative of the constitutional rights revolution during the Civil War and Reconstruction hastened Angell, Bergh, and others to take action. On a personal level, Angell became an animal protectionist in 1864 when he executed his will, which included provisions for "awakening public sentiment on this subject [of animal cruelty]." He directed his trustees to use the remainder of his estate to "be expended . . . in common schools, Sabbath schools, or other schools . . . such books, tracts, or pamphlets as in their judgment will tend most to impress upon the minds of youth their duty towards those domestic animals which God may make dependent upon them."[4]

Yet the origins of Angell's gospel of kindness predated the Civil War era: "It is proper for me here to say, that from my childhood I had been extremely fond of animals. . . . I had seen, and personally interfered in, a number of cases of cruelty to them, and had heard of many others."[5] Born in 1823 to a Baptist minister and deeply pious mother, George Angell came of age during the extraordinary theological and social ferment of the Second Great Awakening. This chapter contends that this era of evangelical revivalism and social reform was essential to the birth of an organized animal welfare movement after the Civil War. The Second Great Awakening put a native-born Protestant stamp on the universalizing mission of animal kindness. The Awakening stressed the potential for human perfectibility on this earth, rather than passive acceptance of God's will. Religious revivalism highlighted the power of free moral agency to combat social injustice. This proactive view of humanity accelerated major antebellum reform movements, most notably abolition and temperance, both of which strongly influenced the structure, scale, and moral tenor of postbellum animal protection societies.

The Second Great Awakening also marked the era in which copious new state and local anticruelty legislation was passed. These laws were similar in scope to Great Britain's first animal welfare law passed in Parliament in 1822, "An Act to Prevent the Cruel and Improper Treatment of Cattle" ("cattle" being broadly defined to include all livestock). Similarly, Great Britain's early animal protection movement grew and flourished in a cultural and social climate of evangelical revivalism.[6] Antebellum American laws meted out stiff fines for those convicted of public cruelty toward designated domestic animals. Section 26 of the Revised State Statutes of New York in 1829 punished convicted defendants who "maliciously kill, maim or wound any horse, ox or other cattle, or any sheep, belonging to another [or himself/herself], or shall maliciously and cruelly beat or torture any such animal," with a fine and/or prison time. A new state statute in Massachusetts in 1836 stated, "Every person who shall cruelly beat or torture any horse, ox or other animal, whether belonging to himself or another, shall be punished by imprisonment in the county jail for not more than one year or by fine not exceeding one hundred dollars." An anticruelty law for the City of Philadelphia in 1855 echoed the statutes in New York and Massachusetts, but with one notable difference: convicted defendants were ordered to pay escalating fines for subsequent offenses.[7] Animals, however, were still considered solely as property under the common-law system during the antebellum era—with no attendant recognition of their status as sentient beings possessing the right to protection.[8] Further, only police officers held the powers of enforcement, which drastically curtailed prosecution.

Despite these barriers to full-scale implementation, the advent of new animal welfare laws signaled an important historical turn during the Second Great Awakening. This era of revivalism and reform did more than simply create the social, cultural, and political conditions for a postbellum animal welfare movement. Instead, a growing emphasis on kindness toward "the least among us" made animal protection an important moral imperative in its own right. Contemporary theologians of the Awakening addressed the treatment of animals in their sermons and jeremiads, as did the popular religious literature of the day. Novelists incorporated animal mercy into their plotlines. Abolitionists and temperance advocates made pleas for animal kindness in tracts, memoirs, poems, and songs, which linked generations of reform in sentiment and deed, for there was ample overlap among these movements. The antebellum communications revolution in printing technologies, internal improvements, and new forms of transportation cohered these diverse textual sources into a far-reaching mandate for kindness.[9] The ubiquity of print media defined antebellum animal advocacy as a textual movement, a critical "structures of feeling," which triggered changes in consciousness as a necessary precondition for direct action after the Civil War.[10]

But the early seeds of direct engagement were already sprouting. The affluent Quaker merchant and first president of the Pennsylvania SPCA, Samuel Morris Waln, later reflected that local animal protection activities were already so prevalent in Philadelphia during the 1850s that a nascent movement was on the brink of solidification and institutionalization. Yet, as he put it, "the unhappy civil war . . . caused the plan to be deferred."[11] In other words, Waln argued that the Civil War temporarily delayed rather than hastened the formal institutionalization of animal advocacy.

Theological and Popular Foundations for a Gospel of Kindness

The Second Great Awakening's ecumenical emphasis on free moral agency, the emotional conversion experience, and social reform primed a national audience for a complementary message of animal kindness. The Second Great Awakening, historian Sydney E. Ahlstrom observes, was a continuation of a "great international Protestant upheaval," beginning in the eighteenth century with the growth of continental pietism, Great Britain's Evangelical Revival, and America's Great Awakening.[12] A proliferation of concern for animals accompanied the evangelical movements in Europe and Great Britain as well. In America, waves of Protestant revival meetings rocked Kentucky, Tennessee, the Northeast, and the frontier country of the Western Reserve in Ohio from the 1790s through the 1830s. Interdenominational in scope, the Awakening appealed to ordinary people and nurtured the growth of plain-spoken mainline denominations, including Methodism and the Baptist Church. Revival ministers preached a vision of God's steady love, but only for those who actively chose a righteous path. They believed that people sinned on their own accord; thus, the unrepentant were responsible for their own damnation.

Emotional intensity was at the heart of the revival experience, just as deep feeling guided the transformative experience of becoming an animal advocate. Timothy Dwight, a Congregationalist theologian and emotionally charged preacher, spearheaded the revivals at Yale College, where he served as president. Dwight's sermons were so compelling that some people wrongly cast him as the sole inspiration for the waves of revivalism that hit the New Haven area in 1802.[13] Charles Grandison Finney, the immensely popular Presbyterian minister and lawyer, preached captivating nighttime sermons. His revivals were marvelous performances, complete with an "anxious seat," whose occupants would be addressed directly and visibly shamed by their indecision. He exhorted the congregation to pray for the conversion of these tentative souls.[14] During Finney's marathon public sermons, audience members swooned. When he threw an imaginary brick at the devil, people ducked. While slowly sweeping his long arm from ceiling to floor to reinforce a sinner's fall into hell, congregants in the rear seats stood up to watch the terrifying descent.[15] Frances Willard, a devoted animal protectionist and president of the Woman's Christian Temperance Union, experienced Finney's sermons in Ohio as a young child in the early 1840s. Her mother recalled: "[Frances] said his great light eyes, white eyebrows, and vigorous manner were to her like a combination of thunder and lightning; lightning in his look, thunder in his voice."[16]

The emotional intensity and anxiety of the revival experience touched George Angell directly through his youthful epistolary relationship with his mother, Rebekah, who spent two hours by herself in silent prayer virtually every day. She worried ceaselessly about the state of George's soul: "A mother's love you can never know my anxiety for you is past description. I know the snares of youth and the temptations of the adversary to your soul are placed on every side. Your morals are in danger of being polluted and your soul destroyed. And what can be done? I have tried to wrestle with God for you. I have engaged Godly friends to do the same. Thousands of prayers have been offered for you the ten years of your life and yet you remain in unbelief."[17] Widowed in 1827 with no means of financial support, Rebekah had returned to teaching and regretfully placed young George, her only child, in the care of distant relatives for the remainder of his childhood. Her fretful daily missives to her son were simultaneously apocalyptic and prosaic: "Can you endure eternal burning? I send the socks now. Please send me those that need footing."[18] She urged George to attend a revival, embrace conversion, and gain salvation: "Is there any revival in the church where you worship or in any of the churches in the City? If so do be induced to attend where God is pouring out his holy spirit and strive for an interest in the Savior's love. . . . The Lord is doing wonders in many places multitudes are embracing the offers of mercy and coming to the Saviour. And now my son while the waters are troubled do step in and be healed of your sins. Now the Saviour stands with arms extended to receive you, if you will only come to him."[19]

Rebekah may have remained anxious about the state of her son's soul, but George welcomed the broader spiritual and secular mandates of the Second Great Awakening. He believed that humankind had the capacity for self-improvement because people were free moral agents. He prized self-sufficiency, shunned debt while working his way through college and law school, and preferred, as he put it, "to paddle my own canoe."[20] His dedication to animal stewardship also reflected the views of key theologians of the Awakening. Charles Grandison Finney and Timothy Dwight each acknowledged the significance of animals in their spoken and written words.

Dwight's sermons connected his theological views of humanity's duties toward our "fellow creatures" to a maze of interrelated topics: manners, cleanliness, marriage, virtue, drunkenness, chastity, childrearing, avarice, and charity. In Dwight's cosmos, biblical dominion represented humanity's moral obligation to serve as good stewards to animals. Dwight was a Sabbatarian, committed to making Sunday (the day that God rested in Genesis) a day of spiritual contemplation, godly fortification, and repose. Dwight argued that the Sunday Sabbath applied equally to laboring animals. He used Proverbs 10:12, "A righteous man regards the life of his beast," to make his theological case. In a society where virtually all aspects of commerce, agriculture, and transportation were powered by animal muscle, Dwight's call for a creaturely Sabbath extended the totalizing reach of the Sabbatarian movement to the most quotidian labor. At the same time, he observed that animal kindness demonstrated the boundless extent of God's mercy.

> The goodness of this glorious Being is forcibly displayed in the provision, which he has made, for the rest and comfort of labouring animals, in the Moral Law. In the hands even of prudent and humane masters, it is clearly seen, that such animals are sufficiently employed when they labour six days of the week, and are released to rest and refreshment on the seventh. God, who perfectly knew what their strength was able to bear, and who perfectly foresaw how greatly they would be oppressed by avarice and cruelty, was pleased, in this solemn manner, and at this early period, to provide for their relief, by securing to them the quiet and restoration of one day in seven. In this merciful

provision, the divine tenderness is displayed in a most amiable and edifying manner. The humble character of even these beings did not place them below the compassionate care of God. Elsewhere, he has commanded us to supply them with food. Here, he has commanded us to furnish them with rest. In both cases, he has taught us, that the Lord is good and kind to all, and that his tender mercies are over all the works of his hands.[21]

Charles Grandison Finney found a clear mandate for God's benevolence in his biblical exegesis, *Skeletons of a Course of Theological Lectures* (1840), which analyzed the "letter" and "true spirit" of the Sixth Commandment— "Thou shalt not kill"—in relation to people and animals. His lecture included a broad list of Commandment violations, which placed prohibitions against animal cruelty next to interdictions against other forms of human brutality:

V. Some cases to be regarded as violations of this command. 1. All abuse, neglect, or treatment of animals, whereby their life is shortened. 2. All sporting with the life of animals. 3. All such treatment of human beings, as tends to injure their health and destroy their lives. 4. All dueling. 5. Every unnecessary violation of the laws of life and health, either in men or animals. 6. Every unnecessary disregard of the command to multiply the number of human beings. 7. Every selfish disposition to lessen the amount of animal life.[22]

Killing animals for food and in self-defense were the only forms of violent dominion that Finney found biblically justifiable. He validated the act of slaying animals for food by turning to Genesis 9:3 "Every moving thing that liveth shall be meat for you; even as the green herb have I given you all things." And in Genesis 9:5, he found corroboration for "the destruction of those beasts that are injurious to men," as an act of self-defense from imminent or anticipated harm, "to slay them before they have committed their depredations."[23] Like Timothy Dwight, Finney saw biblical dominion and stewardship as complementary theological precepts.

Finney's interpretation of the Sixth Commandment included all "creatures," which made animal and human mercy indissoluble. He viewed prohibitions against dueling and blood sports as interconnected imperatives. He coupled animal kindness with pronatalism to condemn any barrier to human or animal reproduction. Finney made this point explicitly to denounce abortion: "[The Sixth Commandment] prohibits the use of means to destroy the existence of human beings in embryo."[24] Finney's theological commitment to unfettered reproduction and animal mercy were future-focused imperatives to build a stronger civilization with morally fortified citizens. The fate of the child was essential to both.

Other theologians of the Second Great Awakening were equally interested in children and animals, believing that Christian childrearing should emphasize kindness to animals to safeguard the moral integrity of future generations.[25] Timothy Dwight argued that salvation was impossible unless parents taught their children to acknowledge personal sin and to learn kindness as a powerful antidote.[26] Dwight asserted that swift parental intervention was crucial to promote a child's continued moral development.

> Every child should be invariably instructed to exercise kindness towards animals, and to shun cruelty even to an insect. The plundering of birds' nests, and the capture of their young, is in all ordinary cases, notwithstanding it is so generally allowed, an employment, fitted only to harden the heart, and prepare it to be insensible to human sufferings. Still worse is the deplorable practice, extensively allowed also, of setting up poultry as a mark, to be destroyed by gradual torture. Worse still is the practice, so widely and shamefully extended in some parts of this country, of cockfighting; abominable for its cruelty, and detestable for its fraud. Children should never injure animals without reproof solemnly administered, nor, as the case may be, without punishment.[27]

As citizens-in-formation, children were living repositories for new class-inflected ways of thinking about the interconnections among animal abuse, character development, and futurity. Dwight's emphasis on self-control and its counterpart, parental prevention, complemented an emergent middle-class creed of internalized time discipline in an industrializing market economy. Moral sobriety and delayed gratification were part and parcel to a new ideal of capital accumulation tied to the clock, rather than older, sensory modes of preindustrial timekeeping, such as the "cattle clock" (i.e., the daily regimen of livestock care), which were bound to the diurnal and seasonal rhythms of the natural world. According to historian E. P. Thompson, changing market relations heralded a transformation in temporal relations: "Time is now currency: it is not passed but spent."[28] Dwight's articulations of an embryonic gospel of kindness placed time discipline and thoughtful moral uplift in stark juxtaposition with impulsivity and consequent animal brutality.

Dwight's case studies of childhood cruelty also tied the treatment of animals to the growing sanctity of the domestic sphere among the nascent middle class. The nesting bird and her babies were common popular tropes for home and family, while poultry provided extra "egg money" for mothers and children. Historian Katherine Grier explains that the gentle cultivation and stewardship of pets and children inside the antebellum household represented a "domestic ethic of kindness," which stressed patience, discipline, and delayed gratification—all of which were self-identified moral and temporal values of the growing middle class.[29] In the first half of the nineteenth century, the budding industrial economy gradually separated the home from the market, and the former was idealized as a restorative, soothing, spiritual balm to counter the crass hustle of the marketplace.[30] Dwight's vivid reference to the plundered bird's nest, the poultry used as target practice, and the vicious cockfight illustrated the ways in which animal cruelty desecrated this powerful domestic ideal.

Harriet Beecher Stowe used these tropes of childhood cruelty throughout her long writing career to demonstrate the essential importance of a mother's moral power to right a wayward child with animal kindness. In *Uncle Tom's Cabin* (1852), Mrs. Bird punished her sons severely, "whipped and tumbled off to bed, without any supper," when she learned that they had joined some "graceless" neighbor boys in stoning a kitten.[31] Stowe's short story, "A Talk about Birds," also accentuated the mother's role as a moral compass and bearer of animal kindness. The story opened with young Jamie traipsing after two "strange" boys who spoke jollily about killing birds for idle sport: "Come along with us—we are going to have fun. We have got our pockets full of stones, and we are going to kill birds with them; it's the best fun in the world."[32] Jamie's mother witnessed the whole exchange from afar, called him off, and gently explained how a songbird—beautiful, sentient—was a marvel of God's creation and needed humane stewardship: "The Bible says, his *tender* mercies are over all his works; he is not merely good to everything, but he is tender and careful in all he does, as a mother is tender in taking care of a little helpless infant."[33] Bonding biblical and maternal stewardship into a singular lesson of kindness to all creatures, Stowe treated such domestic lessons as a moral springboard for expansive social change.

Frances Willard's mother guided her children with firm, biblical lessons of animal mercy. Fifty years later, Frances recalled the power of her mother's moral influence in action when she and her sister, Mary, were quick to stop errant male playmates from harming nesting birds during their wooded sojourns in Wisconsin during the late 1840s: "'You may climb the trees and look, if you want to see the eggs or little ones, but you can't hurt a birdie, big or small, in *our* pasture.' The boys said their mother told them the same thing, and they only wanted to 'look.' So Mary and I showed them under the leafy covert some of the brown thrush's housekeeping, and the robin's, too, and didn't want to kill the pretty creatures God had made."[34] Willard reflected upon her mother's lessons of animal kindness as the bedrock of her awakening moral consciousness. (Indeed, her very first essay as a schoolgirl was a paean to her beloved kitten.)[35] Collectively, Willard, Stowe, Dwight, and other writers consistently paid close attention to pets, poultry, livestock, and wild birds: that is to say, domestic animals living in close proximity with their human stewards and wild animals whose nest-building and fastidious "housekeeping" enacted middle-class domestic ideals. Birds straddled these relations of proximity because they were also popular caged pets inside the home. Literary scholar Brigitte Nicole Fielder suggests that familiar animals "might also be understood as familial—that is, as figured in affective kinship relations or through larger notions of national kinship and belonging—by virtue of their proximity to humans in domestic spaces."[36] Enfolded into the national "family" through kindly stewardship, animals and children created the building blocks for moral national belonging.

During the antebellum communications revolution, a popular literature on animal topics now reached a national audience. The Sunday school movement, an enduring innovation of the Second Great Awakening, was a fertile site of popular productions of animal mercy. Formed in 1824, the American Sunday-School Union encouraged the development of Sunday school curricula and published extensive educational literature.[37] Diverse animal topics were common—from creation stories and zoological bestiaries to human relationships with pets and livestock. In 1847, the American Sunday-School Union published a cautionary tale about an orphan boy circus star, John "Slim Jack" Ward, who ultimately paid for his fame with a fatal fall. *Slim Jack, or the History of a Circus-Boy* portrayed circus life as boozy, thrilling, dishonest, and brutal, noting that intelligent audience members would not be fooled by animal tricks: "Their knowledge of the nature and habits of these animals told them that in the discipline necessary to teach them these things, they had suffered inexpressible torture, and they had so much feeling for the dumb beasts, that they could not look long at them with any pleasure."[38]

The American Sunday-School Union also used animals as subjects of biblical exegesis. Published in 1845, *Kindness to Animals, Or, The Sin of Cruelty Exposed and Rebuked* placed human-animal relationships at the center of the story of Original Sin. Prior to the fall, Adam, Eve, and the wild animals were fast friends in a creaturely utopia:

Was it not a wonderful and a beautiful sight? There, in a very delicious garden, full of all manner of rich fruit and bright flowers, with soft warm air, and calm sunshine, was the first and only man in all the world! He was righteous and good, without any malice, or cruelty, or covetousness, or pride in his heart, looking with delight upon the creatures that came about him as their right ruler, to receive their names. Can you not fancy how he must have admired the noble and beautiful creatures as they meekly and lovingly came to him?"[39]

After Eve took the fateful bite of the apple from the Tree of Knowledge, wild animals became vicious and humanity discarded gentle stewardship for brutal dominion: "This sad curse was on the animals too; not by their fault, poor things! but by man's dreadful sin. For, you see, it was God who made them subject to man; and when man became a rebel and traitor to God, the creatures turned against him, and against each other."[40]

As a manifestation of Original Sin, animal cruelty was tied to other sins that resulted from the loss of self-control. *Kindness to Animals* reminded its young readers that stewardship was an effective antidote to sinful greed. Modulation, as a demonstration of self-mastery, was the handmaiden of animal mercy. Despite animals' legal status as property, this Sunday school text argued that they were embodiments of divine creation, rather than human acquisitiveness: "How perfectly the Lord knows and numbers all the works of his hands, and how tenderly he cares for them all. This is one of the things that we are apt to forget when we have a beast, or a bird, or a fish, or an insect, in our power."[41]

Kindness to Animals used animal anecdotes to address two other significant areas of antebellum reform: education and the asylum movement. To segue from Genesis to stories of individual animals, its anonymous author wrote about adopting an impoverished deaf and dumb seven-year-old Irish boy named Jack while traveling abroad. The author recounted how proper education and gentle tutelage transformed the boy. Although never able to gain full speech during his brief life, Jack learned to communicate and he was tender and pious, especially in defense of animals:

> How often has Jack, when he saw a thoughtless boy hurting a dog, or any other animal, gone up to him, and said, on his fingers, in an very quiet, gentle, but earnest manner, "God see—God angry." He felt much for the dumb beast, suffering pain; but more for the boy who was forgetting that the Lord's hand would yet punish him, when he

least expected it: for Jack very well knew that the Bible says, "He shall have judgment without mercy that hath showed no mercy."[42]

Jack's transformation mirrored a growing cultural focus on the moral development of children as the keystone to American civilization. In 1836, William H. McGuffey published the first *Eclectic Readers*, a ubiquitous set of school reading books with strong moral lessons that reached a circulation of some 120 million copies by the end of the nineteenth century.[43] Kindness to animals was an integral part of McGuffey's moral pedagogy: "The boys should be kind to their horses. It is best not to whip them. When they are done riding, they will give the horses some hay or corn"; "'Why Hattie, you are not sorry puss got the rat, are you?' 'No, I can not say I am sorry she got it; but I do not like to see even a rat suffer pain' "; "'Shall we take the [bird's] nest, Rose?' 'Oh no, Willie! We must not take it; but we will come and look at it again, some time.'" Other lessons in the *First Reader* highlighted brave Ponto, the hero dog that saved Rose from drowning; Rab, the patient dog that guarded the children's dolls and baskets; and the protective mother songbird that made a little girl realize just how much her own mother loved her.[44]

Dogs were central characters in the *Eclectic Third Reader's* digest of famous literary excerpts: "The little boy and the little dog were great friends. Frisk loved him dearly, much better than he did any one else, perhaps, because he recollected that Harry was his earliest and firmest friend during a time of great trouble." One could also read bestiaries of horses, lions, eagles, tigers, and elephants; meditations on the differences between people and animals; and cautionary tales of impulsive behavior, such as the "Effects of Rashness," a story of a wealthy Persian man who killed his loyal dog after falsely assuming the dog had hurt his baby, when in fact the dog had saved the baby from a snake in the nursery.[45] Used in public school curricula across the nation, McGuffey's *Eclectic Readers* made animal kindness a pedagogical building block of proper American citizenship.

This instructional accent on animal mercy amplified a parallel antebellum movement against corporal punishment in schools, asylums, prisons, and other public institutions.[46] Innovative new animal training manuals likewise demonstrated the effectiveness of learning through kindness instead of fear. John S. Rarey, the internationally famous "Great American Horse Tamer," gentled seemingly wild and incorrigible horses with touch, habituation, rewards, and a fundamental respect for equine intelligence. Rarey generally avoided the whip, spurs, and other modes of coercive discipline.

His bestselling (and widely plagiarized) primer, *The Modern Art of Taming Wild Horses* (1855), and his sensational live equine gentling exhibitions made him an instrumental voice in diverse reform movements against the physical punishment of defenseless people and animals.[47] As a consultant and inspector with the Union Army during the Civil War, Rarey found an even more authoritative platform from which to broadcast his mandates for kindness.[48] Rarey died of a stroke at the age of thirty-eight in 1866, but he cast a long shadow on the humane movement: Rarey was regularly memorialized in *Our Dumb Animals* as a fundamental lever of social change. George Angell remembered, "The grandest preaching we have ever had in Boston, came from Rarey, when he taught us the moral philosophy of love with reference to the horse."[49]

Future animal welfare leaders also venerated the antebellum asylum reformer Dorothea Dix as a kindness pioneer. The MSPCA, for example, erected a horse fountain at Boston's Custom Square in Dix's memory in 1888.[50] Future animal protectionists were indebted to asylum activists for their compelling uses of language and innovative forms of reportage. Asylum reformers used the suffering animal as a referent for the suffering person. Often shackled in chains and housed in prisons and almshouses, mentally ill Americans, as well as the physically and developmentally disabled, were commonly depicted as animals, deprived of reason, and subjected to beatings and neglect. Dix effectively deployed a new genre of sociological writing, the sensational exposé, to rally public support for asylum reform.[51] In 1847, Dix testified in front of the Tennessee General Assembly to lobby for the construction of a new state mental hospital. As in other legislatures across the nation, her testimony in Tennessee included gruesome accounts of the inhumane care she had witnessed: "Pining in cells and dungeons, pent in log-cabins, bound with ropes, restrained by leathern throngs, burthened with chains—now wandering at large, alone and neglected, endangering the security of property, often inimical to human life. . . . The highly excited patients shut into those wretched cells in the cellar, damp, cold, and unventilated as they are, are not fit for any human creature, much less for the treatment of the sick."[52] In making the hidden bondage of vulnerable asylum inmates visible, Dix addressed a common goal across diverse fields of antebellum reform: to render suffering visible through vivid language, illustrations, and graphic narrative. Nowhere was this explicit visualization of the suffering body more apparent than in the abolitionist movement.

FOUNTAIN WE ERECTED IN CUSTOM HOUSE SQUARE
IN MEMORY OF DOROTHEA L. DIX.

FIGURE 1.1. In 1888 the MSPCA erected an equine water fountain in Boston to honor the memory of antebellum asylum reformer Dorothea Dix, an important inspiration for postbellum animal advocacy. "Fountain We Erected in Custom House Square in Memory of Dorothea L. Dix," *Our Dumb Animals*, September 1900, 45.

Slavery, Drunkenness, and the Loss of Free Moral Agency

Abolitionists used the treatment of animals as a litmus test for good character. They twinned animal mercy with antislavery activism and animal abuse with slaveholding. The abolitionist language of cruelty and kindness permeated animal protectionist rhetoric, as well. The African American abolitionist newspaper, *The Colored American*, used Timothy Dwight's theology of animal kindness to remind readers that childhood animal cruelty was hardly innocent, but instead a harbinger of adult wretchedness: "Boys who kill squirrels will rob the poor innocent and harmless birds of their young, set old growler, the great dog, at the poor terrified cat, and pull off the wings of the tortured fly. They learn to love cruelty and that is extremely wicked."[53]

Several theologians of the Second Great Awakening participated directly in abolition. Oberlin College, where Charles Grandison Finney was professor and then president, was a hub of antislavery activism. Raising the theological possibility of total sanctification, ministers promulgated the moral urgency of ending slavery. Simultaneously, the rapid expansion of the Union—from eighteen states in 1814 to thirty-three on the eve of the Civil War—put the fractious question of whether new states would be slave or free at the center of the nation's future. In the contemporaneous climate of evangelical revivalism and social reform across the Atlantic, the British Parliament abolished slavery in the British Empire in 1833, which intensified the escalating moral divide between slavery supporters and abolitionists in the United States.

In the 1830s, American abolitionist writers increasingly focused on the slave's excruciating bodily suffering, a corpus of literature that historian Elizabeth Clark identifies as a new genre, the cruelty narrative. Comprised of tracts, reports, autobiographical ex-slave narratives (after 1840), and sentimental fiction, cruelty narratives pulled their readers into a sympathetic relationship with suffering slaves, based on the recognition of humanity's universal capacity to feel pain. Clark locates the roots of what she calls the "sympathetic or affective mode of moral reasoning" in the ethical sentimentalism of the English philosopher Ashley Cooper, the third earl of Shaftesbury (1671–1713). Evangelicalism, she writes, made Americans receptive to this form of moral thought in the United States; religious revivalism stressed the centrality of the emotional conversion experience, one's intimate, personal relationship with God, and the belief in the universality of Christian benevolence as a trigger for social reform.[54]

Liberal Protestant denominations, such as Unitarians and Quakers, rejected predestinarian Calvinist beliefs in pain as an inevitable and necessary stimulus for moral development. Instead, they treated suffering as direct proof of human wrongdoing.[55] Simultaneous medical innovations in pain management, such as the use of nitrous oxide gas and ether anesthesia, redefined pain itself as preventable, no longer an inevitable symptom of God's wrath. As a result, humanity's new ability to manage pain diminished God's omniscience in favor of human agency.[56] Historian James Turner identifies the advent of analgesics and anesthesia as a major catalyst for postbellum animal welfare activism in a society where pain was now actively prevented rather than passively tolerated.[57] Innovative technologies of pain control also spurred the development of new popular print cultures singularly focused on pain: the abolitionist cruelty narrative, Gothic fiction, the urban mystery, and the shocking penny press exposé.[58] Historian Karen Halttunen contends that these cultural forms were bound together by a shared sensibility of "spectatorial sympathy," in which vivid language and visual material enabled readers to visualize and thus prevent suffering through acts of affective kinship, or the ability to feel fully the suffering of others.[59] The popular eighteenth-century moral philosophers of the Scottish Enlightenment believed that sight was the most powerful of the five senses and therefore, the key to unlocking the feeling of sympathy.[60]

American abolitionists shared this belief in the primacy of seeing as a means for sparking sympathy and consequent social change. They amplified the affective power of the popular cruelty narrative with graphic illustrations of slavery. Lydia Maria Child included grisly images of shackles, stakes, and cuffs in *An Appeal in Favor of that Class of Americans called Africans* (1833), and Henry Bibb illustrated his autobiographical slave narrative, *Narrative of the Life and Adventures of Henry Bibb, an American Slave, Written by Himself* (1849), with stark pictures of bound and naked enslaved men and women beaten by wicked slaveholders.[61]

Suffering human bodies also illuminated the shared histories of slaveholding, livestock husbandry, and brutal mastery. Slaveholders ordered slaves to tend livestock, which, as historian Philip Morgan suggests, "encouraged the manager [overseer] to think of his human and animal charges in similar ways and treat them as such."[62] Slaveholders described enslaved human beings as "stock," women as "breeding wenches," the slave market as "like a herd of cattle," or as "Horses in a Market." Slaveholders applied the same brutal methods of animal "taming" and domestication to enslaved human beings: beating, "breaking," branding, chaining, whipping, buying, selling, and castration.[63] After the Civil War, animal protectionists evoked this interconnected history of violent mastery using explicit narratives and illustrations of animal bondage—from acts of outright violence, such as grisly floggings with a bullwhip, to subtle artifacts of fashionable torture, such as the choking checkrein, and the exposed docked tail. Animal advocates also displayed physical artifacts of mastery at world's fairs and traveling shows to remind their audiences of the suffering physical consequences of dominion and fashion.[64]

The nation's most famous cruelty narrative, *Uncle Tom's Cabin* (1852), reinforced the synergetic relationship between the treatment of animals, human bondage, and moral character. Animal cruelty helped define the violent, amoral universe of the slaveholder. Master Tom, for one, stoned and drowned George's beloved dog, Carlo, who was a gift from George's wife, Eliza.[65] In contrast to the evil Master Tom, the kindly Mrs. Bird protected animals and she vehemently condemned the passage of the federal Fugitive Slave Law in 1850. She openly admitted to her husband, a senator who had voted for the law, that she would break the law on biblical principle, if given the chance: "Things have got to a pretty pass, if a woman can't give a warm supper and a bed to poor, starving creatures, just because they are slaves, and have been abused and oppressed all their lives, poor things. . . . Now, John, I don't know anything about politics, but I can read my Bible; and there I see that I must feed the hungry, clothe the naked, and comfort the desolate; and that Bible I mean to follow."[66]

Stowe's depictions of "creatures" potentially conflated African American slaves and animals in ways that could reinforce, rather than destroy, racialist hierarchies. During the antebellum era, the theory of polygenesis was born, a new school of scientific racism that claimed separate animal origins for specific racial groups. The proponents of polygenesis included Louis Agassiz, Samuel Morton, and Josiah Nott, all of whom roundly rejected monogenesis—that is, a common origin for humanity.[67] Bridgette Fielder contends that Stowe and other abolitionists used animals strategically in cruelty narratives to affirm the common humanity of the enslaved by way of contrast to animals, and to demonstrate the immorality of animalization, or treating people "*as though* they were animals."[68] Although these connections rooted in metaphor and simile potentially reified rather than defied animalization, they were generative for an embryonic movement in animal protection: Stowe's juxtaposition of kindness, bondage, and suffering helped shape a symbiotic movement language and an expansive field of reform. George Angell referred directly to the novel in 1890 when he funded the publication of *Black Beauty* (first issued in England in 1877) in the United States. He advertised the American edition as "the *Uncle Tom's Cabin* of the horse," to make an urgent, familiar cry for social justice through moral suasion.[69] In so doing, Angell spread the gospel of animal kindness to new audiences, helped make *Black Beauty* an enduring classic, and reminded readers of the formative theological and social ties among animal protection and abolitionism.

Angell also had direct personal ties to abolitionism. In 1852, the year that *Uncle Tom's Cabin* was published, Angell became a law partner with

Stowe's attorney, the prominent Boston abolitionist Samuel E. Sewall.[70] Descended from a distinguished colonial New England family of jurists, ministers, merchants, and abolitionists, Sewall was closely connected to virtually every aspect of the antebellum antislavery movement. He helped establish the *Liberator* with his good friend William Lloyd Garrison in 1831 and served as a contributing columnist. Garrison readily credited Sewall for the paper's survival: "I never should have been able to continue the paper. He was the man who gave money again and again, never expecting and never asking for the return of it."[71] Sewall fought the legality of the Fugitive Slave Law; he represented Thomas Sims in 1851 and Anthony Burns in 1854. These enslaved men had escaped to Massachusetts, but were court-ordered back into southern bondage.[72] Throughout his legal career, Sewall readily offered his expertise to African American students who wished to become lawyers. Sewall also maintained regular contact with John Brown, who frequently visited Boston to raise funds in the 1850s. Although Sewall was shocked by Brown's raid on Harper's Ferry, he provided Brown with legal assistance and raised money for Brown's wife and twenty children.[73] Sewall was elected to the Massachusetts Senate in 1851 as a member of the Free Soil Party, where he lobbied hard for abolition and women's marital property rights. Sewall's commitment to abolition made him increasingly attentive to the women's rights movement. He supported universal suffrage. He spearheaded new asylum regulations in Massachusetts after a vengeful husband threw Sewall's female client into an asylum on charges of "insanity" when she sought a divorce. Sewall rallied against coverture in favor of equal marital property rights.[74] In short, Sewall's activist fields coalesced into an expansive, mutually constitutive defense of human rights. George Angell bore intimate witness to his legal partner's reformist strategies and tactics.

Angell keenly remembered the hubbub of abolitionism and other social activism at his law practice: "[Sewall] spent almost half his time in endeavoring to protect the weak and defenceless. His private office was headquarters for nearly all the abolitionists and Free-Soil men in the Commonwealth—John Brown and a multitude of others. He frequently had there Sumner, Wilson, Andrew, Garrison, and Wendell Phillips. I should think that almost a peck measure of keys intended to open prisons and jails for the freeing of alleged slaves were kept at his office by the committee of safety."[75] In 1866, Angell and Sewall amicably ended their fourteen-year law partnership, which spanned a singular watershed period in the history of American slavery and freedom. Although Angell never possessed Sewall's stature in the abolition movement, his direct proximity to antislavery activism indelibly shaped his moral consciousness and future work in animal protection.

Other abolitionists participated in Angell's emergent gospel of kindness through their mutual admiration for John Rarey, the horse trainer. William Lloyd Garrison breathlessly attended Rarey's spectacular traveling show in Boston. He was so moved by Rarey's rousing disquisitions and exhibitions of merciful gentling that he published a virtual fan letter to Rarey in the *Liberator*: "Dear Sir—Though wholly a stranger to you, permit me to express the high gratification I have felt in listening to your sensible and excellent instruction. . . . You are instructing men, not less than subduing horses. . . . The field of your labors expands to a boundless extent. You are needed every where in the two-fold capacity of teacher and savior. . . . Love responds to love; friendship to friendship; gentleness to gentleness; and likewise force to force, and hatred to hatred."[76] In the same open letter to Rarey, Garrison mentioned his first experience with animal protectionism at Dublin in 1840 when he met William H. Drummond, author of *The Rights of Animals, and Man's Obligation to Treat Them with Humanity*: "My heart actually leaped within me as I read the expressive title, 'The Rights of Animals!' I was myself then, as now, engaged in vindicating 'The Rights of Man'; but here was a claim even for animals, affirming the possession, their part, of certain absolute and inherent rights."[77] In a similar spirit of expansive uplift, the Canadian sculptor Hamilton McCarthy coined the verb "to Rareyfy" in his poem, "Rarey, the Equine King": "Let gospel teachers learn to show/ How love begets its kind;/ Deal not so much damnation round,/ But Rareyfy mankind."[78]

Caroline Earle White, the founder of the Women's Branch of the Pennsylvania SPCA (1869) was likewise immersed in abolitionism during her formative years. She was raised in a prominent abolitionist household in Philadelphia, where her parents, Thomas and Mary, were movement leaders. Her father, a successful attorney, ran as the Liberty Party's vice presidential candidate in 1840, and like Samuel Sewall, he represented numerous slaves and freedmen. Caroline's brother, George, was also an abolitionist lawyer, and her uncle, John Milton Earle, was a member of the Free Soil Party and a close associate of Senator Charles Sumner of Massachusetts. Her mother was cousin to abolitionist and women's rights activist Lucretia Mott. Caroline herself participated in antislavery conventions and made charitable donations to abolitionist groups.[79] Her childhood activism provided both a moral springboard and an invaluable wellspring of practical experience for her future activism in the animal welfare movement.

Decades after the Civil War, animal advocates repeatedly reminded their constituents of the historical links between abolition, nation building, and the humane movement with reverential stories about President Abraham Lincoln. The Great Emancipator appeared in the pages of *Our Dumb Animals* and the *National Humane Review* as steadfast in his kindness to animals throughout his life, adopting stray dogs and cats and treating horses with gentleness.[80] Although young Lincoln "grew up in a land of wild plenty," he reportedly refused to hunt and fish: "He was, from the first, tender hearted with animals."[81] The *National Humane Review* published undated correspondence from Lincoln to Senator John C. Calhoun of South Carolina, in which he voiced his horror at witnessing a slave auction in New Orleans: "John I guess it takes a queer fellow like me to sympathise with the put upon and down trodden. Those blacks, John, don't live—they simply exist. I never trapped an animal in my life and slavery to me is just THAT both filling my soul with abhorrence."[82] Animal protectionists readily invoked Lincoln's memory, and by association, abolitionism, because the Civil War and subsequent Reconstruction Amendments radically expanded American ideas about freedom, property, and the rights of citizenship. Susan Pearson points out that these historical associations were generally nonracist because animal advocates connected the status of slaves and animals out of a shared social standing of "mutual defenselessness," rather than a racist notion of shared biological inferiority.[83]

In theory and in practice, abolitionism overlapped considerably with temperance, an antebellum social movement that combated addiction—another form of human bondage and suffering. Together, abolitionism and temperance formed a cornerstone of postbellum animal protectionism. In Washington, DC, the abolitionist newspaper, the *National Era*, explicitly connected drunkenness with animal cruelty and loss of manhood: "But perhaps the man in form is no longer a man. He has thrown away the only thing that had raised him above the brute. He has drowned his reason in a cup. He is drink [*sic*], and his generous horse must suffer! How much nobler is the brute that is beaten, than the brute that beats him!"[84] Similarly, in *Uncle Tom's Cabin* (1852), drunkard Simon Legree was the most vicious slaveholder in the novel, the state of his dilapidated plantation reinforced by the presence of "three or four ferocious-looking dogs."[85]

Antebellum reformers emphatically believed that alcohol was a direct threat to the nation's future. The laboring rhythms of daily life were saturated in drink: multiple shots of the "daily dram" (often shared with an employer) oiled the workingman's hours on the job, anesthetized his aching body, and comprised part of his wages.[86] Workingmen jokingly referred to Monday as

"St. Monday," or "Blue Monday," a day of hangover and recovery after binging on Sunday. Yet in an increasingly mechanized workplace that prized efficiency, a flexible laboring culture combining sociable drinking and work was becoming untenable.[87] Temperance reformers zealously believed that alcohol lubricated the passions, obliterated one's self-control, and unleashed unspeakable acts of cruelty on man and beast.

Drunkenness was diametrically opposed to new theologies of self-improvement. Imbibers were held hostage to unbridled passions, spiraling poverty, and violence toward their "fellow creatures." Timothy Dwight declared that drunkenness was "nearly allied with Suicide. It is equally certain means of shortening life." In the rubble of individual autonomy lay what Dwight called "a mass of flesh, in which a soul once lived, thought, animated, and controlled. . . . It has become palsied, lifeless, and for the period, extinct, under a shock of which it was unable to sustain."[88] Although temperance groups disagreed among themselves whether moderation or prohibition was their goal, organizations such as the American Society for the Promotion of Temperance (better known as the American Temperance Society [1826]) and the Washington Temperance Society (1840) agreed that drunkenness was socially ruinous. Spearheaded by middle-class reformers and sustained by workingmen's societies and women's "home visits" to intemperate households, temperance was the most widespread reform movement of the era. Temperance reformers used moral suasion as their primary weapon, but they also turned to the state, successfully securing the passage of new laws against liquor trafficking and consumption, beginning with Maine in 1846.

In spirit, theory, and practice, the antebellum temperance movement paved a continuous activist path for the postbellum animal welfare movement. Like temperance, animal advocacy rested upon a theology of manly and feminine self-control, gentle comportment, and emotional reserve. Two key antebellum temperance constituencies—women and children—engaged in modes of activism that influenced the tactics of the postbellum animal welfare movement. "Taking the pledge" to check one's passions and impulsivity was an essential part of both movements. The Band of Hope, a working-class children's temperance organization founded in Leeds, England, in 1847, celebrated "taking the pledge" to abstain from alcohol, tobacco, and profane language at weekly meetings: "I hereby solemnly promise to abstain from the use of all Intoxicating Liquors as a beverage. I also promise to abstain from the use of Tobacco in all forms, and all Profane Language."[89] Rank-and-file meetings were filled with testimonials and songs, such as: "We Do Not Swear," "Touch Not the Cup," or "The Anti-Tobacco Pledge," all of which were set to popular tunes of the day.[90]

In the affirmative solidarity of frequent meetings, Band of Hope members steeled themselves against temptation and loss of self-control. They sang, read Scripture, prayed, discussed, and pledged to avoid alcohol, profanity, and tobacco. Kindness to animals strengthened children against these potentially irresistible dangers. For example, an illustrated afterword entitled "The Silent Appeal" in the *Young Volunteer Campaign Melodist* featured little Nellie Montgomery and her "faithful old house dog," who politely begged for a bit of the girl's bowl of bread and milk. Nellie immediately brought the dog a full plate of food from the kitchen and resumed her meal. "[The dog] seemed to be very grateful to her for her thoughtful kindness of heart and ready sympathy. . . . We hope all our Young Volunteers will be as kind to these noble animals, for they all love Cold Water, and never drink whiskey, smoke tobacco, or swear. Little Nellie's dog loves the sparkling water of Silver Creek better than the old toper loves his bottle."[91] Rejecting vice, the water-loving housedog was a virtuous exemplar for young children.

FIGURE 1.2. Children's temperance groups believed that kindness to animals fortified a child's moral character against the temptations of drink, tobacco, and profanity. "The Silent Appeal," Sydney Herbert, *The Young Volunteer Campaign Melodist* (Boston: James M. Usher, 1864), back cover.

Thomas Timmins, an English Unitarian minister and RSPCA member, used the Band of Hope as his model for the Universal Mercy Band Movement, British Empire Division, which was a successful animal advocacy organization for English children.[92] In 1882, Timmins and George Angell used this organization as a blueprint to create the Bands of Mercy, an international children's animal welfare and humane education group. In five short years, the US Band sprouted 5,703 branches with approximately 400,000 members; it grew to 53,642 branches in 1903; 90,000 branches (containing over 3 million signers) in 1914, and 157,057 branches in 1926. *Our Dumb Animals* proudly chronicled the movement's expansion each month.[93] Similar to the Band of Hope, each Band of Mercy member was required to take the following pledge: "I will try to be kind to all harmless living creatures, and try to protect them from cruel usage."[94]

The Bands of Hope and its animal protectionist descendants used a universal, inclusionary rhetoric of kindness. Yet other antebellum temperance activists used animals to construct a nativist language of exclusion. Nativist temperance advocates commonly targeted Irish Americans (who comprised approximately 2.5 million new immigrants between 1815 and 1854).[95] Hired to work the most dangerous jobs that built modern America—canal dredging, railroad construction, ditch digging, quarry work, grinding tools, and mining—Irish American laborers were routinely fired for inebriated acts of "gratification merely animal."[96] Degraded as drunks whose allegiance lay with Rome, not the United States, Irish Catholics were often characterized as dogs "despised and kicked about," pigs living in "dung hills, vile refuse," and "driven like horses."[97] Nativist political groups, such as the American Republicans (1843), and the secret Order of the Star Spangled Banner (1849), which metamorphosed into the Know Nothings in the 1850s, had close ties to the antebellum anti-liquor movement.[98] Their exclusionary vision of the nation denied full citizenship to recent Irish Catholic immigrants—similar to popular representations of American Indians as stumbling drunkards who were unfit for citizenship.[99] While historically disconnected from this nativist strand of temperance, animal protectionists embraced a similar movement language of "barbarism," "savagery," and "civilization" to distinguish drunken animal abusers from their sober, civilized betters. This language was teleological and racial—used to mark otherness with tacit geographical referents, such as "barbarians" from the North African Barbary Coast, as well as more generalized racial constructions of immigrants as "wild," foreign, and "heathen."[100]

Nonetheless, the antebellum temperance movement was large enough to offer a welcoming political platform for other groups denied the full rights of citizenship. Women, in particular, were active participants in temperance reform, gaining a new public voice through their private moral authority in the home. Confronting drunkenness head-on, female temperance workers appealed directly to the moral imperative of sobriety and kindly comportment to effect social change in an era when they were still denied the vote. Women's moral status, however, privileged a normative ideal of affluent Euroamerican womanhood as the primary agent of civilization, a face of antebellum reform that would also generally characterize the female membership of postwar animal protectionism.[101]

The Second Great Awakening and its contemporaneous social movements embodied a new liberal theology of free moral agency that discarded predestinarianism in favor of potential perfectibility. Rooted in biblical exegesis, metaphors of animal kindness and suffering in the antislavery and temperance movements were significant structures of feeling that presaged the birth of new institutions, strategies, and tactics dedicated specifically to animals.[102] Moreover, future animal protectionists often had direct professional or familial ties to these antebellum movements, which gave them invaluable exposure to grassroots organizing and institution building. As a legacy of this reformist era, the Woman's Christian Temperance Union (WCTU) and its Department of Mercy widened its anti-alcohol movement into an expansive moral plea for animals and their human stewards.

2

"A World of Kindness Is a Copy of Heaven"

ANIMALS, MORAL UPLIFT, AND THE WOMAN'S
CHRISTIAN TEMPERANCE UNION

IN THE NOVEMBER 1887 issue of *Our Dumb Animals*, George Angell heralded the new "Age of Woman." He proclaimed that "woman" would "throw her influence into the grand work of regenerating the world" in an era riven by crime, cruelty, partisan rancor, and class conflict.[1] Angell pointed to the all-female Woman's Christian Temperance Union and its "great temperance army of two hundred thousand Christian women," as a model of respectable women's activism. He envisioned the WCTU as a "vanguard of the greater army," a transnational phalanx of Christian women dedicated to public reform: "One of these days, we think, it will drop the T., and stand before the world as 'The Woman's Christian Union,' for temperance, humanity, and God."[2] Angell was impressed that the WCTU had printed 50 million pages of temperance literature in 1886, a record that the Massachusetts SPCA (MSPCA), with 5 million pages to its credit that year, strove to emulate.[3]

In 1874 women temperance activists founded the WCTU after a sustained "Woman's Crusade" of public prayers, hymn singing, and petitioning in protest against newly loosened state liquor laws during the depression of 1873. Eliza Daniel Stewart (also known as "Mother Stewart") recalled that "in several places even the dogs, whose masters were saloon-keepers, invariably manifested an interest—and may I say, sympathy—for the Crusaders."[4] The WCTU soon became the largest women's movement in the nation (only the transnational American women's missionary movement was larger).[5] The WCTU evolved into a sprawling reform movement comprising thirty-seven departments, whose areas of support ranged from the eight-hour day to the humane treatment of prisoners.[6] Angell eagerly sought the opportunity for collaboration.

He found a receptive audience. WCTU president Frances Willard had supported animal protection since childhood. Willard wrote glowingly to Angell, "I look upon your mission as a sacred one."[7] In 1887, she invited Angell to give a keynote speech at the WCTU's national convention in Nashville. Although Angell was unable to attend, he published his speech in its entirety in a supplemental issue of *Our Dumb Animals*. He offered WCTU members an unlimited supply of gratis humane literature and he launched Bands of Mercy within existing children's temperance groups, such as the Loyal Temperance Legions and Bands of Hope.[8] Angell also gave speeches, such as the provocatively titled, "How Drinking Men Treat Their Horses," to stress the shared mission of the WCTU and the MSPCA.[9] Willard enthusiastically coupled the two, as well: "Nothing has made men madder in their rage toward the defenseless than the drink delirium, hence to teach the ethics of kindness to animals is germane to the white-ribbon gospel. God speed the Band of Mercy."[10]

WCTU leaders welcomed the opportunity to work with Angell, but they were hardly dependent on his aid for they already possessed extensive women's networks of animal advocacy. Most notably, Mary Frances Lovell of Bryn Mawr was a founding member of the Women's Branch of the Pennsylvania SPCA in 1869, an antivivisection leader, and the originator of a statewide Band of Mercy in 1889.[11] A year later, Frances Willard tapped Lovell to become national superintendent of the WCTU's newest prong in its "Do Everything" platform, the Department of Mercy, which formalized the WCTU's commitment to fighting drunkenness, animal cruelty, and family violence. Lovell juggled her leadership duties with her work as associate editor of the *Journal of Zoöphily*, the monthly magazine of the American Anti-Vivisection Society (AAVS), which also provided the WCTU with an additional media platform.[12] Lovell possessed extensive transnational ties to other animal advocates, many of whom were members of the World WCTU, forged over decades of activism in the field. As national superintendent of the Department of Mercy, Lovell collaborated with other women's groups and humane organizations, such as the National Association of Colored Women, the Audubon Society, and the Woman's Foreign Missionary Society.

The WCTU welcomed animal kindness into its self-styled "white ribbon gospel," a vision of civilization created by benevolent acts of moral suasion and individual uplift to protect home and family.[13] While the centrality of women's participation in animal advocacy has been well recognized, the WCTU's role in the humane movement has been less so.[14] For example, it is well known that the WCTU funded public drinking fountains as a cooling, sober alternative to the tempting saloons nearby, but it is less known that the organization also sponsored the construction of water troughs for thirsty laboring animals.[15] Perhaps the WCTU's cooperative "Do Everything" policy overshadowed the individual activities of its myriad departments. But it is precisely the WCTU's intersectionality among multiple fields of reform that demonstrates the wide reach of the humane movement in the late nineteenth and early twentieth centuries. Accordingly, the Department of Mercy worked closely with other WCTU departments, such as the Departments of Purity in Literature and Art, and Penal and Reformatory Work, to build an interconnected gospel of kindness leaving few areas of reform untouched. The organization also benefitted from the WCTU's emphasis on local grassroots organizing.[16] The Department of Mercy made its mark seemingly everywhere: from large urban centers like Los Angeles to scattered rural hamlets, such as Maine Prairie, Minnesota, where local Mercy activists journeyed five miles away from the town each week to post animal welfare flyers on the railroad depot wall.[17]

Mercy activists believed that animal protection was an act of Christian stewardship. They sought alliances with church leaders and peppered their publications with scriptural imperatives to give credence to their work: "Open thy mouth for the dumb" (Proverbs 31:8); "He giveth to the beast his food, and to the young ravens which cry" (Psalms 145:9).[18] George Angell admiringly characterized the WCTU as altruistic and apolitical, "without one selfish purpose or thought, seeking only the glory of God and the welfare of mankind."[19] While Angell extolled the WCTU as an exemplary model of Victorian womanhood, the lived experiences of its leadership often defied cultural norms. The majority of the WCTU's officers participated in the paid labor market at various points in their lives, and 20 percent remained single in an era in which over 90 percent of all adult American women were married.[20] The organization's normative language of home and family diffused the lived experiences of its leadership and helped transform potentially unconventional positions into a defense of traditional gender roles. In 1876, for example, Francis Willard justified her support for women's suffrage as "home protection," arguing that votes for women would protect the home from the dangers of drink.[21]

While a valorization of marriage and motherhood gave the WCTU its voice, it also limited the organization's tactical decisions. Mercy members avoided confrontations on the street in favor of moral suasion inside the church, school, doctor's office, and home, which firmly connected the

WCTU to antebellum traditions of women's activism. Put another way, Mercy women embraced strategic essentialism to achieve their goals.[22] They assumed that women's and girls' special moral status made them virtually incapable of harming animals. As a result, they pursued men and boys as their primary subjects of uplift—fully in line with the broader animal welfare movement, which most often represented the (human) body of kindness as female and white. The MSPCA enshrined this intersectional dynamic into its official seal depicting a female angel of mercy confronting a ragged carter beating his horse. In the early 1890s, rank-and-file Mercy activists created children's humane education programs, as well as adult informational outreach and lobbying. In the early 1900s, they increasingly viewed animal kindness as a humanitarian template for an all-encompassing civilizing project, which spurred a growing focus on prisoners, working girls, and other human rights issues. Because animals were seemingly apolitical subjects, they represented a neutral conduit to potentially controversial fields of political change in an age before women had the full rights of American citizenship. Yet this shifting emphasis also meant that animals themselves increasingly were replaced by other concerns, an erasure that ultimately led to the Department's demise.

From Help Mates to Leadership: Building Women's Organizations and Networks

At the inception of the humane movement, women cast themselves as helpmates to male leadership, preferring to work behind the scenes away from the public eye. In this phase of the movement, women were just as reluctant as their temperance allies to seek leadership positions in organizations containing men. Mary Lovell's friend and associate, Caroline Earle White, launched the original petition drive to incorporate the Pennsylvania SPCA (PSPCA) in 1867, but immediately became a foot soldier thereafter. White readily supported female suffrage but was hesitant to push for women's leadership roles in the PSPCA because its officers possessed the powers of arrest, which invariably led to flashy public confrontations with animal abusers in the streets. These physical showdowns would have been wholly inappropriate acts of public disruption for a respectable upper-class woman. White expressed her preference for moral suasion as a more appropriate form of women's activism in a letter to Henry Bergh: "If I were a man, I am quite sure that I should follow your example but as it has pleased Almighty God to create me a woman, I must be satisfied with a more limited sphere of labor, and do

NO BLINDERS NOR CHECK-REIN.

FIGURES 2.1 AND 2.2. Humane advocates commonly represented human exemplars of kindness as white and female. (Top) "No Blinders or Checkrein," *Our Dumb Animals*, June 1888, 36. (Bottom) Illustration used in MSPCA Seal, *Our Dumb Animals*, August 1888, 25.

the little good I can with my tongue."[23] Moral suasion through words, rather than body politics in the streets, made women's place subordinate in the early male-led SPCAs. Yet Bergh's chief counsel, Elbridge Gerry, recognized the importance of such behind-the-scenes support: "Whenever Mr. Bergh was censured by one man he was endorsed by fifty ladies. . . . Without their aid . . . the society . . . would never have made such rapid progress."[24]

Yet Caroline Earle White and Mary Lovell embraced leadership opportunities in the SPCA movement when they built their own all-female institutions—just as the WCTU would do in the 1870s. With the encouragement of the PSPCA's president, Samuel Morris Waln, White founded the Women's Branch of the PSPCA in 1869 as a women's auxiliary. Also known as the Women's PSPCA, this new organization was an "auxiliary" in name only, however. Under White's leadership, the Women's Branch significantly changed the course of institutional animal advocacy in the United States. Among its many achievements, it pioneered the sheltering movement, which used private and municipal partnerships to build new facilities to house lost pets and stray animals in the hopes that reunion and adoption, rather than extermination, would prevail.[25] The Women's Branch instituted new humane methods of capturing strays, as well.[26] Although rounding up strays potentially placed women in the streets, the shelter itself was a de facto domestic space, which reinforced, rather than challenged, the ideal of separate spheres for women and men.

Women's Branch leaders adopted the same conservative approach when they launched the American antivivisection movement. Alarmed by the rising frequency of experiments on animals in Gilded Age science classrooms and research laboratories, Caroline Earle White founded the American Anti-Vivisection Society in 1883 after she met Frances Power Cobbe, the British antivivisectionist and feminist activist. Cobbe's organization, the Victoria Street Society, had already achieved considerable success in persuading Parliament to pass Great Britain's first antivivisection law, the Cruelty to Animals Act (1876), which limited vivisection to those experiments that could help save a human life, and mandated anesthesia for all vertebrate experiments.[27] White received a state charter from the Pennsylvania legislature to incorporate the new organization, yet she chose not to serve as its official leader.[28] She and fellow female founders concluded that their work would be taken more seriously if a man served as the AAVS's first president.[29] With the legitimizing mantle of male leadership in place, women antivivisectionists lobbied successfully for laws banning animal experimentation in six states, and they effectively blocked all state bills that would have given medical researchers unlimited access to animals from local pounds.[30] In negotiating the limitations and possibilities for women's leadership in the humane movement, Caroline Earle White, Mary Lovell, and their colleagues created a blueprint for the WCTU's Department of Mercy.

Bird protection represented a third formative organizational prong for the Department of Mercy. Even though women virtually singlehandedly resuscitated the bird conservation movement in the late nineteenth century, they were reticent to assume formal leadership roles in heterosocial organizations. Conservationist and sportsman George Bird Grinnell organized the first Audubon Society in the 1880s, but his group crumbled within two years because it grew too fast and became organizationally unwieldy. In 1896, a group of elite Boston women resurrected Grinnell's moribund organization to fight the fashionable bird hat. The reincarnated Audubon Society, spurred on by the Boston women, expanded rapidly, but the establishment of state and local branches helped to structure and maintain its growth. Like the AAVS, the Audubon women enlisted prominent men to serve as their leaders, but women still made up approximately 80 percent of the membership of state Audubon Societies.[31]

Early Fields of Activity

Bird protection and antivivisectionism were central to the Department of Mercy's first collaborative activities. This protectionist plan targeted domestic animals and wild nest-builders living in close proximity to human beings, which enfolded these creatures into the domestic sphere. Over time, Mercy activists, influenced by the conservation movement and new threats of extinction, expanded their protectionist field to include other wild animals, especially the furbearing mammalian victims of the steel trap. They supported the efforts of the AAVS in the courts and state legislatures to regulate, and later to end, vivisection, arguing that the practice tortured animals and ossified the souls of its human practitioners, especially in schools filled with impressionable children. Mercy members placed humane education literature in classrooms, doctors' offices, and university medical schools to reach vivisectionists directly.

Mercy superintendents juxtaposed annual reports with traumatic stories of cruelty. In 1894, Oregon's Mercy superintendent, Mrs. Louise P. Rounds, dryly enumerated the number of county and local supervisors, public postings of animal welfare laws, and the number of pages distributed, and then presented a horrifying anecdote to steel members' dedication to antivivisection. A college professor "choked a cat to death to let the students see how it struggled in dying. Since he was threatened with arrest he kills before cutting, but starves a few days at first. He also varnished a cat to prove that skin was the third lung."[32]

Mercy advocates viewed the bird hat as a comparable form of butchery. Elaborately built out of the feathers, wings, heads, and sometimes the whole bodies of songbirds, owls, herons, egrets, gulls, terns, and hummingbirds, this millinery confection decimated entire rookeries. Newspaper coverage presented the feather trade as a wholesale assault on domestic life, as nesting homes were destroyed in the name of commerce and fashion, especially in southern rookeries, where bird parents were snatched and slaughtered, leaving vulnerable orphan hatchlings abandoned in the nest.[33] Activists rejoiced at the passage of the federal Lacey Act in 1900, which created the nation's first wildlife refuges and reinforced existing state laws by prohibiting the interstate commerce of specific birds. Other legislation banned the sale of native songbirds for the cage trade.

Local and state Mercy Departments created youth groups, dispensed humane literature, such as "The Appeal to Women not to Wear Birds or Their Plumage," in strategic places of authority, including doctor's offices and churches. They convinced people to take the Bird Pledge as a demonstration of avian devotion. Superintendents held Bird Day celebrations and Bird Socials in conjunction with Arbor Day; still others hosted a Bird Welcome each spring, an occasion for song, recitation, and "an instructive essay in relation to birds."[34] In all areas of their animal protection work, Mercy activists sought support from those members of society deemed to have the greatest moral influence: school superintendents, teachers, newspaper editors, physicians, and most significantly, ministers.

"Christ among the Cattle"

The support of religious officials lent moral and spiritual legitimacy to a women's movement that scientists, doctors, hunters, railroad officials, and meatpackers routinely scorned. Dr. William W. Keen floridly described how women antivivisectionists were possessed by the "most violent and vindictive passions" in their letters to him, which hysterically addressed him as "Arch-Fiend."[35] Keen dismissively nodded to Mary Lovell's journal, *Zoöphily*, as his amusing "stand-by": "Of course its columns, like those of all its tribe, are filled with much fiction, but it often reminds me of the good-humored epigram of a witty husband to his wife, 'My dear, you are usually wrong, but you are never dull . . .' I find it very entertaining."[36] Given the spiritual and moral validation that alliances with religious authorities could bring to the movement, Lovell openly expressed her frustration when church leaders responded lackadaisically to her calls for support: "I am amazed over the indifference of the church to this matter of humane teaching. . . . I have attended church all my life, but have never yet heard an entire sermon on the subject of mercy to the helpless."[37]

Lovell's frustrations reflected her organization's mixed record in reaching ministers.[38] Only two denominations—the Presbyterians and the eighth provincial synod of the Episcopal Church in the Midwest—reported animal welfare work as part of their formal activities.[39] And even among these denominations, humane leaders met resistance. The Reverend Charles Scanlon, general secretary of the Presbyterian Church's Board of Temperance and Moral Welfare, openly disparaged his reluctant colleagues of the cloth, while urging humane groups to remain resolute: "I have gone to a good many churches when they did not let me in, and I have had a feeling they did not let the Lord in, either. So maybe, they won't let you in. . . . Get them filled with enthusiasm and knowledge and zeal, and they will be just as earnest on that as on everything else."[40]

The Department of Mercy actively sought relationships with ministers who looked remarkably like its own membership: mainline Protestant, white, and native born.[41] The Department of Mercy's emphasis on soliciting support from respectable, mainline Protestant leadership meant that its members missed opportunities for alliances with smaller sects and individuals, such as the self-described lay "evangelical Unitarian" minister, temperance activist, and newspaper worker Anderson H. Wimbish of St. Paul, Minnesota, who considered "a feeling of mercy and protection for all dumb animals, however humble their estate" to be a cornerstone of an upright moral life.[42]

The media visibility of traditional men and women of the cloth exceeded their actual numbers in the movement because they were such valuable allies. Religious leaders wrote columns for humane periodicals, such as Sister M. Fides Shepperson's "Cloister Chords." Religious periodicals, such as the *Christian Recorder*, published the latest news about state legislation and antivivisection activism.[43] Local ministers occasionally preached "Humane Sunday" sermons, which Mercy members circulated nationwide in an effort to enlist clergy in the movement. Published in 1906, *Christ among the Cattle* was a consistent favorite.[44] Its author, Frederic Rowland Marvin, was a Congregational minister in Portland, Oregon, who preached that the humble birth of Jesus in a manger brimming with creatures signaled the birth of the gospel of kindness: "Was not our Savior's advent associated with beasts of the stall to teach us lessons of respect for and kindness toward the animal world?"[45] In 1914, the American Anti-Vivisection Society became the first animal protection group to adopt Humane Sunday formally in its home state of Pennsylvania.[46] In May 1915, the American Humane Association (AHA) brought Humane Sunday, also known as Mercy Sunday, to a national audience as part of its new weeklong event designed primarily for children. Be Kind to Animals Week included educational activities in local schools and humane societies, such as poster and essay contests, radio addresses, film, parades, pageants, and public lectures.[47]

Animal advocates encouraged ministerial participation by publishing boilerplate Humane Sunday programs. The *National Humane Review* suggested that Humane Sunday assume the structure of an ordinary Christian service, which ultimately reinforced the Protestant inflection of the humane movement, for there was no reference to Catholic communion, Jewish services, or any other religious practices. Humane publications suggested specific prayers, hymns, and scriptural references, a pledge of kindness to animals, and a sermon focusing on such animal-friendly topics as Barry, the heroic St.

FIGURE 2.3. Founded in 1915, "Be Kind to Animals Week" was an educational event designed for children. Activities in schools and humane societies included parades, poster and essay contests, radio shows, and public lectures. "Be Kind to Animals Week," *Our Dumb Animals*, April 1926, 161.

Bernard, St. Francis of Assisi (despite the absence of other Catholic service elements), Clara Barton, or "some noble woman who began her life of service to mankind by first ministering to the lowly creatures." Sung to the familiar tune of "Stand Up, Stand Up for Jesus," the opening hymn, "Be Kind to All God's Creatures," set a tone of stewardship for the entire service.[48]

Like other animal advocacy groups, the Department of Mercy did not affiliate itself directly with the most famous socio-religious movement of its day, the Social Gospel. Still, as a demonstration of the wide appeal of the humane movement, individual Social Gospel ministers, such as Baptist theologian Walter Rauschenbusch, preached animal kindness. Rauschenbusch's prayer, "For this World," made a forceful plea for biblical stewardship and ecological kinship: "Enlarge within us the sense of fellowship with all the living things, our little brothers, to whom thou hast given this earth as their home in common with us. We remember with shame that in the past we have exercised the high dominion of man with ruthless cruelty."[49] Nonetheless, the absence of direct organizational ties between these popular movements was hardly surprising: animal activists emphasized the collective transformation of the individual consciousness rather than explicitly using Christianity to demand structural social and economic change.

Activist ministers and Mercy members coupled animal advocacy with contemporary social purity activism. Humane advocates believed that animal cruelty, like salacious and violent popular culture, incited the baser passions. Therefore, local Departments of Mercy worked closely with the WCTU's Department of Purity in Literature and Art. When the Presbyterian Church officially adopted an animal welfare platform in 1920, church leaders housed this program in its Board of Temperance and Moral Welfare—a location that affirmed the relationship between animal kindness and individual moral restraint.[50]

The Department of Mercy was equally concerned with the destructive power of new popular media technologies in its collaborative interdepartmental censorship campaigns. At its Central Committee Meeting on March 29, 1898, the Minnesota WCTU petitioned to ban boxing films: "To prohibit, so far as the power of Congress extends, the reproduction of prize fights by the kinetoscope or kindred devices ... and the interstate and mail circulation of extended newspaper descriptions of such fights."[51] The Department of Mercy noted that its members objected to the distribution of the fight between Bob Fitzsimmons and James J. Corbett "with so much force that the display was a complete failure when the veriscope came."[52] Mercy activists argued that boxing should be strictly limited to live exhibitions because film could be endlessly reproduced, thereby spreading the sport's moral danger far and wide.

Yet the WCTU and other animal protectionists were by no means hostile to new media. They readily seized new cultural forms to broadcast their gospel of kindness: the penny press, half-tone photography, buttons, novels, magazines, stereoscope cards, international exhibitions, film, and radio. Mary Lovell recognized the enormous communicative power of her radio broadcasts for the Women's PSPCA: "It is an excellent way of reaching the public and I intend to use the opportunity whenever it is offered to me."[53] In "Man and Beast: A Humane Sermon," Dr. S. Parkes Cadman, the radio minister for the Federal Council of Churches of Christ in America, used the airwaves to promulgate animal mercy as a litmus test of individual morality.[54] After the Eastman Kodak Company introduced its portable Brownie camera in 1900, John G. Shortall of the Illinois Humane Society announced that every officer now would carry a camera to "take snap-shot pictures of the victims for use as evidence in court."[55] Other organizations questioned whether disturbing photographs of abuse would be effective in the court of public opinion. Board members of the St. Paul SPCA, for instance, debated whether they should publish photographs of animals "in their best condition," or at their worst, to rally financial support for the construction of a new animal shelter in December 1923.[56]

Popular media helped propel the humane movement, but Mercy activists believed that in the hands of children, media could be an agent of moral corruption. They found an effective ally in Reverend Frederic Rowland Marvin, author of *Christ among the Cattle* (1906). Children's baser instincts, Marvin warned, were repeatedly tested by modern urban life and its tantalizing array of popular amusements and prurient dime novels, which could encourage cruelty to animals. Marvin preached that children who learned cruelty became hardened and vulnerable to criminality. The Roman emperor Nero, for example, was cruel to animals as a boy, and then as an adult burned Christian women and children in sacks coated with combustible tar: "Nero, when a youth, took great pleasure in tormenting animals. He transfixed them with the spear, cut off their feet and then set them at liberty. . . . A childhood of cruel sports prepared Nero for a career of inexpressible infamy."[57]

Marvin and the WCTU believed that the fate of civilization was intimately tied to proper childhood development—a conviction that persists in the American Humane Association's trademarked theory of "The Link" between childhood animal cruelty and adult violence.[58] To combat the dangerous consequences of the "snares of youth," the WCTU strove for moral resiliency through its youth groups, the Loyal Temperance Legions, Bands of Hope, and Bands of Mercy. Adult group leaders stressed the pivotal influence that humane education played in reaching children before it was too late.

"Heart and Soul Education"

WCTU Mercy members believed in the moral plasticity of the child. Working with other animal protectionists, they urged school officials to support humane education initiatives as a form of character building. They rejected the implications of recapitulation theory, a popular strand of contemporary social thought, as a threat to the gospel of kindness. Psychologist G. Stanley Hall, the primary architect of recapitulation theory, argued that white boys should go hunting to experience the "primitive" world of their evolutionary ancestors, which would allow them to advance properly into civilized men. He recalled that his own youthful adventures gunning down hawks, eagles, and small mammals on his family farm in western Massachusetts had been essential to forming his adult moral consciousness: "[Hunting] may have stimulated the very strong reaction of later years, which now makes it almost impossible for me to give pain to any animal."[59]

WCTU members acknowledged that youthful animal cruelty was often the product of impulsive curiosity. Mrs. E. M. Deardorff, a Mercy superintendent in Los Angeles, who counseled thousands of boys, realized that many children had little intrinsic sense that it was wrong to kill birds: "Many are boys of 15 and 16, some older. Only about a dozen knew that birds were of any value, and hundreds had been killing them. One boy of 15 said he had killed 32 on one Sunday."[60] Such moral immaturity made humane education all the more imperative, lest children mature into callous adults. Animal advocates cautioned that the adult vivisectionist was essentially a "boy" suffering from arrested development who never learned kindness.[61] AAVS leaders ominously predicted that even the sight of animal experimentation in the classroom was sufficient to revive and normalize acts of childhood cruelty for budding scientists: "Can you not in your mind's eye discern the rekindling of latent, or perhaps partially obliterated ferocity and cruelty in the sort of young men who have almost outgrown a boyhood of injustice and torment practiced upon cats, birds, and dogs, or sisters and even mothers?"[62] Department of Mercy activists, like other Progressive-era reformers, believed that nurture trumped nature.

Mercy activists and their allies devoted the majority of their work to humane education programs. George Angell, in his dual capacity as president of the MSPCA and the "father of humane education" as head of the American Humane Education Association (1889), pushed for the expansion of new WCTU-sponsored Bands of Mercy as vectors of "heart and soul" education. Bands of Mercy met after school and in Sunday school under adult supervision. Children sang Mercy songs, played games, offered testimony regarding animal cruelty cases witnessed and prevented, wrote humane stories, made art to foster kindness, and engaged in community service projects to protect animals. Lovell, Willard, and Angell argued that without the moral fortress of humane education, children could easily become hardened criminals.

Local Departments of Mercy collaborated with teachers and school superintendents across the country, inside and outside the classroom, and in formal instruction. They regarded the nation's diverse, growing student population at the turn of the twentieth century as a critical audience for pedagogies of kindness. With the advent of new compulsory attendance laws during the Progressive era, student enrollment swelled in US schools, public and private.

BAND OF MERCY, ORDER OF THE ROUND TABLE

FIGURE 2.4. Established in 1882, the American Bands of Mercy was a children's animal welfare organization that grew quickly into a transnational movement, owing to the support of missionaries, teachers, and temperance advocates. "Band of Mercy, Order of the Round Table," [Birmingham, AL], May 1926, 192.

According to US Census figures, 17,072,000 children in grades kindergarten through twelve in 1900 were enrolled in school. In 1920, that number had climbed to 24,049,000.[63] Mercy chapters sponsored school humane contests and dispensed humane fiction and informational pamphlets to teachers. Mercy superintendents lobbied local and state legislators to pass humane education laws and gladly reported their successes (sixteen states had passed compulsory humane education laws in 1912).[64] But they remained frustrated by the absence of compulsory enforcement provisions in these laws. Only New York, Oklahoma, and Illinois included punitive enforcement measures, such as cutting state funds for salaries and school budgets to punish districts for ignoring the law.[65]

WCTU activists argued that humane education offered a tacitly spiritual—if not denominationally explicit—bulwark against rising secularism in the public schools. Superintendent E. M. Deardorff of Los Angeles contended that rough contact sports had become a de facto religion in modern America: "The Bible has been driven out from our schools and football has gone in, but I do not believe there is a school in Los Angeles today where humane education is being pursued."[66] Similarly, Mercy members believed that humane education, working in dialogue with concurrent experiential nature study pedagogies, could counteract the creeping ugliness of modern science education and its reliance upon gruesome vivisection and godless evolutionary explanations of creation.

To validate the success of humane education, Mercy Departments highlighted youthful testimonies of moral change. Deardorff, who won the county prize for most widespread Mercy activity in 1906, reported that among the 2,000 children she had organized into Young Defenders' Leagues and Bands of Mercy in Los Angeles that year, there was a dramatic sea change in the ways that boys treated birds: "Of their own accord many broke up their air guns and tore up their sling-shots, and some put up targets to shoot at. Many guns and sling-shots were brought to Mrs. Deardorff with the remark, "I thought you might like to have it, and I have no more use for it." Parents who had promised to buy guns were told by their boys not to buy them."[67]

The Department of Mercy strongly recommended two children's novels in its humane education programs: *Black Beauty* (1877), and *Beautiful Joe* (1893). Both stories urged children to build a moral civilization through individual acts of animal kindness. Both tied cruelty to drunkenness. In a clear nod to creaturely sentience, Beauty (a horse) and Joe (a dog) "wrote" their autobiographies in the first person voice, an authorial strategy that bonded readers affectively to the characters. Born on an English country estate, Black

Beauty had an idyllic early life. Joe, by contrast, suffered as a young dog at the hand of his malicious owner, Jenkins, a slovenly idler and drunk, who slashed Joe's ears and tail in a fit of rage.

Black Beauty's English author, Anna Sewell, was intimately familiar with pain and horses. As a teenager, she suffered crippling ankle injuries in a fall, which left her dependent on horse-drawn carriages for the rest of her life and subsequently able to observe laboring horses at length. Largely credited with mobilizing a campaign against the fashionable driving rein or checkrein (which forced a horse's head to be painfully arched or extended), *Black Beauty* was a rallying call to improve the lives of the cab horse and the cab driver in the author's England. Sewell, however, did not live to witness her novel's enormous impact: she died just five months after its publication.[68]

Margaret Marshall Saunders, the daughter of a minister, grew up among animals in Milton, Nova Scotia. The author of twenty-four novels, Saunders wrote under her ambiguously gendered middle name so that audiences would not know she was a woman. She embraced writing as a vehicle for social reform, championing the welfare of animals, the rights of women and children, and urban beautification. *Beautiful Joe* was a fictionalized version of actual events: her brother's father-in-law rescued a mutilated brown dog who became a family favorite. Saunders moved her story to small-town Maine in order to qualify as an entry for George Angell's literary contest, which sought to publish an American version of *Black Beauty*. In 1890, Angell's American Humane Education Society had sponsored the publication of Sewell's novel in the United States to great success.[69] Yet *Black Beauty*'s focus on England's landed aristocracy and working-class cabbies rendered it distinctly foreign. Angell's desire to market a homegrown *Black Beauty* was therefore a patriotic call to make "the Uncle Tom's Cabin of the Horse" an American production.

Moral suasion anchored both novels. Sewell and Saunders beseeched readers of all ages to be active, fearless stewards and to intervene and prosecute acts of cruelty. As a drunken carter beat his team in *Black Beauty*, a gentleman interceded and threatened the man with arrest. The gentleman later explained his actions to Beauty's owner: "My doctrine is this, that if we see cruelty or wrong that we have the power to stop, and do nothing, we make ourselves sharers in the guilt."[70] Passivity was akin to condoning cruelty. In *Beautiful Joe*, Cousin Harry risked his own safety to rescue Joe from the frenzied, knife-wielding Jenkins. Harry carried the bleeding dog to his pious, animal-loving relatives, the Morris family, where Joe healed and lived happily for the rest of his life. Jenkins, meanwhile, was arrested on cruelty charges and his wife and children were removed from the diseased, trash-strewn, sty-like home: "[Mrs. Jenkins'] pan of soft-mixed bread she often left uncovered in the kitchen, and sometimes the hens walked in and sat in it."[71] The physical removal of the children represented the standard policy of the period: extrication from a harmful environment was considered essential to saving children.[72]

At the tidy Morris farm, by contrast, the parents and five children were exemplary moral stewards: they carefully tended their chickens, two loyal dogs, a guinea pig named Jeff, fifteen to twenty rabbits, a cat, pigeons, and a dozen canaries. The Morris family constantly entreated others, such as their wealthy, canine-averse friend, Mrs. Montague, to welcome animals into their lives. Mrs. Morris observed that while her daughters were naturally inclined to compassion, animal stewardship had transformed her sons: "The end of it all is, that my boys, in caring for these dumb creatures, have become unselfish and thoughtful. . . . They are getting a heart education, added to the intellectual education of their schools."[73]

Complementing the WCTU's larger temperance mission, the novels graphically conveyed the dangers of alcohol. Black Beauty's fine knees were damaged when the intoxicated groom Reuben Smith whipped him into galloping home after throwing a shoe. Frothing, torn, and bleeding, Beauty crashed "with violence on both of my knees" and Smith fell to his death, leaving behind a wife and six small children. Now injured and an economic liability, Black Beauty was sold, thus beginning his downward spiral into the heart of industrial London as a cab horse. Beauty's stable mate, a distinguished equine veteran of the Crimean War named Captain, died after an inebriated drayman barreled into him. A young girl was also killed. Beauty's beloved owner, Jerry Barker, was outraged: "I only wish all the drunkards could be put in a lunatic asylum, instead of being allowed to run foul of sober people. . . . If there's one devil that I should like to see in the bottomless pit more than another, it's the drink devil."[74]

The "drink devil" wrought steady destruction throughout *Beautiful Joe*. Mrs. Montague's washerwoman was beaten by her drunken husband and performed her work "standing over her tub . . . and dropping tears into the water."[75] When Cousin Harry, Laura, and Beautiful Joe traveled to the country cottage of a drunken ne'er-do-well, Howard Algernon Barron, to collect a debt for Harry's father, they were greeted by a horrific scene: Barron had left a note on the table deeding Harry's father the livestock as payment for the debt. The chained animals were either starving or dead. Joe watched as Laura immediately released them: "The first thing the cow did was to lick her calf, but it was quite dead. . . . Her head was like the head of a skeleton, and her eyes had such a famished look, that I turned away, sick at heart, to think that she had suffered so."[76]

The cow and several other animals survived owing to restorative care, but the fate of drunken Barron was sealed. Some boys discovered his decomposing body months later in a deep wooded ravine where he had tumbled in an inebriated stupor. The novel's penultimate episode of drunken devastation was a catastrophic hotel fire that killed ten people and scores of animals. Some "fast young men" had accidentally started the fire late at night while playing cards and drinking smuggled wine until they had become "stupid"; they knocked over an oil lamp, panicked when the flames spread, and ran to seek help instead of putting out the fire themselves. By then, it was too late; the entire hotel was engulfed in flames.

The emotional power of *Black Beauty* and *Beautiful Joe* made the novels effective and affective tools of persuasion for children and adult audiences. Both were runaway bestsellers. (In fact, *Beautiful Joe* was the first Canadian book to sell a million copies, although today it is largely forgotten. *Black Beauty*, however, is still highly popular.)[77] WCTU Mercy activists distributed copies in faraway places, such as the isolated wooded community of Maine Prairie, Minnesota, where an energetic local chapter circulated the Mercy Pledge, along with copies of *Black Beauty* and other humane literature to area lumber camps.[78] Additionally, the Minnesota WCTU dedicated an entire branch of its organization to supplying itinerant bands of woodsmen searching for work with "good and wholesome reading" to combat the prurient temptations of pornography.[79]

By the 1890s, humane education had become a central plank of the movement, and with it, a special focus on children. Neither, however, were formal components of the nation's first SPCA in 1866. While Henry Bergh embraced animal kindness as an artifact of proper childrearing, he and his colleagues at the ASPCA targeted public acts of neglect and physical cruelty toward laboring animals, food animals, and animals in blood sports. The street, not the inner domestic sanctum of the home, was the first theater of anticruelty enforcement.

In April 1874, children abruptly entered the ASPCA's agenda in a hail of publicity after its leaders rescued eight-year-old Mary Ellen Wilson and arrested her violent caretaker, Mrs. Mary Connolly. When Mary Ellen was just two years old, Connolly and her husband Francis indentured her from Blackwell's Island asylum. A homebound, terminally ill neighbor routinely heard the child's screams, adults yelling, and ominous thumps through the thin walls. The woman implored Etta Angell Wheeler, a "Bible visitor," to check on the child.[80] Appalled by what she saw, Wheeler approached her minister and New York City police to intervene: they told her that she needed direct evidence of abuse to secure an arrest. At the suggestion of her niece who argued that "[Mary Ellen] is a little animal, surely," Wheeler contacted Bergh. His powerful legal counsel, Elbridge T. Gerry, quickly secured a writ to remove Mary Ellen, and Mrs. Connolly was arrested.[81]

The hearing and trial saturated local newspapers. Alonzo S. Evans, the ASPCA officer who retrieved Mary Ellen from the Connolly residence, testified that the ragged girl whose forehead and extremities had been brutally cut with a pair of scissors, "ran crouching into a corner, and raised her hands as if fearing a blow."[82] Articles repeatedly described Mary Ellen's battered appearance in virtually animalistic terms, stressing a subterranean world of domestic cruelty that lay hidden just below the surface of American civilization:

> Shoeless and almost naked by day, and with but the slender covering of a little blanket, stretched over a bare floor, at night, the child was kept in close confinement in a back room.... She was set to do household work beyond her strength, under the terror of a raw cowhide, whose frequent application had made her little body black and blue. The wanton and unremitting cruelty of the woman Connolly, who had the courage to come on the stand and brazenly defend her inhumanity, forms an awful revelation of the barbarism that lurks amid our Christian civilization.[83]

After Connolly was convicted, Gerry and Bergh helped create the nation's first organization to protect abused children, the New York Society for the Prevention of Cruelty to Children (NYSPCC). Subsequent organizations around the country fused animal and child protection work into singular humane societies. Created in 1877 as a consortium of local and state animal protection societies, the American Humane Association (AHA) dedicated its early years to fighting for better enforcement of the nation's first federal anticruelty law, the "28-Hour Law," passed in 1873, which guaranteed food, rest, and water stops for livestock every twenty-eight hours during railroad transit to distant urban markets. The AHA's efforts culminated with the passage of a new 28-Hour Law in 1906, which implemented a stronger inspection and documentation process at each stop handled through the US Department of Agriculture's Bureau of Animal Industry. While pushing to mandate humane care for food animals in transit, several member societies pressed for more active attention to protecting children; as a result, the AHA became a dual-focused organization.[84]

THE CATTLE TRAIN.

FIGURE 2.5. In the absence of truly effective federal legislation to provide regular feed and water for livestock during long railroad journeys, animal advocates encouraged individual acts of kindness, especially among children. "The Cattle Train," *Our Dumb Animals*, April 1887, 111.

Local SPCAs also threw themselves into child protection work, even when their names would suggest an exclusive focus on animal welfare. Some of these organizations eventually changed their names to reflect their expanded efforts. The St. Paul SPCA, for example, became the Society for the Prevention of Cruelty in 1899, even though it already had included animals and people in its protectionist fold for years.[85] Its daily complaint ledgers documented a violent industrial landscape of neglect, abandonment, and abuse. Side-by-side entries physically contrasted cases of mistreated children and animals. For example, in Case 45 on May 16, 1891, an agent found an emaciated horse imprisoned in a stall without food and water. The next day, Case 48 chronicled the neglect of four small children, ages nine months to seven years, who were locked in a house all day while their mother peddled vegetables.[86] Dog fighting, dog poisonings, drunken parents, horse floggings (including detailed mention of a Bible salesman who was told he "should know better" after he was arrested for beating his horse), starving children, suicidal fathers, overloaded horses, club-footed children wandering the streets, battered women and children, and abandoned horses, poultry, children, women, and the elderly populated the pages of the complaint ledgers.[87]

Neighborly surveillance generated the majority of the St. Paul SPCA abuse case reports. Neighbors reported instances of abuse in person, via telephone, and by letter. On May 7, 1917, for example, a concerned neighbor contacted Agent Bailey because a withered horse had been lying in a nearby alley for three days. Agent Bailey's crisp cursive summarized the horse's fate: "Shot."[88] Given the potential for retaliation, neighbors were unlikely to intervene directly when an act of violence was in progress. One letter, for instance, entreated a St. Paul SPCA officer to take a child from a drunken mother: "Dear Madam, I wish you would please do me a favor and look after Mrs.____. Mrs.____ has an adopted child, and she gets drunk, and abuses the child. She does nothing but rush the can with men and goes to bad company. She was so drunk Thursday that she could not stand. The child will never be anything as long as she has her. So I wished you would please see to this Mrs.____."[89] As members of a watchful community, neighbors, especially women at home tending children, represented the eyes and ears of the humane movement. They were rarely official members of protectionist societies but played a key role in the movement's surveillance ecology, working hand in glove with humane officers to police the social order.

WCTU members treated human rights and animal welfare as inseparable. The Minnesota WCTU denounced feather fashions and vivisection in its annual list of resolutions for 1895, which also forcefully condemned lynching: "We believe that when women have a share in making the laws, such atrocities will disappear from the earth."[90] The Minnesota WCTU resolved to petition the governor of New York to pardon fifteen-year-old Maria Barberi, who had been sentenced to death for slitting the throat of her bootblack boyfriend, Domenico Cataldo. News media luridly characterized Barberi as a bold seductress who was getting what she deserved.[91] But the Minnesota WCTU asserted that Barberi had acted in self-defense as a victim of violence at the hand of a man who "had committed the foulest wrong against her."[92] WCTU leaders vehemently denounced domestic violence of any kind; however, many members did not question women's status in the patriarchal home. For these women, domesticity legitimized their participation in social reform with a stamp of moral authority.[93]

"Social Reform of the Very Highest Order"

In the early twentieth century, the Department of Mercy increasingly called for a sweeping program of "universal kindness," which treated humane education as the linchpin for "social reform of the very highest order."[94] While superintendents still coordinated activities related to bird protection and antivivisection, other types of social reform eventually dominated annual reports. Mercy reports came to regard animals as ancillary beings, whose mistreatment was melded into a larger critique of domestic violence, poverty, labor, and inequality. Put another way, animals began to disappear from the WCTU department whose very creation had been predicated upon a commitment to their welfare. In short, animals became conduits to a larger humane idea. In 1904, Mary Lovell put it plainly: "There is no better basis for social reform than the specific teaching of kindness to every living creature."[95] Using the ideal of animal kindness—rather than the explicit practice of protecting animal bodies—as a catalyst for action, Mercy superintendents devoted more and more of their efforts to interrelated areas of humanitarian concern: prison reform, African American education, international disaster relief, poverty, and child labor. Animal kindness became a building block for other fields of activism.

Founded in 1877, the WCTU's Department of Penal and Reformatory Work gave rank-and-file Mercy members immediate access to the prison system. They distributed humane literature to prisoners; they lectured inmates on animal kindness; and they organized Bands of Mercy solely made up of prisoners' children, "as the reform of the parent may come through teaching the children."[96] Extolling the connection between kindness, compliance, and conformity, Mercy leaders contended that children "trained in habits of kindness to the dependent lower creation become . . . more amenable to authority, and better in their general conduct."[97] In other words, children, like animals, could be "tamed" and domesticated with kindness for the betterment of civilization. Indeed, Mercy annual reports explicitly praised the virtues of humane education in making the children of prisoners more compliant. In a program unique to Nebraska's Department of Mercy, Mrs. Mina D. Plumb worked closely with women prisoners: "The women in our state prison wished to do something to make the poor children happy last Christmas, and begged us to let them dress dolls for them. I sent twenty-five dolls, and the women prisoners were so happy doing this work for others that for a time they forgot their own misery."[98] Across the country, thousands of children joined special Bands of Mercy dedicated to youth whose parents were incarcerated.[99]

As a show of her commitment to prison reform, Mary Lovell even asked a warden to lock her in a prison cell so that she could better comprehend the sensory experience of incarceration. She also worked closely with individual ex-convicts "to better their social position" after they were released back into society.[100] Yet because Mercy activists emphasized individual character building through humane education, they did not openly condemn the systemic structural forces that trapped people in prison, such as poverty or racism.

In a national organization the size of the WCTU, there was no single message about race. In the North and West, a few local unions were racially integrated, but all remained segregated in the South. Yet until the 1890s, black and white southern local unions were members of integrated state WCTU unions. With the solidification of Jim Crowism, state WCTU unions in the South became segregated; black state unions were now known as "# 2 Unions."[101] While most southerners were ambivalent about women's public activism in the 1880s, white and black audiences warmly received Frances Willard during her first southern tour in 1881. Raised in a strongly antislavery household in Wisconsin, Willard kept any sectional sentiments private in favor of publicly stressing a unifying national message regarding the dangers of drink.[102] Southern whites generally did not protest when Willard and other northern white temperance leaders crossed the color line to speak to black audiences because these activists preached a language of personal uplift and accommodation that sat comfortably with racist notions of black intemperance, immorality, and the benevolent civilizing project of the white man's burden.[103] Further, Willard's "white" ribbon gospel was explicitly racist at times. Willard portrayed African American men as drunken sexual predators and white southern women as spiritually chaste and temperate, which sparked a bitter exchange with civil rights activist Ida B. Wells in 1894–5. Although Wells and Willard had much in common as temperance advocates who publicly denounced lynching, Willard's racist views of African American masculinity and white female purity foreclosed a potential alliance.[104]

Southern African American WCTU unions wedded the gospel of kindness to ideologies of racial uplift. Perhaps no WCTU member made this nexus more forcefully than Mrs. Lucinda (Lucy) Simpson Thurman, an African American leader in several WCTU fields. Born in Canada and based in Jackson, Michigan, Thurman had previously served as the WCTU's National Superintendent of the Department of Work among Colored People. In recognition of her pioneering temperance work in Texas in the late 1890s, African American WCTU members in the Lone Star State called their unions "Thurman WCTUs."[105] Thurman was nationally recognized as the Department of Mercy's most effective organizer in 1907.[106] She was at the vanguard of the WCTU's prison reform work across the South, visiting inmates and giving speeches at convict camps.[107] She "was surprised and touched at the interest aroused in the hearts of the convicts, as for the first time many of them heard a plea for kindness to animals." She also distributed thousands of pages of humane literature at jails.[108]

Lucy Thurman helped the National Association of Colored Women create its own Department of Mercy in 1907, with Mrs. S. F. Williams, a principal in New Orleans, as its superintendent.[109] Two years later, Williams reported that 1,673 African American pupils were members of forty-seven Bands of Mercy in New Orleans: "These Bands not only make the pupils kind, but teach them how to put their kind feelings to practical use and are a potent factor in the development of character."[110] A Texas superintendent highlighted the work of an African Methodist Episcopal (AME) pastor who preached twenty-five humane sermons in 1915.[111] The following year, Mrs. Kyle of Dallas reported that she was trying to organize a black Teamsters' League dedicated to easing the lives of laboring animals.[112]

Collaborating with black educators, clubwomen, and ministers, Mercy activists worked with African American children in segregated southern public schools throughout the lower South. In 1899, Lucy Thurman's transcontinental travels for the WCTU included a one-month stay in Vicksburg, Mississippi, where she addressed approximately 600 black children, who were performing "plantation work ... a wonderful field for the Department of Mercy."[113] Mrs. Florence Campbell, a black Tennessee teacher, counseled her large, seventy-four-member Band of Mercy against the use of steel traps to harvest wild furbearing animals in 1903. The state Department of Mercy's annual report lauded her effectiveness: "She gave one of the large boys who was very fond of hunting and trapping, the leaflet called 'Amos Hunt and His Steel Trap.' He read it, and when he handed it back to her he said, 'Mrs. Campbell, I am through with setting steel traps. I can never do it again after reading that.'"[114]

Widely reprinted for humane curricula after its publication in 1883, Cynthia M. Fairchild's cautionary tale of Amos Hunt described the moral awakening of a fatherless boy. Amos Hunt supplemented his family's meager subsistence on a three-acre farm with the sale of the skins of furbearing animals he trapped in the woods. When Amos accidentally became ensnared while checking his traps, he quickly understood just how much his furbearing victims agonized: "Poor little creature! This may be a just punishment for my cruelty. I know now how much my captives have suffered!"[115] Amos offered the ensnared mink pieces of his own lunch, which allowed him to save a creature he had nearly killed.

A neighbor rescued both at dawn. Amos named the mink "Tippet"; he was gentled quickly, and became a cherished, long-lived family pet. Amos never used the steel trap again, replacing all with new humane "cage-traps."[116]

The popularity of the Amos Hunt story among WCTU Mercy activists who worked with African American children reflected a complementary commitment to cruelty prevention and racial uplift. The domestication of Amos, as well as the gentling of the fierce, wild mink, embodied the gospel of kindness as a discourse of civilization. The story's ubiquity reflected the biases of an urban activist base generally unfamiliar with rural practices of gritty subsistence and survival. Historian Steven Hahn notes that trapping, hunting, and fishing were long-standing practices in the rural South, especially among African Americans and poor whites. Before the Civil War, unenclosed private land functioned as a commons, where the de facto "hunter's law" of unmitigated access dominated.[117] After Emancipation, freedmen rejected sharecropping, contracts, and poverty wages in favor of building new lives as independent farmers. Access to game, fish, and furbearing animals signified an important component of this hard-won freedom. Yet stringent, reactionary new local game, fencing, and trespass laws passed in the immediate aftermath of Radical Reconstruction threatened to destroy the ideal of the commons. These new laws served two purposes: to control a mobile black labor force and to monetize the market "as the proper arbiter of social relationships."[118] Subsistence practices remained a vital part of black freedom yet troubled the gospel of kindness. WCTU Mercy activists and other animal protectionists denounced hunters and trappers as "barbarians" because animals died slowly in writhing pain. They also thought that peripatetic hunters and trappers undermined a settled yeoman farmer ideal. As agents of civilization, they strove to intervene, rescue, and elevate children into proper subjects for future citizenship.

African American WCTU activists found receptive allies among other proponents of racial uplift and self-help. Booker T. Washington encouraged the Bands of Mercy movement at Tuskegee Institute with this the same spirit of accommodationism. Lucy Thurman reported "fine work" there, noting that teachers were "glad to receive and distribute humane literature, and impress on their pupils the necessity for kindness to animals."[119] The Hampton Institute created its own Band in 1883. The MSPCA and the American Humane Education Society jointly supported programs at black educational institutions. The Jarvis Christian Institute, a high school in Hawkins, Texas, enrolled its students in Bands of Mercy. Its president, J. N. Ervin, created a twenty-acre campus as "an asylum" for wild animals, while Professor William Wilson offered lessons in humane husbandry to benefit the campus's farm animals.[120]

These black institutions primarily envisioned an agricultural future for their students, which sat comfortably with contemporary Euroamerican racial norms—in the same way that W. E. B. DuBois's vision of an African American elite comprised of the "Talented Tenth" seemed dangerous.

Lucy Thurman insisted that animal kindness provided the most effective foundation for a just world that would eventually culminate in full equality: "The more I work for this department, the more interested I become in it. It seems to me that everything hinges upon it."[121] Using humane education as a gentle springboard to counteracting other forms of structural inequality, Mercy activists became involved in antipoverty work. In 1915, Mrs. Patterson, a superintendent of Humane Education in Mississippi, reported that she had organized twenty-four Bands of Mercy among African Americans, in addition to "car[ing] personally for the poor and sick, even for two who were insane from pellagra, and for whom there was no room in the state asylum." That same year, Mrs. Patterson worked closely with fellow WCTU members and the Southern Methodist Episcopal Church to halt the public execution of an African American man in Starkville.[122] As a seemingly neutral political space, animal protection provided a potentially benign vehicle for broaching volatile social issues. Animals, unlike people, could not "talk back."[123] They could not make demands on their own terms. In recognition of their own powers of articulation, humane organizations underscored their mission to give voice to animals. The masthead on every issue of the MSPCA's *Our Dumb Animals* reminded readers, "We speak for those that cannot speak for themselves," which provided an opening for myriad fields of reform.

The Department of Mercy's annual reports painted a bleak national panorama of inequality, but its members dispelled direct calls for structural change with glowing individual success stories. Mrs. Evelyn A. Curtis, the superintendent for the Mitchell, South Dakota, union reported in 1911 that local Mercy members adopted three orphaned babies; took impoverished women into their own homes; gave money, clothing, bedding, and food to poor families; made 1,859 visits to the sick; and ninety-five visits to institutions; gave 1,230 carriage rides to disabled people; and distributed a veritable mountain of animal welfare literature around Mitchell.[124] Mrs. Plumb of Nebraska aided an impoverished widow who was struggling to support seven children without her late husband's Civil War pension in 1912. A state senator subsequently promised to seek special legislation on the widow's behalf so that she could claim her pension. That same year, Mrs. Patterson of Mississippi closed a brothel in her town, kept an elderly woman out of an insane asylum, "ministered to the sick and poor," visited prisoners, and she convinced the directors of a local playground to take the Mercy Pledge. She also removed from a violent home a nine-year-old boy who was "an expert thief, having a natural genius for picking locks," placing him in the home of a fellow Mercy member who transformed the boy into a model citizen, "now truthful and trusted."[125]

The WCTU ameliorated the working conditions of women and children through individual acts of rescue. In 1909, Mrs. Mollie A. Kyle, Mercy superintendent and president of her local WCTU of Port Gibson, Mississippi, brought a cooling electric fan and "abundant ice water" to young female telephone operators, who spent long, cramped working hours trapped in "a glare of light and heat."[126] In 1910, a Mercy superintendent discovered a seventeen-year-old Indiana girl in a state of near collapse, toiling in a big-city medical laboratory for $4.00 a week, "without other resources, poisoned by chemicals, worn out, without proper clothing, and so discouraged that she was meditating suicide."

> The superintendent took the girl into her own home, made her decent clothes, and after giving her a rest, had her taught bookkeeping by her husband. The young girl worked hard to qualify herself and now has an office position at $8.00 per week, has friends and clothes like other girls, is studying stenography, and is developing into a beautiful and sensible girl. The superintendent says, "If I never do more than help this poor child out of her trouble I shall feel that I have not lived in vain. She often tells me that she is the happiest girl in the whole city, and when I think of her state of mind one year ago, the change seems wonderful."[127]

The superintendent's triumph was permanent in that it gave the girl the tools for self-improvement. The good-hearted benefactor was at the center of WCTU humane success stories. She provided the deserving poor with decent clothing, shelter, food, etiquette training, and educational opportunities, which echoed Mr. Greyson and Mr. Whitney of Horatio Alger's *Ragged Dick*: these respectable, kindly men nurtured Dick Hunter's innate pluck to help him become a gentleman.[128] The benefactor played a critical role in the Mercy Department's two most widely distributed children's novels, *Black Beauty* and *Beautiful Joe*. Black Beauty experienced a harrowing odyssey of owners but was eventually sold to a gentlemanly benefactor, the aptly named Mr. Thoroughgood, who nursed Beauty back to life. Mr. Thoroughgood finally sold Beauty—with the promise to take him back—to three gentle ladies, whose groom turned out to be Beauty's beloved first groom, Joe Green. The novel closed with this happy reunion.

The novels drew a sharp distinction between the deserving and undeserving poor. In *Beautiful Joe*, Mrs. Morris frequently gave money and modest presents to hardworking poor people. The lazy, mean Jenkins, however, deserved penury and imprisonment. When Jenkins tried unsuccessfully to rob a family friend of the Morrises, Joe alerted the family and foiled the crime with his keen nose: "I went and sniffed under the door. There was a smell there; a strong smell like beggars and poor people. It smelled like Jenkins. It *was* Jenkins."[129] Yet the novel's virtuous poor deserved a philanthropic safety net. Cousin Harry bemoaned the plight of hard-working day laborers while in New York City: "We should take better care of them, we should not herd them together like cattle, and when we get rich, we should carry them along with us, and give them a part of our gains, for without them we would be as poor as they are."[130] Harry's solution to the problems between capital and labor rested on voluntary acts of private philanthropy rather than labor solidarity or state-sponsored wealth redistribution.

Still, Mercy activists, like George Angell, also turned to the protectionist powers of the state. Mercy reports lobbied state legislators to ban child labor, protect the rights of women workers, provide equal pay for equal work, and prevent workplace hazards. Alongside a push for compulsory humane education laws and state statutes against tail docking, vivisection, and feather fashions, the Department of Mercy lobbied for federal bans on the rod in the classroom, floggings in prisons, and capital punishment. They persistently called for a prohibition amendment to the Constitution.[131] Moreover, in partnership with the World WCTU, Mercy women sent money, food, and clothing to Armenian orphans, starving children in India, and the drought-stricken community of Terrell, Texas.[132] In short, the WCTU's language of temperance and animal kindness became an idiom for transnational benevolence, or "universal kindness," that vastly exceeded the reach of its antebellum antecedents.

Yet their emphasis on individual initiative, rather than collective action, limited their reach. Mercy activists and their compatriots abhorred conflicts between labor and capital, arguing that the gospel of kindness was the only way to prevent radical upheaval. In a speech slated for the WCTU, George Angell publicly equated labor militancy with acts of violence: "All the criminals of the future are children now; the anarchists, the men who may throw railroad trains off the track, or put dynamite under our churches, or burn half a city some windy night. They are all children now and we are educating them. Shall we give them an education of mercy or not?"[133] In the shadow of the Haymarket bombing at Chicago in 1886, in which eleven people were killed during a labor rally in support of the eight-hour day, Angell was gravely concerned with what he saw as creeping anarchy and believed that heart and soul education, steeped in "kindness to God's lower creatures," would stop incipient class warfare.

The WCTU's rejection of labor radicalism also possessed an occasional nativist accent, which surfaced periodically with the arrival of millions of immigrants from Southern and Eastern Europe.[134] Frances Willard's Tenth Annual Address in 1889 portrayed a nation under foreign siege: "America has become the dumping ground of European cities. . . . To-day we have a hundred thousand anarchists among us in this country who claim to have twenty-five thousand drilled soldiers at their call. . . . It has been said that the explosion of a little nitro-glycerine under a few water mains would make our great city [Chicago] uninhabitable; the blowing up of a few railway bridges would bring famine; the pumping of atmospheric air into the gas mains and the application of a match would tear up every street and level every house."[135]

Rejecting strikes outright, animal advocates preached in favor of individual acts of philanthropy to aid suffering workers and called for state arbitration for disputes between workers and business owners. In 1903, *Our Dumb Animals* sponsored a contest with a $200.00 prize for the best plan to prevent strikes. The winner, Amos Judson Bailey, a Congregational pastor, recommended the creation of government-sponsored Industrial Courts in each state to adjudicate labor conflicts. If strikers in industries critical to the public interest refused to let the Industrial Court mediate their disputes, then the government would have the power to replace those workers with a reserve Industrial Corps of the US Army, or some other dedicated body.[136]

Should any reader be unsure of the MSPCA's stand on labor militancy, an engraving next to the article in 1903 made the organization's views clear: a factory was shown in sky-high flames bordered by a long, precise row of ramrod-straight police with guns drawn. Scattered bodies lay in the foreground, the most visible of which was a lifeless young man, still clutching a fiery club, his limp arm held by his horrified wife shielding two frightened children nestled in her arms. The caption read, "Very bad business which humane education and 'Bands of Mercy' in all our schools would prevent."[137] The MSPCA's antipathy to strikes endured into the New Deal, an era of intense industrial labor organizing and strikes. During a walkout at Chicago's Union Stock Yards in 1934, which left thousands of livestock without food and water, *Our Dumb Animals* condemned the work stoppage: "We pity the women and children of the Stock-yards' strikers who will suffer from loss of wages but have only unqualified condemnation for the men guilty of such inhuman cruelty."[138] Stressing the immoral consequences of labor solidarity, the essay ignored the inhumane working conditions and low wages that prompted the strike in the first place.

VERY BAD BUSINESS WHICH HUMANE EDUCATION AND "BANDS OF MERCY" IN ALL OUR SCHOOLS WOULD PREVENT.

FIGURE 2.6. Humane leaders were keenly sensitive to human and animal exploitation, but generally abhorred labor radicalism. "Very Bad Business Which Humane Education and 'Bands of Mercy' in All Our Schools Would Prevent," *Our Dumb Animals*, November 1903, 68.

Just as Marx and Engels had observed in *The Communist Manifesto*, the movement's raison d'etre was fundamentally conservative.[139] The MSPCA and the Department of Mercy advocated a traditional course of moral improvement for individual workers, an approach that ultimately thwarted any wider solidarity with labor and civil rights groups. Upton Sinclair, for one, might seem to have been a logical ally because his bestseller, *The Jungle* (1906), openly questioned the ethics of slaughtering animals: "And yet somehow the most matter-of-fact person could not help thinking of the hogs, they were so innocent, they came so very trustingly; and they were so very human in their protests—and so perfectly within their rights!"[140] Nonetheless, Sinclair's muckraking socialist indictment against the meat industry called for unionism and larger structural change—a scale of radicalism that the MSPCA and the WCTU rejected. The Department of Mercy believed so strongly in the power of individual transformation through humane education that in 1915 its leaders decided to change its name to the Department of Humane Education as a more accurate reflection of its work.

Aftermath: The Antivivisection Movement Endures

The name change was short-lived. In 1916, the Department of Humane Education submitted its final annual report. Even though humane education activities remained an enduring part of the WCTU's web of transnational, state, and local unions, the formal national department was officially absorbed into the WCTU's juvenile wing, the Loyal Temperance Legion Branch.[141] Mary Frances Lovell remained an active WCTU member for the rest of her life, but she devoted herself almost exclusively to antivivisectionism through her leadership and editorial duties at the AAVS.[142] A month before she died from injuries suffered in a fall, she gave her final radio address for the Women's Pennsylvania SPCA, sounding the themes that had dominated the Department of Mercy/Humane Education under her leadership: moral corruption, cruelty, and crime; the dangers of popular culture; and "the hardening effect on the character" in contemporary medical school training: "Medical students have been known to laugh over the tortures of the unfortunate creatures who are used as subjects."[143] Only humane education, she reiterated, as she had for decades, could save American civilization.

Lovell loathed how the medical community deftly appropriated the humane movement's language of civilization and humanitarianism to serve its own pro-vivisection agenda. She despised the newfangled serums used to inoculate people from potentially fatal diseases. She contended that the "serum mongers" were exploiting the "hysterical imagination" by exaggerating the frequency of rabies, a disease whose existence she and a handful of doctors openly questioned. She maintained that animals and children suffered more readily from serum injections, "these filthy and dangerous products of disease." Lovell described a disaster in Lübeck, Germany, where seventy-three children died in 1929–1930 after the bacteriologist and physician Albert Calmette injected them with an experimental tuberculosis vaccine accidentally contaminated with deadly bacilli: "Think of 76 [73] children killed—murdered because of the gross materialistic fad of injecting a product of disease as a preventive of disease! And let all humanitarians bear in mind the fact that the development of these murderous fads is the culmination of atrociously cruel experiments carried on year after year on the bodies of animals."[144]

In contrast to the Department of Mercy's retreat from animals, Lovell kept the actual "bodies of animals" in view as she connected animal experimentation to historical traditions of medical research on the bodies of the most vulnerable human beings—the poor, people of color, children, and women. In England, these associations triggered the famous "Brown Dog Riots," at Battersea. In 1906, a group of antivivisectionists and civic leaders erected a monument at Battersea in memory of a small brown dog twice vivisected by medical researchers in 1903. The unassuming statue quickly became a theater of confrontation between pro-vivisectionist medical students and local working-class residents, who resented the presence of the wealthy, arrogant interlopers in their neighborhood. Rioting was so persistent that officials dismantled the statue permanently in 1910.[145] Over the next decade, the relationship between defenseless animals and marginalized people became even more potentially damning: scientists, using animal bodies, produced new serum antibodies which, in turn, were tested on vulnerable human subjects. Pamphlets, such as "Human Vivisection," produced by an American group, the Vivisection Reform Society, chronicled these experiments in chilling detail.[146] Experimental inoculation provided antivivisectionists with perhaps their most powerful moral weapon: conclusive evidence of humanity's biological kinship with animals.

Kinship, rather than Christian stewardship, ultimately signaled the greatest difference between the WCTU and the AAVS. While the Department of Mercy vehemently condemned animal suffering, the organization paid

FIGURE 2.7. The American Anti-Vivisection Society forcefully addressed the interconnected histories of animal experimentation and medical research on the most vulnerable human beings. This sign at the organization's headquarters points upward to the moral high ground of antivivisectionism and downward to the subterranean ethical quagmire of experimentation on animals and children. "Sign Post Erected at Woodland Avenue Entrance to the Antivivisection Building," *Starry Cross*, July 1936, 101.

special attention to the human consequences of performing and/or witnessing vivisection. By contrast, Mary Lovell and the antivivisection movement charted a more comprehensive consideration of rights by collapsing the species divide. Scientific experimentation on living creatures, they argued, was physically and spiritually harmful to all sentient beings; tragedies such as the Lübeck tuberculosis inoculation project proved that vaccines could kill people as well as the countless animals destroyed during the research process. By the 1920s, the AAVS and its allies from Great Britain, Europe, and India demanded an end to all forms of animal experimentation and the abolition of vaccines, which they believed to be ineffective at best, and deadly at worst.

The growing radicalism of the AAVS generated periodic tensions with other animal welfare organizations like the American Humane Association and the ASPCA, because mainstream groups became progressively conciliatory toward the medical community to avoid alienation. Yet mainstream alliances still endured. Coalitions between the AAVS and other groups lobbied successfully for the passage of several state laws ending animal experimentation in public schools, as well as effectively blocking the passage of state pound seizure laws, which would have given vivisectionists easy access to lost pets at local pounds.[147] While the AAVS openly challenged medical discourses of progress and civilization, the organization still had strong ties to the broader humane movement.

In her last radio address, Mary Lovell linked animal protection to the status of American civilization in the wider world: "We are all members of a nation which for many reasons is before the critical eyes of the world."[148] Lovell's words evoked a long history of American women's activism that drew on feminine authority in the home to legitimize women's moral guardianship of the nation and globe. Kindly animal stewardship was an essential element of this feminine civilizing project.[149] Because animals could not "talk back," they were flexible bodies and open to interpretation. The Department of Mercy brought women out of the home and into the classroom, doctor's office, laboratory, church, backwoods logging camp, and state legislature. In the early twentieth century, some of these women ventured into the predominantly masculine public space of the streets as a testament to their growing visibility in political life. Here, humane activists and local media represented acts of animal cruelty as markers of racial, ethnic, gendered, and class difference, thus transforming animal-human relations into a referendum on American identity formation and the acceptable boundaries of proper American behavior and citizenship.

3

From Dog Eaters to Mule Beaters

REPRESENTING THE ACCUSED AS ALIEN OTHER

ON MARCH 8, 1906, Pound Master Vachet of Los Angeles issued a formal announcement at City Hall to address the "epidemic of thefts" of over 200 "high class dogs" since January 1. He noted that virtually all of the missing canines were bull or fox terriers with short white fur. He immediately suspected twenty-five visiting Bontoc Igorots from Luzon, Philippines, who had been hired to eat dogs at an ethnological show at Chutes Park.[1] The performances began on same date as the first canine disappearance. The Igorots had become conspicuously "fat and glossy" in just two months, and even more damningly they supposedly coveted the flesh of white dogs. Vachet described how a web of underground contacts provided access to the canines: "My boys are confident that the Nigs get 'em. One of the deputies told me the other morning that the night before he stopped a boy leading a white fox terrier down near Chutes Park. He says the boy confided to him that he was taking the dog to the park and that a fellow there would give a dollar for him. . . . The Blacks have a way of hooking up with the street gamins that brings them plenty of dog meat."[2]

While none of the Igorots were arrested for dog stealing during their 149-day stay, they remained racially and culturally suspect.[3] The Los Angeles WCTU Department of Mercy activist E. M. Deardorff rallied 996 people to sign a petition to the Chutes Park management that put an end to performances of dog killing, even though dog eating remained in the show.[4] Represented as "heathen dog-eaters" in popular media, the Igorots were a sensational living reminder of America's new overseas empire.[5] The "dog-eating Igorot" entered the American imagination in 1904, when the troupe performed in the Philippine Village at the Louisiana Purchase Exposition at St. Louis, where similar rumors of clandestine dog snatchings filled local media.⁶ Although Bontoc Igorots traditionally ate dog meat only for ceremonial occasions, such as weddings, funerals, and after battle, their American performances required a daily dog diet to retain their commercial appeal.⁷ Immersed in culturally specific ideals regarding dogs as man's best friend in a civilized society, American journalists and animal advocates used a familiar racial trope to define the dog-eating Igorot—the unassimilable Other.⁸

This chapter explores the ways in which humane advocates, journalists, and law enforcement officials transformed public interactions with animals into signs of American belonging and exclusion. They regarded animal kindness as a marker of proper American comportment, good citizenship, and higher civilization. They lauded the temperate driver who promptly fed, watered, groomed, and rested his undocked, uncropped working animals, guiding his charges with kind words rather than the whip or the strangulating checkrein, which painfully confined a horse's neck and head. Humane advocates prided cleanliness and the separation of animal and human domiciles. They possessed culturally specific ideas about the most humane way to slaughter food animals. They extolled the unadorned horse as the embodiment of civic virtue. They praised women who rejected feather fashions as exemplars of civilization. In each interaction, humane advocates filtered their definitions of proper and improper American animal practices through the optics of race, gender, and class in four interrelated arenas of public engagement: labor, custom, fashion, and entertainment. Additionally, their longstanding concern with "in" and "out" groups in America's pluralistic society became even more acute during the extended immigration wave between 1890 and 1920.⁹ Millions of new immigrants from Southern and Eastern Europe, Mexico, and Asia, as well as those Americans who recently gained citizenship rights after the Civil War, were frequently in the crosshairs of animal welfare conflict.

Although this chapter tells a national story, New York City and Los Angeles receive special attention. The ASPCA was founded in New York in 1866, and the Los Angeles SPCA (also called the Humane Society in the press) followed in 1877. As Los Angeles expanded in the early decades of the twentieth century, the humane movement took hold in communities across Los Angeles County, such as the leafy city of Pasadena, which founded its own busy humane society in 1894. Its activities were extensively covered in local newspapers.¹⁰

Print media was a persuasive means of public communication and representation for the humane movement. Reportage in animal cruelty cases had the power to transform a defendant, already marginalized on the basis of race, class, or immigrant status, into an unassimilable alien. Yet some humane leaders used the gospel of kindness to critique inequality rather than to reinforce it. These advocates denounced nativism and racism, as well as cruelty to animals. They stressed the social imperative of humane education for all Americans—rich, poor, immigrant, and native-born—to nurture their vision of a compassionate citizenry. Paradoxically, these cosmopolitan animal welfare activists shared a key conviction with their nativist brethren: both believed that animal mercy was a signature American value. Across the political spectrum, the association between American identity, animals, and benevolent conduct was far-reaching because animals permeated virtually every aspect of the nation's public social and cultural life.

Civilizing the Streets: Animals, Labor, Surveillance, and Conflict

Newspaper headlines described chaotic confrontations between accused animal abusers, protectionists, and pushing crowds, which regularly snarled traffic to a standstill: "Peddler Is Mobbed as Heat Fells Pony," or "Woman Blocks City Traffic in Pity for Mail Wagon Horse."[11] While women typically avoided public confrontations in the early years of animal protectionism, they became increasingly visible in the early twentieth century, when suffrage activists and trade unionists took their social movements to the streets. Newspapers routinely described the accused in racial, ethnic, classed, and gendered language. Additionally, laboring conditions further marginalized people who were dependent on animal muscle. During the Gilded Age and Progressive Era, teamsters were frequently at the center of animal welfare conflicts. Unlike the independent antebellum carter who owned his horse, two-wheeled cart, and supplies, post–Civil War teamsters were essentially proletarians working for wages as "haulers" for other companies. They often were African American and Irish and were routinely castigated in popular media for smelling like horses and for their fraternal culture of drinking and rough talk. In 1895, the *Nation* characterized them as "one of the lowest classes of the community."[12]

ASPCA founder and president Henry Bergh was at the center of the earliest journalistic narratives of the movement in New York City.[13] Bergh wore his police-like uniform and flashed his badge, an instant visual reminder of the ASPCA's legal power to arrest anyone who violated the state's animal welfare statute.[14] He frequently blocked traffic by physically placing himself in front of overloaded horse cars until either more horses were added or passengers disembarked, much to the irritation of drivers and passengers alike. He also successfully pushed for changes to the city's traffic patterns. In 1874, street railways began stopping only at street corners, abandoning the older practice of constantly stopping on demand. This change benefited horses, for their legs no longer faced the stress of repeated stopping and starting.[15]

Humane leaders and law enforcement officials set their sights on civilizing the ethnically diverse, animal-powered labor force that was building

FIGURE 3.1. Confrontations between SPCA officers and overloaded horse cars were virtual theaters of conflict on the streets in a muscle-powered world. "It Took Courage to Stop Overloaded Street Carts," *National Humane Review,* April 1941, 4.

modern Los Angeles. Aided by animal muscle, laborers were constantly visible in backbreaking occupations. They hauled lumber, brick, scrap, and refuse; they graded the city's steep terrain for road construction in new hillside neighborhoods like Bel Air and Hollywood Hills; they built bridges; and they poured gravel, tar, and macadam. In each of these animal-powered jobs, workers clashed with humane officers. Even though animal welfare leaders idealized the primacy of heart and soul education over prosecution, humane education programs were generally aimed at schoolchildren, not laboring men. Animal welfare advocates also prosecuted people for training horses (and dogs) with "primitive Mexican methods" and for breaking horses using the "Spanish-style," in which a horse was starved into submission and then trained for ordinary riding, haulage, or bronco riding. Such labeling hardened these associations between ethnicity and animal cruelty, especially as a contrast to the gentling techniques of the virtually sainted white Ohio native, John Solomon Rarey, the "Famous Horse Tamer," whose gospel of kindness embraced positive reinforcement to train even the most incorrigible horses.[16]

The majority of workplace cases in the *Los Angeles Times* involved horses that were starved, abandoned, overworked, or beaten. This coverage revealed that anticruelty laws generally addressed the actual act of abuse rather than the indirect intent to commit animal cruelty. As a result, these laws typically prosecuted individual workers instead of the employers who gave the orders to drive faster, carry a heavier load, or ferry more passengers. In other words, an individual teamster or conductor who obeyed company orders could be liable for prosecution—even if he strenuously disagreed with his boss. In 1868, New York's *People v. Tisdale* set a precedent for other state anticruelty laws, ruling that an employee, not an employer, was legally accountable in an animal cruelty case.[17] (Henry Bergh himself recognized the unfairness of prosecuting teamsters for overloading, especially with fines running as high as $300.00, but the law favored owners, not drivers.)[18] Consequently, when John F. Carrillo of Los Angeles was convicted of animal cruelty for beating a team of four horses while hauling gravel for a contractor in April 1903, he was personally liable, not his employer.[19]

Occasionally, however, contracting firms and haulage companies were prosecuted, especially in cases when an animal's wretched condition was clearly the product of sustained neglect. In July 1904, the Pasadena Humane Society and the Los Angeles SPCA jointly arrested the owners and management of Robert Sherer & Company, a local grading company, on twelve counts of cruelty, "for torturing, tormenting, and working stock unfit for labor."[20] Many of the firm's exhausted and malnourished mules were barely able to stand; others had giant fistulas and tumors. Sherer boasted that he would simply ship his stock to Arizona, outside the jurisdiction of Los Angeles County, and would fight all charges in court. Humane authorities intercepted the mules at the rail yard to provide medical treatment and to hold the animals as collateral. Sherer, meanwhile, temporarily disappeared, thus demonstrating a common strategy to avoid prosecution.[21]

Ramish and Marsh, a Los Angeles contracting firm, was also repeatedly convicted of animal cruelty and neglect for the poor condition of the horses and mules in its grading camps. Adolph Ramish regularly paid fines of $200.00 and more, but seemed unconcerned with the sorry state of his equine fleet. He merely regarded these fines and legal fees as an unavoidable business expense. As proof of his ability to make money even in the face of continued animal cruelty prosecution and penalties, Ramish plowed his considerable contracting profits into building a sprawling real estate and entertainment empire.[22]

Individual laborers, by contrast, possessed few financial and legal resources to answer charges of animal cruelty and neglect, a power dynamic amply documented in local newspapers. In August 1894, Wong Si Sue was arrested for abandoning a horse in Los Angeles; two months later, William Morales was arrested for starving a horse, which was shot on the spot.[23] On July 24, 1900, a foundering horse belonging to a Chinese vegetable seller was reported to the SPCA and shot. The owner sold the carcass to a fertilizer company for $1.50.[24] On June 13, 1904, an Italian fishmonger, Antonio "Goo-Goo Eyes" Peters, described as "one of the dirtiest characters of the harbor city [San Pedro]," was arrested for overloading and neglecting a sickly old horse.[25] The rare instance in which an individual laborer was able to pay a fine was a newsworthy exception that proved the rule. In October 1903, Charles Johnson, an African American driver, faced a $20.00 fine after he was convicted of beating, abandoning, and then selling an injured horse. "Much to the surprise of the officers," Johnson pulled a $20.00 gold piece from his pocket, paid his fine, and walked away.[26]

A fine or an arrest could be economically disastrous for individual laborers. Paradoxically, the same could be said for animals: anticruelty laws dedicated to protecting animals could unintentionally imperil them. This predicament vexed the animal protection movement throughout its history in the United States and abroad. The ASPCA, for example, became New York City's leading killer of horses from 1887 and 1897. Perversely, the ASPCA unwittingly supported affluent herd owners by shooting their horses because insurance companies would deny a claim to an owner who shot a suffering animal himself.²⁷ Such class-based ironies existed in London, where Section 39 of the Metropolitan Police Act of 1839 banned the use of dogs to pull carts within the city limits to prevent canine hardship.²⁸ Yet dogs were indispensable to the poor as an affordable alternative to expensive horses and donkeys, which were subject to stiff tolls when hitched to a cart.²⁹ Deprived of their livelihood, the poor could no longer afford to keep their dogs. On the morning the new Act took effect, impoverished owners killed their dogs by the thousands because abandoned dogs, ever loyal to their owners, would find their way home. As historian M. B. McMullan puts it, "The measure, purporting to be for their benefit, resulted in their slaughter."³⁰

"We Speak for Those That Cannot Speak for Themselves"

The press often represented poor and immigrant subjects in animal cruelty cases in their "own" voices. This speech was characteristically accented in phonetically exaggerated minstrel-like language, which echoed the intentional misspellings and punning speech of popular nineteenth-century American humorists.³¹ In September 1866, the *New York Herald* reported that Maria Colvin, "a burly female of Holland birth," obtained an injunction against a young Irishwoman named Bridget Bolton, who had kicked Colvin's dog. According to Colvin's court testimony, "I say, 'Bridget, vat for you do dis, eh? De little tog don't hurt you, does he?' Den she says dat she vould keek me too if it wasn't for fear of de law."³² The thick transliteration rendered a violent incident into a virtually unintelligible comic tangle. In October 1905, Mrs. James Lewis, a Canadian washerwoman of African descent, resisted arrest in California after her neighbor complained about her emaciated horse housed in a barren yard. The *Los Angeles Times* translated the confrontation into a familiar minstrelesque representation of southern black dialect: "I'se a British subjec', I is, an' I doan' want none o' you' white trash comin' roun' heah a-feedin' my horse. D'ye heah me now, git off dis heah place." In compliance with California law, the humane officers seized the starving horse and shot it.³³

If the transliterated voices of the immigrant poor sounded crude, humane leaders spoke in a vastly different register. They penned erudite opinion pieces and letters to newspapers, beseeching the public. Henry Bergh's elegant pleas appeared frequently in New York City newspapers: "I shall remain at my post, and fight the 'battle of the brutes' until that day shall arrive, which I trust may never dawn, when the people of this State shall command me to desist."³⁴ Bergh's elevated prose mirrored the elegant settings in which SPCA monthly board meetings took place. Newspapers described sophisticated WASP-y society affairs, replete with genteel entertainment: violin and vocal solos, poetry readings, tea, cakes, and literary recitations.³⁵ Animal protectionists believed that their mission of kindness transcended social and cultural differences through a singular universal message of mercy and moral uplift. Yet these moments of articulation in local newspapers formed their own axes of belonging and exclusion.

"Deemed too Dirty for Swine"

Voyeuristic sensory reportage from impoverished neighborhoods underscored the prevalence of animal cruelty. Slaughterhouses often figured into stories about poverty and animals, if for no other reason than because these facilities were overwhelmingly located in poor neighborhoods. On January 27, 1885, the *New York Times* reported that the Ladies' Health Protective Association, "richly dressed in furs and silks," made a sanitation inspection tour of East Side slaughterhouses. Titled "The East Side Pests," the story noted that the ladies passed "a colony of Italians . . . in quarters that would be deemed too dirty for swine." A subsequent article distorted poverty into inassimilable pestilence: "Their front steps were slats nailed on piles, and their front yard was a reeking barge of city garbage ornamented with dead cats and decaying refuse." Moral decay complemented this diseased domestic environment as the reporter observed a "drove of cattle tortured by small boys." The neighborhood was so horrific that the newspaper described the nearby slaughterhouse as "neat and orderly" by comparison.³⁶

In 1907, the *Los Angeles Times* similarly targeted Chinese immigrant hygiene while discussing the passage of a municipal ordinance mandating strict sanitation standards and inspection protocol at local slaughterhouses. The article ghoulishly described a "score of filthy shacks just outside of the city limits" that supplied meat to Chinatown: "The killing is done in a primitive manner, and the entrails, etc., of animals are cast aside on the ground, where they rot in the hot sunshine. The odor that is wafted to occupants of passing vehicles is staggering. The Chinese do not seem to notice it. Every morning they drive out from the city in a wagon, do their killing and hasty dressing, bring back the carcasses and dispose of them in the city."³⁷ Although the reporter acknowledged the willingness of Chinese slaughterhouse owners to comply with the new ordinance, the story conveyed a willful rejection of assimilationist values.³⁸

A wide range of cultural forms, from vaudeville to international expositions, reinforced anti-immigrant ideologies at the turn of the twentieth century. Dystopian fantasies of fecund immigrants and eugenicist theories of selective breeding and human improvement hastened the formation of nativist groups such as the Immigration Restriction League (1894). Sociologist Edward Ross argued in 1902 that exploding immigrant birthrates would invariably lead to the "race suicide" of "old-stock" white Americans, a point echoed in eugenicist Madison Grant's *The Passing of the Great Race* (1916).[39] Fears of immigrant contagion shaped formal policy at every level of government. When the bubonic plague—a flea-borne bacterium transmitted to humans living in rodent-infested areas—hit San Francisco on March 6, 1900, public health officials immediately quarantined Chinatown because the first victim, Chick Gin, lived there. A few months earlier in Honolulu, city officials similarly opted to burn most of Chinatown to contain the plague and to save the city's reputation.[40]

Dog Days

In a doppelganger of official policies to contain human contagion, the racial and class hierarchies of canine purebreds and mixed breeds shaped municipal dog policy in the nineteenth and early twentieth centuries. Quite simply, breed status determined which dogs lived and died. In an era before vaccination, city dog laws addressed rabies prevention. Stray dogs were believed to be the primary vector of the disease. Civilization, according to the Department of Health in New York City, was dependent on municipal canine control: "The experience of all civilized communities has shown that the existence of large numbers of stray dogs favors the spread of rabies.... it should be acknowledged that the community is responsible for the size of its stray dog population, just as it is for the cleaning of its streets or the disposal of its garbage."[41] Louis Pasteur successfully vaccinated the first human rabies victim in 1885, but killed-virus vaccines for dogs and cats were rarely available until the 1930s.[42] Before then, cities tried to prevent outbreaks by instituting dog ordinances, which mandated periodic muzzling, occasional "shoot on sight" orders for unmuzzled dogs, and strict enforcement of leash and licensing laws.[43] While stray cats were even more common owing to their remarkable fecundity, municipal authorities generally ignored them because they were profoundly intractable.

The centerpiece of the urban dog ordinance was the annual stray roundup during the "dog days of summer" (originally named after Sirius, the dog star) because people erroneously believed that rabies proliferated in hot weather.[44] Mere mention of rabies sparked public panic and screaming newspaper headlines, such as in 1903, when multiple cases were reported in New York, Chicago, and other cities: "Dog Bites Nine Persons: Big Newfoundland Spreads Terror Down Town," and "Rabies Raging in Chicago."[45] Rabies notwithstanding, loose urban dogs could be aggressive and were dangerous trajectories for infectious disease. In 1910, the New York City Department of Health listed 3,792 reported dog bites in the city limits.[46] While only 152 dogs tested positive for rabies that year, the prevalence of urban strays made dogs a special target of social and epidemiological control.[47]

Newspapers characterized these animals with the same nativist language used to describe migrant laborers and immigrant ethnic and racial groups. Strays were demonized as "mongrel curs," "vermin," and "contagion."[48] Motivated by additional pay running as high as thirty cents per dog caught, dogcatchers took to the streets, zealously dragging, throwing, and lassoing strays into crowded wagons bound for the newly opened municipal pound, which received thousands of unlucky canines each summer. Packs of poor boys and men also participated, enticed by the prospect of receiving as much as a fifty-cent bounty for each dog captured or killed.[49] Emboldened by the prospect of easy cash, dogcatchers were often just as brutal to neighborhood residents as they were to local strays. In 1877, a deputy dogcatcher with a history of violence in New York City was imprisoned after he drew his revolver and threatened to shoot Mrs. Sarah A. Ross, an African American who refused to turn over her unlicensed dog. Even during his sentencing, he vowed to "have the satisfaction of seeing Sarah's dog hanged."[50] On August 10, 1882, a dogcatcher was incarcerated after killing a fourteen-year-old Harlem boy named James Doyle who was shielding his dog in his arms. The dogcatcher reportedly fired his pistol in a fit of rage after a group of boys pelted him with rocks while warning their neighbors, "The dog-catchers are coming! Look out for your dogs!" Dogcatchers routinely harassed the neighborhood's Irish laborers, seizing and killing beloved "mongrels of little value" with impunity. Consequently, tempers quickly flared.[51] On July 14, 1886, dogcatchers in pursuit of a small neighborhood Spitz prompted several hundred Polish Jewish immigrants on Hester Street to unhitch the dogcatchers' wagon, scare away the horses, and to attempt the release of a "score of yelping curs of all breeds and sizes already ensnared" before one of the dogcatchers fired his gun. A local resident sustained minor injuries; the dogcatchers were subsequently arrested and jailed for felonious assault.[52]

Pedigreed dogs and their owners were also vulnerable during summer dog seizures—although less so than working-class residents and mixed breed strays. Dogcatchers routinely stole expensive, "high-class" purebreds from backyards, from the arms of an owner, off the leash, or under the pretense of confiscating an animal for violating muzzling ordinances.[53] Unscrupulous dogcatchers sold these dogs for quick cash or brought them to the pound to receive bonus pay. On the morning of Christmas Eve in 1889, for instance, Thomas Maitland, a lawyer, stood on his porch in New York City watching his purebred setter, terrier, and a French poodle as they strolled out front. Suddenly, three dogcatchers pounced on the dogs. A journalist noted, "Mrs. Maitland saw the row and screamed so that the frightened dog catchers fled with only the terrier."[54]

Mixed breeds fared worse than their purebred brethren at the city pound. These public facilities typically had separate cages for purebred dogs "of the finer class," while the mixed breed "curs of low degree" were housed en masse, usually without food or water, and were "permitted to associate promiscuously with each other."[55] At New York City's East 16th Street pound in 1883, Pound Master John McMahon gave pet owners forty-eight hours to pick up their mixed breed dogs in exchange for a $3.00 fine. After the deadline had passed, unclaimed canines were placed in a "grim iron cage" outfitted to hold 100 dogs and drowned in the East River. Yet "particularly fine animals" were held longer with the expectation that they would be claimed and paid for.[56]

The dogcatchers' conduct and the bleak conditions at municipal pounds prompted the Women's Pennsylvania SPCA (WPSPCA) to jump headlong into humane municipal stray reform in 1869. Inspired by an innovative new facility at Battersea, England, the WPSPCA captured strays with large nets rather than dangerous lassos and wire nooses; they banned the practice of throwing strays into wagons and they kept dogs in separate compartments in transit on specially designed shock-absorbent wagons. They hired their own dogcatchers, rather than relying on a graft-ridden system of mayoral appointees; they abolished the practice of incentivizing the capture of strays, and they kept scrupulous accounting records, which reduced kickbacks and outright theft. Insisting that rabies was no more common in summer than at other times of the year, they instituted a year-round stray capture policy, which eased the city's frantic spectacle of the annual summer roundup. They leased the dog pound from the City of Philadelphia, renamed it a "shelter," and revamped the facility, providing food, water, separate housing, and shade for all animals. They prohibited the practice of clubbing dogs to death in full view of other dogs in favor of a separate room where animals were euthanized with carbonous oxide gas, or chloroform, although puppies and kittens were still drowned during the facility's early years.[57] With few exceptions, they eventually euthanized unclaimed animals for want of precious space and supplies.

While other groups eventually followed the WPSPCA's lead, calls for sheltering reform were initially met with resistance. Many of the oldest animal protection groups were reluctant to embrace sheltering initiatives for fear of spreading their resources too thin. They were, however, openly critical of status quo municipal dog policies, such as muzzle ordinances, canine bounty hunting, and corrupt appointments.[58] Henry Bergh argued that the media outcry against rabies was unnecessary because the virus was rare. Health statistics collected during the Progressive Era supported Bergh's earlier conclusions. For example, nationally, there were fewer than 100 reported rabies deaths each year from 1901 to 1910. During the first eight months of 1911, New York City's Department of Health reported seven confirmed cases of human rabies, seventy confirmed cases of dog rabies, and 2,462 dog bites. By contrast, pneumonia was New York City's deadliest disease, killing 10,057 residents in 1911.[59]

In the face of growing membership pressures, the ASPCA gradually, if reluctantly, embraced the tenets of sheltering: the organization began prosecuting local dogcatchers for cruelty in 1877 and eventually took charge of New York's municipal stray and licensing policy in 1894, abolishing the pound, and building a new shelter in the city and in Brooklyn.[60] The Massachusetts SPCA (MSPCA) eventually moved into sheltering, as well.

Historian Bernard Unti observes that women initiated, rather than followed, the sheltering movement. New animal rescue leagues, such as those in Boston (1899), Chicago (1899), and New York City's Bide-A-Wee Home (1903), sought no enforcement powers during their state incorporation proceedings because they wanted to focus exclusively on sheltering and care for strays rather than prosecution—a policy that complemented traditional notions of separate spheres for women and men. (The Bide-A-Wee Home pioneered another innovation that would eventually become mainstream a century later: its facility practiced a no-kill policy for all, but terminally ill or chronically suffering animals.) Sheltering advocates responded to public criticism regarding the movement's alleged indifference to poor pet owners by offering to subsidize the cost of licensing and veterinary care.[61] In 1908, women led the new Los Angeles Humane League's successful takeover of the city pound. Women organizers ran a telephone and postcard campaign, culminating with the presentation of 14,000 signatures to the city council to abolish "the present brutal system."[62] The new shelter allowed poor families to pay the facility's new $2.00 annual dog license, as well as any shelter fines, in installments: "This is reversing the old order which heartlessly tore the children's pets from them because there were fees to be earned."[63] Yet racial and class hierarchies still remained at the Los Angeles Humane League's new shelter. "Worthless" mixed breed dogs were euthanized after three days of impoundment, while healthy purebreds faced a brighter future: "The well bred dogs, those that appear to be useful and healthy will be spared and homes will be sought for them. In this way the canine caste will be preserved in the survival of the fittest."[64]

Cultural Practice as Animal Cruelty

Animals were intimately tied to normative ideas about cultural assimilation. Italian immigrants were routinely prosecuted for hunting songbirds, a diet staple in their native Italy.[65] The *New York Times* scorned subsistence passerine hunters at the Bronx Zoological Park as "creatures made in fairly convincing imitation of human beings," even though there was a "trace of an excuse in their ignorance" because the majority of "these criminals" were impoverished Italian immigrants. Their inassimilable behavior tempted the newspaper to reconsider (half-jokingly) its opposition to corporal punishment "to advocate the prolonged application to each of them, when caught, of an oaken or hickory club about four feet long and from two to three inches in diameter. We don't really think that a proper remedy for the evil, but it would have certain charms for the observer."[66] In another incident, game wardens chased and fired shots into the air to frighten an Italian man as he hunted but warned that next time they would shoot to hit.[67] The American Ornithological Union (AOU) gave avian law enforcement its stamp of approval. The AOU indicted Italian immigrants for harming American agriculture because they hunted insectivorous birds, which protected crops from damaging insect pests.[68]

Animal protectionists took special aim at Jewish slaughter practices. Under the exacting rules of kosher slaughter, or *shechita*, an animal had to be fully conscious when its throat was slit, a process thought to be quick, painless, and humane. Repeatedly, animal welfare leaders rejected *shechita* as "barbaric," arguing that rendering an animal unconscious through a blow to the head or (starting in the 1920s) an electrical jolt was an act of mercy. In 1867, Henry Bergh pleaded with New York City rabbis and kosher butchers to stun animals before slaughter, as well as to stop the practice of dangling conscious animals by a chain. Bergh was rebuffed and reluctantly agreed to

FIGURE 3.2. William Temple Hornaday, director of the New York Zoological Park, wedded nativism and conservationism when he condemned immigrants for killing passerines for food. "Aliens We Kill the Song Birds," in William T. Hornaday, *Our Vanishing Wildlife: Its Extermination and Preservation* (New York: New York Zoological Society, 1913), 55.

stop interfering with Jewish customs—although other animal welfare leaders did not.[69] Baptist minister and MSPCA president Francis Rowley clashed with Jewish leaders over kosher slaughter. In 1913, Rowley outlined his opposition in a controversial pamphlet, "Slaughter-House Reform in the United States and the Opposing Forces." Jewish leaders responded decisively: The New York *Hebrew Standard* called Rowley "a bigoted and implacable enemy of *shechitah (shechita)*" noting that he was "again at work in his efforts to discredit the Jewish methods of slaughtering before the bar of American public opinion. He grounds his opposition to *shechitah* upon its fancied inhumane character, when in truth the very reverse is the case."[70] Rowley publicly confronted hundreds of rabbis "clothed in their official vestments," as well as Jewish lawyers and representatives from the packinghouses, when the MSPCA unsuccessfully lobbied the Massachusetts legislature to require stunning prior to slaughter.[71] Rabbis were outraged by what they saw as Rowley's flagrant disregard for the Torah's dietary laws of *kashruth*. Rowley insisted that he respected Judaism: "I dread more than I can say the accusation of being an anti-Semite, an antagonist of the Jew."[72] Rowley was quick to condemn anti-Semitic violence, calling such "treatment by the Christians for centuries the greatest shame of history."[73]

It would be a mistake, however, to conclude that kosher slaughter posed an irrevocable religious divide in the humane movement. For one, several rabbis were SPCA leaders, such as Rabbi Max Samfield, the founder of the Tennessee SPCA, and Rabbi Abram Simon, the founder of the Sacramento SPCA.[74] In a lecture to the Young Men's Hebrew Association in 1880, Henry Bergh noted that cruelty to animals was absent in Jewish entertainment traditions, and that the Jewish Saturday Sabbath gave animals a day of rest—just like the Christian Sunday Sabbath: "The Jews had no pigeon shoots, no bull fights, dog fights or cockfights, nor did their ladies, as some of ours are reported to have done, shoot buffaloes in the wantonness of slaughter."[75] George Angell also praised Jewish animal customs, such as prohibitions against slaughtering diseased animals, and he freely cited studies showing that Jews, on average, lived five years longer than Christians because of their healthful dietary practices and humane animal care.[76]

Nonetheless, by insisting on unconsciousness as the singular, incontrovertible litmus test for a merciful death, American humane leaders and their allies abroad tacitly denied the humane precepts of kosher slaughter. A British Admiralty committee on humane slaughter unanimously agreed in 1904.[77] When the ASPCA sponsored a contest in 1922 with a $15,000 prize to improve humane slaughtering methods, its leaders publicly stated that stunning cattle prior to slaughter was "essential" to any winning entry.[78]

As a counterpoint to *shechita*, industrial meat producers promoted the modern American slaughterhouse as humane and efficient. Its common features included an assembly-line design; after stunning and slaughter, carcasses were immediately suspended above the slick floor to maximize air circulation during dressing; adjacent vaults of ice kept the entire process cool and sanitized.[79] Meat industry proponents pointed to Chicago's vast, 640-acre Union Stock Yards and "Packingtown" as an exemplar of the modern system. Opening on Christmas Day in 1865, the Union Stock Yards quickly became the nation's epicenter of industrial meat production. While antebellum centers of slaughter, such as Cincinnati, sourced local livestock from the Ohio River Valley, Gilded Age meat producers used the nation's expansive railroad networks to bring millions of animals to market from faraway western rangelands and midwestern farms at railroad terminuses stationed within the vast stockyard grounds.[80] In 1900, 50,000 cattle, 200,000 hogs, 30,000 sheep, and 5,000 horses could be accommodated at any given time.[81] Journalist W. Joseph Grand's flattering account of the complex extolled its transparency and maximal productivity: "From the tips of the long tossing horns of the Texas steer to the end of his tail nothing is lost ... parts of the same animal may eventually be scattered to the four quarters of the globe."[82] Grand's *Illustrated History of the Union Stockyards* was a guidebook for the thousands of tourists who flocked to the Yards to behold a spectacular dis-embodiment of American capitalism: "Every factory in the Union Stockyards is wide open for public inspection, and indeed, so far above public expectation is the management of the factories that it is entirely to their interest to help the public to examine into their methods."[83]

Packinghouse titans extolled Chicago's Union Stock Yards as a marvel of modern capitalism, but muckraking journalists and animal welfare leaders indicted the vast compound as a glaring colossus of cruelty. As a long-standing proponent of food safety legislation decades before the Pure Food and Drug Act of 1906, George Angell disguised himself in laborer's clothing to gain entry into the interior regions of the Union Stock Yards so that he could bear witness "to the inhumane conditions, and plead for those who were dumb yet keenly suffered."[84] Upton Sinclair's novel, *The Jungle* (1906), chronicled the grim lives of Lithuanian immigrants Jurgis and Ona Rudkus, who toiled under wretched conditions at Packingtown, tightly quartered among thousands of fellow immigrant workers and their families, virtually cheek and jowl with doomed livestock. Shortly after arriving in Chicago, Jurgis visited a packinghouse and its ceaseless assembly line of hog slaughter, "staring openmouthed, lost in wonder," remarking quietly, "*Dieve*—but I'm glad I'm not a hog!" While Jurgis survived the slaughterhouse, many fellow workers died or lost limbs. Sinclair merged the brutalization of animals and workers into a rallying cry for socialism in America.[85]

"For Justice and Fair Play"

The enforcement of anticruelty laws often targeted laboring people who were reliant on muscle power or traded in animal products, but humane leaders emphatically believed that the gospel of kindness offered an effective weapon against American bigotry. It is especially notable that several African Americans were movement leaders in the South, therefore representing a surprising degree of racial diversity then and now. Animal welfare leaders condemned racial violence, and they freely shared stories of individual metamorphosis. In 1892, Miss M. M. Murphy, the principal at San Francisco's Jefferson School, instituted a school-wide humane education curriculum.

The metamorphosis of the student body was dramatic. Before 1892, gangs of "young barbarians" assaulted immigrants and stray animals on the streets and schoolyard:

> A few years ago a Chinaman was unsafe thereabout. If he wasn't forced into unequal hand-to-hand battle he was pelted with stones and made to think that existence in this country had more penalties than the annual poll-tax. Woe to the stray dog or cat, which ran into the territory of the young barbarians south of Market Street. The cur was terrorized with an pendant of old oyster cans, and his noisy flight furnished amusement for many a block, while the feline became a target for slingshot and brickbat till she either succumbed to the assault or escaped under some friendly house.[86]

Bigoted boy mobs were "tamed" and transformed into compassionate citizens once exposed to humane education. Murphy formed each class into a separate Band of Mercy. Every Friday afternoon, some 350 students gathered in color-coded badge groups in the Assembly Room. After reciting the Band of Mercy Pledge, children shared stories and testimonials of how they actively defended destitute immigrants and animals. One boy, Dominick Syce, recalled scolding a racist boy: "One day a Chinaman with a bag o' rags on his back was going along, and a boy began firing stones at him. The Chinaman began to run, and the boy kept a-chasing of him and firing at him, until I runs up and sticks out my foot and trips the boy head over heels.... He jumps up wild and yells, 'What's the matter of you?' 'I'm all right,' I says, 'How d'you like it yourself. Now go and throw stones at another Chinaman, will you?'"[87] In just four years after the founding of the Bands of Mercy, the Jefferson School had become virtually unrecognizable from its former violent self: "The children don't fight as they used to; they don't stone cats, or tie tin cans to the tails of dogs, or molest the sons of the Flowery Kingdom."[88]

George Angell and Francis Rowley believed that animal advocacy and civil rights activism were inseparable. *Our Dumb Animals* regularly chronicled the activities of southern African American animal protectionists who worked closely with the MSPCA and the American Humane Education Society (AHES), most notably the Reverend F. (Frederick) Rivers Barnwell, John W. Lemon, and Seymour Carroll. Collectively, these activists performed the majority of their humane work, as well as their human welfare advocacy, in the church and the school—two key institutions in post-Emancipation black society espousing racial uplift and self-help.[89] Based in Fort Worth,

Barnwell was a vigorous and peripatetic field officer for the AHES throughout Texas and the Lower South. He lectured, staged lantern slide exhibitions, established new Bands of Mercy, coordinated birdhouse building competitions at African American schools, and preached humane sermons to tens of thousands of people each year.[90] Barnwell blended these extensive activities with his other professional and social justice responsibilities: he was a Baptist minister, hymnal composer, educator, field marshal for the Red Cross during World War I, and director of Negro Health Services and director of the Tuberculosis Association of Texas starting in the 1930s.[91]

The Reverend John W. Lemon of Ark, Virginia, organized more than 500 Bands of Mercy and gave more than 800 school addresses, lectures, and sermons across Alabama and Virginia from 1910 to 1927. He coordinated church groups, club meetings and Sunday school gatherings, dispensed literature, and created humane exhibits at county fairs and humane floats in local street parades.[92] Lemon's lectures on animal kindness and civilization dovetailed with his other human-centered topics on racism and economic inequality.

FIGURE 3.3. The Reverend Frederick Rivers Barnwell of Fort Worth (pictured to the left with students and teacher members of a local African American Band of Mercy) was a field secretary for the American Humane Education Society starting in the 1920s. He and other black southern AHES leaders espoused a synthetic social justice project of animal kindness, self-help, and racial uplift. "Band of Mercy of Gay Street School, Fort Worth, Texas," *Our Dumb Animals*, July 1927, 110.

Our Dumb Animals noted that "[Lemon] has labored with unremitting zeal to liberate his race from the crowded, demoralizing, one-room log cabin; from the pernicious and blighting rental and mortgage system that has long existed, into the respectability and independence of the real American home, and thus helping themselves to secure for themselves better race relationships."[93] Although Lemon's lectures acknowledged structural inequality, they emphasized self-uplift and self-help, which individualized and diffused a more sweeping call for social change.[94]

Seymour Carroll's activism also struck an accommodationist tone in the spirit of his father, the Baptist Reverend Richard Carroll, a personal friend of Booker T. Washington and a field representative for the American Humane Education Society.[95] During Carroll's childhood on his family's farm in Richland County, South Carolina, his father ran an industrial school for orphans and held humane education meetings. Young Seymour held impromptu sermons with the other children, who brought dogs, cats, and chickens to the services. In 1928, he lobbied successfully for the passage of the Anti-Steel Trap Law in South Carolina, the first of its kind in the nation. In recognition of Carroll's leadership, Governor John Gardiner Richards invited him to stand at the signing ceremony.[96] Although trapping provided a source of food and income for the rural poor, Carroll and other activists vigorously fought it because it caused protracted suffering. They also believed that trapping was morally akin to poaching, promoting subsistence, itinerancy, and tacit theft over an ideal of agricultural stewardship, ownership, and capital accumulation.

Carroll was the youngest field representative of the American Humane Education Society and its most widely traveled. *Our Dumb Animals* described his breadth of activity as "limited only by the speed of his Ford car." He logged 1,000 to 2,000 miles a month giving upward of 100 speeches to schoolchildren and dozens of talks to adults at "enthusiastic mass meetings," and he handed out a "great quantity" of humane literature.[97] He organized Bands of Mercy and Junior Humane Societies in tandem with his activities for the National Association of Teachers in Colored Schools and the National Baptist Sunday School Congress. Owing to the extent of his service work, the *Spartanburg Herald* called Seymour the "negro social and welfare worker of the state."[98]

Occasionally Carroll made explicit references to human rights abuses in the Jim Crow South. Speaking at an AME church service in his official capacity as field secretary of the Negro Branch of the State Council of Defense just days before the United States entered World War I, Carroll exhorted black

South Carolinians to enlist in the military as a patriotic claim to citizenship even when tested by racial violence: "In slavery, in freedom, in oppression, in war or peace we have not deceived or betrayed our trust as American citizens."[99] Because he publicly acknowledged racism and economic inequality, his animal welfare work occasionally became dangerous. After giving a speech in 1923 at a Baptist church in Princeton, South Carolina, which denounced debt peonage as virtual slavery, he narrowly escaped being lynched.[100]

Our Dumb Animals reported Carroll's harrowing experience as part of its consistent condemnation of American racial violence. "Thirty-four citizens of our glorious country—the land of the brave and the free—lynched during 1926. Shot, 19; hanged, 7; hanged and shot, 3; burned, 2; manner of deaths unknown, 3. Taken from police officers and jails by mobs, 18. Of thirty-four thus murdered, 28 were colored. We have millions and millions to spend to enforce some laws; how much is being spent to guarantee to our own citizens within our borders the rights that are theirs under the constitution?"[101] During World War I, *Our Dumb Animals* contended that the frequency of lynching and race rioting at home threatened the nation's benevolent stature abroad: "There are evidently men among us as savage and cruel as any we have denounced across the sea."[102] In particular, "the horrors of the East St. Louis debauch of arson, torture, and murder, at the very hour when the nation is professedly standing as the defender of manhood rights and human freedom, must seem incredible to the civilized world."[103]

Barnwell, Carroll, Lemon, Rowley, and Angell believed that the gospel of kindness was antiracist to its core, a universal expression of American ideals of mercy and self-determination. *Our Dumb Animals* repeated this conviction, time and again: "This magazine has stood, from the day of its inception, for justice and fair play. It has by no means confined its interest to animals. Men, women, children, the victims of greed, oppression, injustice, prejudice, have found on its pages an outspoken championship."[104] In 1915, the MSPCA joined the National Association for the Advancement of Colored People (NAACP) in calling Americans to boycott D. W. Griffith's feature-length film, *The Birth of a Nation*, for its racist content: "Not only does it falsify the character of the Negro of war times and imply that he is still unfit for citizenship in an enlightened republic, and present him in guises that excite hostility against him, but it appears to have been most skillfully and deliberately planned to arouse and widen in the North that prejudice against the Negro that has characterized the worst elements of the South."[105]

Yet the movement's antiracist message often remained unheard, especially in the years before humane education became widespread. For example, the

African American newspaper, the *Christian Recorder*, criticized the humane movement for its silence after two black Texans were lynched in 1887 for defending themselves in a robbery: "Where is the Society for Prevention of Cruelty to Animals, that spends hundreds of thousands of dollars, seeing to it that men do not maltreat their donkeys and dogs; that they do not protect the animal life that resides in the humanity of the black man? O, where is Christianity?"[106] Despite a wellspring of genuine antiracist sentiment among the humane movement's leadership, day-to-day policing often reinforced existing forms of racial, ethnic, and economic inequality. Additionally, African American humane leaders, like their white colleagues, were college-educated elites whose class status may have made them less sensitive to the challenges of urban and rural laborers whose livelihood depended on animal bodies.

Cruel Fashions

Animal advocates treated bird hats, docked tails, and the checkrein as violent examples of un-American decadence. As the foot soldiers of the humane movement, women participated widely in these campaigns using an intersectional language of morality, motherhood, and civilization. But women just as often found themselves the target of fellow animal protectionists who demonized them as hypocrites for wearing fur and feathers while preaching the gospel of kindness. A Californian, for example, observed, "I stood in the streets of Oakland last week . . . and saw a woman wearing a plumed hat and costly furs seeking to have a workman arrested for driving a lame horse."[107]

Class, racial, and ethnic difference defined gendered notions of kindness, cruelty, and fashion. Millinery advertisements wooed consumers with images of upper-class European elegance and civilized refinement, while bird protectionists used discourses of savagery to compare Euroamerican bird hat enthusiasts to American Indians, among other people of color. Women who succumbed to feather fashions, they reasoned, had abandoned white civilization.[108] At the annual convention of the American Humane Association (AHA) at Chicago in 1906, J. Howard Moore elicited "tears and hysterical denials" from furious AHA members, some of whom walked out during his speech, "The Cost of a Skin":

> Nobody but a barbarian would adorn her head with the carcass of a bird or the heads of grinning weasels. Such things appeal only to the vulgarian. Such a woman is about as attractive as if adorned with a

string of skulls, for she excites pity and is a murderess. When I think that in this day of advanced action and supposed refinement brutalities such as are necessary to secure the furs of these little animals are practiced, I am heartily ashamed of the race to which I belong.[109]

Moore's inflammatory words were hardly in isolation. In 1907, the General Federation of Women's Clubs deployed a racialized message of feminine kindness when it announced a ban on the bird hat at its upcoming biennial meeting: "Feathers and scalps, rapine and blood . . . are the accompaniments of savage life. Better things are expected of civilization."[110]

Animal advocates were equally critical of young, working-class immigrant women who enthusiastically spent their hard-earned wages on cheap, ready-to-wear clothing and bird hats.[111] William T. Hornaday, director of the New York Zoological Park, recoiled at the chopped bird bodies displayed in shop windows within 100 feet of the Fourth National Conservation Congress at Indianapolis in 1912: "I counted 11 stuffed heads and 11 complete sets of plumes. . . . And while I looked, a large lady approached, pointed her finger at the remains of a greater bird of paradise, and with grim determination, said to her shopping companion: 'There! I want one o' them, an' I'm agoin' to *have* it, too!'"[112] Hornaday's dialect-inflected description rendered the shopper into a monstrous burlesque of merciful womanhood. Not only did laboring bird hat consumers defy affluent notions of domestic propriety by working in factories and other heterosocial spaces, they attempted to cross class lines by aping the fashions of the debauched rich.

Although feathers had been part of American fashion since the colonial era, animal advocates at the turn of the twentieth century repeatedly characterized the bird hat as foreign. The *Los Angeles Times* urged women to "Spare That Hat," because feather fashions were an expression of European profligacy, "a base and debasing custom, that was born beyond our boundaries, and inflicted on us like a foreign plague," which had no place in America: "Think of it, America, which stands, if it stands for anything, for civic liberty, for religious culture, for the noblest development of manhood, for the purity and beauty of womanhood, and those divine and far-reaching sympathies for all that is free and pure and sweet and worthy to exist because given and beloved of God."[113]

The composition of the feather trade, or, in William T. Hornaday's words, the "millinery octopus," contributed to these perceptions of foreignness and racial otherness.[114] Out of the eight largest firms in the National Millinery Association in 1911, Jewish businessmen—readily perceived in nativist terms as foreign—owned at least six.¹¹⁵ Questions of cruelty were intertwined with references to the marginalized people employed in the feather trade. The ASPCA called the South the "Black Belt of cruelty" because the organization assumed that African American hunters and trappers dominated the bird slaughter trade: "It is a normal sight to see Negro boys coming into towns early in the morning carrying long strings of dead robins."¹¹⁶ Back in New York City, shop floor conditions were miserable as immigrant female laborers fashioned dead birds into hats. The suffocating air was heavy with feathery particulate, which lodged in workers' lungs.¹¹⁷ The Lower East Side was the center of American millinery production. Russian Jewish immigrant women and their American-born daughters comprised the majority of the workforce. Italian American women and girls made up the second-largest ethnic group at these factories.¹¹⁸ Ostrich feather workers went on strike from October 1888 to April 1889 to protest wage cuts and to preserve their right to remain in the Working Women's Union. They lost: not only were wages reduced, but many strikers also lost their jobs.¹¹⁹

Jews participated in every aspect of the global ostrich feather trade in Britain, South Africa, and the United States, as investors, farm and factory owners, middlemen, and laborers.¹²⁰ Ostrich feather manufacturers stressed the distinction between their farmed plumes—painlessly (they argued) taken from live ostriches—and the fancy feather trade, which dealt in wild feathers plucked from slaughtered egrets and herons, among others. As a result, Audubon Societies generally exempted ostrich feathers from anti-plumage lobbying. Mary Lovell agreed after visiting several California ostrich farms: "I can vouch for those feathers . . . there was no cruelty practiced there."¹²¹

Yet Jewish Americans were still implicated in the political dimensions of the fancy feather trade. In 1911, the New York assemblyman Aaron J. Levy represented the business interests of his Jewish supporters in the American Millinery Association when he unsuccessfully attempted to repeal the new Dutcher Law, which banned the sale of wild American bird plumage in the state of New York (only game birds and domestic fowl were exempt).¹²² Levy's politicking outraged other Jewish constituents, who rallied successfully to defeat the bill using the ideals of animal kindness and respectable womanhood to define the tenets of proper Judaism:¹²³

> Let us Jews not participate in this tragedy. We Jews are merciful children of the Merciful. We were the first in the world to preach about mercy to animals. In our Temple there were no other images except those of Cheruvim—birds. Let us help protect these charming forest

enchanters. As Jews, we urge Assemblyman Levy to leave this bill for others, and let himself, as a Jew help defeat such a bill that is neither Jewish, nor humane, nor just. Let us hope that the Jewish milliners will finally withdraw this bill, and that the Jewish women will be the first truly civilized, and will refuse as head wear the little dead bodies of the pretty forest songsters.[124]

Reflecting cultural stereotypes of the virtuous or vainglorious woman, humane advocates placed women at the center of other forms of fashionable cruelty, including ear cropping for dogs and tail docking for both dogs and horses and the checkrein. On the streets of Los Angeles, author and freethinker Channing Severance observed, "Women are given credit for being naturally sympathetic, and one would expect them to have some regard for a dumb animal, but I have seen them every day as cold and heartless as a stone when pride is leading them to put on style with an overdrawn check-rein."[125] The British author of a popular guide to horse care described the genteel lady riding a docked mare "in season" as "a disgusting and indecent sight which should not be tolerated in a civilised society."[126] Similar to the bird hat, docking and the checkrein were generally practiced by the rich—whom George Angell dubbed "the bobtail aristocracy"—thus giving humane activists a powerful rebuttal to critics who accused them of harassing the poor.[127]

Docking and cropping proponents claimed that these practices made horses and dogs more useful. Kennel club breed standards mandated ear cropping and tail docking to ensure excellent conformation and utility, especially for hunting breeds, whose ears and tails might otherwise become ensnared in thick cover. Equine docking supporters used a similar rationale of fashion and safety for severing the tailbone. Docking had ancient English roots; its popularity fluctuated over the centuries, but steadily increased in the 1870s as the demands of haulage escalated in the industrializing world. Docking advocates asserted that the practice was necessary for draft and cab horses to prevent tails from becoming dangerously tangled during transportation and sport. They also reasoned that docking strengthened the spine and presented a clean, uninterrupted muscular line of the body.[128]

Although animal welfare activists condemned canine cropping and docking, they felt powerless to stop these practices in an unregulated marketplace. Instead, they channeled their energies into banning equine docking and the checkrein—cruel fashions that stood a chance of defeat because horses were highly visible sources of public conveyance and haulage. Humane organizations prosecuted these animal fashions under existing state anticruelty laws, in addition to spearheading state legislation in Massachusetts (1894), Michigan (1901), California (1907), and elsewhere.[129] Their efforts to ban the checkrein wholesale, however, generally failed, and even laws that banned tail docking proved difficult to enforce, especially with the sale of horses across state lines.[130] Although the California statute required that docked horses imported from other states be registered at the county clerk's office within sixty days of arrival, few owners faced prosecution for failing to do so.[131]

Because law enforcement was uneven, animal protectionists channeled their resources into winning over the court of public opinion through humane education literature, which emphasized the Old World origins of docking and the checkrein. In *Black Beauty*, Anna Sewell portrayed the wealthy proponents of docking and the checkrein as shallow fashion plates who recklessly abused their privileged station instead of honoring it through acts of stewardship. The spirited but ill-fated chestnut mare Ginger could barely breathe under the strangling immobilization of the checkrein, while Sir Oliver, Black Beauty's bobtailed friend, suffered a lifetime of torment, unable to swat biting flies away from his body: "I was tied up, and made fast so that I could not stir, and then they came and cut off my long, beautiful tail, through the flesh, and through the bone, and took it away."[132] Sewell's wrenching story of bobbed and maimed British horses helped catalyze a wider popular movement in England against painful equine fashions.[133] As part of marketing the book to American audiences, George Angell hitched Sewell's vision of proper stewardship to American ideals of unadorned civic virtue.

Courtroom deliberations also tied cruel fashions to foreignness. In 1878, the ASPCA prosecuted the management of New York City's Polo Club for docking the tail of its celebrity "Indian" polo pony, "the Custer Mare" (she had been owned by the late General Custer). In a graphic gesture, Henry Bergh and Elbridge Gerry brought a bunch of docked tails into the courtroom. This gruesome physical evidence, including a tail freshly "dripping with blood," was intended to counter the defense's claim that docking was relatively painless if performed properly. During the trial, the *New York Times* reported that Assistant District Attorney Herring was unsparing in his criticism of the defendants: "He handled the members of the Polo Club without gloves, characterizing them as a clique of snobs and would-be aristocrats, who endeavored by importing the fashionable vices of England to give themselves an air of selectness."[134] The Polo Club's lawyers convinced the jury that the pony had not suffered as a result of the docking because she "fed as usual" soon after the surgery.[135] Nonetheless, Herring's Anglophobic views of docking were widely shared by other Americans who believed that "Anglomaniacs . . . who wish to be considered in the swim" brought this corrupted fashion to the United States.[136] In 1903, President Theodore Roosevelt ordered the sale of all docked horses in the White House stables—lest anyone think that he was un-American or beholden to corrupt Old World cultural norms.[137]

Birds, horses, and dogs were the primary animal subjects of the fin de siècle movement to ban cruel fashions. As domesticated companions and workers, wild nest-builders, or caged parlor pets, they possessed a vital place in the domestic imaginary. In 1925, wild furbearing mammals joined this circle of concern with the creation of the Anti-Steel Trap League. While the WCTU Mercy activist Lucy Thurman and other humane educators had dispensed "Amos Hunt and His Steel Trap" and other anti-trapping pamphlets to children for decades, the tipping point for the formation of an official anti-trapping organization came with the growing threat of extinction. The booming post–World War I consumer economy and the attendant popularity of cheap mass-produced fur fashions accelerated the disappearance of furbearing mammals.[138] In 1921, the federal Biologic Survey declared an impending ecological disaster caused by the national "craze for furs."[139] Regional extinctions of fishers, martens, Arctic fox, and beaver united conservationists and animal welfare activists in a shared campaign against trapping similar to the coalition that successfully lobbied for passage of the federal Lacey Act in 1900 in the face of looming avian extinctions.[140]

The late 1920s saw the growth of state anti-trapping legislation in South Carolina, Georgia, and Massachusetts.[141] The intersectional politics of race, gender, and class shaped the ideological tone of the movement. Activists emphatically decried the soulless vanity of fur-wearing female consumers. *Our Dumb Animals* asked rhetorically: "Are women largely responsible for this immense traffic in trapped furs . . . ? If responsible, do they realize it? If they realize it, do they care? . . . Women, my sisters, the answer is up to you."[142] Activists depicted amateur subsistence trappers and professionals alike as lazy and indifferent, setting their steel-jaw traps in a wilderness they did not own, and profiting from the spoils of interminable suffering. Worse yet, trap sellers threatened to corrupt impressionable children because they advertised in juvenile magazines, wooing young consumers with promises of outdoor adventure and easy money, such as, "Trapping for Fun and Profit."[143] Lucy Thurman and Seymour Carroll regularly included anti-trapping curricula in their programs with rural southern black children, in part, as a project of racial uplift. They strove to mentor African American children away from an extractive and nomadic lifestyle predicated on animal cruelty and precarious subsistence, in favor of a steady and upwardly mobile future in which full citizenship would eventually be achieved through accommodationist strategies of self-improvement.

"Brutes in the Shape of a Man": Animals in Public Entertainment

A widely syndicated article on dog fighting in 1866 explained "How Human Brutes in New York Amuse Themselves."[144] The article highlighted the most infamous contemporary dog and rat fighter, a squat, pock-faced, "beastly" Irish American Catholic saloonkeeper named Christopher Keyburn, better known as Kit Burns, who operated dog fights in a hidden pit in the back of his building.[145] New York State banned animal fights in 1856 and the amended state anticruelty statute in 1867 explicitly prohibited aiding, attending, or "keeping a place for cock fighting, bull baiting, dog fighting, etc."[146] Although Burns repeatedly clashed with the ASPCA, he was seldom caught in the act of a dogfight or rat baiting.[147] The "unmistakable odor of dog which extends even into the street" hinted at the illegal activities within, yet Burns designed his saloon and fighting pit with evasion in mind. A long hallway with "dark and tortuous passages" and a "short and rickety staircase" connected the saloon with the "damp and unwholesome" fighting pit in the basement. Sentinels were posted to keep watch. When the police and ASPCA agents arrived, only the blood-spattered pit left clues of prior activity.[148] Even when prosecuted, Burns escaped conviction by shrewdly arguing in court that rats were vermin, not animals, and as a result, exempt from anticruelty laws.[149] Burns also dodged prosecution by moving around. In 1868, he cleverly turned his old Water Street fighting pit into a Christian revival meeting. When interviewed there about Kit's "wicked life," his father replied, "I'm sorry he has dogfights and all that, but I'm more sorry he's sometimes given to drink."[150] Bergh led a successful raid in December 1870, but Burns avoided prosecution a final time. While awaiting trial, Burns caught pneumonia and died at the age of thirty-nine.

Illustrations magnified the sheer kinetic violence of dogfighting and rat baiting by representing the human participants and spectators as animals. Hairy, simian bodies—sometimes labeled as immigrant Irish Catholics—with misshapen, thick faces, rotten teeth, and small, glittering eyes reinforced lingering racist beliefs in polygenesis, or separate origins for different ethnic and racial groups and social classes. They also resembled representations of

Irish Americans in other popular entertainments, such as vaudeville, where primates occasionally played Irish characters. The musical acrobatic team, Goggin and Davis, for one, incorporated simian costuming into their vaudeville comedy act of an ape and a policeman.[151]

Cockfighting was similarly portrayed through the optics of inassimilable difference. Although cockfighting was a global sport with transnational origins, the *Los Angeles Times* declared that it and other "Latin" blood sports were a barrier to the city's prosperity because globetrotting tourists claimed to witness more animal cruelty in Los Angeles than in any other city in the world: "Doubtless this trait has descended to the Latin races from the days when gentlewomen gloated over the spectacle of innocent maidens and children being torn to pieces in the public arena by lions and tigers, or ravished by gladiators, dressed in the skins of animals."[152] The newspaper reported Sunday afternoon battles between dedicated animal protection officers and raucous, Sabbath-breaking cock fighters. In 1900, a politically powerful Latino gangster, Ignacio Bilderrain, was convicted of trying to bribe a Los Angeles humane officer at a cockfight. Bilderrain's lawyers successfully

FIGURE 3.4. Irish American saloonkeeper Christopher Keyburn, better known as Kit Burns, ran New York City's most notorious dogfighting and rat-baiting operation during the Gilded Age. Burns and other blood sport enthusiasts were often represented in snarling, animalized form. "A Dog Fight at Kit Burns,'" in James D. McCabe, *The Secrets of the Great City* (Philadelphia: Jones Brothers, 1868), facing 388.

overturned his conviction by arguing that the humane officer had no powers of arrest because the SPCA had ignored state incorporation laws when creating its bylaws. Bilderrain walked free; the SPCA was forcibly dissolved and had to be reorganized the following year. Meanwhile the Sunday cockfights continued.[153]

In May 1904, six humane officers descended on one of Bilderrain's cockfights in a thicket of willows near the Los Angeles River and the Sentous slaughterhouse. A wealthy butcher, C. David Frey, was fatally shot as he fled in his carriage. The *Los Angeles Times* described a chaotic scene at the coroner's inquest, with Frey's supporters forming a "scowling knot" outside, chanting "Lynch the ___ pale face!"[154] Despite a claim of self-defense, humane officer C. F. Carpenter was charged, convicted, and imprisoned for manslaughter.[155] Dr. Hugh H. Walker, a local humane leader, concluded that in light of Carpenter's conviction, religion and humane education, rather than surveillance, might be the most effective ways to end gambling and the cockfight.[156] Other ministers echoed Walker's call for local churches to lead the fight against vice.

Blood sports attracted diverse, boisterous crowds, which made them seemingly more menacing to ideals of civic virtue and the public good. Given the wide focus of animal protectionism on laboring animals and blood sports, critics charged that affluent activists were primarily dedicated to policing the poor. When Officer Carpenter was convicted in 1904, the deputy district attorney criticized the Los Angeles SPCA for running moralistic interference at the popular cockfight: "[They] hound these men who go up the river to enjoy a sport handed down to them by the people of Mexico for the past 400 years."[157]

The animal welfare movement policed elite blood sports like coursing, fox hunting, and pigeon shooting. But they were often unsuccessful in prosecuting the rich. Wealthy defendants had powerful legal representation and extensive political connections.[158] Successful pigeon shooting bans, for example, only came after decades of activism: in Massachusetts (1879) and New York (1902), but not in Pennsylvania, where all efforts were defeated.[159] The powerful membership of exclusive gun and hunt clubs were formidable foes to the passage of anti-shooting legislation. Animal advocates had better luck monitoring the welfare of individual horses in racing and polo under existing anticruelty statutes, but wholesale prohibitions proved all but impossible.

Animal advocates worked hard to regulate the burgeoning film industry. Unlike ephemeral live blood sports, movies possessed the dangers of endlessly reproducible permanence. The staged (and sometimes actual) violence of a recorded cockfight, feline boxing match, or bullfight could "live" forever in film. Protectionists focused on two aspects of film: the actual treatment of the animal actors during production and the representational power of the film's storyline in which the illusion of cruelty could be created by clever camera work. Humane activists successfully lobbied the industry's self-regulatory body, the National Board of Censors, to add animal cruelty to its Production Code in 1925—to prevent and censor animal cruelty just as vigorously as other forms of lascivious conduct were suppressed under Will H. Hays. The amended Code also stipulated that any attendant or employee caught being cruel to animals would be dismissed.[160]

Enforcement, however, was spotty. Approximately 150 horses were recklessly killed in the making of the chariot race scenes in *Ben-Hur: A Tale of the Christ* (1925). After a horse was intentionally driven off a seventy-foot cliff in *Jesse James* (1939), the AHA became increasingly vigilant in monitoring the welfare of the creaturely actors on movie sets. The AHA was given the authority to evaluate scripts in progress and to place an AHA representative on the set to enforce humane treatment.[161] Throughout the history of the Production Code, the collaborative relationship between animal welfare activists and purity reformers demonstrated their mutual concern with individual moral conduct.

Film, like other forms of American entertainment, used racialized tropes of civilization and savagery to represent its heroes and villains as animal defenders and abusers, respectively. Furthermore, it is important to remember that the racially segregated social milieu for watching a movie amplified cinematic representations of animalized racial inequality and citizenship denied.[162] On screen, representations of animal cruelty and kindness broadcast American definitions of the worthy citizen and the hopelessly unassimilated. Native Americans, in particular, were depicted cinematically as unredeemable "savages."

Released in 1913, D. W. Griffith's twenty-nine minute short film, *The Battle at Elderbush Gulch*, made animals essential to its representations of Native American unfitness for citizenship. In the film's first scene, two tearful white girls clutching their beloved puppies in a basket were sent by stagecoach to live with their uncles in a western frontier town. An opening caption signaled the film as a story of manifest destiny: "A tale of the sturdy Americans whose lifework was the conquest of the Great West." Once the girls arrived at their uncles' home, an ominous caption foreshadowed conflict: "That evening, at the nearby Indian village, the Feast of Dogs is celebrated." The girls fretted because the uncles refused to let the puppies inside the cabin. Two Indians lying in wait snatched the dogs by the ears. Sally, the older girl, tried to intervene and was taken hostage. Her uncle appeared, shot one of the men, and Sally ran back to the cabin, puppies in hand. In retaliation, the Indians invaded the town. The US Cavalry roared onto the scene, the Indians were quickly vanquished, and white settler civilization was saved. Best of all, the uncles finally agreed that the puppies could stay inside.[163]

Foreshadowing the racial politics of D. W. Griffith's epic film, *The Birth of a Nation* two years later, *The Battle at Elderbush Gulch* portrayed white women, children, and house pets as linchpins of American civilization. Banished from their appropriate place in the household, the puppies were left to wander away from the safety of the built environment into the Indian wilderness, where they were in danger of being eaten as part of the Feast of Dogs. While concepts of civilization and nation rested on mutually constitutive ideas of settler domesticity and animal kindness, the dog-eating Indians were represented, by contrast, as primitive drifters sleeping on the bare ground in ephemeral encampments made of sticks and skins. They instinctively went to war, as the subsequent caption put their intentions into words: "At dawn, a war-dance lashes the passions of the Indians into a savage hatred." While the film's conclusion rested with the Indians' demise, the story's final moments went to the dogs, now welcomed inside as a testament to civilization won on the frontier.

The film's normative performances of citizenship and animal kindness complemented the assimiliationist goals of contemporary Indian boarding schools. Curricular materials accentuated animal kindness as a bellwether of future citizenship. Although humane leaders were not directly involved in federal education programs on Indian reservations, their influence was clear. Teacher manuals, textbooks, and songsters stressed animal stewardship as indispensable for preparing pupils to become independent farmers: "The aim of this course of training [in the ninth year] is the development of the individual and his preparation for citizenship. . . . The course should include lessons on cleanliness and neatness, gentleness, politeness, kindness to others, *kindness to animals*, love for parents, benefactors . . ."[164]

American civics textbooks similarly exhorted immigrant and native-born children to practice animal kindness as a pathway to proper citizenship. *The Teaching of Civics* (1913) encouraged children to "always protect birds and other animals."[165] *Civics and Citizenship* (1934 edition) contained tests of moral judgment, which asked its youthful readers if the following activity, for example, was morally acceptable: "Shooting at song-birds to test your skill with an air rifle."¹⁶⁶ Author Henry Noble Sherwood ominously intoned that without a rigorous civics education, the nation's moral future was fragile: "Poor training in childhood and youth is poor preparation for citizenship."¹⁶⁷ Published in 1905, Waldo Sherman's *Civics: Studies in American Citizenship*, proposed local ordinances for the fictional town of Collegeville that addressed matters of comportment and moral behavior, including "disorderly assemblages, cock-fights, dog-fights, prize-fights, sparring matches, and all brutal or depraving exhibitions of sport."¹⁶⁸ The kindly regulation and protection of animal bodies was essential to municipal order in fictional Collegeville. Further, the assimilative reach of the civics textbook extended far beyond the American classroom in a new age of American empire building at the turn of the century.

From the dog-eating Igorots at ethnological exhibitions to the dog-eating American Indians in *The Battle at Elderbush Gulch*, representations of animal cruelty and unassimilated difference in the United States were mutually constitutive and culturally contingent. Kindness to animals was a litmus test for national belonging and exclusion, which could be both liberatory and oppressive. Animal mercy also helped to define the borders of right conduct in America's overseas empire. In reporting an ongoing court battle regarding humane poultry transport methods in 1899, the *Los Angeles Times* gestured to the new empire in its characterization of carrying chicken by their feet: "with their heads pointed toward the Philippines."¹⁶⁹ Traveling to the Philippines and other new American territories, the next chapter explores the ways in which the gospel of kindness played an essential role in defining the quotidian and ideological contours of American benevolence and exceptionalism in the new empire.

4

An Empire of Kindness

AMERICAN ANIMAL WELFARE POLICY AND MORAL EXPANSIONISM OVERSEAS

ON FEBRUARY 15, 1898, the USS *Maine* exploded at Havana Harbor in Cuba. Bellicose yellow journalists and politicians demanded a declaration of war against Spain. George Angell, by contrast, demanded peace. On the pages of *Our Dumb Animals*, he proclaimed, "A war frenzy has smitten thousands of weak minds. Physical retaliation, the first thought that occurs to lower animals, is everywhere being threatened against Spain."[1] Angell called upon "every clergyman in America to pray in his home and his pulpit the Almighty to save our nation from the curse of war. . . . *If this is faithfully done we shall have no war.*"[2]

Angell called the public's attention to "*all the animal creations* that suffer so terribly in wars."[3] During the Philippine-American War (1899–1902), more than 90 percent of all work animals died during a rinderpest epidemic.[4] Angell was equally attentive to the human costs of war. He denounced American atrocities in the Philippines, including coercive *corvée* (unpaid) labor, village burnings, drowning by the "water cure" (or waterboarding in contemporary parlance), and slow death through starvation rationings in reconcentrated (concentration camp) villages, also known as *reconcentrados*.[5] *Our Dumb Animals* reprinted contemporary poems, such as "Malevolent Assimilation" and "To the Filipino," alongside Angell's own furious polemics, such as "Shooting Boys in the Philippines":[6] "To be sure we paid Spain twenty millions of dollars for the privilege of shooting them, and so shifted from Spain's shoulders to ours a war *which she was mightily glad to get rid of* and which, saying nothing of the loss *and suffering* of human and animal life, has cost us up to the present moment *more than six hundred millions of dollars.*"[7]

Yet Angell was no isolationist. His vision of animal compassion and stewardship complemented the expansion of American values overseas. Although opposed to formal imperialism, Angell and other animal advocates supported the peaceable spread of American representative government, free trade, industrial development, and Protestant evangelism around the world. Nor were humane advocates unilateral pacifists. Many supported war when the United States appeared to be fighting for a higher moral purpose rather than territorial or economic gain. The Reverend Francis Rowley, Angell's successor at the Massachusetts Society for the Prevention of Cruelty to Animals (MSPCA), endorsed America's entry into World War I in 1917, even though he had been a bitter critic of American militarism at the turn of the century: "Had the United States gone into this war to gain a single foot of territory, or to add to its glory or its power, this magazine, to be true to its record, could only have denounced such a step. We cannot think of this war ... as other than one in self-defense and on behalf of human liberty."[8]

Similarly, humane leaders applauded the patriotic service of horses, mules, elephants, camels, and dogs on the battlefields during World War I. In 1916, the American Humane Association instituted the Red Star Animal Relief (Red Star, for short) to provide care for the millions of horses serving with the nation's future wartime allies, as well as the nearly 100,000 horses and mules serving with the American Expeditionary Forces currently engaged in a border war with Pancho Villa's revolutionary forces on the Rio Grande under filthy and overcrowded conditions.[9] Humane publications regaled readers with stories from the Western Front to convey the importance of supporting America's heroic "sub-human army" through a donation to the Red Star Animal Relief: "Side by side with his heroic masters, he fights on, torn with shot and shell; gassed; squirted with liquid fire; bombed from the skies; blown up by subterranean mines; drowned at sea on his way to the front.... We can at least help him."[10] After the Armistice, the MSPCA sponsored a $50,000 peace endowment "in memory of the million horses and dogs who served and suffered and died in the Great War."[11] Other writings pleaded, "We helped you win—now help us to freedom from abuse" as a direct patriotic demand for the right to protection.[12]

Animal protectionists, however, denounced the Spanish-American War and the subsequent Philippine-American War as unbridled imperialism. George Angell, a lifelong Lincoln Republican, blamed President Roosevelt for fomenting a new jingoistic culture of chest-thumping militarism. In 1907, Angell believed that his open condemnation of Roosevelt's hunting trips prompted federal administrators in Washington, DC, to pull *Our Dumb Animals* from local public schools, by order of the president. Angell noted that this act of censorship had only served to advertise *Our Dumb Animals* because subscription rates soared as a result of the controversy's media coverage.[13] While Angell recognized the president's "much good work," he also observed that the MSPCA had long doubted TR's judgment, even publicly opposing Roosevelt's appointment as assistant secretary of the navy in 1897: "because we felt sure if he received that appointment we should get into a war with something about something. We failed, and the Cuban and Philippine wars have cost thousands of lives, hundreds of millions of dollars, an enormous increase of our pension list, and the end is not yet. . . . [W]e cannot help thinking of him as a powder mill, liable at any time to explode and do vast damage."[14] Angell enjoyed productive relationships with other presidents, but relations between the MSPCA and Roosevelt remained permanently strained: "Our experiences with President Roosevelt have not been of the happiest. We have never had any faith in his humanity and grave doubts of his being anything more deserving of praise than a political partisan seeking first, last, and only, the profit of Theodore Roosevelt."[15]

Despite an emphatic rejection of Roosevelt's ardor for military expansionism, early twentieth-century humane leaders joined missionaries, temperance advocates, and other social reformers to propagate assimilative American values of free moral agency, personal uplift, and civilization to build a self-styled empire of kindness.[16] These informal transnational actors often tacitly embraced notions of the white man's burden as part of their call to educate and enlighten their brethren of color abroad. Gendered ideologies of moral empire building and animal protection were predicated on an ideal of sober, thrifty, industrious manliness, and chaste, respectable femininity.

This chapter analyzes the ways in which American policymakers and animal advocates promulgated a gospel of kindness in the empire to remap the moral contours of the modern world. At the turn of the century, animal protectionism had become so widespread that even policymakers with no direct ties to the movement, such as William Howard Taft—whom Angell criticized as a Roosevelt lackey in other contexts—made humane legislation in the empire an essential part of their civilizing project.[17] In other words, the same architects of American expansionism that humane leaders criticized for their aggressive militarism made animal welfare a priority in the daily operations of local, provincial, and territorial administration. These policies, however, periodically clashed with culturally specific practices.

Animal protectionism overseas, as at home, exposed the movement's paradoxical impulses: promoting freedom from animal pain and suffering, on the one hand, and circumscribing human freedom through programs of political, social, and moral control, on the other. Although material from Cuba, Puerto Rico, and Hawaii is included, this chapter focuses primarily on the Occupied Philippines, where a sustained American military and civilian presence generated a remarkable trail of historical evidence related to animals.[18] With the exception of the indigenous carabao, these animals represented virtually the same species that activists worked hard to protect in the United States. That is to say, policymakers and protectionists focused on the domestic creatures and wild birds that people most frequently encountered in their daily lives.

Americans' imperial engagement with animals took place on a biological level as well as a political and cultural one. As part of building a commercial empire, American officials ferried honeybees and bumblebees to the Philippines (via Honolulu) to promote beekeeping on the Islands. They imported American jacks to mate with native donkeys throughout the empire, as well as jennets and Morgan horses, using contemporary theories of hybrid vigor to improve stock overseas. They also introduced Maltese milch goats as a way to promote dairying. They attempted to cultivate California redwood and hemlock-fir in the Philippines in a futile effort to find a wood distasteful to the native white ant, a voracious and ubiquitous pest that readily decimated wooden buildings and furniture.[19]

Microbes played an important part of this biological exchange. The rapacious global spread of anthrax, rinderpest, surra, glanders, and other fatal livestock diseases dictated US customs regulations overseas.[20] The destructiveness of these diseases prompted US veterinarians and bacteriologists abroad to perform experiments on animals in order to find cures—a move that shocked the American antivivisection movement. Activists feared that offshore animal experimentation would signal the end of humane oversight. Animal protectionists in the United States petitioned unsuccessfully for a ban on vivisection, specifically targeting Philippine macaques, which were being used to test experimental vaccines against smallpox. Novelist and reformer Elizabeth Stuart Phelps Ward wrote to her personal acquaintance President Roosevelt, protesting this practice as "bad precedent" for animals in the new empire, especially since many major American research institutions now regulated vivisection. Ward and her colleagues feared that US scientists were effectively taking vivisection offshore as a way to avoid potential oversight at home.[21]

Law, Surveillance, and Daily Life in the New Empire

Animal welfare laws were instruments of US authority overseas, but the jurisdiction and punitive scope of each law varied. Hawaii's expansive animal welfare law was part of the Laws of Hawaii that took effect when Congress annexed the Islands by simple majority in July 1898; it stipulated that "'animal' or 'dumb animal' shall be held to include every living creature; the words 'torture,' 'torment,' or 'cruelty' shall be held to include every act, omission, or neglect whereby unjustifiable physical pain, suffering, or death is caused or permitted." The law further defined the accused "owner" or "person" to include "corporations as well as individuals."[22] On August 17, 1899, Brigadier General George W. Davis issued General Order No. 122, which established the Protectora de los Animales in Puerto Rico and granted this humane organization the powers of arrest, as well as the authority to support itself with funds "arising from fines imposed for infringement of its regulations."[23] The activities of the Protectora de los Animales were limited to San Juan, which frustrated animal protectionists in other parts of the Island, such as Ella Payne, an American schoolteacher in Mayagüez, who implored the Bureau of Insular Affairs in 1913 to fund a humane organization with enforcement powers in her town.[24] In Cuba, the earliest animal welfare policy also took the form of a military order. On April 19, 1900, Brigadier General Adna R. Chaffee signed Order 165 on behalf of the Military Governor of Cuba, which banned cockfighting beginning on June 1 and fined each violator $500.[25]

As head of the Philippine Commission and first civil governor of the US Occupied Philippines, William Howard Taft argued that cruelty to animals by Filipinos demonstrated their unfitness for citizenship: "The idea that these people can govern themselves is as ill-founded as any proposition that [William Jennings] Bryan advances. They are cruel to animals and cruel to their fellows when occasion arises. They need the training of fifty or a hundred years before they shall even realize what Anglo-Saxon liberty is."[26] Shortly after Taft assumed office in the Philippines, his administration, working in cooperation with Filipino elites, established an elaborate Municipal Code for the entire country that structured the legal minutia of local governance, including laws against animal cruelty. On February 6, 1902, the Municipal Board of Manila enacted its own "Ordinance for the Prevention of Cruelty to Animals." In five comprehensive sections, the ordinance mandated new modes of comportment and surveillance, replete with stiff fines of $100.00 and imprisonment of up to six months for those who failed to comply.[27]

Manila's Municipal Code represented the first of several pieces of animal welfare legislation passed during the decades-long American Occupation.[28]

The Philippine Commission incorporated the Philippines SPCA in 1905 as a policing body to provide an additional layer of official enforcement. Similar to blueprint anticruelty legislation in the United States, the act declared that SPCA agents in Manila and in the provinces "shall have the power and authority of a police officer" to "enforce laws which may be in force in relation to cruelty to animals or the protection of animals in the Philippine Islands and generally to do and perform all things which may tend in any way to alleviate the suffering of animals and promote their welfare." The law authorized the police "wherever organized" across the Islands to assist local SPCAs with the enforcement of "all such laws." The involvement of municipal police in the Philippines SPCA was critical to its success. As in the United States and elsewhere in the empire, the authority of the Philippines SPCA as a private organization to enforce public laws placed it in a murky juridical sphere; it was privately run, elected its officers by its own undisclosed rules, and raised money independently, yet it was vested with public policing powers and the right to raise revenues through fines collected.[29]

The majority of anticruelty legislation during the Occupation focused on people's encounters with individual domestic animals. Policymakers treated wild animals in the aggregate, as subjects of new conservation legislation and scientific research. Birds, in particular, were of special interest—just as they were among local Audubon societies and WCTU Departments of Mercy in the United States.[30] Conservation advocacy groups, such as the American Ornithologists' Union, urged the War Department's Bureau of Insular Affairs to ban the export of birds and plumage.[31] In response, the Philippine Commission enacted a series of bird-related acts that established closed hunting seasons on specific birds and dictated how birds were to be killed.[32] While the Occupation Government's Bureau of Science was dedicated to bird conservation, it also did a brisk business in bird skins (dead birds) with museums around the world, a contrary move that officials justified in the name of scientific research and public education.[33]

The Philippine feather trade remained virtually unregulated until the passage of An Act for the Protection of Game and Fish in 1916, which included a ban on hunting or trading any designated "protected bird" under the law. Nonetheless, Section 7A allowed "any person of good repute" over the age of fifteen to obtain an official permit for collecting nests, eggs, and bodies of protected species for "scientific purposes only."[34] This legislation also broadened the scope of surveillance by expanding the policing powers of extant enforcement groups on the Islands to include animal protection. The Philippine Constabulary, local police, extension agents, and other officials were legally transformed into deputy game wardens, "with full authority to enforce the provisions of this act and to arrest offenders against it."[35] Instituted shortly after the establishment of civilian US government in the Philippines in 1901, the Philippine Constabulary was a powerful insular police force and its officers, as deputy game wardens, now played a direct role in policing animal activities on the Islands.[36] Additionally, administrative orders from the Philippines Department of Agriculture and Natural Resources transformed designated public places—playgrounds, public schools, parks, and cemeteries—into bird sanctuaries and game refuges. Anyone found harming birds or eggs in such places could be fined up to 200 pesos.[37] Public spaces, therefore, were effectively transformed into zones of ecological conservation and social control.

Anticruelty laws worked in tandem with other animal laws to bring Progressive-era rationalization and order to daily life in an empire powered primarily by muscle. Urban capitals, such as Honolulu, Havana, and Manila were crowded with creatures cheek by jowl. Merchants, passersby, bicycles, carriages, and sputtering automobiles jockeyed for space with cattle herds plodding to pungent city stockyards and dairies, stray dogs, poultry, and horse-drawn trolleys in a virtual sensorium of empire, which as historian Andrew Rotter suggests, helped define the ideological meanings of colonial encounters.[38] Sections 355–358 of a law entitled "Obstruction of Streets" in the Laws of Hawaii contained explicit instructions for hitching and fastening horses, mules, and any draft animal to promote the orderly flow of traffic. Section 355, for example, prevented animals from blocking transportation arteries: "No person shall hitch or fasten any horse or other animal to any ornamental or shade tree in the streets or sidewalks, or to any frame around such tree."[39] American authorities regarded the efficient, unencumbered movement of animal and human traffic in public spaces as an essential building block of commerce, infrastructural growth, and modern civilization in the empire.

American media attributed public displays of orderly animal and human interactions in Havana to good American stewardship. Newspapers and animal welfare publications credited Mrs. Jeannette Ryder, an American SPCA activist and wife of a physician living in Cuba since 1902, as the primary agent of change. The American press described Ryder as the embodiment of benevolent, respectable womanhood: "One little American woman, working single-handed, within the last decade has instilled into the Cuban mind a new idea—that man's inhumanity to dumb brutes is an iniquitous thing."[40] The gendered social stigmas that kept Caroline Earle White and other white, affluent, female Gilded Age animal protectionists off the streets and inside the classroom and animal shelter were dissolving during the Progressive Era. Women's escalating participation in public reform movements and entry into higher education brought them into direct public contact with animal abusers in the United States and abroad. In this changing social milieu, Jeannette Ryder was so ubiquitous on the streets that any white American woman was reportedly assumed to be her, prompting local teamsters and carters to behave kindly for fear of arrest.

To highlight Ryder's achievements in Cuba, American media routinely referred to the streets of Havana prior to her arrival as an uncivilized "hades of horror." Markets were "full of fowl with wings twisted out of joint to keep them still," stacked for days in tightly packed coops without food or water; stray cats and dogs "filthy with sores"; thin, bedraggled hackney coach horses and omnibus mules with running wounds: "In all the community not a human voice of protest arose against conditions which were bad in themselves but infinitely worse in their ultimate effect on citizens who tolerated them."[41] Mrs. Ryder, who founded the El Bando de Piedad de la Isla de Cuba (the Cuban Group for Compassion) in 1905 and a local Band of Mercy in 1906, remonstrated with local cartmen, gained the goodwill of local policemen and judges, and enlisted boys in her Band of Mercy to carry injured animals in baskets and barrows to her animal shelter. Youthful Cubans allegedly felt so empowered as deputized humane agents that they reported acts of animal cruelty to local law enforcement: "[The accused] knows the grinning policeman on the corner will cooperate with the 'kiddie,' and down in the court room, if he lets the case go so far, the Judge will remind him that the law is with the child. Thus it has come about that Cuba is developing citizens not ashamed to feel pity or to act upon pity's impulse."[42]

As members of Ryder's Band of Mercy, Cuban children constituted a body of inchoate citizens. Ryder made her Band of Mercy a democratically elected organization, with each leadership position chosen by popular vote; the group created a set of bylaws that all were expected to obey, therefore (according to popular media) imparting the tenets of proper citizenship and representative government to each boy: "In this manner the little boys learned the meaning of law and the respect citizens must have for it."[43] Ryder expanded her sheltering work to include poor children, who received free medical care at her clinic across the street from her facility for abandoned animals. No longer the "hades of horror," Jeannette Ryder's Havana now had an elegant granite water fountain at San Francisco Square funded by American philanthropists, which served two purposes: to refresh the city's horses and dogs and to memorialize a fellow animal protectionist and founding member of the local Band of Mercy, Señora Brigida Cecilia Martinez Viuda de Arredonda, who was crushed to death on July 11, 1910, by an angry driver, who backed his wagon into her after she stopped him for flogging his mules and carrying a burdensome load.[44] The Arredonda fountain memorial was both a testament to the humane movement's power to transform urban environments and the dangers of public confrontation, especially in regard to an organization with direct ties to American rule in Cuba. Arredonda was Cuban, but her work with the Band of Mercy potentially marked her as an American collaborator.

Colonial Canine Control

American policymakers prioritized dog management as an essential part of public health, safety, and colonial order. Occupation authorities in the Philippines developed municipal canine control policies that were often even more far-reaching than their American precedents. They established a public pound, a municipal dog census, and exacting rules for licensing, muzzling, capture, impoundment, and notification. Toward the end of the military phase of the Occupation in 1901, the American provost marshal general issued a series of health and police orders for the City of Manila that became a blueprint for subsequent legal action regarding stray dogs during the civilian Occupation.[45] Ordinance 13 required the Department of Licenses and Municipal Revenue to keep a register of licensed dogs, noting their breed, sex, color, and name. The police were required to pick up strays, impound them for a period of no longer than three days, and publish a description of each dog in the *Official Gazette* (printed in English and Spanish)—after which the dogs would either be destroyed or sold to the highest bidder.[46] Under this order, officers and inspectors from the Department of Licenses and Municipal Revenue possessed "full police powers for the purpose of enforcing any of the provisions of this ordinance." These officials could shoot on sight any aggressive, uncollared, unlicensed, and unleashed dog outside a private residence, thus extending the authority to destroy dogs in the Occupied Philippines to other parties beyond traditional agents of animal control. At the same time, municipal dog policy in the United States became more circumscribed because SPCAs and humane societies were now assuming the duties of urban dog control under the auspices of the burgeoning shelter movement.

Ordinance 13 empowered Manila neighbors to participate in canine surveillance with legal authority to initiate lethal action against annoying dogs.

An unattractive—but otherwise quiet—dog was vulnerable to destruction if five neighbors deemed it a nuisance and petitioned the superintendent of police: "Any dog which ... is, by reason of disease, malformation, or accident, an object of disgust ... may be declared a nuisance by the superintendent of police," and then killed within three days.[47] As in the United States, local authorities were legally empowered to issue muzzling orders for unattended dogs and did so readily, especially during summer, when rabies was feared to spread more quickly. In 1911, the Philippine Commission reported that forty-eight dog-bite victims in the City of Manila had been vaccinated at the new free Pasteur institute in Manila, which also offered free treatment to provincial residents.[48] More than two decades later, rabies was still deemed to be a serious municipal public health threat, which motivated officials to impose severe punishments in the Revised Ordinances of Manila in 1927 for any dog owner who failed to muzzle a wandering canine—a maximum fine of 200 pesos, six months in prison, or both. Dog owners were also liable for any civil damages to victims.[49]

Fear of rabies contagion fueled dog extermination campaigns around the world. In nineteenth-century England, rabies policies were enmeshed with class-inflected anxieties about social contamination and rising numbers of disaffected urban proletarians, human and canine.[50] Dog licensing laws invariably burdened the poor, who were readily stigmatized by animal protectionists and public health authorities alike for even owning dogs without the means to care for them. Without a license, a dog was vulnerable to seizure and extermination. Dogs belonging to poor people were deemed to be especially peevish, ill-bred, and susceptible to rabies. Although the affluent commonly did not purchase dog licenses, they could easily pay impoundment fees to retrieve their dogs. As additional levers of rabies control and social control, the Metropolitan Streets Act of 1867 and the Rabies Orders of 1886 and 1887 gave local police the authority to order muzzling for dogs off-leash. Unmuzzled dogs could be destroyed on sight.[51] When Louis Pasteur proved that rabies was transmitted through saliva, not spontaneous generation, his scientific findings validated the muzzling measures already in effect in the 1880s. As historian Harriet Ritvo puts it, "Not only did Pasteur's discoveries vindicate the policies of surveillance and punishment that had increasingly been favored by medical experts and national public health authorities, they also encouraged officials to extend these measures and to enforce them more vigorously."[52]

British officials, like their American counterparts, extended their dog policies to their empire. In colonial India, Section 144 of the Criminal Procedure Code, created in 1861, gave local magistrates expansive powers to issue orders "in urgent cases of nuisance or apprehended danger," which were (and still are) used to prohibit unlawful assembly, defined usually as any group of five or more people.[53] Section 144 also applied to potentially rabid street dogs because an unleashed dog in public constituted a form of unlawful assembly and was subject to immediate destruction. The owner of the deceased dog, often living in poverty, also faced prosecution in front of a magistrate for "disobedience."[54]

During the Meiji Restoration, indigenous street dogs were nearly annihilated in many parts of Japan as the result of new regulations for rabies prevention. Any dog found in violation of licensing, collar, and leash laws was subject to extermination. A lucrative bounty law allowed anyone to kill street dogs for profit.[55] Dogcatchers rarely killed foreign breeds owned by Westerners and Japanese elites for fear of antagonizing the rich and politically powerful.[56] By contrast, Japanese dog policy treated indigenous street dogs as dirty, racially degenerate, and potentially rabid. The ostensibly feral status of the native dog reflected the ostensibly degenerate status of indigenous people, such as the Ainu, the native hunter-gatherers of Hokkaido, whose canines were essential partners in hunting and fishing.[57] The Colonization Agency at Hokkaido established extensive ranching and agricultural operations as part of the Meiji government's new expansionist settlement and modernization initiatives. The Colonization Agency justified mass canine slaughter by claiming that native wolves and "feral" dogs were variously rabid or livestock killers. The annihilation of indigenous dogs hastened the virtual erasure of the Ainu society. Historian Aaron Skabelund observes that this complementary extermination policy achieved the Meiji government's broader goals: "In the end the deer population, Ainu culture, and wolves and Ainu dogs were decimated."[58]

American Occupation officials in the Philippines sought to control indigenous interactions with dogs, particularly Bontoc Igorot traditions of ritual dog eating. Yet the significance of this cultural practice to American colonial policy was primarily symbolic. As a marker of barbarism in the American popular imagination, dog eating represented a cultural justification for assimilative empire building, even though actual colonial policy did little to stop it. After the Philippine Commission established a summer capital in the cool highlands of Baguio, Luzon, Occupation authorities instituted a new municipal code in 1903 prohibiting the purchase of dogs in the city market "and within a radius distance of said market." Violators were fined a small charge of one to five pesos.[59] The law tacitly recognized Americans' endless fascination with Igorot dog eating, a cultural practice that was quickly exploited for profit in live traveling performances at American world's fairs.[60]

Anthropologists, government officials, teachers, and missionaries whetted American consumer demand for orientalist cultural productions by sending home lurid descriptions of muscular, bare, heavily tattooed, hyper-masculine Igorot "wild men," who lived in mountainous jungles, hunting enemy heads, feasting on roasted dogs to restore their vitality after battle, and worshipping animal spirits.[61] R. F. Barton, an American teacher who worked with the Bontoc Igorots in the early twentieth century, painstakingly detailed the medicinal uses of canine body parts for fertility and well-being, in addition to the precise techniques that boys and men used to slaughter a dog: "The animal is starved for a day or so, then given all the cooked rice it can eat. After a wait of three or four hours, it is slowly beaten to death or near death with a stick. The ante-mortem pounding is believed to make the flesh tender and bring out the flavor. The stomach and intestines with the partially digested rice are said to be a rare delicacy." Although Bontoc Igorots ate dog meat primarily on special occasions, Barton surmised that local demand for dog flesh was so strong that he told prospective students that dog would be served on the lunch menu as an inducement to enroll.[62]

Baguio's dog market continued in plain sight on Sundays, in spite of the prohibition. The law, in other words, was essentially unenforced, serving chiefly as an emblematic gesture of America's civilizing mission. *Our Dumb Animals* indirectly criticized the absence of American enforcement in noting that the sale of dogs for food was common: "The dogs are purchased to be eaten—a practice that is little less than savagery and must pass away before a people or nation, however, progressive, will be considered fit for independence and self-government."[63]

Docked Tails and Other Forms of Vice

In 1912, American officials banned equine tail docking in the Philippines. The law also barred importing equines already docked, even those from the military. Influenced by the anti-docking movement at home, officials worried that legal docking in the empire would contradict benevolent American values. For an administration trying to legitimate its authority with an exceptionalist gospel of kindness, the docked tail was a visible show of American brutality because docking was highly uncommon among Filipinos. Owners of animals already docked prior to 1912 were grandfathered, but they were required to present a certificate of ownership to the treasurer of their municipality, register their animal, and pay an annual tax of two pesos. Anyone refusing to comply would face a maximum fine of fifty pesos.[64] As the embodiment of bodily integrity and republican virtue, the undocked horse was a visible reminder of American ideals of animal mercy as well as a check on those Americans who might fall prey to the whims of other vices.

US officials in the empire embedded animal laws into the moral dictates of proper comportment and bodily containment. Revised versions of the Manila Municipal Code placed animal cruelty laws in a chapter called "Offenses against Public Morals." In 1908, this chapter also contained laws against obscene advertising, intoxication, vagrancy, gambling, and a range of "indecent acts," such as wearing minimal dress, using profane speech, and possessing obscene literature and images. Other chapters dealt specifically with laws against prostitution, liquor, and gambling. And still others covered myriad "Offences," including prohibitions against noisemakers in public, firecrackers, bells, kite flying, and the use of multicolored confetti. Public grooming was regulated as well, stipulating that barbers be neat, "with short, well-trimmed nails," and wear a "clean white shirt." Other grooming practices were banned outright, such as eyelid scraping and ear cleaning.[65] It is no accident that animal cruelty laws were enfolded into a larger set of bodily regulations: all were tantamount to an ethic of moral free agency and sober, obedient self-management—all of which were building blocks for the gospel of kindness.

Occupation officials displayed, nonetheless, a marked degree of practical flexibility with respect to vice and the body. Alcohol, though frowned on, was readily available in US territories. The Minnesota Woman's Christian Temperance Union condemned "the shipment of immense and still increasing quantities of intoxicating liquors from this country to our recently acquired territory, and their sale therein: and this under the protection of our country's flag."[66] Although gambling, the opium trade, and prostitution were illegal under US Occupation laws, vice flowed freely on the Islands, to the disgust of the Minnesota WCTU and other moral reformers: "The fruits of this policy are already seen in the debauchment of the nation's wards and in the surprise and disgust with which the better element among them looks upon this horrible misrepresentation of American and Christian civilization."[67] Working in Manila in 1908, the Episcopal bishop, Mercer Johnston, declared: "From the beginning the Civil Government in these Islands has been far too tender-eyed towards the opium traffic, the liquor traffic and the gambling traffic."[68]

American officials privately admitted as much. Secretary of War Elihu Root and Governor General Taft agreed upon the government-mandated medical care of prostitutes after venereal disease became rampant among US troops: "Result better than futile attempt at total suppression in Oriental city of three hundred thousand producing greater evil."[69] Taft, however, was quick to distinguish between pragmatic and flexible vice policies for US military personnel and the unwavering moral surveillance that he deemed essential to civilian governance. He noted in a terse telegram that the Occupation government's civilian moral policing had already proven successful in Manila: "Crimes of violence now comparatively few. Gambling greatly decreased. Native Vino shops in Manila in August, 1898, 4,000. Now reduced to 400. American saloons including hotel and restaurants reduced from 224 in February, 1900, to 88, now."[70]

Taft may have idealized his administration's moral standards as steadfast, but US civilian governance and animal policies on the Islands were susceptible to local pressures, as the fate of the cockfight shows. At the turn of the twentieth century, US authorities promptly banned cockfighting in Cuba, Puerto Rico, Hawaii, and the Philippines, a policy move that mirrored anti-cockfighting legislation in the United States, where thirty-six out of forty-eight states, along with the District of Columbia, had passed prohibitions by 1915.[71] American policymakers and reformers despised the cockfight for virtually the same reasons that people at home and in the empire loved it. Cockfighting promoted autonomous populist cultures of male camaraderie, fueled by gambling and liquor. Cockers (practitioners) came from all social classes. Fighting cocks were accessible and affordable (although some champion strains were expensive). Unlike the costly bullfight and its elaborate Plaza de Toros (bullring), the cockpit was easily constructed: a circle in the dirt could suffice. While cockfights almost always ended with the death of a combatant, cockers in countless cultural locations took painstaking care of their roosters for two years before entering the fighting pit. They fed their birds a special diet, provided daily conditioning exercises, and cradled and stroked these sociable animals to enhance the bonding process, which, in turn, made the birds more responsive fighters.[72] The earliest fighting cocks originated in India and Southeast Asia and eventually populated other parts of the world as a consequence of global trade and colonialism.[73] Despite the sport's far-flung origins, individual practitioners treated the cockfight as an inviolate indigenous tradition. Consequently, American cockfighting bans in the empire sparked enormous controversy and even outright rebellion.

Cockfighting in the Philippines

The cockfight had multiple meanings in the US Occupied Philippines. For the American military, it was a troublesome wrinkle in wartime strategy.

For some Filipino nationalists, it represented cultural degradation; for other Filipinos, it was the proud embodiment of cultural nationalism. For US civilian leaders, it catalyzed confrontations with Protestant missionaries, who, in turn, used cockfighting to condemn Catholicism. While war raged against the US military in the Philippine provinces of Batangas and Laguna, Brigadier General J. F. Bell banned cockfighting for the duration of the insurrection because, in his words, it was "a source of very considerable revenue to insurgents and a convenient means of enabling the insurgent element to secretly mingle, impose upon and intrigue with the portion of the people who may prefer to be peaceful."[74] Manila's first municipal animal cruelty ordinance also banned cockfighting outright in 1902.[75]

Military officials in the Philippines primarily used the ban as a practical means of social and political control. The cockfight, especially when held on festival days for saints, was a raucous, ritualistic masculine spectacle, replete with betting, drinking, and occasional brawling. And as Brigadier General Bell observed, it also provided a potent occasion for sharing information and spreading the insurrection. More than a decade earlier, Dr. José Rizal acknowledged the potentially subversive power of the cockfight in his nationalistic novel, *Noli Me Tangere* (Touch Me Not), published in 1887. He described a Sunday cockfight as a site of social leveling, where rich and poor sit together at the matches, and where an underdog rooster (read nation) defeats a larger, more powerful foe: "This is what happens among nations. When a small one defeats a big one, they relate the tale for centuries and centuries."[76] Similarly, cocker and author Angel Lansang treated the cockfight as a key to Filipino identity and heritage: "By all means then let us propagate our national pastime. It is here that we can assert and preserve our dignity as a free and independent country. After all, cockfighting is a precious heritage handed down to us by our brave ancestors and its traditions have been written in blood. Let us make of our national sport a symbol of our country."[77]

Conflicts over the cockfight, however, did not automatically signify a showdown between indigenous nationalist cockers and foreign empire builders. While the sport was a popular masculine pastime across the Islands, Filipino independence leaders sometimes diverged from their countrymen. In *Nole Me Tangere*, Rizal criticized the ritual for sapping people of their money and judgment:

> Cockfighting... is one of the people's vices, even more transcendental than opium among the Chinese. The poor man goes there to risk what he has, wishing to get money without working. The rich man goes as

a distraction, using the money left over from his feasting and the purchase of masses. But the fortune he wagers is his own, the gamecock is brought up with great care, perhaps with greater care than his own son, who succeeds his father in the cockpit.[78]

Emilio Aguinaldo shared Rizal's view of the cockfight as a moral threat to Philippine independence. In particular, he despised gambling and thus closed the cockpits during his brief tenure as president of the First Philippine Republic, declaring: "Gambling more than anything else in the Philippines is the mother of crime."[79]

American Protestant missionaries in the Occupied Philippines condemned the cockfight as a gory and profligate form of vice, freely quoting Rizal and Aguinaldo to support their own platform of purity reform.[80] Arthur Judson Brown, secretary of the Board of Foreign Missions of the Presbyterian Church in the United States, reduced the enormous ethnic diversity of the Philippines Islands to a lazy, fatalistic, barely dressed Filipino "type" who gambled everything on the cockfight:

> The unwillingness of the Filipino to work is a serious problem in the development of the Islands. He does not lead "the strenuous life." Rich soil, perpetual summer, and simple wants are not conducive to hard labor. . . . At Escalante, I found a disgusted contractor who could not induce men to load a *lorcha* (sailboat) at any price because they had won enough for their immediate necessities at the Sunday cockfight, and they would not work till the money was spent.[81]

To American missionaries, the native cockfighter represented a stark contrast to industrious middle-class manly ideals; his dependency on blood sport made him unfit for independence in his current state. But he was potentially redeemable. Because liberal Protestants posited that souls could be saved, they believed that a combined gospel of Christianity, kindness, and physical vigor could prepare indigenous men for eventual citizenship.

American Occupation authorities considered baseball a wholesome alternative to the cockfight. The zoologist and Philippine Commission member Dean Worcester reported that baseball was successfully combating the lure of the cockpit in building sober, physically fit future citizens:

> Baseball not only strengthens the muscles of the players, it sharpens their wits. Furthermore it empties the cockpits to such an extent that

their beneficiaries have attempted to secure legislation restricting the time which it may be played. It has done more toward abolishing cockfighting than have the laws of the commission and the efforts of the Moral Progress League combined. It is indeed a startling sight to see two opposing teams of youthful savages in Bukidnon or Bontoc "playing the game" with obvious full knowledge of its refinements, while their ordinarily silent and reserved parents "root" with unbridled enthusiasm![82]

For Worcester, baseball's ascendancy over the cockfight was a triumph of civilization, powered by sober fitness and team building over inebriated decadence. The Bureau of Education instituted a baseball-centric athletic curriculum in public schools to build the "spirit of fair play and sportsmanship, hitherto lacking" on the Islands. By 1914, roughly 80 percent of the student body participated.[83]

Foes of the cockfight routinely blamed the Catholic Church for the blood sport's popularity. American Protestant missionaries reasoned that Filipino cockers, bound to the pope and Catholic Church, possessed little free moral agency. The extractive friar system encouraged men to gamble on cockfights, which generously filled the coffers of the Spanish colonial state through heavy taxation.[84] Missionaries erroneously assumed that Spanish Catholic colonial outsiders introduced cockfighting to the Philippines, even though the sport had been popular long before the first Spanish explorers and missionaries arrived in 1565.[85] Protestant missionaries conflated transubstantiation in the Catholic Mass with animism. Bearing witness to the intimate relationship between men and their roosters, Bruce Lesher Kershner, a missionary with the Disciples of Christ, observed that Filipinos took their game cocks to church and fed them Holy Water and the Communion wafer to fortify the birds for battle: "Not unfrequently he would slip the wafer from his tongue where it had been placed by the priest when at Communion, and putting it in his handkerchief, carry it to his chicken. He believed that the chicken which had eaten the body of Christ was invincible."[86] In viewing the cockfight as a metonym for Catholicism, Protestant missionaries deemed Filipino Catholics to be just as un-Christian as the polytheistic tribal peoples they proselytized in other mission fields. In so doing, these missionaries participated in a long American tradition of anti-Catholic sentiment.[87]

Cockfighting foes soon suspected that Occupation officials preferred to ignore the cockfight rather than confront it, because the Occupation Government quickly lifted the newly established ban in 1902 in favor of regulation and taxation as the insurrection slowly dissipated.[88] The Revised Municipal Code of Manila in 1911 attempted to distance the Occupation Government from its Spanish colonial predecessors, arguing that its interest in the cockfight was not remunerative, nor (as a secular government) tied to state-sponsored Catholic rituals and festivals: "At the present time cockfights do not possess the official character that they had in the time of the Spanish Government, when the Government monopolized the exploitation of this sport."[89]

Moral critics, however, described the move from prohibition to regulation as a reincarnation of Spanish rule, a betrayal of sober republican virtue.[90] Homer C. Stuntz, field secretary of the Middle Atlantic Division of the Board of Foreign Missions, denounced American leniency and complicity in the cockpits in a newspaper editorial: "Cockfighting is the gambling passion of the Filipinos, and the Catholic Church as well as the Government has worked it for what is in it. It is very offensive: It shows the subtle clutch the Catholics have on our politics there."[91]

Evangelical objections to the Occupation Government's liberal cockfighting policies escalated in 1908 when a festival triggered a showdown between business-minded pragmatists and moral idealists. Early that year, Manila's municipal government granted a private American consortium, the Carnival Association, permission to hold cockfights during the Manila Carnival in late February. American animal protectionists and the Evangelical Union, a federation of evangelical Protestant churches working in the Philippines, were furious. Letters and telegrams of protest poured into the War Department and the White House. Based in Manila, the Episcopal bishop Mercer Johnston was notably vocal. On February 23, 1908, he preached a sermon dedicated to the controversy, "A Covenant with Death, an Agreement with Hell," as part of a large protest meeting consisting of approximately 2,500 people, including members of the Philippine Teachers Association, more than 600 Filipino high school and university students, and American women.[92] Johnston condemned the Occupation Government for its collusion in the cockfight:

> Were I a Filipino, I would hate or despise the American who trafficked in the vices of my people, and withstand him to the face, at all hazards. What then shall we say of this contract? Is it not a covenant with death? Is it not an agreement with hell? Are not those Americans who are parties to it, especially those American officials, courting death, moral death, both for themselves and their country? . . . Yonder cockpit is as a house swept and garnished, awaiting the evil spirits invited

thither by the Carnival Association.... Yonder cock-pit is as a whited sepulcher, hungering for dead men's bones and soon to be filled with all uncleanness.[93]

Johnston warned that unprincipled American policies were dangerously laissez-faire, promoting a "business morality" that could lead to political radicalism.[94] Evangelical leaders remained confident that wherever evangelical Protestants lived in the Philippines, the noxious cockfight would wither away and wholesome, physically fortifying activities like baseball would blossom in its place. An evangelical newspaper published in Dumaguete, Negros Oriental, bluntly stated that Protestantism was killing the cockfight: "In two places where members of the Methodist Church are largely in control, cockpits and all gambling places have been abolished. Revenues are used in improving those towns and awakening a better interest in decent places of abode."[95]

American officials remained unmoved. They kept the cockpits open. Clarence Edwards, head of the Bureau of Insular Affairs in Washington, DC, noted that ordinary Filipinos, as well as many Americans on the Islands, overwhelmingly favored cockfighting. Edwards wryly concluded that "opposition [was] being fathered by a few ministers who desired to advertise themselves."[96] Indeed, the sport was so popular among Occupation forces in the Philippines that American soldiers introduced a fierce new chicken strain known as the Texas, which soon became the most coveted fighting stock on the Islands.[97] The proliferation of the Texas strain was proof of the cockfight's cross-cultural popularity in the Philippines, the embodiment of cultural fraternization and exchange among colonizer and colonized.

Cockfighting in Cuba

In Cuba, purity reformers saw the cockfight as a keystone of the island's illicit pull for American travelers. Ever since American mining and sugar enterprises established operations in Cuba in the early nineteenth century, transient businessmen, seamen, entertainers, fugitives, schemers, crooks, tourists, prostitutes, and deserters flocked there in search of profit and pleasure.[98] Drinking, prostitution, gambling, and complementary betting-based animal sports drove a rollicking vice economy catering to Americans.

In the initial stages of US rule in Cuba, there appeared to be little dissent between animal advocates, their missionary allies, and American officials, who collectively propagated a shared gospel of creaturely kindness and respectability. US Military Order No. 165 banned cockfighting; No. 217 subsequently punished anyone who even witnessed or "aided" an animal fight, providing for harsh fines and potential prison time. Despite these severe measures, the fights simply moved to the countryside or to private grounds after the closure of urban public cockpits, where they continued, hidden in plain sight.[99] In 1903, pro-cocker members of the Cuban Congress sponsored a lottery bill to repeal both US military orders, but President Tomás Estrada Palma—a strong American ally—threatened a swift presidential veto. In his message to Congress on January 6, 1904, President Palma argued that the American ban on blood sports and gambling was a crucial demonstration of an advancing Cuban civilization "in perfect harmony with the Revolutionary Program of the fathers of the present country, and of all who raised the flag of independence."[100]

Many Cubans, however, rejected Palma's vision of virtuous nationhood. In 1907, the cockfight abruptly became the catalyst for a political showdown pitting Palma and his American allies against anti-American Cuban nationalists.[101] How did a blood sport become implicated in a battle over nation building? In late September 1906, General José Miguel Gómez and fellow members of the Republican Liberal party rebelled against the reelection of President Palma, whom they dismissed as an American dupe. Palma appealed to American authorities and troops quickly returned to Cuba. Two weeks later, on October 13, Charles E. Magoon was installed as US Provisional Governor. At the same time, the Rural Guard, a paramilitary Cuban arm of the American military, intensified its policing activities, especially in enforcing the cockfighting ban. In correspondence with Secretary of War Taft, Magoon acknowledged that the Rural Guard's motive was revenge: "I am assured by many persons, and I think the assertion is in a measure true, that the Rural Guards are 'getting even' with the men of the insurgent forces."[102]

The trouble intensified in January 1907, when an American banker in Havana staged a large cockfight. Between 200 to 300 people attended, including American officers as well as General Gómez, Major General Pino Guerra, and other leaders of the 1906 rebellion. During the cockfight, two members of the Rural Guard heard the telltale shouts and squawks. Everyone scattered, except for Gómez, Guerra, and their friends, who seized the public opportunity to defy the ban and the Rural Guard. They were promptly arrested and fined $50 apiece. Gómez instantly demanded a repeal of the prohibition in his newspaper, *El Rebelde*, and a pro-cockfighting protest movement was born.

The cause spread quickly as Gómez and his allies orchestrated huge local parades, rallies, and petitions across Cuba. Each petition defended cockfighting with the same language of virtuous citizenship and cultural nationalism that President Palma used to justify the ban. Local mayors and other politicians sent pages of testimony to Magoon describing a "monstrous manifestation" of citizens taking to the streets, as thousands of cockfight supporters assembled in myriad public spaces. Magoon chronicled these protests in his correspondence with Secretary of War Taft: "The demonstrations in favor of repealing the law take the form of a parade, which, after passing through the streets, stops in front of the Mayor's office and presents him with a request to advise me of the demonstration and ask me to issue the desired decree. This the Mayor does, either by telegram or letter."[103] In one such decree, Antonio Ruiz, president of a pro-cockfighting committee in Cienfuegos, presented a "Manifest to the Public in General": "The time has come when all Cubans, lovers of their traditions, should combine in one solid mass, and as one man work without rest to obtain the reestablishment of the cockfights."[104]

Ruiz and other Cubans denounced the ban as an American-led assault on their rights of citizenship. They highlighted the democratic character of the rallies and parades, "in which all classes of society are represented, as also all the towns and cities of the Island."[105] Narciso Lopez Quintana of Havana beseeched Magoon to lift the ban and thereby restore civil liberties: "We, therefore, in this public and peaceful demonstration, appear before you today almost convinced that you will do us justice . . . in behalf of the reputation conceded to us by the civilized nations as a cultured people."[106]

Petitioners asserted that hardworking laborers had a right to preserve their indigenous traditions of male leisure and conviviality, particularly in rural areas where little other amusement was available after long days of agricultural toil. Writing from Nueva Gerona in the Isle of Pines (Isla de la Juventud), D. M. Pearcy "and many others" offered an earnest portrait of a moral, patriotic, and industrious people, describing themselves with the same syntax of suffering and mercy that humane activists used to defend animals.

> The cock-fight was not an imported sport bringing with it the pernicious vice of gambling. No, it appeared as a compensation to the hardworking country laborer. The people of Cuba who do not live in cities away from all business center and who limit themselves to the cultivation of the soil to earn their living, without the lenitive [sic] offered by the amusements to be found in all cities, felt the natural melancholy of those who suffer, and found in the diversion it now acclaims some relief to sustain its hope in the future. And the amusement . . . became a necessity which your kindness can gratify.[107]

Cuban pleas to kindness and suffering only steeled the opposition. Focusing on the cockfight's violence to the twin bodies of rooster and nation, animal protectionists vehemently protested the possibility of repeal as a grave contradiction of American values. George Angell beseeched Magoon "in behalf of the more than two millions of members of our American Bands of Mercy" to preserve the ban.[108] John L. Shortall, president of the Illinois Humane Society, envisioned "a serious backward step for Cuba, whereas should the law remain in force it would be a marked evidence of progress and would be uplifting in Cuba, and encouraging to those who are striving for better things."[109] ASPCA president Alfred Wagstaff declared, "It was the fervent hope of the friends of humanity that whenever the flag of the United States was planted, the dumb animals might share in the benefits of an advancing civilization."[110] Cuban animal protectionists, such as Magdalena Peñarredonda, also connected the legitimacy of American leadership abroad to its commitment to animal welfare: "I do not believe that an American Governor, who represents a country where the ideas of commiseration and pity towards the irrational animals are so thoroughly observed and practiced, will permit that a struggle between two unfortunate animals which tear themselves to pieces and bleed to death with horrible sufferings, should be the means of pleasure and gain in Cuba."[111]

American sugar growers also wanted to preserve the cockfighting ban but purely for economic, not humanitarian, reasons. They argued that cockfighting made plantation workers unruly: laborers often skipped work for days after a cockfight, thus slowing the production of a highly profitable crop that dominated the Cuban economy.[112] A delegation of mill owners went a step further, approaching Magoon in 1906 and 1907 to preserve the cockfight ban in conjunction with pushing for new prohibitions on dancing, and "playing musical instruments at any time, day or night" during the cane harvest to discipline laboring bodies into a totalizing experience of surveillance on and off the job.[113]

US officials in Washington, DC, repeatedly assured animal advocates that the ban would stand. Yet Governor Magoon privately wondered if the law was actually undermining US authority: "It is not advisable . . . to have a law on the statue [sic] books which is openly and flagrantly violated, thereby lessening respect for the law making and enforcing departments of government."[114] As an alternative, he presented the Philippine law as culturally flexible and therefore a more durable model of American governance because it gave each municipality the power to legislate its own cockfighting policy. "I think such course is proper here."[115]

By April 1907, the situation had become so heated that trains and other modes of public conveyance became theaters of conflict. Rural Guards roamed the countryside, snatching chickens and arresting the owners, including wealthy planters who happened to be caught traveling on trains with their birds, in defiance of American military orders.[116] As late as February 26, 1908, Secretary of War Taft urged Governor Magoon "not to interfere with this order in any way."[117] Yet the escalating national crisis forced a solution in which the political and economic power of American sugar growers and the moral sway of animal welfare activists and evangelicals could no longer carry the day. On January 28, 1909, home rule returned to Cuba, and the leader of the pro-cockfight movement, General José Miguel Gómez of the Liberal Party, was elected president. In July the Cuban Congress repealed the ban in favor of letting each municipality legislate its own cockfighting laws.[118] Colonel Frank E. McIntyre of the federal Bureau of Insular Affairs criticized the repeal as "the lie," which would keep "a back country Cuban family ... in thatch-roofed huts" with American blessing—and permanently inassimilable.[119] Cockfighting enthusiasts, however, saw the repeal as a vindication of their struggles for cultural and political self-determination in a country under virtual U.S. sovereignty.

FIGURE 4.1. In Cuba, as in other countries, the cockfight was a highly adaptive form of popular fraternal leisure, which could be staged almost anywhere, including the Havana alleyway pictured in this postcard. "Cuban Cockfight," postcard, Havana, Cuba, 1912, Record Group 350, General Classified Files, Entry 5A (1898-1913), Cockfighting prohibition (Cuba), Box 213, File 1660, 350:150:56:8:6, National Archives at College Park, College Park, MD.

Cockfighting in Puerto Rico

On March 10, 1904, the American civil government in Puerto Rico prohibited cockfighting, along with other bird and quadruped fights. Guilty parties faced a $50 fine and/or a month in jail.[120] As in other parts of the empire, American authorities reasoned that cockfighting was a signature of inassimilable difference, a catalyst for idleness, permanent poverty, Catholic fatalism, and wholesale violence to birds and men. American journalist William Dinwiddie noted that after a long, orderly cockfight, "the crowd moved straightaway from a cock-fight to a solemn Catholic ceremony."[121] American officials read the cockfight as yet another expression of corruption traceable to Spanish colonial politics of collusion and patronage with local elites.[122]

US Governor H. M. Towner was convinced that the ban preserved public peace: "The fights of the cocks were nearly always the commencement of fights by the people. Drinking led to drunkenness and drunkenness led to quarrels and assaults, even to murder. . . . To be prepared for a cockfight in these days, as now, the jibaro (peasant) must have money, liquor, and a gun or knife. To hurt, to harm, to kill—that is the object lesson of cock fighting."[123] Towner's description of human violence, however, represented the exception, not the rule; most cockfights were sober, methodical affairs based on exacting rules of pitting well-matched birds and strict observance of time limits.[124] Still the intimate circumstances of the matches—the close proximity of fighting birds, men, strong drink, money, and bloodshed—demonstrated the ways in which human beings and animals both were potential victims of the cockfight.

Puerto Rican cockers simultaneously appealed to ideals of cultural nationalism and citizenship to defend their sport.[125] To be sure, most simply ignored the ban, particularly in rural areas. Second, Puerto Ricans based their right to fight on their legal status as American citizens. Passed by the US Congress in 1917, the Jones-Shafroth Act gave Puerto Ricans limited American citizenship. Cockers reasoned that they possessed the authority to legalize their sport through state, not federal, jurisprudence, just like an individual American state. They articulated their rights in cultural terms rather than as a claim to independent nationhood (i.e., in contrast to Cuba and the Philippines). Writing from Rio Piedras in 1920, Manuel Jiménez Santa urged the Puerto Rican Senate and US Secretary of State Bainbridge Colby to repeal the ban: "The fact is that here, though American citizens, we are persecuted by the police force, because of following a tradition. . . . Porto Rico, deprived of her traditional cockfights, is a Ruin."[126] Santa warned that

America's international stature was now in jeopardy: "The United States of America, by its conduct in Porto Rico, is digging the grave for its prestige as a colonizing nation in the opinion of the peoples of South America, who, with astonishment and terror, look upon these things done by a nation which sent its armies to fight for the democracy and freedom of the world."[127]

As in other colonial settings, Manuel Jiménez Santa evoked the same patriotic ideal of republican virtue to argue in favor of cockfighting that critics used to denounce it. Although the ban remained during the 1920s, cockers received an unexpected boost in 1927 when prizefighting, another form of violent corporal spectacle, was legalized. An American government commission regulated boxing thereafter and took a healthy share of the considerable profits. Boxing soared in popularity and new fancy stadiums dotted the landscape.[128] Cockers saw this success as a clear sign to renew their repeal movement because they had long allied themselves politically with boxing interests. Lobbying groups agreed, and in 1928, the Puerto Rican legislature voted to repeal the cockfighting ban.

The US governor, Horace M. Towner, immediately vetoed the bill, supported by Protestant missionaries and local animal advocates, In his address to the Puerto Rican House of Representatives, Towner called the original ban, a "wise and patriotic act ... a great benefit to the country. ... Such sports were common in a barbarous and cruel age, but are being abandoned in a more humane and kindly era."[129] Similarly, journalists observed that Puerto Ricans were leaving the cockpit in favor of the wholesome American bullpen.[130] Other foes contended that cockfighting encouraged impulsive, addictive behavior: "The jíbaro pays no attention, saving his breath for the secret pit, the dashing fury of his little bird, the hot argument of epic narrative afterward."[131] According to such logic, the peasant cocker lived in the moment, dependent on capricious excitement; possessing little interest in sober capital accumulation, he would remain forever incapable of self-government if cockfighting were legalized.

Yet economic concerns during the Great Depression trumped the moral imperative of protecting birds and men. In 1933, the new US administration of Governor Robert H. Gore decided legalization would make Puerto Rico's tourist economy more attractive to American visitors.[132] "We must create more lures for the tourist-minded man and woman. ... We must have the recreation to satisfy the spirit that is ever seeking something new. And to gratify that, you can offer the oldest sport known to original man—a sport that I participated in as a boy in my Kentucky home."[133]

A coalition of animal protectionists, US officials, purity reformers, and missionaries denounced the repeal as a shocking, profit-minded repudiation of the nation's moral responsibilities abroad. According to the former secretary of state of Puerto Rico under President Wilson, Martín Travieso: "This is just a sample of what our new Governor is doing to demoralize our people, to expose us to the contempt and ridicule of other civilized communities and to destroy the wonderful work done by the people of this island during the thirty-five years of our life under the American flag."[134] Animal welfare leaders, such as N. J. Walker of the American Humane Association, feared Puerto Rico's new law would create a precedent for the legalization of cockfighting across the United States.[135] Nonetheless, the economic argument prevailed. Cockfighting remained—and still remains—legal in Puerto Rico. The cockfight quickly became a significant lure for US tourists seeking leisure and nearby exoticism.[136] Like other human and animal interactions in the empire, the shifting status of the cockfight helped American expansionists justify their empire of kindness rising phoenix-like from the ashes of Spanish imperialism. The fighting cock, however, remained a political and cultural minefield whose fate was tied to competing visions of cultural identity, citizenship, civilization, and self-determination.

The Philippine Public School Classroom as Animal Sanctuary

American policymakers and animal advocates saw Philippine public school classrooms as prime locations for cultivating future citizens with assimilationist values of animal kindness. In 1901, the Philippine Commission enacted Act No. 74, known as the Organic School Act, which established a new public school system in the Occupied Philippines prohibiting religious instruction.[137] Humane education initiatives, which were often folded into civics curricula, offered a valuable opportunity for implicit religious instruction in a state-mandated secular system. New compulsory attendance laws dramatically expanded enrollment, thus widening the reach of new humane education programs, and municipal governments provided significant funding for local schools. After 1907, the Philippine Assembly made generous annual appropriations for public education. Between 1901 and 1906, the number of elementary-age Filipinos attending public school more than tripled.[138] Given the enormous ethnic and cultural diversity of a country comprising more than 7,000 islands, American officials' commitment to educational secularism was as much a desire for efficient, standardized governance as it was a high-minded constitutional commitment to the separation of church and state.[139]

American religious leaders worried that the Organic Act's secular mandate would leave Filipino students bereft of moral guidance.[140] In rhetoric reminiscent of the cockfight debate, evangelical Protestants and Catholics each claimed that the other had greater influence with Occupation officials.[141] Recognizing a potential moral vacuum, the MSPCA and its sister organization, the American Humane Education Society (AHES), jumped at the opportunity to spread the gospel of kindness in the secular colonial classroom, where the American-led Bureau of Education had adopted English as the lingua franca of public instruction.[142] Despite its name, the MSPCA's work extended far beyond Massachusetts. The organization consistently supported transnational animal protectionism, often in concert with its allies in education, missionary work, and temperance reform. The MSPCA and AHES donated thousands of English-language copies of *Our Dumb Animals*, *Black Beauty*, and *Beautiful Joe* to Philippine public schools. The MSPCA also funded new Bands of Mercy and supported missionary work with children.

ROUND THE GLOBE GOES THE BE KIND TO ANIMALS MOTTO
Recent picture of the Band of Mercy Council in Cebu, Philippine Islands. Each young man represents a Band; the General Secretary, Atanasio S. Montayre, in the center.

FIGURE 4.2. The MSPCA donated animal welfare literature and other humane education materials to Philippine Bands of Mercy during the American Occupation. "Round the Globe Goes the Be Kind to Animals Motto (Cebu, Philippines, Band of Mercy Council)," *Our Dumb Animals*, March 1928, 37.

The ideals of the teachers themselves complemented the MSPCA's goals. The Filipino educational administrator and author Gilbert S. Perez remembered the 509 original American public schoolteachers who landed in the Philippines on the USS *Thomas* on August 21, 1901, as selfless humanitarians. He characterized the "Thomasites" as a "new army that was unarmed," which successfully schooled Filipino pupils to embrace the assimilative appeal of American representative government: "These pioneer American teachers were delighted to see their pupils react to a recitation of Lincoln's Gettysburg Address and Patrick Henry's speech to the Virginia Assembly exactly as the pupils at home would react."[143] At the end of the Occupation Government's first year, the secretary of public instruction reported to the Philippine Commission that humane education would combat morally questionable behavior among students and native teachers, who skipped school to attend cockfights.[144] John A. Staunton, deputy division superintendent of education for the province of Cebu, stressed the need for new kindness curricula: "Instruction of children in the wickedness of cruelty to animals I need only to mention to commend to your attention. May the day soon come when Filipino cattle will not be starved for three days previous to slaughter and when chickens will not be plucked before they are killed."[145] Staunton, like other American animal advocates, pointed to quick, insensate slaughter as a marker of advanced civilization.

Birds dominated kindness pedagogies in the Occupied Philippines. As strikingly beautiful artistic subjects in drawing and painting classes, birds on the wing and in the nest were visual and literary metaphors for home and family in didactic children's stories.[146] Fluttering close to humanity in a liminal zone between wild and tame, birds were also popular subjects for anthropomorphized conservation stories. Filipino children encountered birds and other animals through grammar exercises, classroom seatwork, school gardens, birdhouses, and art projects.

Birds were so important to the complementary projects of animal kindness and national uplift in the Occupied Philippines and in the United States that "Bird Day" became a day of civic celebration. As a prominent feature of the annual holiday calendar (along with Mother's Day, and patriotic holidays, such as the Fourth of July, and Rizal Day, which honored the slain Filipino patriot José Rizal), Bird Day encouraged children to think ecologically. First instituted in the United States on May 4, 1894, by School Superintendent Charles Almanzo Babcock in Oil City, Pennsylvania, Bird Day blossomed into an international phenomenon and was often celebrated in conjunction with Arbor Day, a holiday for tree planting. By the 1920s, a singular Bird and Arbor Day was one of many holidays intended to promote America's higher humanitarian purpose in its empire. The ubiquity of this holiday attested to the enduring influence of two Progressive-era educational currents in the United States: the nature study movement and John Dewey's pragmatic educational philosophies.[147] These interconnected movements cast a long shadow in the Philippines, where American educators stressed the pedagogical and therapeutic power of active learning with an emphasis on wild animals and the environment.[148] As a result, Bird and Arbor Day was filled with tree planting, gardening, and birdhouse construction, in effect, activities that required direct physical engagement with the learning process.[149]

FIGURE 4.3. Bird and Arbor Day was an important part of the humane education movement in the American Occupied Philippines. Public schoolchildren built birdhouses and planted bird-friendly vegetation as part of moral lessons in avian kindness. "Making Bird Houses," in Antonio Nera, *Nature Study Readers, Book Four* (Rizal, PI: Oriental Commercial Co., 1933), Record Group 350, Philippine Materials Collection, Entry 95, 121.16 Catalogue—Course of Study and Textbooks, 121.144, V658, 350:150:58:22:5, National Archives at College Park, College Park, MD.

Art classes dominated humane curricula and nature study courses. They promoted animal kindness and gentle comportment through an aesthetic emphasis on harmony and beauty in the natural world. Art manuals highlighted the importance of radiating lines, rhythm, symmetry, and color harmony to create pleasant, tranquil representations of animals and rural society.[150] Birds and animal-powered agricultural labor were common subjects for visualizing an ideal yeoman Filipino citizenry. Manuals directed teachers to have their students construct bird posters out of paper silhouettes, crayons, and paint, along with suggested captions that reinforced ideologies of animal kindness: "Protect Bird Life"; "Save the Birds"; "Birds Help the Farmers"; "Birds Beautify"; "Feed the Birds"; and "Birds Save the Crops."[151] Their emphasis on birds as agents of civilization complemented the views of animal protectionists in the United States, such as the WCTU's Department of Mercy and the MSPCA. *Our Dumb Animals* characterized insectivorous birds as "little patriots of the air," who "help us to be successful as they busy themselves in destroying myriads of the enemies to the growing crops."[152] Kindness to birds helped guarantee the country's food supply, a concrete consequence of benevolent nation building in the United States and its empire.

Philippine education manuals noted that aesthetic appreciation cultivated an ethic of stewardship and conservation in an age of creeping extinctions: "An interest in and a love of birds may be created by emphasizing their beauty of song or color, the way they help us by killing the worms that destroy plants, etc. . . . It is for the teachers to stimulate the children to take such an interest in nature, and in birds in particular, that it will be impossible for them ever to kill the small, harmless birds which are far too scarce now."[153] Bird literature in Philippine classrooms taught students about indigenous species and habitat requirements. Students also learned how to observe birds, care for the injured, and catalogue abandoned nests and eggs in garden classes. Official publications urged teachers to stress that insectivorous and rodent-eating birds were the "farmer's friend" and to encourage boys to monitor each other's behavior around birds:

> In rural communities, the garden class may form a "police" organization for the protection of birds, having each member of the class act as a policeman to watch and report other boys who wantonly shoot birds. Such mischievous boys should be given a heart-to-heart talk by the garden teacher or by the principal of the school or in some other way to feel the ill effects of their acts. . . . For lack of something else

to busy themselves with, boys usually spend their vacation on farms killing birds with sling shots, blow guns, shot guns, and every other conceivable means of taking life. For this reason, something about the protection of birds should also be included in the closing programs of schools.[154]

Grammars of animal kindness formed another cornerstone of humane education in Philippine public schools. The act of learning the American English language was saturated with imperatives for animal mercy: from the importance of providing one's dog with adequate food to the case of compassionate children hosting a funeral for a deceased pet bird. Exercises in comma placement and tenses, and drills in capitalization and punctuation helped structure ideas about animal welfare. For instance, an exercise for seventh-graders, "The Boy Who Robbed Birds' Nests," required students to change the verbs in the numbered sections into the past tense while receiving a moral lesson about the personal consequences of animal cruelty:

1. I know a boy who is fond of catching birds. He sometimes even
2. takes the eggs out of the nest. He does not think about how sorry the
3. mother bird will be when she finds that her pretty blue eggs are
4. gone.
5. This boy goes to the forest to find birds. On his way he meets
6. two of his friends. He tells them what he intends to do and asks
7. them to go along. They tell him that God punishes naughty boys
8. who rob birds' nests. He says that he doesn't care and that he intends
9. to go anyway. He goes farther and farther into the deep
10. woods, so far that he loses himself and can't find his way out. He
11. sits down and cries and wishes he had not come.[155]

Exercises featuring animals accompanied lessons in American patriotism, Philippine hygiene, industry, grooming, manners, and the process of readying oneself for citizenship. Kindness was taught along with the moral consequences of bad behavior, as in the example of a man riddled with a lifetime of guilt for wantonly killing a bird.[156] In 1910, an educational circular, "Morals and Right Conduct," included "Duty toward the Lower Animals" in its program of moral training—as a pointed rebuttal to religious critics who claimed that secular education offered nothing moral.[157] In close proximity to cheery sheet music for a "Song of Cleanliness," "I Have Two Hands," or "Philippines, My Philippines," one could find complementary seatwork exercises explaining the heroic deeds of American Revolutionary patriots and exhortations to perform one's patriotic part by joining the army.[158]

School curricula used the Philippine home to promote American notions of civilization. One primary grade exercise included a Home Improvement Card, which contained a student checklist for proper domestic hygiene, much of which depended on one's proximity to animals: in addition to questions about general cleanliness and private bathrooms in the home, the checklist asked about the presence of animals and whether the property was fenced to keep out wandering livestock.[159] American and Philippine educators lauded the separation of people and itinerant domestic animals as a sign of modern progress.

Citizenship was a major preoccupation in humane education materials. Instructions for art posters included kindness to animals as a central topic for any "Good Citizenship" project.[160] Exercises for Philippine educational achievement tests spanned the pantheon of kindness—animal mercy, good manners, beauty, self-control, neatness—and love of country. The Pledge of Allegiance to the US flag was omnipresent. Students were tested on their cadence and inflection in recitation exercises that included the following: "1. Do an act of kindness every day. Manners make the man," or "3. The Philippines is a free country, although it is not yet an independent nation. Its people are a free people. 35. "Hundreds of birds that go singing by, hundreds of birds in the sunny weather."[161]

Throughout these declarations of Filipino freedom and eventual independence, American educators envisioned an animal-powered agricultural future for their students. Textbooks urged pupils—as future agriculturalists, conservationists, and citizens—to treat birds as the good friend of the farmer.[162] Frank L. Crone, acting director of education in the Philippines, stressed a gendered division of agricultural education as the primary goal of rural teachers in the 1910s: "The rural school should teach the girls housekeeping and cooking, and the boys love for animals, crops, and the use of tools, even if this must be done at the expense of certain cultural subjects."[163] The proper care of animals complemented a personal regimen of thrift, industry, cleanliness, sobriety, patriotism, and environmental stewardship, which offered proof of benevolent assimilation in practice. Sustained pedagogies of animal kindness also served another civilizing purpose: to rewrite the violent legacies of imperial conquest with a program of merciful uplift.

At the dawning of the "American Century," animal protectionists condemned American military expansion. As moral empire builders, however, they promoted their own expansionist project of benevolence through an

FIGURE 4.4. Philippine public school lessons stressed the civilizing power of proper hygiene during the American Occupation. As part of educational mandates to keep hands clean, classroom materials directed children to keep livestock fenced and housed away from the home. "Keep Hands Clean, Help Mother," *Course of Study in Drawing for Normal Schools—Bureau of Education* (Manila: Bureau of Printing, 1929), 23, Record Group 350, Philippine Materials Collection, Entry 95, 121.143 Courses of Study, V654, 350:150:58:22:5, National Archives at College Park, College Park, MD.

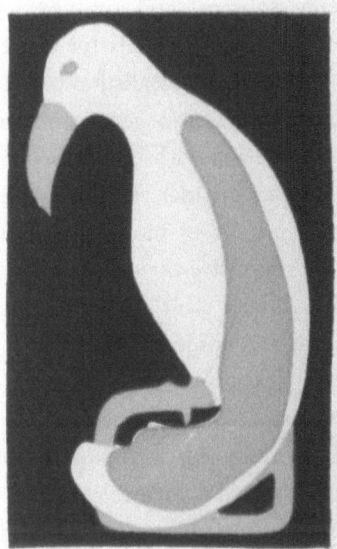

FIGURE 4.5. Humane education curricula in Philippine public schools during the American Occupation included art projects, which emphasized the relationship between animal kindness, civic pride, and future citizenship. "Birds Beautify Our Town; Be Kind to Animals," *Course of Study in Drawing for Normal Schools—Bureau of Education* (Manila: Bureau of Printing, 1929), 23, Record Group 350, Philippine Materials Collection, Entry 95, 121.143 Courses of Study, V654, 350:150:58:22:5, National Archives at College Park, College Park, MD.

interconnected program of animal mercy, sobriety, and anti-vice reform. Although animal protectionists praised American officials for instituting a wide spectrum of humane legislation abroad, their idealism often clashed with the pragmatic, day-to-day business of American governance in the empire. These animal welfare laws, in conjunction with humane education programs in public schools, codified America's broader mission overseas in two interrelated ways: as a humanitarian project of moral improvement, and as a universalizing manifestation of Progressive-era order and reform. Humane activists likewise sincerely believed that their empire of kindness could build a peaceful modern world in practice, not just in theory.

Indigenous nationalist movements also expressed themselves through animal bodies, which, as the example of the cockfight suggests, challenged American authority both politically and culturally. After Filipino lawmakers drafted a new constitution in 1935, which charted a path to eventual independence, they slowly dismantled various forms of American hegemony. During the sessions of the First Commonwealth National Assembly in 1936, legislators voted to abolish the considerable policing authority of the SPCA Philippines, "to withdraw from agents of the Society for the Prevention of Cruelty to Animals of the Philippines the power and authority to make arrests for violations of the law against cruelty to animals and for the protection of animals and to abolish the privilege granted the said society to share in the amount of the fines collected for such violations."[164] Stripped of these powers, the SPCA Philippines was no longer an arm of American governance. During the formative stages of American empire building, subject people often viewed animal welfare activism as simply formal empire building by another name. In the face of indigenous resistance and pushback, American policymakers and animal protectionists eventually realized that humane education and practical recognition of pluralistic traditions constituted a more effective animal welfare policy than exclusion and criminalization. This faith in humane education was especially apparent in colonial India; here American political influence was scant, but American humane advocates forged strong ties with missionaries and Indian reformers as part of a shared commitment to moral uplift through the gospel of kindness.

5

"A Country Rich in Cattle"

GOSPELS OF KINDNESS IN COLONIAL SOUTH ASIA

IN JULY 1900, George Angell declared that America's international priorities were egregiously misplaced. The United States was waging a costly war in the Philippines but doing nothing to help starving people in India: "If we could have had our way, every dollar our government has been spending in the Philippines, and every dollar the British government has been spending in South Africa, should have gone to the starving in India. From our moderate means we have thought it our duty to make several contributions."[1] As part of its global gospel of kindness, the Massachusetts SPCA (MSPCA) offered aid to a country in peril. The drop in global silver prices had severely devalued the Indian rupee in the 1890s; a series of monsoon failures had plunged the Deccan region of western India into famine; and a plague epidemic had decimated the population. Between 1895 and 1905, India's total population declined for the only time since census figures had been taken.[2] Just as Angell condemned human rights abuses in the United States and its empire, he argued that extravagant British imperial celebrations were an outrage during such disastrous times. When King Edward VII was crowned emperor of India at the opulent Durbar of Delhi in 1903, *Our Dumb Animals* roundly condemned the lavish spectacle of forty-thousand soldiers, hundreds of elephants, and the "vast exhibition of jewels and riches" as conduct unbecoming for a nation claiming to rule by a higher moral purpose: "It all seems more like the stories of the 'Arabian Nights' than of things actually done. Then our thoughts go back to the calls made on us . . . to send money to the starving millions of India, and then we take up dispatch from London this January 10th telling that all this folly has cost nearly *five millions of dollars*, while '*the majority of the people of India are continually on the threshold of starvation.*'"[3]

American animal advocates turned to colonial South Asia as a source of imperial critique and cultural fascination. They condemned gaudy British colonial pageants and hunts, but they heartily approved of British social reform in India. They viewed the abolition of child marriage, *sati* (widow burning), and the passage of new animal welfare laws as interconnected gospels of kindness to rescue and uplift the "unenlightened" East. These tensions mirrored America's ambivalent relationship with Great Britain writ large: critical of formal imperialism, on the one hand, but fully supportive of the exceptionalist moral mandate of "gentle English government," on the other.

American animal protectionists were captivated by Indian religious traditions of vegetarianism and *ahimsa* (nonviolence) as well as the subcontinent's abundant charismatic megafauna. They romanticized India's culture and history to celebrate and to critique the humane movement. In so doing, they both affirmed and challenged European and American traditions of orientalism. An imperialism of European and American thought and culture, orientalism represented diverse Asian and Middle Eastern countries in undifferentiated terms as irrational and ahistorical.[4] Cultural producers brought a wealth of orientalist representations of India to American audiences: live elephants and tigers, translations of Hindu texts, handicrafts, and field reports of headhunters, sacred cows, and sadhus (Hindu holy men) who reclined on beds of nails.[5] Henry David Thoreau and other American transcendentalists embraced hybrid cosmologies of Hindu, Buddhist, and Christian thought through their exposure to newly translated Indian religious texts, which European philologists, such as Max Müller, made accessible to new Western audiences in the nineteenth century. Animals were commonly at the center of these popular and textual forms of Indian orientalism.

The sustained interest of American animal advocates in colonial India was unusual in one respect. While law enforcement was a central component of animal protectionism in America and its empire, colonial India remained outside formal American jurisdiction. India primarily served as a field for American humane education—as a model of nonviolence and vegetarian animal kindness on the one hand, and as a subject for moral uplift on the other. American humane organizations supported missionaries in the South Asian field and forged alliances with South Asian social reformers and nationalists. Additionally, Americans used Indian ideas about animals either to support or to condemn the Indian independence movement. American and British empire builders believed in animal protectionism as a linchpin of higher civilization, which suggests that humane advocates around the world shared a common teleological language of animal protectionism. However, the colonial India example underscores the ways in which cultural and political differences bear on transnational histories of animal advocacy.[6] The experiences of caste, religious pluralism, and British colonialism shaped South Asian ideologies of animal kindness and nationalism in culturally specific ways, helping to sow the seeds of Hindu cultural nationalism and Muslim demonization in the twentieth century.

"From Cruel Head-Hunters to Christians": Missionaries of Animal Kindness in India

India had been an American missionary field since 1813, when evangelical members of Parliament successfully spearheaded the Charter Act, which lifted a ban on missionaries in Indian provinces. Mainline American missionaries acquainted home audiences with Indian animal cosmologies in field reports brimming with sacred cows and sensational, hybridized animal/human religious icons, such as Ganesh, the elephant-headed god, or Hanuman, the monkey god. As greater numbers of American women attained a college degree in the 1870s, they increasingly became missionaries, especially those who were unmarried. At the turn of the twentieth century, American and British women comprised the two largest groups of Western female missionaries in the subcontinent.[7]

American and British animal advocates collaborated with missionaries and social reformers to bring the complementary gospels of Jesus Christ and humane education to India through the Bands of Mercy movement.[8] Women, working as teachers in conjunction with their other missionary duties, often led local Indian Bands of Mercy, just as they did in classrooms across America.[9] Moreover, *Black Beauty* was a popular text in Indian Bands of Mercy, where it was translated into Hindi and Telugu.[10] Individual Bands were often secular, as in America, but the movement's historical roots were evangelical and colonial. When the English Unitarian minister Thomas Timmins co-founded the American Bands of Mercy with George Angell in 1882, he modeled this new humane education society on an eponymous group he helped lead in England.[11] Timmins also led the Universal Mercy Band Movement, British Empire Division.[12] The Universal Mercy Band advertised itself as "Educational—Unsectarian—Non-Political: Teaches Kindness, Justice, and Mercy, to every Creature both Human and Dumb, and Protection for all from Cruel Treatment, especially Women, Children, and

Dumb Creatures."[13] The coupling of women, children, and animals as ostensibly "unsectarian" and "nonpolitical" defined the humane movement worldwide.[14] Although disavowing formal militarism as an instrument of empire building, George Angell described the growth and influence of the Bands of Mercy worldwide as an "army" for moral expansionism.[15] Missionaries similarly used military metaphors to characterize their peaceable project of uplift. American Methodist Episcopal missionary James Thoburn portrayed American and Canadian churches as "the final invaders of India; but theirs is a great peaceful enterprise, the obligations of which they joyfully accept in union with the Christian forces of Great Britain."[16]

Missionaries reported to *Our Dumb Animals* that the gospels of Christ and animal kindness had uplifted formerly "savage" populations. For example, Mrs. N. Agnes Robb, an American missionary in Sura, Assam, and Band of Mercy leader, proudly reported the rapid march of civilization using familiar orientalist tropes of cruelty and enlightened progress:

> Not much more than half a century ago these people were wild savages and cruel head-hunters, though they were not cannibals so far as we know. Now there are many schools and more than 5,000 Christians. There are forty-one members, big and little, in the Band, and would be more if I could give more time to it. Some of the big boys and girls who joined have graduated from our school here this year and gone home to their villages. Some of them, I feel sure, are interested enough to teach along humane lines if they do not really organize Bands. The seed has been sown and I pray the good work may spread.[17]

Another Band of Mercy in Ferozepur [Firozpur], Punjab, was created in 1911. Later known as the Animals' Friend Society, this organization combined animal protection activities with programs of proper self-management. Echoing the humane education activities in Philippine classrooms, Punjabi children built birdhouses and cultivated bird-friendly gardens. From Fort Worth to Manila, humane education programs were often quite literally built around the birdhouse—a zone of edifying domestic contact between wilderness and civilization. With the growing threat of extinction owing to avian habitat loss and the global feather trade, the act of building a birdhouse promoted wildlife conservation. It also "harmoniously develops the head, heart and hand" as part of a synergistic pedagogy in hands-on learning and moral elevation: humane curricula stressed that the study of birds offered students instructive models of fidelity and family devotion.[18]

American missionaries used dirt, sanitation, and the proximity of human habitation to animals as critical markers of civilization. Bands of Mercy members in Firozpur practiced Booker T. Washington's "gospel of the toothbrush," by promoting "natural and humane diet" and good hygiene. They were mindful of the interconnected dangers of grime and cruelty: "just as dirt is the hot-bed of disease, so the cruel heart is the fruitful source of much crime."[19] These redemptive, teleological connections between animal kindness, cleanliness, Christianity, and proximity complemented an imperial imaginary of the white man's burden throughout America's transnational missionary field. In Hawaii, where American missionaries had been active since 1820, breathless accounts of trash, nudity, smoke, fleas, lice, "the rudest hovels," and domestic animals filled the pages of missionary periodicals in vivid reportage that resembled Marshall Saunders's descriptions of the filthy, sty-like home belonging to Jenkins, who tortured Beautiful Joe.[20] In 1838, a missionary wrote from Waimea, Oahu, "Night comes on; men, women, and children, the married and unmarried, fowls, dogs, and cats, and sometimes pigs even, lie down to sleep.... In this respect all things are common."[21]

As a component of evangelization, some American missionaries demonized South Asian traditions of ahimsa as signs of moral perversion. Missionary publications listed a cornucopia of animal species, from insects to cows, which Jain and Hindu veterinary personnel treated in *pinjrapoles* (animal hospitals). According to James Thoburn, "their chief peculiarity is their abnormal regard for life, whether of man, beast, bird, or insect.... Snakes are not excluded, but children are not admitted. It is said that even vermin are tolerated and protected."[22] The sacred cow was considered to be the most decadent Hindu creature in a land of human starvation. Stories focused on the thin, holy "ill-fed kine" wandering the streets and fields, the sickest of which were housed in special *gaushalas* (cow sanctuaries) dedicated to their care.[23] The *Heathen Woman's Friend* regaled young readers in its "Children's Department" with the special challenges of converting cow-worshipping Hindus to Christianity:

> Did you ever hear of such a thing?... If a Hindu boy should see you eating the flesh of a cow, he would be almost as much shocked as if you were making your dinner off the flesh of a man.... Shall we not all do our best to give the people of India the knowledge of the true God and of his Son Jesus Christ, so that they will no longer consider cows holy, and bow in homage before them?[24]

Yet American missionaries were hardly in ideological lockstep. Exposure to Indian religions occasionally prompted a reevaluation of the place of humanity in relation to animals. T. J. Scott, for one, arrived in northern India at the turn of the twentieth century embracing traditional Protestant ideals of animal mercy and Christian stewardship. His missionary handbook, *India Mission Jubilee of the Methodist Episcopal Church in Southern Asia,* instructed its Methodist Episcopal missionaries to proselytize the "principles of reverence towards God," which included "humility, kindness to the lower orders of creation, and other kindred Christian virtues."[25] After Scott became immersed in India's diverse religious traditions of ahimsa, vegetarianism, cow worship, and animalized Hindu deities, he began to think differently about animals, reconsidering his former notions of Christian stewardship and beneficent dominion in favor of interspecies kinship:

> My India experience of quite a lifetime gave me a more appreciative idea of our kinship to the higher animals, domestic in our homes and fellow citizens on our streets.... I once observed a Hindu on the street with his arm around the neck of his cow as they walked along. "You seem to like your cow," said I. "She is my mother," was the reply, and he kissed her on the mouth. I once observed a Parsee... as he passed a horse on the street of Bombay, bow deferentially to it.... Few persons fully grasp the resemblance of animal physiology and psychology to our own. We do the animal injustice, ignore his rights and misinterpret his actions.[26]

Published in the *Methodist Review* in 1918, Scott's essay, "Our Dumb Fellow Creatures," mirrored the polemical strategies of *Our Dumb Animals* in its plea for kindness. Using anecdotes of animal sentience and intelligence, the essay celebrated India's pluralistic religious traditions to argue for physiological and spiritual kinship among human beings and animals. Scott's syncretic, cosmopolitan worldview reflected the views of other liberal Protestant missionaries in India, such as the American Methodist Episcopal missionary and author Eli Stanley Jones, a vocal advocate of Indian sovereignty and racial equality. Jones was a personal friend and advisor to Mahatma Gandhi, and his biography of Gandhi introduced Martin Luther King Jr. to Gandhian principles of ahimsa. Jones's famous early work, *The Christ of the Indian Road* (1925), sold more than a million copies.[27]

The Indian reformer and nationalist Pandita Ramabai Sarasvati forged her own gospel of kindness out of her pluralistic experiences with Hinduism and Christianity. A Brahmin who converted to Christianity while living in England as a young woman, Ramabai is best known as a child-widow advocate and educator. She was also a dedicated animal protectionist who worked with American humane leaders, temperance activists, and missionaries. She established close ties with George Angell and WCTU president Frances Willard during her popular lecture tour in the United States from 1886 to 1888. She also served as a national lecturer for the WCTU in India.[28] A widowed mother and vegetarian, Ramabai was a charismatic speaker who attracted enthusiastic crowds wherever she traveled. In December 1887, progressive reformers founded the American Ramabai Association to fund her Indian educational initiatives. Frances Willard served as vice president. The group raised so much money that Ramabai was able to open her boarding school for child-widows, the Sharada Sadan, immediately after she returned to India in 1889.[29]

Ramabai and Angell corresponded regularly during her American tour. She blasted the bird hat and asked Angell to send her pamphlets that she could hand out during her lecture stops. Like her brethren in the American animal welfare movement, Ramabai appealed to essentialistic notions of female virtue: "As I travel around this country I see thousands of young ladies and old women, as well as little children, wearing whole and half bodies of birds on their bonnets. It shocks and grieves me. There is cruelty enough in my own country, but our gentlewomen do not at present think of beautifying themselves with dead birds. Please send me some leaflets on this subject, and I will distribute them on trains and street-cars, as well as give them to my friends. God bless you and your humane work."[30] Angell gladly complied and Ramabai was true to her word. The Reverend T. DeWitt Talmage of Brooklyn wrote to Angell, "This morning I had put in my hand a leaflet from the [MSPCA]. It contained a letter from Pundita Ramabai of India, which she says there is more wrong done [to] the birds in America than in India."[31] In the years ahead, Angell sent boxes of material to Ramabai in India, which she used in her new humane curriculum at the Sharada Sadan.[32] In gratitude, Ramabai wrote that her humane education program was "a monument to our dear friend Mr. Angell, God bless him! Through him I learned what a good influence this has over children."[33]

In her best-selling account of her travels, *The Peoples of the United States,* Ramabai recounted her revulsion at the popularity of hunting and meat eating in America.[34] Yet she rejected the chauvinistic notion that ahimsa made Indian traditions morally superior to the decadent West. She readily acknowledged that Indian religious prohibitions against animal cruelty hardly mitigated the incidence of actual abuse. She was equally uneasy when American missionary organizations made similarly exceptionalist claims, such as the Bombay-based American Mission, in its monthly children's magazine, *Balabodha Meva* (Moral Instruction for Children), which heralded the United States as a singular bastion of "great kindness." Ramabai recognized the complexity of human and animal relationships in her rebuttal: "In [Indian] villages, and sometimes even in cities, there are families which keep milk cows; the women and children of these families love the cows and calves as if they were family members. It is terrible that traders, milkmen, and butchers ill-treat cattle; and all must strive to put a stop to this ill-treatment. But it is not true that such ill-treatment does not exist in America."[35]

Ramabai's affective modes of representing physical and emotional abuse in her speeches and writings galvanized her American supporters through the animalization of children and the humanization of animals. Her stories echoed the reportage of Mary Ellen Wilson, the battered girl whose abuse at the hand of her cruel guardian prompted ASPCA leaders to establish the Society for the Prevention of Cruelty to Children in 1874. Ramabai's examples included a thirteen-year-old Indian girl who was betrothed in babyhood, sent to live with her mother-in-law as a toddler, shunned once her adult husband died, and subsequently "starved, beaten, her body often balanced through a ring suspended from the ceiling, she became prematurely old."[36] Photographs of shorn and branded child-widows, along with the testimony of the girls themselves, corroborated textual narratives of cruelty similar to the ubiquitous visual images and written accounts of battered animals. Ramabai's Indian male critics attempted to delegitimize her work through metaphors of abject animals, such as the street dog living on the margins of society: "Those who have neither husband nor sons to serve are of no more value than the street-dogs and crows, and might as well live like them. They can easily get a crust of bread and a handful of rice to subsist upon!"[37] In the midst of the famine in 1897, Ramabai observed that hardship had pulverized what little humanity remained in many of her new students: "Some are little better than brute beasts. The filthy habits they have acquired during this period of famine have become second nature with them. It will take a long time to civilize and teach them. We can do all things in the power of the Lord."[38]

Echoing the MSPCA's imperative to speak on behalf of animals, Ramabai and her American benefactors described the Sharada Sadan as "an answer to centuries of mute protest from India's women." Ramabai, like her friend and WCTU colleague Frances Willard, rallied supporters with Scripture to

A Country Rich in Cattle 159

The child-widow described with the brass water pots.

Tara, a child-widow eleven years old. She was branded with hot irons.

FIGURE 5.1. MSPCA president George Angell and WCTU president Frances Willard were enthusiastic supporters of the South Asian reformer, nationalist, and vegetarian Christian, Pandita Ramabai Sarasvati, who instituted humane education programs into her curricula at Sharada Sadan, her school for child-widows in Maharashtra, which included Tara, pictured here. "Tara, A Child-Widow Eleven Years Old," in Clementina Butler, *Pandita Ramabai Sarasvati: Pioneer in the Movement for the Education of the Child-Widow of India* (New York: Fleming H. Revell), facing 24.

"Open thy mouth for the dumb" (Proverbs 31:8), among other biblical exhortations to animal mercy.[39] Both were dedicated to eradicating the mutually reinforcing cruelties of domestic abuse and animal violence through an interdependent program of Christian uplift and education. Ramabai's accounts of violence toward Indian women and girls were especially compelling to American and British women long steeped in the ideological imperative to "rescue" the benighted women of the East from brutish husbands and fathers.[40]

The presence of domestic animals magnified the Sharada Sadan's status as a domestic sanctuary. American visitors reported that as a stark "before and after" contrast to the frail child-widows who entered the school, long-term residents were healthy and happily ensconced with pets. The presence of contented, pampered milk cows, buffalo, and "a little ox, who is a great pet," amplified the aura of civilized calm in this domestic female refuge where the gospel of kindness was a way of life.[41]

"Gentle English Government": Colonial Animal Welfare Legislation in the Age of Crown Rule

In 1887, *Our Dumb Animals* glowingly reported some impressive statistics: India's largest animal protection society, the Calcutta SPCA (CSPCA), had the highest number of arrests for animal cruelty in the world, leading to 7,126 prosecutions and an extraordinarily high 7,042 convictions in 1886. Steeped in orientalist assumptions about Indian piety, *Our Dumb Animals* attributed the arrest and prosecution rate in Calcutta (Kolkata) to an indigenous grassroots commitment to ahimsa, while overlooking how CSPCA policing represented an arm of the colonial state.[42]

While Indians embraced animal protectionism within their own religious traditions, they viewed colonial SPCA officers as an Anglo face on a fickle and abusive system of policing. Similar to colonial subjects in the American empire, Indian laborers and professionals rejected the high-minded notion that Anglo SPCA officers were guardians of mercy. Instead, they saw these uniformed agents in racial and political terms, as racially exclusive Anglo-Saxon bodies of social control; indeed, the organization virtually excluded Indians until the early 1930s. Raj Bahdur N. N. Banerjee, a public prosecutor and major advisor to the government of Bengal, observed "that for some time past the Society had been looked upon by a large section of the Indian public of Calcutta as a close[d] Corporation from which Indians, even of eminent positions in public life, had been excluded without any adequate reasons."[43] Prior to the 1930s, the income of the CSPCA—like other Indian SPCAs—was generated by fines, which naturally motivated the Society to prosecute vigorously.[44] For Indian subjects, the public presence of British SPCA officials embodied the exclusionary power of the colonial state. Its punitive reach extended into the intimate, prosaic rhythms of daily life, heightening social and cultural divisions.

Changes to the CSPCA's membership and enforcement policies occurred only after the CSPCA and local police clashed directly with Calcutta's carters. In February 1930, the CSPCA ordered a citywide ban on bullock driving between the hours of noon and 3:00 PM, scheduled to begin on April 1 and lasting through the hot season so that the animals could rest. Violators were to be arrested and charged with animal cruelty. Because the ban would severely disrupt the carters' livelihood, their labor union quickly organized an extensive opposition movement.[45] On April 1, the carters staged a massive strike. At noon, 25,000 to 30,000 carters unhitched their bullocks at the city's busiest intersection, led them away, and returned to their carts to protest the new ordinance. Local police, with CSPCA officers at their sides, responded with an overwhelming show of force: they shot and killed seven carters and injured hundreds.⁴⁶

Relations between the carters and the CSPCA had long been bad, a microcosm of colonial tensions that even distant British officials recognized: "It is upon the overloading and treatment of the buffaloes that the main controversy in Calcutta has so long centered."⁴⁷ Calcutta carters and other city workers profoundly distrusted what appeared to be a racist, imperial organization working hand in glove with the hated police. In the aftermath of the bloody Carters' Strike, British officials lifted the driving ban in Calcutta during the hot season; they funded the CSPCA with a government grant instead of revenue from fines; and they opened the organization to Indian membership.⁴⁸ The burgeoning Indian independence movement provided the broader political context for the Carters' Strike and its deadly consequences: the strike occurred in the midst of Mahatma Gandhi's internationally publicized Salt Satyagraha (Salt March) to the Sea, which protested the Raj's monopoly on salt manufacture and its prohibitive tax on Indian producers. Although Calcutta's midday ban on bullock driving had no literal connection to the imperial salt tax, the carters saw both as equally reprehensible symbols of colonial oppression. British ideals of animal kindness ignored the daily rhythms and contingencies of local labor, thereby threatening to destroy the carters' occupational future.

The timing of the earliest British colonial animal welfare legislation in 1857 paved the way for enduring Indian suspicions. British officials enacted the first of these laws at virtually the same time they consolidated formal control of the subcontinent during the Sepoy Rebellion. Applying only to the railway station of Howrah (a major transportation hub near Calcutta), the governor-general of India in Council authorized police officers to arrest without a warrant and to fine any person they witnessed committing an act of animal cruelty. Over the next thirty-three years, twenty-two new colonial anticruelty laws regulated local and regional interactions with animals across the subcontinent as part of Crown Rule.⁴⁹

The government of India passed its most comprehensive animal welfare legislation on March 21, 1890. The Prevention of Cruelty to Animals Act, Act XI of 1890 (PCA Act), was the first anticruelty law to cover the entire subcontinent and beyond. Drawing heavily on local precedents, the PCA Act codified proper kindly conduct in everyday public life.⁵⁰ Significantly, the law allowed local officials to "opt out" of any section they deemed to be unenforceable according to specific circumstances, which made it similar

FIGURE 5.2. Calcutta's bullock carters, pictured here at Howrah Station in 1926, clashed repeatedly with the British-run Calcutta SPCA. Carters felt that colonial animal welfare laws were an oppressive form of social and economic control, while animal advocates viewed such laws as a linchpin of higher civilization. "Goods Shed, Howrah Station, Calcutta, India," *Our Dumb Animals*, May 1926, 185.

to the model of local autonomy that American officials would adopt in the Occupied Philippines a decade later.[51] As an additional show of plasticity and commitment to secular colonial governance, the act exempted religious rites, rituals, and cultural traditions involving animals.[52] It relied upon public witnessing and surveillance to catch perpetrators "in any street or in any other place, whether open or closed, to which the public have access, or within sight of any person in any street or in any such other place."[53] The definition of cruelty itself was intertwined with these specific locations and the daily public theater of animal labor and commerce. As a result, the law primarily targeted indigent, uneducated, lower-caste, and lower-class urban agrarians whose livelihood was dependent on animals. Lawmakers characterized animal cruelty and neglect as a moral problem rather than a structural consequence of poverty. In the same way, they assumed that poor people readily embraced vices like gambling and drunkenness alongside a passion for cockfighting, described as "no doubt a barbarous practice," whose crowds were described as "aboriginals," "the lower castes of Hindus," and "country people."[54]

Despite its allowances for local flexibility, the PCA Act remained a prong of colonial rule. The law reached into private spaces because it granted high-ranking police officers expansive powers to issue themselves search warrants to investigate potential or actual violations of the law after receiving credible written notice.[55] The PCA Act also expanded the authority of the police to seize or kill any sick or abused animal.[56] In the early twentieth century, the act's judicial reach was extended beyond the subcontinent to British colonies in East Africa and the British Residency at Aden (in modern-day Yemen). In 1908, Major C. P. G. Griffin (Commander, Aden Troops) recounted how he burst from his bungalow in his pajamas to stop a driver beating a camel cart heavily overloaded with grain: "I saw the driver repeatedly prod the camel in the anus, he then threw a heavy stone at the camel's head and finally swung himself on the camel's head and pulled at the nose string until it broke away. The man had worked himself into a frenzy of cruelty. I was in my sleeping suit at the time, but . . . put a stop to further cruelty, and had the cart unloaded."[57]

Drivers and hostlers stood dumbfounded as officers summarily shot animals deemed to be hopelessly injured or ill. Police ordered sick, chafed, neglected, starving, and overworked animals that had a chance at recovery to stay at a pinjrapole (infirmary), where owners were liable for the cost of any food, board, and veterinary care—expenses that were exorbitant for struggling laborers, who often responded by simply abandoning their animals there. Abandonment was so endemic that the government of India modified the PCA Act in 1933 to give SPCA and other law enforcement authorities the power to force owners to pick up and pay for those animals that were incurable and thus unsalable.[58] The distrusted figure of the colonial policeman, a long-standing symbol of capriciousness and corruption, worked hand in glove with SPCA officials, thereby putting an Indian face on quotidian matters of British rule. During the Carters' Strike in 1930, the direct collusion of the Calcutta police and the all-Anglo CSPCA transformed what might have remained a tense standoff into a catastrophe.[59]

Like contemporaneous legislation in the United States, the PCA Act did little to protect wild animals. Crown officials argued that the mass destruction of wild animal "vermin" was a necessary function of good government. Each provincial government issued a highly detailed annual report, the "Extermination of Wild Animals and Venomous Snakes," which catalogued an immense death toll of human beings and cattle killed by specific wild animal species each year, as well as the tens of thousands of wild animals killed.[60] The tiger, for one, faced annihilation by the 1930s because it was seen as a threat to livestock and human civilization; it was also coveted as a colonial hunting trophy and a visible token of political power. For British imperialists and indigenous princely rulers alike, killing a tiger was a hallmark of strong rule.[61] American missionary reports from South Asia echoed these views: "A tiger . . . was shot within the town of Jaffna [Sri Lanka]. Very providentially, it was killed before it had done much injury."[62] Framed as a matter of public good, some colonial manuals suggested that captured tigers should be beaten to death, shot by torch, or even baited with a mace-like ball filled with food that slowly eviscerated the animal from within once swallowed.[63]

Even *Beautiful Joe*, the winning manuscript entry in the American Humane Education Society's 1893 literary contest, tacitly condoned killing apex predators as a necessary condition of civilization. The kindly farmer Mr. Wood argued that protecting his property justified the shooting of a mother bear pillaging his corn crop, using the examples of elite British blood sport and colonial hunting to explain that the ethics of killing animals were morally situational: "I'll tell you what I've no patience with, and that's with these English folks that dress themselves up, and take fine horses and packs of dogs, and tear over the country after one little fox or rabbit. Bah, it's contemptible. Now if they were hunting cruel, man-eating tigers, or animals that destroy property, it would be a different thing."[64]

While viewing hunting as permissible under limited circumstances, American activists emphatically condemned hunting for sport, particularly as a profligate expression of imperial authority. A cartoon in *Our Dumb Animals* depicted a large buck with an impressive rack bound and dragged from hunting lands labeled, "The Imperial Forest: No Trespassing," and placed in front of a portly king sitting with a gun in a well-appointed edifice embossed with the Scottish lion rampant. A pile of slain deer lay nearby. Entitled "Royal Sport: Its Pains and Perils," the cartoon made a mockery of fair chase by depicting the British colonial hunt as a canned, corporate enterprise, complete with a large staff of soldiers/servants.[65] Its publication in 1909 coincided with another canned hunt slightly closer to home: Theodore Roosevelt's African safari, which *Our Dumb Animals* condemned repeatedly with gruesome reports of TR's slaughter in the field, including an ostrich pair he shot on their nest: "And this is what Mr. Roosevelt calls 'sport.'"[66] American humane groups supported the efforts of Labhshankar Laxmidas and other Indian animal advocates who demanded new humane laws to protect Indian game animals from British and indigenous princely slaughter: "Thousands of poor ducks and other birds are killed for the sake of mere amusement by cruel pleasure-seekers. . . . Admiring reports of such idle butcheries of innocents are published in newspapers, and so the cruel fashion goes on unchecked."[67] Despite such efforts, the PCA Act did little to protect wild animals.

FIGURE 5.3. American animal advocates and their South Asian allies condemned the imperial hunt as an extravagant, wasteful spectacle of cruelty, as well as a mockery of any standard of fair chase. "Royal Sport, Its Pains and Perils," *Our Dumb Animals*, June 1909, 4.

Ritual slaughter was exempted under the PCA Act to mitigate potential cultural conflict in the aftermath of the Sepoy Rebellion, which began after British military officers ordered Hindu and Muslim soldiers to load their new Enfield muzzle-loading rifles with cartridges greased with pig and cow fat. (This order violated religious dietary laws against pig and cow consumption because soldiers had to rip the paper cartridges open with their teeth before pouring the gunpowder down the muzzle.) Yet slaughter remained a flashpoint among pluralistic constituents in colonial India, as in the United States, where *shechita*, or kosher slaughter, was still controversial.[68] Colonial officials used animal sacrifice as tacit proof of India's unfitness for self-government in lurid, orientalist terms. Writer and educator Lockwood Kipling spent the majority of his adult life in India, where scenes of ritual goat and buffalo sacrifice to the Hindu goddess Kali in Calcutta thoroughly riveted him: "There may be seen thousands of people gloating in delirious excitement over rivers of blood."[69]

Missionaries, government authorities, and animal welfare advocates alike compiled sensational, voyeuristic slaughter chronicles.[70] Labhshankar Laxmidas, who published regularly in the *National Humane Review*, denounced the government of India for its hypocritical inconsistency in exempting religious slaughter under the PCA Act while prohibiting other religious-based social customs that did violence to women and girls:

> Seeing that they stopped sati, or widow-burning, and female infanticide, and passed the Age of Consent Act without the least risk, I feel sure that they are quite able to protect animals from religious tortures. If they will do their sacred duty they will deserve the gratitude of thousands of kind-hearted men and women not only in India, but in England also, and the silent blessings of poor, defenceless creatures that are at present mercilessly tortured by cruel-hearted men.[71]

Laxmidas argued that animal protection had the same legislative urgency as human rights abuses. He contended that animal protection was a "sacred duty" that would instantiate humanitarian governance. Animal advocates and their missionary allies pushed the Raj to conduct a formal investigation of animal sacrifice in 1907, but the British ultimately upheld the policy of non-interference under the PCA Act. Nonetheless, colonial investigators concluded that informal moral suasion (i.e., humane education) was permissible.[72] In addition to concerns about undue suffering, critics of animal sacrifice prized the legitimacy and inerrancy of printed textual traditions over idiosyncratic local oral practices.[73] Historians observe that the growing currency of textual purity was a product of the transnational colonial experience, which involved the religious cross-fertilization of Protestant missionaries, Orientalist translators, colonial officials, and indigenous reformist religious movements like the Brahmo Samaj and the Arya Samaj, which incorporated Western theologies into their hybrid social thought.[74]

Vegetarianism

On September 11, 1893, the ascetic Hindu monk Swami Vivekananda gave the first of several dazzling speeches on religious pluralism and peace at the Columbian Exposition's Parliament of Religions at Chicago. A charismatic orator, Vivekananda blended the teachings of his Hindu guru, Ramakrishna, with Deism, Unitarianism, Universalism, and the Indian Brahmo Samaj. He traveled the nation thereafter, and newspapers tracked his every move: from his speaking engagements to his founding of the American Vedanta Society in 1894.[75] Many American media outlets dismissed Vivekananda as a crank or a fraud. The *Missionary Herald* cynically described his orange garb as "gorgeous robes of rich materials and bright colors … simply to catch the American fancy and appeal to the sentimentalism of hearers."[76]

Vivekananda, however, reached a wide, receptive American audience that was beginning to rethink the ethics of meat eating. His visit to Chicago came on the heels of a historic gathering of international vegetarians to discuss dietary reform and the "civilizing" benefits of a meatless diet, which was sponsored by the fair's Department of Temperance. The meeting attracted more than 200 delegates, including representatives from India.[77] Vivekananda, however, went even further. He explicitly wedded vegetarianism and animal advocacy into an expansive gospel of kindness and Indian exceptionalism. In churches, private homes, and lecture halls across the nation, Vivekananda vigorously argued that Indian vegetarianism separated "enlightened" India from the "savage" West. At a meeting of the V Club in New York City on May 2, 1894, he rebutted those Americans who thought vegetarianism simply represented a functional solution to Hinduism's theological conundrum of the transmigration of souls, or, put another way, the fear of cannibalizing one's ancestors. Vivekananda maintained that vegetarianism was an expression of Hindu animal kindness; American meat eating, by contrast, was a symptom of American barbarism:

> Nearly three-quarters of the people of India are vegetarians. They are so because they are too kind to kill animals for food. In this country, when animals are injured, it is the custom to kill them. In India, it is

the rule to send them to a hospital. In approaching Bombay, the first thing the traveler comes across is a very large hospital for animals. This has been the practice for 4,000 years.[78]

To be sure, some early vegetarians in America tacitly recognized the connections between dietary practice and animal cruelty. For example, the Philadelphia Bible-Christian Church, also known as the "Vegetarian Church," was founded in 1817 by a dissident immigrant group of former members of the Bible-Christian Church of Salford, England. They believed that the Bible commanded Christians to avoid meat and liquor, as well as other forms of violent dominion, including slavery, war, and capital punishment, thus making vegetarianism their keystone of antebellum reform.[79] But few early vegetarians explicitly addressed animal suffering. In the 1830s, Sylvester Graham and his vegetarian followers, known as "Grahamites," believed that meat eating was a form of intemperance akin to alcohol consumption, which stimulated the "animal" passions of violence and sexual desire, thereby rendering people more animal-like.[80] Graham imbued his vegetarian mission of moral reform with the evangelical language of conversion during the Second Great Awakening.[81] After the Civil War, Americans embraced vegetarianism primarily for health reasons. Michigan impresario Dr. John Harvey Kellogg enticed thousands of people to his Battle Creek Sanitarium beginning in the 1870s with his spirited prescriptions of vegetarianism, temperance, sexual abstinence, and other forms of "biologic living."[82]

South Asian animal advocates helped bring vegetarianism to the American humane movement. Vivekananda and Ramabai, among others, made their case in person. Still others pleaded for a merciful vegetarian diet in their writing, which appeared in American humane periodicals and vegetarian publications. In the *Vegetarian Magazine*, Labhshankar Laxmidas bluntly wrote that Hindus would be hard-pressed to convert to Christianity when its missionaries ate beef: "We Hindus worship the cow, while you Christians murder and eat her."[83] Even though the vast majority of American animal protectionists still ate meat at the turn of the twentieth century, South Asian gospels of vegetarian kindness found an increasingly receptive audience at a time when the nation's meat industry had become a symbol of corruption and a public health hazard. The five largest meat producers—including Swift and Armour—became derisively known as the "Beef Trust" in the 1880s because they set meat prices, curried political influence, and cut deals with railroad companies (which often held controlling interests in stockyards and packinghouses). Meat companies faced charges of endangerment, which reached a fever pitch during the Spanish-American War, when thousands of American troops became ill from consuming "embalmed" canned meat. The ongoing scandal of tainted meat reached a critical mass when Upton Sinclair's muckraking bestseller, *The Jungle*, spurred passage of the federal Pure Food and Drug Act in 1906.[84] The miasmal environmental conditions of the meat industry in Chicago triggered the growth of a thriving local vegetarian consumer culture at the turn of the twentieth century; the city was home to vegetarian publications, restaurants, and health food stores.[85]

Modern industrial methods of livestock transport, delivery, and slaughter amplified the humane movement's growing receptivity to Indian pleas for vegetarian kindness. Labhshankar Laxmidas pointed directly to the agonizing conditions of production when urging his American Christian readers to become vegetarians: "I feel pain that such a noble religion should not command its followers to be strict vegetarians, thus preventing them from being the cause of unutterable cruelties of the cattle boat, the train and slaughter house to millions upon millions of poor innocent animals as helpless as their own little children and as sentient as themselves."[86]

While antebellum slaughterhouses in Cincinnati had pioneered industrial assembly-line methods of killing, livestock generally traveled short distances to the city's stockyards from nearby farms in the fertile Ohio River Valley.[87] After the Civil War, livestock often traveled for days in fetid, tightly packed railroad cars without food and water, from distant western rangelands and other rural hinterlands to urban stockyards. Frequently, these beleaguered bleating and bawling animals landed at Chicago's vast 640-acre Union Stock Yards, which replaced Cincinnati as the nation's "Porkopolis" in 1865.[88] Because newborn calves and lambs were still too wobbly to walk from rail yard to stockyard, teamsters bound and stacked them onto carts. This transportation method was so grisly that it prompted the nation's first animal welfare organization to deploy its newly incorporated powers of arrest. On April 11, 1866, an ASPCA officer arrested a German butcher driving a cart piled with bawling calves, including one whose eye had been impaled.[89] The suffering of food animals in transit also was the catalyst for the 28-Hour Law in 1873, the nation's first federal animal welfare law, which stipulated that livestock in transit must receive food, water, and rest stops every twenty-eight hours. Owing in large part to his good personal relationship with George Angell, President Rutherford B. Hayes actively supported subsequent efforts to improve the wretched conditions of railroad transport.[90] Conditions were so bad that some hailed the advent of the refrigerated rail car in 1878 (commissioned by meat manufacturer Gustavus Swift) as a merciful innovation because livestock could now be slaughtered prior to shipment: "The long journey on the hoof, so injurious to the animal, is avoided."[91] As a testament to Progressive-era reform, a new 28-Hour Law was passed in 1906 to replace the original legislation, which was largely ineffective. This law initiated a more rigorous system of certification and federal oversight through the Bureau of Animal Industry to ensure compliance at water, feed, and rest stations across the nation.[92] Nonetheless, railroad transport and subsequent truck travel remained sites of prolonged suffering.

The sensory experience of visiting a sprawling modern stockyard and slaughterhouse was a watershed moment for many animal protectionists. After Mary Lovell traveled to the Union Stock Yards in her forties, she was so profoundly shaken that she never ate meat again. She emphatically agreed with Laxmidas's characterization of slaughterhouses as "Hells upon Earth," in her subsequent writings about vegetarian kindness in the pages of the *Starry Cross*.[93] Lovell's experiences in Chicago were hardly in isolation. In the final pages of *The Jungle*, Upton Sinclair espoused vegetarianism as part of the novel's prescribed socialist awakening through the rhetorical musings of Dr. Schliemann, "Eventually those who want to eat meat will have to do their own killing—and how long do you think the custom would survive then?"[94] Even W. Joseph Grand's celebratory history of the Union Stock Yards recognized the miserable status of the modern pig in 1896: "Fifty years ago, he was a 'pioneer hog,' sharing pioneer conditions. A sty and trough were unknown to him. He found his own food and bed.... What has the hog of today?... There is no chance for grass to grow under so many feet, he never tastes herbage, his food is usually corn and swill, while he drinks from a pool in which some other hog is wallowing and stirring up the mud."[95]

Although *Our Dumb Animals* remained officially neutral about meat consumption, the magazine used South Asian traditions of ahimsa to condemn American slaughter practices. One essay urged American readers to reject the cruel consequences of unbridled modern consumerism, "where the cow, which has mothered our children, is fatted up and sent to the butcher so soon as her milk supply ceases to bring in its full pennyworth of profit," in favor of learning bovine kindness from India: "The sacred bulls still wander unharmed, the oxen are the wealth of the people, and the milch kine their dearest possession."[96]

In an age of industrial meat production, British Indophile activist and writer Henry Salt found a receptive American audience for his pluralistic cosmologies of ahimsa and vegetarianism. Salt was born in India, the son of a colonel in the Royal Bengal Artillery. Although he and his mother moved to

England when he was an infant, he retained a lifelong interest in South Asian Buddhism and Brahmanism, and he fiercely supported Indian independence. He urged his friends to read the Hindu devotional poem, the *Bhagavad Gita*, and wrote widely of his commitment to vegetarianism as a linchpin of a humane civilization. His pioneering polemic, *Animals' Rights Considered in Relation to Social Progress* (1892), made an explicit case for vegetarianism as a necessary component of the humane movement.

Salt was widely admired among animal advocates in America and India, including Mary Lovell, George Angell, Francis Rowley, and most famously, Mahatma Gandhi. He introduced Gandhi to the work of Henry David Thoreau whose writings on civil disobedience influenced Gandhi's approach to the *Swaraj* (self-rule) movement.[97] In reading Salt's biography of Thoreau, Gandhi would encounter a worldview strikingly similar to his own. Salt lauded Thoreau's vegetarianism, asceticism, and pluralistic spiritual beliefs, which were evident in his large library of diverse religious texts, including the *Bhagavad Gita*, the *Vedas*, and the *Laws of Manu*, which he read in French and German translations. When a Harvard visitor at Walden told Thoreau that he was studying "the Scriptures," Thoreau immediately replied, "But *which*?"[98] Salt noted that Thoreau's "extraordinary sympathy with animals was one of the most singular and pleasing features in [his] character."[99] In portraying Thoreau as a pioneering American humanitarian, Salt stressed how his "sense of brotherhood" and "singular humanity to animals" were inextricably tied to his vegetarian "faith in the humanities of diet."[100] Put another way, Salt's Thoreau offered a groundbreaking pluralistic American gospel of vegetarian kindness to animals. In his other writings, Salt accentuated the incompatibility between animal protectionism and meat eating in the baldest terms through imaginary arguments between vegetarians and skeptics: "Vegetarian: 'Not cruel, I suppose?' Bon Vivant: 'Cruel! I subscribe regularly to the Society for the Prevention of Cruelty to Animals.' Vegetarian: 'And *eat* them.' "[101]

In the late nineteenth and early twentieth centuries, the Theosophists also introduced American audiences to hybridized South Asian traditions of ahimsa and vegetarianism. Founded in 1875 by a Ukrainian occultist, Madame Helena Blavatsky, and an American Civil War colonel, Henry Steel Olcott, in New York City, Theosophy was a colorful, prismatic fusion of myriad transnational religious philosophies, including American spirit rapping, Mesmerism, Hinduism, Buddhism, and Blavatsky's vivid visions of "Himalayan Masters" who guided the universe.[102] Bathed in romantic orientalist notions of Indian piety, Theosophists argued that the spiritual East

(India) represented the basis for all spiritual thought. Olcott and Blavatsky sold everything they owned to move to India in late 1878.

Many Indians quickly denounced the émigré Theosophists as charlatan mystics, but the organization gained a wide permanent following in India, Sri Lanka, Britain, and the United States.[103] In Britain, Theosophist physician Anna Kingsford wrote vividly about the dangers of meat consumption and the virtues of vegetarianism using civilizationist language that echoed Sylvester Graham: "If we are to justify ourselves in killing and eating [animals] because some of the fiercer races among them kill and eat one another, we might by the same logic, decend [sic] to their plane in respect of all other practices attractive to low-minded and vicious men, and revert to polygamy, disregard of personal rights, and still worse manners. For if certain animals see no harm in bloodshed, neither do they see harm in theft, rapine, and seduction."[104] In the United States, Katherine Tingley led the Theosophical Society of America (renamed the United Brotherhood of Theosophists); she lectured widely at home and abroad against poverty, capital punishment, and vivisection.[105] In 1900 she established the Raja-Yoga Academy, a sprawling headquarters at Point Loma, California, where vegetarianism was a guiding tenet.[106] Americans also became acquainted with Theosophy on the pages of *Our Dumb Animals*. In April 1904, for example, the magazine reported that Theosophists were holding a worldwide day of prayer against vivisection.[107]

The example of India also prompted American animal advocates to criticize contemporary impounding practices, euthanasia, and rabies prevention policies, particularly the violent urban spectacle of the American summertime dog roundup. In 1909, a reader of *Our Dumb Animals* stressed the superlative kindness of the Jains as a contrast to the uneven record of the American humane movement: "The Jains are strict vegetarians, and will not kill anything that breathes, even for food. . . . They differ from you [the MSPCA] in one respect, in that animals, whatever their condition, are never 'mercifully put to death.' These kind-hearted people build houses for birds, and place food and water for them in public places. They will not even kill a fly or mosquito."[108] The example of India even made an appearance at a eulogy for George Angell, who died on March 16, 1909. The Reverend Thomas Van Ness remembered how Angell's commitment to stewardship rebutted South Asian critiques of Christian animal cruelty: "While strong, vigorous, and educational, [Christianity] yet has small respect for sentient life, the animal, the bird, the water creature. To the gentle followers of Buddha one can easily understand why Christianity presents this aspect of cruelty. If the reproach is merited it has been lifted from the Western nations by the work of George T. Angell."[109]

Cow Protection

Many American animal advocates idealized South Asian religious traditions of ahimsa and vegetarianism. In colonial India, however, a dangerous vegetarian Hindu cow protection movement was taking shape at the turn of the twentieth century. Colonial legislation and judicial rulings played a central role in sparking and sustaining this movement. Despite Queen Victoria's official statement of religious non-interference in the post-Mutiny Proclamation of 1858, British policies helped foster a reactionary new identity politics among Hindus who felt that their religion was under siege. In 1888 the British North-Western Provincial High Court declared that cows were not sacred and consequently were not covered under Section 295 of the Indian Penal Code.[110]

For Hindus who already perceived the colonial state to be a tacit agent of Christian evangelism, the ruling posed a direct threat to their religious identity. Soon thereafter, the cow protection movement formed in the Punjab and then spread across Uttar Pradesh and other parts of northern India. Hindu elites spearheaded the movement in urban environments. Cow protection spread into rural areas via itinerant orators, wandering holy men, and printed materials.[111] Participants devoted themselves to saving the lives of cattle slated for religious sacrifice and ordinary butchering. Cow protection societies targeted Muslims who sacrificed cattle as part of Baqar Eid (in ceremonial observance of the sacrifice of Ishmael by Ibrahim), and they assailed low-caste Hindus who sold cattle to Muslims for sacrificial purposes, slaughtered cows themselves, or worked with leather. The colonial state further fanned suspicions when it transferred Hindu officials, such as *tahsildars* (tax collectors), who were involved in cow protection.[112]

Cow protection activities ranged from benign acts of stewardship to outright violence. Some activists simply purchased cattle destined for slaughter and placed them in well-funded gaushalas. Other activists were provocateurs.[113] In the village of Akhop (in the modern state of Uttar Pradesh), four men led twenty-five others armed with *lathis* (heavy sticks) to the home of a local Muslim. The mob demanded 100 rupees as a subscription to the local cow protection fund and threatened to pillage his home if he did not join. All four were sentenced to three months of "rigourous imprisonment" and two of the four were also fined 100 rupees.[114] Hindu leatherworkers and agents who were engaged in the cow trade with Muslims were harassed, beaten, and bullied in the courts. At still other times, cow protection activism turned deadly. In 1893, huge Hindu mobs in eastern Uttar Pradesh killed a dozen Muslims practicing their legal right to sacrifice, along with several Muslim bystanders.[115] The *New York Times* editorialized that the cow riots evoked memories of the Sepoy Rebellion of 1857, arguing that stronger colonial rule was necessary through liberal use of "the stick."[116] Ultimately, cow protectionism helped consolidate the formation of a wider Hindu public opposed to British rule but also increasingly intolerant of diverse religious practices.

Mahatma Gandhi remained steadfast in his nationalist commitment to religious and cultural pluralism, a position that enhanced his considerable popularity among Americans. *Time Magazine*, for example, named him its "Man of the Year" for 1930. Gandhi, however, also actively supported cow protection. His weekly journal, *Young India*, his newspaper, the *Harijan* (Untouchable), and his lectures charted his complicated relationship with the cow. In some respects, Gandhi seemed to embrace the same sort of Hindu exceptionalism that he flatly rejected elsewhere as a potential form of social fragmentation: "Cow protection is the gift of Hinduism to the world. And Hinduism will live so long as there are Hindus to protect the cow."[117] Gandhi justified the sacred status of the selfless, steady cow, with her bountiful milk, as a civilizing life force responsible for the birth of agriculture and a more reliable source of sustenance than the human mother: "Mother cow is in many ways better than the mother who gave us birth. Our mother gives us milk for a couple of years and then expects us to serve her when we grow up. Mother cow expects from us nothing but grass and grain."[118] Because of the cow's centrality to life and civilization, Gandhi claimed that cow protection was the foundation of ahimsa: "A Hindu who protects the cow should protect every animal."[119]

Yet while Gandhi believed wholeheartedly in what he called "cow service," he flatly rejected state legislation that would prohibit cow slaughter, unless the "intelligent majority of its Musalman [Muslim] population" supported it.[120] Like other transnational animal advocates, Gandhi asserted that real change was only possible through interfaith friendship and education, in other words, moral suasion and humane education: "[Hindus] must trust by befriending Musalmans, that the latter will, of their own accord, give up cow sacrifice out of regard for their Hindu neighbors. . . . Cow slaughter can never be stopped by law. Knowledge, education, and the spirit of kindliness toward her alone, can put an end to it."[121] Gandhi believed that state-mandated religious freedom would best ensure the transformation of individual hearts and minds.

Gandhi unequivocally rejected cow protection by force. He denounced Hindus who snatched cows and goats away from Muslims at fairs, and he emphatically condemned cow protectionists who resorted to violence: "To attempt cow protection by violence is to reduce Hinduism to Satanism and to prostitute to a base end the grand significance of cow protection."[122] Gandhi noted that Hindu cattle dealers, pinjrapole operators, and dairymen accounted for roughly three-quarters of all cattle deaths each year. By contrast, Muslim butchers and participants in Baqar Eid accounted for only a quarter of all annual cattle deaths.[123] Gandhi concluded that the state should control all aspects of the cattle market, especially the ownership and operation of all dairies, to guarantee inexpensive and healthful milk for the poor.[124] In essence, he believed that structural change, that is, the "economic side of the cow question," would solve the "delicate religious side" of this fractious form of animal protection.[125]

Katherine Mayo and the "Drain Inspector's Report"

American journalist Katherine Mayo was equally interested in cows, but solely for the purpose of discrediting Gandhi and the Indian independence movement writ large in her worldwide bestseller, *Mother India* (1927). An adversary of independence movements wholesale (she was equally hostile to Philippine nationalism), Mayo supported a strong state police force, and she praised the Johnson-Reed Immigration Act of 1924, which virtually banned immigration from Asia to the United States.[126] Although Mayo claimed to be an unbiased American outsider, "unsubsidized, uncommitted, and unattached," the British government supported her work at every turn.[127] Scholars have written widely about Mayo's focus on suffering Indian women and children as a potent affective strategy for burnishing the moral superiority of Western women trying to rescue their vulnerable Eastern sisters from sati, child marriage, female infanticide, and other forms of patriarchal violence.[128] But this universalizing project of female uplift was also dependent on universalizing Christian ideologies of animal mercy.

Mayo fixed her sights on South Asian animals in "Part Four: Mr. Gandhi." Point by point, she challenged Gandhi's writings about cows and animal protection to discredit Hinduism. She flatly dismissed Gandhi's vision of cow service, claiming (and echoing earlier strands of missionary thought) that Hinduism had transformed the cow into a holy parasite: "India is being eaten up by its own cattle. And even at that the cattle are starving."[129] She denied that gaushalas and pinjrapoles represented an indigenous commitment to animal welfare. Rather, these so-called animal sanctuaries and hospitals were dumping grounds for unwanted animals, whose abject status was shared by Indian child brides, discarded widows, and *devadasis* (temple dancers/prostitutes) in a morally corrupt society where mothers reportedly fed opium to fussy babies. Mayo recounted her first visit to a gaushala, recounting scenes of calves packed in tiny pens, separated from their mothers, fed only a "tea-cupful" of milk a day: "Some [cows] had great open sores at which the birds, perched on their hipbones or their staring ribs, picked and tore. Some had broken legs that dangled and flopped as they stirred. Many were diseased. All were obviously starved."[130]

Throughout *Mother India*, Mayo transmogrified ahimsa into a hypocritical philosophy of apathy, cowardice, and implicit torture because it forbade euthanasia: "In the land of ahimsa, the rarest of sins is that of allowing a crumb of food to a starving dog, or equally, of putting him out of his misery."[131] Mayo also obsessively described the practice of *phuka* (increased milk production through physical irritation of the cow's reproductive parts) and flaying goats alive for supple leather, much of which was sold to American merchants, as additional evidence of Indian barbarism.[132]

Mayo repeatedly contended that British India's animal laws were the product of a merciful colonial state, insisting (incorrectly) that all Indian animal welfare policies were strictly British in origin: "Britain, by example and by teaching, has been working for nearly three-quarters of a century to implant her own ideas of mercy on an alien soil. . . . And, given a people still barbarian in their handling of their own women, it is scarcely to be expected that they should yet have taken on a mentality responsive to the appeal of dumb creatures."[133] Mayo even credited the British for a clean, successful Indian-run dairy near Bombay, because its owner had been British trained.[134] Mayo argued that a contemporary movement to Indianize the SPCA was a grave misstep resulting from a foolish and reckless experiment in racial integration: "Dumb creation pays with its body the costs of the experiment."[135]

Indian nationalists dismissed Mayo's diatribe as an outrageous attempt to delegitimize their right to self-determination through hypocritical imperial hyperboles of savagery and kindness. According to Gandhi: "Her case is to perpetuate white domination in India on the plea of India's unfitness to rule herself."[136] While acknowledging that the book was "cleverly and powerfully written," Gandhi likened Mayo's analysis to the quotidian "drain inspector's report" made "with the one purpose of opening and examining the drains of the country . . . to give a graphic description of the stench exhuded [*sic*] by the opened drain. . . . If I open out and describe with punctilious care all the stench exhuded from the drains of London and say 'Behold London,' my facts will be incapable of challenge, but my judgment will be rightly condemned as a travesty of truth. Miss Mayo's book is nothing better, nothing else."[137]

Gandhi and fellow nationalists reversed Mayo's diatribes of Indian suffering into an indictment of American and British cruelty. Hardly the enlightened and exceptional guardians of progressive uplift, British imperialism instead caused India's "ever-growing emasculation," creating a brutal colonial society in which "electrocution is a humaner [sic] method of killing than the tortuous method of roasting alive ... a humane deliverance from the living and ignominious death which we are going through in the present moment."[138] The Punjabi politician and author Lala Lajpat Rai criticized Mayo's strategy of using phuka and goats flayed alive to condemn Indian civilization, when she overlooked cruel British and American fur and feather fashions.[139] The Bengali nationalist poet Rabindranath Tagore chastised Mayo for falsely claiming that Hindus consumed cow dung and urine, while overlooking the "uncivilized" Western carnivore: "as eaters of live creatures or of rotten food, mentioning oysters and cheese for illustration."[140] Tagore juxtaposed ideologies of American moral superiority and Christian virtue with examples of American depravity, ranging from meat eating, consumerism, and sexual titillation in the cinema, to the shocking regularity of lynching.[141]

Charles Freer Andrews, an Anglican priest and close confidante of Gandhi, likewise denounced Mayo's hollow assertions of American superiority in a serialized rebuttal, which appeared in twelve consecutive issues of *Young India* in 1928. While Andrews was wholeheartedly committed to religious pluralism, his discussion of animals bore the stamp of Hindu exceptionalism: "No country in the world can show a higher or nobler record in this direction than Hindu India. ... It is one of the most beautiful things in the world, which has to be seen by western eyes to be understood."[142] His characterization of the United States sounded little different from Mayo's orientalist portrayal of India: sexually debauched, racist, violent, and decadent. Andrews chronicled the shock and disgust of Indian audiences as they read about the treatment of animals in America: the hunt and slaughter of "panic-stricken deer by dogs and men"; the bloody stockyard "shambles of Chicago" from Upton Sinclair's *Jungle*; graphic photographs of blood-sports "undertaken solely for amusement"; and the open acceptance of vivisection as an essential component of scientific progress.[143] Just as diverse Americans—from George Angell to Katherine Mayo—judged Indian civilization to be either "advanced" or "savage" on the basis of its treatment of animals, South Asian critics and their allies used the persistence of animal cruelty to indict America's self-proclaimed benevolence.

A FAMOUS QUOTATION attributed to Mahatma Gandhi acknowledges the ideological connections between animal mercy, civilization, and nationhood: "The greatness of a nation and its moral progress can be judged by the way its animals are treated." Diverse transnational animal advocates shared Gandhi's universalizing sentiments, but for different cultural and political reasons. British empire builders implemented South Asian animal welfare legislation as a cornerstone of colonial uplift, civilization, and benign social control. Conservative American missionaries and their compatriots like Katherine Mayo used Hindu, Buddhist, and Jain traditions of vegetarianism and ahimsa to validate British colonial rule and discredit Indian claims of sovereignty. By contrast, liberal American missionaries and SPCA advocates used these same Indian religious traditions to critique America's own "moral progress" and to expand, in time, the scope of their own gospel of kindness to include vegetarianism in the twentieth century. Indian reformers and independence leaders similarly used the status of animals to validate their own claims of sovereignty and to condemn British and American domination. Across these far-flung cultural fields, class remained a critical flashpoint for conflict between animal protectionists and the accused. Diverse constituents defined their rights of citizenship vis-à-vis their interactions with animals, which also laid bare extant cultural, social, and economic hierarchies.

And yet specific aspects of colonial South Asian animal protectionism were culturally unique. Caste and religion shaped animal welfare politics in ways that were not lost to Indian politicians after Independence in 1947. The animal advocate and member of India's Parliament, Shrimati Rukmini Devi Arundale, announced that India's religious traditions of ahimsa made the nation uniquely positioned for global moral leadership: "India must set a great example to all countries in the world. . . . The very word Ahimsa comes from India; it belongs to us."[144] Yet such universalizing rhetoric portended a cultural divide: cow nationalism grew out of the cleavages of colonial policy, caste, religion, and nationalism. While Gandhi saw cow protection as a universalizing moral call, India's specific historical and cultural circumstances of caste, pluralism, and colonialism spawned a dangerous politics of communalism. Cow protection escalated into cow nationalism, which became a flashpoint for the dangerous social and cultural divisions that bedevil South Asia to this day. In America, cow nationalism also told its own story of nation and empire building—illuminating the history of continental expansion, cattle drives, the mythic Wild West, and the nostalgic masculine figure of the Anglo cowboy vis-à-vis the "barbaric" American Indian. When it took the form of a fighting bull, cow nationalism grappled directly with America's own history of empire building, Spanish imperialism, and the gospel of kindness.

6

"So Thoroughly Un-American"

MAKING HISTORICAL SENSE OF THE BULLFIGHT

LETTERS BOMBARDED TEXAS Governor James V. Allred from far and wide in May and June, 1936: Hastings, Nebraska; Malone, New York; Fergus Falls, Minnesota; Flint, Michigan; Boston; Orlando, Florida; Deerfield, Illinois; Philadelphia; Darlington, Wisconsin; Greenville, South Carolina; Hartford Connecticut; Washington, DC, and elsewhere.[1] The tone was urgent. Mrs. Ella M. Megginson of Webster Groves, Missouri, implored Governor Allred: "Please do not let Texas be the first to introduce anything so thoroughly un-American."[2] What activity was "so thoroughly un-American" that even its mere mention catalyzed a national grassroots letter-writing campaign? Bullfighting. By 1936, a majority of American states had banned bullfighting through statutes against blood sports modeled after New York's revised anticruelty statute (1867). Texas law, however, was vague. While the state's revised statutes in 1879 included language "to prohibit and punish the abuse of animals," there remained no explicit reference to bullfighting.[3]

Animal welfare advocates were doubly horrified to learn that this "un-American" bullfight might take place in Dallas at the Central Centennial Exposition of 1936, where fair organizers promised patrons thrilling and uplifting historical lessons and outsized Texas pride: "No other state has had such a glorious history.... It is good for the world to know the part that Texas has played and may play in building our great western civilization. Every well-informed, true-loyal Texan believes that such information will be helpful to others in their efforts to promote Christian civilization. This is the principal reason that the Texas Centennial should be held."[4]

This language of civilization, progress, Christianity, and patriotism had pervaded American world's fairs ever since the first was held in Philadelphia in 1876.⁵ As a celebration of progressive betterment, world's fairs were ideal sites for animal advocacy. Instructive exhibits of cruelty and mercy provided a thoughtful coda to displays of material progress, such as new engines and canned goods. At Philadelphia, the ASPCA's display documented animal cruelty in multiple media: photographs of sore-ridden work horses, spiked clubs to drive urban livestock, humane pamphlets, and taxidermy bodies of a bulldog mangled in a dogfight and bloodied roosters after a cockfight. A visitor from out of state characterized the ASPCA exhibit as "a sickening evidence of the depravity of human brutes. . . . So long as men are cruel to beasts, they will be cruel to each other; and these Humane Societies should be aided by every one, who feels any desire to see humanity and public morals on a higher plane."⁶

At the Louisiana Purchase Exposition at St. Louis in 1904, the horse celebrity Beautiful Jim Key demonstrated the remarkable consequences of kindness training. He delighted audiences with his performances of equine intelligence and mathematical know-how.⁷ Beautiful Jim's African American owner, William "Doc" Key, was a former slave, Civil War veteran, self-educated veterinarian, impresario, and horse whisperer in the spirit of Jonathan Solomon Rarey. The Keys' exhibitions at St. Louis came with an official stamp of approval from George Angell, who proclaimed Doc Key and Jim Key honorary members of the "Parent American Band of Mercy" in 1900.⁸ The American Anti-Vivisection Society (AAVS) likewise sponsored pedagogical exhibitions at the Louisiana Purchase Exposition, which constituted a chilling, dystopian counter-narrative to American medical progress: "life-like" animal models depicted the grotesque process of experimentation; sharp, menacing instruments used in actual procedures were displayed and informational leaflets warned audiences about pets snatched and tortured in the name of science, such as a medical trial in which two puppies were sewn together.⁹ The shocking evidence of bodily suffering provided a swift, effective tutorial in humane education.

At the same time, the scientific and commercial uses of animal bodies for food, muscle power, and medical advancement were prominently featured in displays of American innovation. At Buffalo's Pan-American exhibition in 1901, the Mexican Exhibits catalogue showcased the "hygienic" Department of Epidemiology and its chemical and bacteriological laboratories where "animals or birds are kept for the practice of scientific experiments."¹⁰ Scientific animal exhibitions generally took place without incident, even when antivivisection displays were shown elsewhere on the fairgrounds.

Bullfights were another story, however. In a prelude to the troubles at the Texas Centennial, the organizers of the Cotton States and International Exposition in Atlanta in 1895 figured that a bloodless Portuguese/French bullfight in the Mexican Village at the Midway would provide fairgoers with an entertaining glimpse of "authentic" Mexican life. The immediate "tremendous and angry chorus of condemnation" surprised fair officials when they announced their plans. As a result, the bullfight was canceled and a group of idled Mexican toreros were left with nothing to do.[11]

By attempting to bring a bullfight to the midway, the Atlanta promoters recognized a common dialectic at international exhibitions: audiences expected entertainment in addition to uplift. Similarly in Dallas, Centennial organizers treated the proposed bullfight as a lucrative complement to the novel pleasures already scheduled on the program: a Midget Village, amateur boxing tournaments, rodeos, a pet parade, beekeeping exhibitions, demonstrations with homing pigeons, football games, a Centennial circus, stock shows, a troupe of Cuban Yanyego Voodoo dancers, jazz, and the Jungle Show featuring the famous Texas-born animal dealer Frank "Bring 'Em Back Alive" Buck.[12]

None of the proposed animal entertainments sparked the kind of national outrage that met the possibility of a bullfight—even when promoters promised a bloodless performance. This wholesale censure was even more striking considering the ubiquitous animal amusements humane activists generally ignored at the Centennial: the rodeo, circus, and stock exhibitions. Fundamentally, the bullfight struck a deep cultural nerve connected to long-standing ideologies of civilization, savagery, and complementary histories of colonial conquest.

This chapter explores the bullfight as an American crucible for articulating ideas about civilization and benevolent nation and empire building. The historical shadow of colonial Spain is essential to understanding American views of the bullfight at the Texas Centennial and elsewhere. The bullfight's cultural meanings broadened after the United States won the majority of Spain's empire in 1898. Holding fast to President McKinley's proclamation of "benevolent assimilation" regarding American rule in the Philippines, animal protectionists, policymakers, religious leaders, and travel writers trumpeted American bullfighting bans across the new empire as concrete proof of American exceptionalism in practice. By contrast, they pointed to the continued popularity of blood sports in Spain as a clear sign of the nation's moral bankruptcy and inevitable decline.

The pernicious "Black Legend," or "Leyenda Negra," influenced the cultural status of the bullfight in America. A long-standing anti-Spanish propaganda campaign waged by rival nations, the Black Legend crystallized when enemies of Spain appropriated the nation's own dissenting views about its imperial project in the Americas to argue that imperial violence and religious intolerance were uniquely Spanish.[13] (Colonial subjects, however, saw little distinction between early Spanish and British conquest.) The sixteenth-century Dominican friar, Bartolomé de las Casas, unwittingly laid the foundation for the Black Legend by condemning his country's enslavement of native Amerindians in his *Brevíssima Relación de la Destrucción de las Indias* (A Very Short Account of the Destruction of the Indies, 1552).[14] The Black Legend flared with greater intensity in the United States during the Mexican War (1846–1848) and the Spanish-American War (1898). A new edition of las Casas published in 1898 fortified American perceptions of Spanish colonialism as antithetical to their own merciful empire of liberty. While anti-Spanish propaganda had circulated transnationally since the sixteenth century, the Black Legend itself remained unnamed until 1912 when a Spanish journalist, Julián Juderías, coined the phrase to protest the ubiquity of anti-Spanish representations.[15]

This chapter ranges geographically from Spain to its former empire in Mexico, the Caribbean, the American borderlands, and Texas. American travel literature and newspaper reportage used the bullfight a stand-in for nation, race, class, gender, and Catholicism. American critics paid close attention to Mexico, a former Spanish colony, an empire in its own right, and a neighboring home to "Latin" blood sports.[16] American tourists eagerly crossed the border for colorful leisure activities and exoticized spectacles, while animal welfare critics apprehensively referred to Mexico's open bullrings as a potential moral contaminant on Texas and the entire US border. The steady flow of American traffic to animal fights underscored the permeability of the border and the potential for spreading moral decay, which critics likened to the endemic infectious diseases that also moved easily across the border.[17] The bullfight entered the diplomatic sphere as a potential source of US tourist dollars to Latin America, and as a target of US humane reform. The transnational history of the bullfight and its American opponents provides a necessary prologue to the controversy at the Texas Centennial during the summer of 1936, when the famous American "Bullfighter from Brooklyn" Sydney Franklin and a Mexican bullfighting syndicate battled an Anglo-Protestant consortium of cultural brokers over the pluralistic meanings of Texas history and American civilization.

Encountering the Bullfight Abroad

Near the end of her life in July 1946, writer Gertrude Stein urged Richard Wright to visit Spain: "You'll see the past there. You'll see what the Western world is made of. Spain is primitive, but lovely. . . . See those bullfights, see that wonderful landscape."[18] Stein's characterization echoed how the Black Legend had translated Spain into "Europe's racialized internal other," a pluralistic, orientalized crossroads of Judaism, Islam, and Catholicism.[19] A traditional tourist destination for northern Europeans and Americans, Spain offered copious regional festivals and feast days, which spectacularly displayed the interconnections of religion, ritual, leisure, and animals. The culture of "Tauromachy," or bullfighting, was entwined with nearly every aspect of festal Catholic Spain.

The bullfight was the keystone of the Spanish travelogue. This focus was of such long duration that as early as 1789, the British officer Alexander Jardine opted to skip a full discussion of bullfighting in his letters from Spain because it was such a familiar topic: "I shall not trouble you with the particulars about the Spanish bull-fights, as they have been so often described."[20] The American periodical *Ballou's Dollar Monthly Magazine* succinctly captured the contradictory allure in 1855: "[Bullfighting] is a barbarous, terrible and sanguinary spectacle, but, unquestionably, full of seduction and excitement."[21] Or, as Ernest Hemingway perceptively noted seventy-seven years later, "Bullfighting is based on the fact that it is the first meeting between the wild animal and a dismounted man. This is the fundamental premise of modern bullfighting."[22] Richard Wright recounted the irresistible lure of this elemental encounter between man and beast in his travelogue, *Pagan Spain*, which devoted twenty-six pages to his experiences at a bullfight in 1954: "I was revolted, but hungry for more. I was indignant, but bewitched, utterly. . . . Man and beast had now become fused into one plastic, slow-moving, terrible waltz of death, the outcome of which hung upon the breath of a split second."[23]

The structure of the modern, familiar *corrida de torro* (bullfight, or literally "running of the bulls"), which took shape in the eighteenth century, was highly ordered. The *corrida* contained a strict division of labor among paid professional *toreros*, or bullfighters, and took place in a formal, often architecturally grand, bullring, or *Plaza de Toros*. Yet other forms of bullfighting were more malleable: virtually any male villager could participate in the free-form *vaquillas* (bullfight with young bulls), *encierros* (running alongside the bulls in transport), or *capea* (amateur fight), which took place in improvised bullrings or village streets. Most American writing about bullfighting addressed the formal, timed corrida de torro, which involved three professional *espadas,* or matadors, and five assistants. Six mature bulls between the ages of four and five years old were killed in precisely programmed increments of twenty minutes for each fight. Each *torero* (the collective term for any paid bullfighter) fought twice. Each fight contained three ritual parts, or *tercios.* The first tercio involved the two mounted *picadors* on horseback, who used a lance or pike to spear the bull's neck muscles. In the second tercio, three *banderilleros* approached the bull on foot and stuck his neck hump with barbed spears (*banderillas*) festooned with fluttery ribbons and paper flowers. In the last tercio, the *espada* or matador, made a series of graceful passes (*veronicas*) in front of the bull using a cape. The last tercio ended when the espada plunged a short sword into the bull's neck, severing his aorta. Known as the *hora de la verdad,* or "moment of truth," the bull died instantly if the espada was skilled.[24] Nonetheless, there was always a chance that the espada would die violently in the bullring, which heightened the corrido's unnerving pull.[25]

American spectators condemned the bullfight for its absence of fair chase. Encircled by thousands of viewers, who "howled like a band of demons," the bull was fatally trapped in the ring.[26] Thomas Ewing Moore, a secretary of the American Diplomatic Service and Secretary of the Legation at Lisbon, recoiled at the inevitability of the bull's demise, concluding that the corrida was a ritual of emasculated cowardice: "To call such a spectacle, or any part of it, sport, or to give it any name which does not stigmatize the calculated cruelty of the strong over the weak, is to condone it. It is a grim exhibition of how far the avoidance of fair-play can be carried."[27] Even Hemingway observed philosophically that bullfighting should not be called a sport: "The formal bullfight is a tragedy, not a sport, and the bull is certain to be killed."[28]

While American critics readily called the corrida as a violent spectacle, they generally paid less attention to the bull's suffering than to the moral consequences of the bullfight experience, including the deafening enthusiasm of the roaring crowds. Once killed in the ring, the bull would be eaten, which ultimately reinforced his near-universal status as a food animal. Fundamentally, the bull was a commodity, whose fate was already sealed: eventually he would be slaughtered for his meat, bones, and hide, even after serving as a valuable breeder because semen potency diminished with age. His death at the bullfight was simply premature.

The suffering and death of the mounted picador horses in the bullring, by contrast, sparked consistent outrage. Wearing blinders, these vulnerable animals could not even anticipate the bull's attack. Equine death in the bullring

FIGURE 6.1. Despite its barrage of color, roaring crowds, and violence, the bullfight was a highly structured three-part blood sport, which ended with the "moment of truth," when the *espada*, or matador, plunged a short sword into the bull's neck, an imminent event captured in this sketch. "Untitled," in John Hay, *Castilian Days* (1871; reprint, Boston: Houghton Mifflin, 1913), 116.

was often spectacularly gruesome. Frenzied by the picador's lance, bulls routinely disemboweled horses with their horns. Journalist and sociologist George E. Vincent wrote of "terribly lacerated" horses making "a wild circuit of the ring and leave a hideous trail of copious blood."[29] Secretary of State John Hay described gory scenes of dangling viscera and dying horses: "It is incredible to see what these poor creatures will endure—carrying their riders at a lumbering gallop over the ring, when their thin sides seem empty of entrails. Sometimes the bull comes upon the dead body of a horse he has killed. The smell of blood and the unmoving helplessness of the victim excite him to the highest pitch. He gores and tramples the carcass, and tosses it in the air with evident enjoyment, until diverted by some living tormentor."[30]

The suffering of the captive picador horses was so graphic that some American commentators indirectly endorsed an older, virtually extinct form of bullfighting that flourished in medieval Spain among the nobility, *toreo de rejones* (bullfighting with lances). In contrast to the rigid corporate structure of the modern bullfight with its *tercios* of picadors, banderilleros, and espada, the individual mounted nobleman of medieval and early modern Spain charged around the ring and took aim at the bull with his lance; the distance between the pivoting horse and bull usually prevented routine equine eviscerations.[31]

American animal advocates pointed to the grisly plight of the picador horse when denouncing the Spanish corrida as a violation of international moral conduct. American diplomat Thomas Ewing Moore called on the League of Nations to ban the Spanish bullfight in the 1920s: "It is a mission far more urgent than handing over majorities to minorities; playing at territorial delimitations . . . engaging in a dozen other futile [League of Nations] tinkerings. Cannot public opinion, so reinforced, lend its authority to an errand of mercy in Spain?"[32] Cardinal Merry del Val of Rome heartily agreed, arguing that bullfighting was worse than prizefighting and "ought to be abolished."[33] In response to widespread international pressure, the administration of Spanish Prime Minister Primo de Rivera mandated the use of thick, protective body pads on picador horses in 1929.[34]

Even with protection, horses were routinely injured and sometimes killed. Ernest Hemingway reflected that the battered condition of such worn-out horses when they entered the ring—frail, old, tattered, and thin—rendered them almost unrecognizable as equines. Hemingway maintained that the death of the picador equine was not tragic because "the tragic climax of the horse's career has occurred off stage at an earlier time; when he was bought by the horse contractor for use in the bull ring."[35] Only those exhausted, decrepit horses no longer possessing any monetary value as laborers were candidates for the bullring. The grim fate of the picador horse was simply one of several ghastly outcomes for the urban cab horse, who was routinely beaten, worked to death, and abandoned in the streets.

Yet the constant outrage over the suffering picador horse suggests that Americans felt differently about horses than bulls. Although equines were commoditized as laboring muscle, entertainment, transportation, hide, and gelatinized bone, their flesh was rarely eaten in the United States and primarily during hard times. (The Harvard Club represented one of the few exceptions, offering horse steak on its menu until the late 1970s.)[36] Horses were central actors in complementary mythologies of American nation building and manifest destiny. They transported Euroamerican settlers across the continent and were important partners with two key cultural figures: the self-reliant cowboy and the Lakota warrior. Taken together, horses, cowboys, and Plains Indians became popular performers in triumphal narratives of American civilization and conquest, such as William F. "Buffalo Bill" Cody's Wild West and Congress of Rough Riders of the World, which traveled across the nation and toured abroad. To be sure, cattle were essential participants in westward expansion, but the horse's charismatic beauty and its centrality to human transportation and agricultural cultivation heightened the interspecies bond. More often than not, people named their horses. The intimacy of riding or driving a sociable fellow creature and communicating through bodily contact, pressure, and sound also intensified the emotional nature of human and horse interactions. The first organized SPCAs tacitly acknowledged this special relationship in making the bedraggled urban cab horse the centerpiece of their protectionist agenda.

Additionally, the horse was slowly transitioning from a laborer to a cherished pet. With the introduction of gasoline-powered automobiles in the 1890s, journalists wrote nostalgically about the impending disappearance of the working horse.[37] While this sentiment was factually premature because horses remained an essential source of power until World War II, it nonetheless signaled a shift in cultural attitudes. A spate of highly sentimental novels featuring horse protagonists, from *Black Beauty* (1877) to *My Friend Flicka* (1941), celebrated the horse as a sentient, soulful companion to humanity. In the context of a long, special historical relationship between Americans and horses, the agonizing demise of the picador horse, represented a special outrage for critics of the corrida.

Americans and other foreign travel writers considered the entire bullfight experience—the pushing crowds, absence of fair chase, and the spectral equine disemboweling—as a sign of a declining civilization.[38] Italian criminal sociologist Cesare Lombroso wrote that bullfighting, the Inquisition, and the flow of easy riches from the New World spawned ignorance, intolerance, and uncontrollable atavism. Lombroso noted that Calomardo, the minister of King Ferdinand VII (1784–1833), had gutted funding for the humanities "and replaced them by schools for bullfighting," a move which hardened the

Spanish into a people "who take delight in the cruel fate of human beings who are torn to pieces in an arena and who deify a torero."[39]

Other critics used the bullfight to indict Spanish Catholicism.[40] Writing in *Our Dumb Animals*, South Carolina poet and novelist Kadra Maysi concluded that the persistence of animal cruelty embodied the "riddle" of devout Spain, particularly in the bullring.[41] The torero often carried amulets and gave thanks to the protection of the saints. US Secretary of State John Hay summarily characterized the toreros as "all very pious, and glad to curry favor with the saints by attributing every success to their intervention." Hay branded the bullring a virtual church in its own right, with a small chapel in the torero waiting area "where these devout ruffians can toss off a prayer or two in the intervals of work." A priest always stood by with a consecrated wafer, "to visa the torero's passport who has to start suddenly for Paradise."[42] Such descriptions reinforced Protestant stereotypes of Catholics as fatalistic, superstitious, and fundamentally animistic in their devotion to animal rituals and transubstantiation. Moreover, they complemented mythologies of the Black Legend with equally powerful Protestant stereotypes of Catholic Spain as the so-called "Sick Man of Europe," stagnant, hidebound by archaic traditions, anti-individualistic, and susceptible to despotism.

American writers judged Spanish Catholic society to be virtually feudal, comprising an all-powerful church and nobility that owned huge tracts of land for breeding generations of bulls. Indeed, *Our Dumb Animals* speculated that bullfighting might wither away during the Second Spanish Republic of the 1930s in part because leftist land reforms had broken up these gigantic medieval church holdings.[43] Even American corrida aficionados, such as Frank L. Kluckhohn of the *New York Times*, made a tacit causal connection among the church, the potential fall of the bullfight, and land redistribution: "Today the poor have come to rule where the rich did, the church has lost its medieval power and the army its feudal position. Not only is the picturesque disappearing and bullfighting with its bright costumes becoming anachronistic, but the bull herds which gave bullfighting its vitality must disappear."[44]

The historical relationship between the Catholic Church and Spanish bullfighting was complicated, however. In 1567, Pope Pius V issued a papal edict that excommunicated all Christian princes who allowed bullfighting in their countries. The edict refused Christian burial to anyone killed in the bullring. Pope Pius was moved to take decisive action by the disturbing numbers of toreros killed in the ring. In the 1500s, bulls often fought in the same arena more than once, which made these intelligent animals dangerously familiar with their surroundings. Because King Philip II and other Spanish royalty ignored the papal edict in the midst of the Protestant Reformation roiling Europe, the church was forced to compromise: bullfighting could continue without papal interference if the bull were to appear only one time in the ring—a concession that translated into a bovine death sentence.[45]

The relationship between the Catholic Church and Spanish bullfighting became increasingly amicable with the rise of the Bourbon dynasty in 1700. During the Spanish Enlightenment, the Bourbon nobility and a new cosmopolitan merchant class rejected (and periodically banned) older Spanish traditions, such as the *toreo de rejones* in favor of continental European (especially French) fashion, manners, gesture, and culture.[46] Severed from its older association with the mounted nobility, the bullfight evolved into a modern, plebian popular form that appealed across socioeconomic classes. The toreros themselves increasingly came from the ranks of a growing urban proletariat, often the former employees of industrial slaughterhouses with experience in killing cows.[47] The three-part corrida was, in short, the product of modernization.

Yet conservative Spaniards and the Catholic Church increasingly viewed bullfighting as a symbol of "timeless," agrarian Spain, thereby clouding its formative ties to urbanization and industrial slaughter in favor of reactionary nation building. Traditionalists rejected French customs as immoral, conspicuous displays of consumption. Because the Francophile Bourbons and their allies had rejected the bullfight, xenophobic traditionalists embraced it even more enthusiastically as a form of cultural nationalism, a bulwark against corrupting outside influences. By 1750, this conservative movement was so dominant that the same aristocracy that had disallowed the bullfight just fifty years earlier became one of its strongest supporters. These cultural nationalists constructed public bullrings, subsidized toreros, and bred tough fighting bulls. In short, elites rejected the cosmopolitan Francophone Enlightenment to become faux plebian populists using the bull as their battle symbol.[48]

Once the Spanish bullfight became a formidable marker of traditionalism and modern identity, church and state were quick to deploy it in the service of national unity. After being roundly defeated by the United States in 1898 in the Spanish-American War, Spanish officials staged patriotic bullfights; crowds wore national colors and the toreros made full-throated nationalistic speeches.[49] In 1899, poet Katharine Lee Bates, author of "America the Beautiful," witnessed jingoistic tauromachy during her travels to *carnival* in Granada: "Notwithstanding all the griefs and losses of the year, Spain has kept her carnival.... One does not need to behold the sickening spectacle [bullfighting] to find out how much these people love it."[50]

American leaders also used the corrida to rally popular opinion in support of military intervention. In a speech before Congress on March 17, 1898, Senator Redfield Proctor of Vermont reported on his recent fact-finding mission to Cuba, where he witnessed General "Butcher" Weyler's pacification policy of *reconcentrado* firsthand. Proctor relayed appalling scenes of Cuban families forcibly rounded up and resettled in barren, barbed wire encampments: "Little children are still walking about with arms and chest terribly emaciated, eyes swollen, and abdomen bloated to three times the natural size. The physicians say these cases are hopeless."[51] Proctor included bullfighting in his broad moral indictment against Spanish violence: "There is a proverb among the Cubans that 'Spanish bulls cannot be bred in Cuba'; that is, that the Cubans, though they are of Spanish blood, are less excitable and of a quieter temperament. Many Cubans whom I met spoke in strong terms against bullfights; that it was a brutal institution introduced and mainly patronized by the Spaniards."[52] Other contemporary American commentators used the bullfight to stand in for Spanish repression and decay in the aftermath of the Spanish-American War. The *Cleveland Gazette* tied Spain's "deadly vapors of stagnation" to its anachronistic bullfights: "Spain should have kept her fences in order and her cattle off the track. The train cannot stop to save material for a bullfight."[53]

American officials pointed to new bullfighting bans in the overseas empire as indisputable proof of America's higher moral purpose as an emancipator, not an imperial power. At a celebration for Cuban president-elect Tomás Palma in 1902, Cubans staged wholesome games and amusements, including baseball, circus performances, and a modified, harmless bullfight. According to the *New York Times*, "The old, brutal bullfights have been prohibited since the American occupation of the island, but lovers of the sport are allowed to regale themselves with a tame imitation, in which a little Cuban bull with padded horns essays combat with the traditional toreadors, picadors, and matadors."[54] Transformed into harmless burlesque through "tame imitation," the bullfight's demise helped American officials and private actors make a case for benevolent assimilation.

American anti-bullfighting policies complemented the views of Cuban nationalists, who considered the corrida and Spanish colonialism to be inseparable. José Martí posited that bullfighting was "a futile bloody spectacle... and against Cuban sentiment for being intimately linked with our colonial past."[55] Reflecting the objectives of American missionaries and policymakers alike in the wake of the Spanish-American War, Cuban nationalists rejected Spanish Catholic traditions in favor of baseball and Protestantism as shared idioms of independence and modernity.[56] While Cuban nationalists quickly denounced the American occupation as a variant of formal imperialism, their enthusiasm for the American bullpen after the demise of the cruel Spanish bullring became an important marker of modern Cuban identity.

Encountering the Bullfight in the American Borderlands

American travel writers, politicians, and humane groups readily applied their representations of Spanish bullfighting to corridas in the United States and the Mexican borderlands. Bullfights were also subject to anticruelty laws in the United States, which applied to blood sports and animal baiting. Corridas regularly appeared along the frontier borderlands and occasionally in American cities with immigrant ethnic neighborhoods. In both locations, animal advocates treated the bullfight as a visceral symbol of disorder, contagion, and frontier lawlessness; consequently, policing the corrida represented another way to define the proper boundaries of American civilization.

Geographically positioned on the physical borderlands of the nation, California's fondness for bullfighting in the immediate aftermath of statehood made it a moral borderland, as well. By 1850, San Francisco's reputation as a rollicking "wide open town" of global commerce, booze, gambling, and entertainment was already well established.[57] There were two bullrings within the city limits, in addition to a popular racetrack and facilities for cockfighting and bear baiting. Blood sports were so prevalent in 1850 that when a grizzly bear and bull were released in a ring at San José, the state's first capital, the California legislature adjourned so that all lawmakers could go see the fight.[58]

There were still traces of this freewheeling culture of blood sport in California at the turn of the twentieth century, even though the state's anticruelty statutes prohibited "the use of animals in fights."[59] When A. H. Beal, president of the Minneapolis Humane Society, visited Los Angeles with his family in 1891, he was "highly pleased" with the city, "the most orderly place of its size in the United States," until he saw a "huge" poster for a bullfight to be held on Christmas Day, "on the anniversary of the advent of the 'Prince of Peace' on the earth, and who brought justice, mercy and kindness to every living creature." In a letter to the *Los Angeles Times*, he expressed his outrage: "It does not seem possible for this relic of barbarism to take place. Such a disgraceful display would not be probable in any Eastern city, Minneapolis, for instance. The authorities would arrest all parties who attempted it."[60] Beal's letter prompted an immediate reply from the secretary of the Los Angeles Humane Society [SPCA], who assured the public that "necessary steps" would be taken to prevent the bullfight.[61] Humane advocates were quick to emphasize their proactive surveillance measures to counter outside claims of lawlessness, which invariably targeted the city's "Latin" population as the primary audience for the bullfight and other blood sports.

Animal welfare officers and their media allies in California readily delineated the bullfight in racial, ethnic, and national terms as a foreign contagion creeping into California from Mexico. A summary report of local humane societies identified the San Diego Humane Society's propinquity to the border and the "character" of the city's population as the "most vexing problems" facing the Society in 1916. The report described Tijuana as a wild town drenched in alcohol and revolution, "where bull-fights and other animal fights are constantly held and where gambling-houses are always wide open." These activities spilled into San Diego, where humane officials discovered training facilities for fighting animals. "It has been very difficult to make any appeal on moral or humane grounds to the Mexican element, and Mexican officials have been found no exception to this rule."[62]

Humane advocates represented bullfighting pockets in the trans-Mississippi West as a racialized borderlands writ large—a rough and tumble periphery far from the civilized center. ASPCA president Henry Bergh, for one, publicly shamed Governor Glick of Kansas in a letter published in the *Kansas City* [Missouri] *Times*, after hearing about a corrida in Dodge City on the Fourth of July, 1884, where "humanity and public decorum have been trampled under foot and the blood-red flag of barbarism elevated above them." Bergh fused his diatribe with patriotic moral certitude: "While the banner of our Nation was being raised in every State, town, and village in the land, amid the thundering of artillery and the cheers of a prosperous and patriotic people, Dodge City alone unblushingly announces to the world that the tastes and habits of the heathen and the savage are to be inaugurated upon its soil."[63] Bergh envisioned what the Founders might say about the bullfight in Dodge City. Channeling their imaginary voices, he cast bullfighting enthusiasts in Kansas as emasculated and un-American: "A portion of the young State of Kansas ignoring all these precious benefits, elects to cast its lot among those few ignorant and effete States remaining in the world."[64]

As Bergh's words suggest, the racialization of the bullfight was in full force even in states far from the border. When reporting a series of arrests following a bullfight in Gillette, Colorado, in 1895, the press emphasized the Mexican identity of the bullfighters, along with a call from the governor for the firing of the local humane society agent "on the ground of incompetency."[65] Emotions ran so high about this bullfight that at the national meeting of the American Humane Association nearly a month later, the delegates moved to censure G. P. Thompson, secretary of the Colorado Humane Society, for failing to prevent the fight.[66]

Animal advocates were just as vigilant in policing mock, bloodless "Charlie Chaplin" bullfights, also known as *charlotada*, in which a Chaplin impersonator performed with a live bull.[67] On several occasions, Newark, New Jersey, was home to a showdown between corrida aficionados and SPCA officers. The newspapers focused on the area's substantial "foreign" Spanish and Portuguese population in explaining the demand for bullfighting in Newark. In August 1924, a bloodless corrida was held at Dreamland Park, where "a colony of Spaniards living near Newark attended the opening performance en masse and cheered hoarsely with memories of old Madrid in their minds." At the conclusion of the mock fight, five Spanish toreros and a park manager were arrested and released on $25 bail for causing "mental anguish and pain to the bulls."[68] The charges were dropped the next day. Yet the men were arrested again just two days later after a second mock bullfight—along with a sixteen-year-old Russian girl "who danced a Spanish dance between combats"—for causing, once again, "mental anguish" to the bull.[69]

One could argue that this heightened emphasis on the bull's emotional welfare signaled an attitudinal shift among critics whose concern in an earlier era was blunted by the bull's status as a food animal. While aspects of the modern meat industry (such as market transport and stunning before slaughter) had been a steady cause for reform in the humane movement, the majority of local protectionists devoted their attention to animal laborers (primarily horses), municipal stray policy (dogs), hunting (wild birds and furbearing animals), and the immoral consequences of blood sports on the public. Mock bullfighting fell into this latter category: critics charged that even bloodless bullfighting was a hothouse of cruelty and moral decline because the bull was still goaded and thus harassed—a form of cruelty in its own right. Many states amended and fortified their laws against blood sports to include prohibitions on animal baiting, which facilitated bans against bloodless bullfighting.[70] Yet mock bullfight supporters stressed the absence of picador horses and painful lances as further evidence of the bloodless bullfight's humane character, a point highlighted by the American Legion when advertising how "no weapons were to have been used" in its burlesque mock bullfight for disabled veterans at Madison Square Garden in February 1922. Nonetheless, the ASPCA successfully blocked the event, along with many others.[71]

Critics contended that the moral consequences of bloodless, "burlesque" bullfights would exacerbate tensions with immigrant populations already resistant to assimilation. In November 1930, actress and animal activist Minnie Maddern Fiske condemned bullfighting as a form of foreign racial contagion in a packed lecture hall at Yale University. Although scheduled to give a speech on contemporary drama, Fiske instead turned her podium into a bully pulpit. She denounced the "invasion of this country" in Newark and strongly warned the crowd about the moral dangers of bullfighting: "Bull-baiting would be a step backward in sport, a step backward to an ancient custom which better civilization long ago abolished, and would be particularly a blow to the efforts to establish humane education in the schools of the United States."[72] Fiske's rallying cry to save American civilization provided a boost to local humane officials' efforts to prevent the Brooklyn matador Sydney Franklin from staging a mock bullfight in Newark on November 30. Approximately fifty Yale students, along with a handful of professors and Princeton University's president, wrote to Newark's mayor, Jerome T. Congleton, in protest. Local religious leaders also participated, including Harry L. Bowlby, general secretary of the Lord's Day Alliance of the United States, who thought that the show would violate New Jersey's State Sunday law. Within days of the uproar, Newark's director of Public Safety, William J. Egan, banned the upcoming bullfight, citing the state's law against animal baiting.[73] In the end, Fiske and her allies triumphed over the "invasion" of the foreign Catholic Latinodad corrida aficionados in a showdown over the contested meanings of cruelty and cultural pluralism.

In the Mexican borderlands, American travel writers and humane advocates characterized bullfighting enthusiasts in much the same way as they did in Spain. They focused on superstitious Catholic "mobs" clinging to an archaic tradition.[74] Critics condemned the absence of fair chase as a clear sign of immorality.[75] They denounced a culture of debauchery—strong tequila, *mescal, pulque* (the "national drink"), and gambling "carried out in sight of the church."[76] Commentators noted with revulsion that bulls often seemed tame, only becoming aggressive once they were harassed inside the ring.[77] Similarly, American critics reserved special condemnation for the treatment of the Mexican picador horses. In 1925, a Mexican newspaper, *El Universal Gráfico*, published a short story, "The Victim," written in the voices of a doomed picador horse and the remorseful former owner who wept over the dying animal he had sold to the bullring. The *Los Angeles Times* enthusiastically proclaimed that the story "vies with Black Beauty," and hailed its publication as a major blow to bullfighting in a corrida-obsessed country whose SPCA movement was reluctant to attack it outright.[78]

Mexico's history and intimate proximity to the United States made its bullfights more socially threatening to American humane leaders than those in distant Spain. Animal welfare advocates warned against the dangerous lure of easy travel to Mexican border towns. Novelist Gwendolen Overton acknowledged that the base temptation of the bullfight was difficult to resist—even for an animal advocate—after crossing the border:

> You say you will not go to a bull-fight probably. At least you do if you happen to be a member of the Humane Society at home, and to have a reputation to keep up. Then when you get to Mexico and the thing is in the very air... and everybody looks at you curiously and uncomprehendingly when you say that bull-fights are barbarous... [s]ome Mexican youth, handsome and polished like so many of his kind, will ask, "Don't you want to go to the bull-fight this afternoon?" and you will say, "Yes." You drown the voice of an importunate conscience by talk and loud laughter, and think you are beginning to enter into the spirit of the thing. You are rather proud of your truly cosmopolitan knack for becoming a Roman in Rome.[79]

Such warnings hardly stopped American tourists from supporting the thriving Mexican bullfighting business. *Our Dumb Animals* routinely mentioned audiences "principally made up of Americans" visiting border towns to watch blood sports, such as a fight between a pet lion goaded with an iron bar and a bull witnessed by 3,000 people in 1903.[80] The problem of the lucrative American tourist market for bullfighting was so chronic that Minnie Maddern Fiske offered delegates at the annual California State Humane Association meeting in 1924 a "substantial cash prize" for any plan that would most persuasively convince American tourists to avoid bullfights at Mexican border towns.[81]

The Mexican Revolution temporarily slowed the tide of American bullfighting tourism but did not stop it. During this era, animal advocates worried that US business investors in Mexico would lobby successfully for an American invasion to protect profitable oil and gas holdings.[82] *Our Dumb Animals* described chaotic scenes of towns torched and caravans of refugee people and animals, "a mass of moving humanity of draft animals of every sort, of hogs and mules and cattle and dogs," crossing the international bridge to reach Laredo, Texas.[83] Amid the flow of refugees, bullfight tourism in Mexican border towns continued. Edward Eccleston, a lecturer with the Luther Burbank Company in San Francisco, juxtaposed grizzly scenes of political violence with bullfighting during a trip to Juárez in 1915:

> I saw many interesting, filthy, and disgusting things. . . . But the bullfight—that is my subject. The Mexicans on both sides of this border are woefully poor. Two dollars, the admission price, is a living for a month. They cannot go the bull-fights. Who, then, supports them? The Americans from all parts of the United States. Their excuse is, "Oh, well, I must see it once," but that once, together with its sometimes repetition, keeps up the most inhuman and diabolical form of sport in the world. . . . How can Americans, and especially Christian Americans, forget themselves so far as to make this one of the largest means of revenue in Mexico?[84]

Eccleston's account confronted American complicity in sustaining Mexican bullfighting, even as he simultaneously trumpeted ideologies of American benevolence: "As a rule I think the Anglo-Saxons, especially here in America, are more compassionate toward our dumb friends than the Latins or their descendants; yet a burning shame lies at the gateway of Christian America from Mexico."[85]

Eccleston and other Americans ignored the fact that bullfighting was controversial in Mexico as well. In the twilight of the Diaz dictatorship, opposition writers accused the government of funding the corrida as a "bread and circuses" distraction from government corruption and socioeconomic inequality.[86] Yet Diaz loyalists also despised the bullfight: founded in 1904, the Mexico SPCA, whose original membership included First Lady Carmen Romero Rubio Diaz, believed that eradication of bullfighting and the cockfight would come gradually, only through generational change, "free from the passion of the past," with humane education in the classroom rather than prosecution in the courtroom.[87] During the Battle of Juárez in 1911, the city's bullring literally became a military theater. Throughout the Mexican Revolution, myriad parties attempted to don the mantle of sober, moral republican virtue by banning the bullfight, gambling, and liquor, similar to other revolutionary leaders like Emilio Aguinaldo of the Philippines, José Martí of Cuba, and the First American Continental Congress.

The bullfighting tourist market in Mexico, however, was simply too lucrative for any ban to last. When Pancho Villa gained control of Juárez in 1914, he found that bullfighting profits helped finance weapons, military uniforms, and provisions for his army. After the United States officially (but reluctantly) recognized the leftist government of Venustiano Carranza in 1915, the Mexican president issued a decree banning bullfighting. In a claim repeated in other revolutionary settings, the *New York Times* stated that President Carranza openly advocated baseball as a replacement for bullfighting.[88] This association between the barbaric bullring and the uplifting bullpen spanned America's overseas empire, from Cuba to the Philippines. Yet President Carranza's bullfighting ban was violated immediately and forgotten within the year, most notably when the mayor of Juárez himself rode a bull into the Plaza de Toros.[89] All the while, the profitable American tourist market provided vital sustenance for Mexican bullfighting.

The enduring popularity of American bullfighting tourism threatened to undermine the high-minded implementation of American rule in the new empire. As a fierce critic of US militarism at the turn of the century, *Our Dumb Animals* alleged that bullfights played a role in the destruction of the USS *Maine* in 1898. George Angell theorized that Captain Charles D. Sigsbee and his officers were so distracted by bullfighting in Havana that they were lax about the ship's security. Angell claimed that the captain, when warned of probable danger to the ship, did nothing because he was too engrossed in the fighting at the Plaza de Toros. Had Sigsbee not been sidetracked by the corrida, Angell charged, he would have ordered additional gunboats to protect the ship in Havana Harbor. Angell was convinced that without the temptations of the bullfight, "it is quite possible that the lives of some three hundred American sailors, plunged in one instant into eternity, might have been saved."[90]

As Angell's unsupported interpretation of the *Maine* disaster suggests, American animal advocates treated the bullfight as an all-encompassing moral problem. This sentiment also was widely shared among supporters of American military intervention abroad. For example, Senator Redfield Proctor's congressional speech urging US military action in Cuba used the bullfight to define Spanish "barbarism" and its antidote, enlightened American progress. During the US occupation of the Philippines, Marie von Piontkowski, president of the Philippines SPCA, argued for bullfighting bans in nationalist terms when the organization successfully prevented a "bullfight project" to be held for a Spanish delegation in 1926: "A real bullfight, with all its horrors, cannot take place in a country under the sovereignty of the United States, where we have an anticruelty ordinance for the protection of all animals."[91] Yet other American humane leaders used the bullfight to undermine such exceptionalist claims. Massachusetts SPCA (SPCA) president Francis Rowley chided his fellow animal advocates for decrying the Mexican corrida while ignoring unspeakable acts of racist violence at home: "Bull-fights in Mexico! What a barbarous state of civilization, or uncivilization, must exist there! But what must the bullfighters and the witnesses of this cruel sport think of our civilization, guilty of weekly lynchings, in which men and women, American citizens, are riddled with bullets, clubbed to death, burned at the stake. Surely we are a great people—in numbers."[92] Rowley's gospel of kindness treated every form of violence as interconnected and mutually constitutive.

Rowley's insistence on a consistent creed of kindness made him a ready critic of any prominent American who attended bullfights abroad. In 1933, a son of President Roosevelt expressed "pleasure at the spectacle" and publicly acknowledged his "gratification" when a bull was dedicated to him in a Spanish corrida. *Our Dumb Animals* condemned his behavior: "The world of thoughtful men and women who have for generations looked with horror upon that relic of barbarism ... will find it hard to believe that the parents of this young man have read of his conduct in Spain with anything but pain and humiliation."[93]

The potential rebirth of the corrida in the American empire panicked humane activists. In 1934, the US ambassador to Cuba, Jefferson Caffery, visited with the famous American torero Sydney Franklin in Havana. Caffery publicly acknowledged that he "had seen many bullfights," an admission that mobilized a vigorous anti-bullfighting letter-writing campaign to the US State Department.[94] Caffrey's frank talk seemed to confirm fears that he was secretly trying to increase American tourism in Cuba during the Great Depression by promoting the bullfight—just as Governor Robert H. Gore had done successfully a year earlier in Puerto Rico by repealing the Island's anti-cockfighting laws.[95] Humane groups across the United States lodged so many complaints with the State Department that the ambassador was forced to make a public denial: "Regarding reports published in the United States that I made a statement favoring the resumption of bullfighting in Cuba, I want to declare emphatically that I made no such statement."[96]

Nonetheless, humane groups had good reason for concern. The American-led National Tourist Corporation actively sought to revive bullfighting in Cuba as a way to compete with Mexico for American tourist dollars.[97] Shortly before Christmas in 1936, Sydney Franklin traveled to Cuba with Ernest Hemingway to discuss with Cuban leaders a plan to lift the ban; yet Franklin and Hemingway abruptly left the country after political officials reportedly demanded $10,000 apiece before they would consider the matter further.[98] A few months later, American humane publications reported that Franklin was bringing 150 of "Spain's best bulls" to Cuba, where "an American-financed syndicate" was building a Plaza de Toros.[99]

The *National Humane Review* speculated that American bullfighting enthusiasts were ultimately seizing the opportunity to profit from "present chaotic social conditions" after the revolution in 1933. This turbulent era in Cuban history was marked by anti-imperialist rallies, student protests, labor strikes, and economic upheaval owing to America's neocolonial control over the Cuban economy, specifically sugar production, pricing, and distribution.[100] In 1937, American humane groups conducted a letter-writing campaign to President Federico Laredo Brú, begging him to resist the tempting prospect of free-flowing bullfighting tourist dollars during the global depression. The most influential anti-bullfighting voices, however, came from within: approximately forty years after the end of Spanish rule, Cuban nationalists still considered the corrida a bloody relic of Spanish colonialism, which they emphatically had no desire to revisit. Dr. Gustavo Odio de Granda, president of the Cuban humane society, Bando de Piedad de Cuba, expressed these sentiments to a receptive *Miami Herald* audience of Cuban exiles: "This in itself is sufficient to make [bullfighting] undesirable for the majority of Cubans."[101] Thus the ban remained, despite the best efforts of Sidney Franklin, Ernest Hemingway, and fellow American bullfighting compadres.[102]

Encountering the Bullfight in Texas

Tensions over bullfighting escalated during the 100th anniversary of Texas independence. Sydney Franklin, the cleverly nicknamed Jewish "El Torero de la Torah," was at the center of virtually every controversy, including an international bullfighting dispute between Spain and Mexico in May 1936. After Spain banned all foreign bullfighters that spring, the Mexican government quickly retaliated with its own embargo on foreign toreros.[103] Franklin assumed that the prohibition would either be lifted or ignored when he was on the Sunday corrida program in the border city of Matamoros on May 17; however, he ended up having to watch the corrida from the stands.[104]

The events leading up to the Matamoros bullfight were even more fraught than the bullfight itself. On May 9, five American ministers in the Rio Grande Valley wrote a resolution demanding that the bullfight be "stricken from the program." Although animal welfare advocates and Protestant clergy had routinely protested even bloodless American bullfights for decades, their method of attack in Mexico had been the boycott rather than an order for outright prohibition, as they had little jurisdiction in another sovereign nation. Nonetheless, thirty area Protestant congregations signed the Matamoros petition, which they submitted to the *Heraldo de Brownsville* in anticipation of ample press coverage. But the paper ignored them. J. Troy Hickman, pastor of the Mercedes Methodist Church, angrily accused the *Heraldo* of censorship and Catholic bias: "If the emphatic action of thirty congregations of Protestant people is not news, then what is news? We feel that in the interest of partisanship you have suppressed our protest, and that we have not received from the *Brownsville Herald* the consideration that we ought to receive. In this group of people are included many of your subscribers and some advertisers."[105] The *Heraldo* published Hickman's letter along with an explanation for the missing story that tacitly denied any Catholic bias: the editors claimed that they had been in a rush to publish a special edition and had "inadvertently" deleted the story, even though the Associated Press carried it elsewhere.[106]

Considerations of animal cruelty were central to the ministers' objections, but it was the specific festival circumstances on May 17, 1936, that triggered their demand for a ban.[107] This particular bullfight was part of the Brownsville Port Celebration held in the twin border cities of Matamoros and Brownsville to commemorate the opening of a new deep-water port in Brownsville, which was expected to expand the economy in South Texas. A watershed moment for the development of the region's transportation, capital, labor, and information networks, the event was to celebrate American progress, prosperity, and civilization—the same ideals, according to the ministers, that would be destroyed by the bullfight.

The Brownsville Port Celebration set the stage for the Texas Centennial, where Sidney Franklin would help sustain an even bigger bullfight controversy. During a twelve-year planning process that involved meticulous historical research and the procurement of local, state, and federal funding, the future Centennial's larger ideological objectives were established: state boosterism, patriotism, economic growth, and a historical salute to Anglo settlement and civilization. In pitching the Centennial to the US Congress, fair officials and Texas politicians presented the story of Texas as the nation's narrative. They noted that Texas was a gateway to lucrative hemispheric markets in Central and South America, a promotional plug with special urgency during the Great Depression. They asserted that Spain had done little to modernize Texas during its long dominion over Mexico, thus privileging an Anglo claim to the state's infrastructural development and modernization.[108] The higher civilizing purpose of the Centennial was clear: a historical pageant of Anglo-Texan free enterprise, nation building, and hemispheric expansionism.

Further, Centennial organizers framed their goals with a religious accent. The Texas Centennial Commission worked closely with white Protestant ministers to make the Centennial year of 1936 "a religious year," in which a massive "Save Texas Revival" or "State Centennial Revival" would coincide with a dedicated revival site on the fairgrounds, the Hall of Religion.[109] Paradoxically, the separation of church and state was essential to the Centennial's presentation of the past. Centennial histories told audiences that Anglo-Texans had fought for their religious freedom against the Mexican government, which had made conversion to Catholicism and tithing to the state church a precondition for land grants and settlement in Coahuila y Tejas. Nonetheless, Centennial officials treated Protestantism as a virtual state religion in the ongoing denominational celebrations at the Hall of Religion from June to November.[110]

The Centennial's educational exhibitions nodded to the cultural contributions of the state's racially diverse population; yet its historical displays highlighted "murderous" Comanche and Apache Indians, "treacherous" Mexicans, and African American slaves who were, by turns, "devoted," "shiftless," and "lusty."[111] While the Hall of Negro Life was perhaps the only public building in the South with integrated bathrooms in 1936, the rest of Fair Park contained segregated washrooms and seating arrangements. Midway concessionaires barred blacks from their shows.[112] Still, the Centennial's integrated Juneteenth celebration on June 19 prompted a white Louisiana official to blast Governor Allred in a "personal protest" letter for the "detestable spectacle" of racial integration at the fairgrounds: "This is certainly a new departure in 'southern hospitality'—permitting negroes and whites to meet on the track on a parity. . . . I had always thought that Texas would be one of the very last states to obliterate the color line."[113]

In the context of the Centennial's racially fraught Anglo-Texan narratives of progress and exclusion, it would seem that there was little room for the bullfight—a cultural form firmly associated with the state's Catholic Spanish and Mexican past. The stage was set for combat in May 1936, when a Dallas attorney, Richard Burton Humphrey, filed an application for a bullfight at the Centennial on behalf of a group of Mexican corrida proprietors—known ominously in the American press as the "Mexican Syndicate." According to Paul Massman, director of exhibit sales and special events at the Dallas exposition, "We have not decided yet to a bull fight here, but, like every other application, this one is being given consideration."[114] Anticipating resistance, Humphrey attempted to quell the protest before it started, first by declaring that bullfighting "was not cruel," and then by comparing it to the rodeo, a cow- and horse-centered entertainment already widely featured on the Centennial program: "A bull fight is far less cruel then the American rodeo, both on the animals and the men. Of course in a bull fight the bull is killed, but it is a painless death."[115]

Centennial officials advertised the rodeo as a major draw that enriched the fair's larger entrepreneurial goals for the Texas cattle industry. The rodeo reliably lured crowds with its death-defying dangers and nostalgic, triumphal Anglo-American reenactments of the western frontier, a tradition that extended back to the popular Wild West shows of the late nineteenth and early twentieth centuries. In May 1936, Centennial press releases enumerated the great cost and spectacular scope of Colonel W. T. Johnson's World Championship Rodeo, slated to run from June 6 (the opening day of the Centennial) to June 21, and then again in November, with massive cash prizes. Over 600 head of livestock were being shipped to Dallas for the event.[116] Stock shows of variegated cattle breeds and individual demonstrations of rodeo skills highlighted the importance of the cattle industry to the entire Centennial enterprise. Although animal welfare activists denounced the rodeo in other contexts, including copious articles in *Our Dumb Animals* and the *National Humane Review*, they funneled their attention exclusively to bullfighting at the Centennial, in part because the rodeo enjoyed such overwhelming state and private support that fighting it would have been futile.[117]

Bullfighting foes used letter-writing campaigns to newspapers and politicians as their primary method of protest. They warned of the dangerous relationship between vice and viciousness, just as their brethren in the WCTU's Department of Mercy had contended in the decades prior to Prohibition. Writing from Brenham, Texas, Methodist minister Oscar W. Hooper declared that the Mexican Syndicate was capitalizing on the "retrograde in public morality" in a state that had regrettably legalized "the evils of the liquor traffic" and "race gambling." Hooper argued that the patriotic and moral stakes of the Centennial were too high to permit a bullfight: "We believe that the moral life of the people of Texas will promptly resent the presumption that Texas has deteriorated to such a point as to advertise her 100 years of progress with such a sickening feature of cruelty and hopeless brutality as the Mexican bullfight would demonstrate in advertising

Texas before the life of this Nation."[118] Feelings were so strong that when a man named Roy Franklin of Amherst, Texas, rode into Dallas atop a bull on June 17, people mistakenly identified him as Sydney Franklin, and the rumors of a bullfight started raging anew.[119]

The relentless protest against the corrida forced bullfighting enthusiasts to scramble for palatable alternatives. Syndicate promoters immediately offered to modify the traditional bullfight in favor of a bloodless corrida within days of their initial plans going public: "There is no specific statute prohibiting bullfights. The only statutes which could prevent it are those pertaining to the cruel treatment of the animals. If we guarantee that the bulls would not be hurt the show would be entirely legal."[120] At the end of May, bullfight enthusiasts brought Sydney Franklin to Dallas to lobby for a modified Centennial bullfight—a bloodless French or Portuguese bullfight, without horses or barbs: "The animal is not even scratched." Franklin maintained that all of the excitement of the bloody bullfight would remain and therefore would still draw huge crowds: "The technical work and skill of the matador and his assistants in handling the huge, enraged animal will supply plenty of thrills. You'd put this exposition on the front page all over the country by staging such fights."[121]

Franklin and his Syndicate colleagues persisted into mid-August, offering to perform a "hickory limb" exhibition, sans swords, a "dexterous, thrilling spectacle with art and style as its most important elements."[122] Franklin maintained that the "bull, too, would enjoy it." He made a similar humane argument in defense of traditional bullfights, asserting that a skillful matador killed the bull painlessly with the sword's fast "death-thrust"; thereafter, the bull meat "quickly reaches the best Spanish restaurant tables at advanced prices."[123] In reminding readers of the *Dallas Morning News* that the bull was always eaten, Franklin reinforced the exotic bullfight's direct ties to the ordinary slaughter of beef cattle, which virtually every Texan could understand.

Although Franklin returned to Dallas in August, no further bullfighting plans at the main fairgrounds materialized. A bullfight took place during the Centennial year in Pittsburg, Texas, as well as a bloodless corrida in Galveston during the city's Fourth of July festivities, far from the central celebration in Dallas. *Our Dumb Animals* maintained that it mattered little whether the corrida was an "actual fight of the typical Spanish form" or a "mock fight" because "the principle involved is the same."[124] Opposition to any form of bullfighting at Dallas remained so fierce that Franklin abandoned the project. Years later, he did not even mention the Centennial flap in his autobiography, *Bullfighter from Brooklyn*.

Franklin literally erased the episode from his own history, but the Centennial bullfight controversy remained intertwined with questions of historical memory, cruelty, cultural pluralism, and Anglo narratives of progress and uplift. Maria Elena Zamora O'Shea, an educator and novelist whose writing celebrated the Spanish and Mexican American origins of Texas history, was disgusted that Centennial organizers would bow to anti-bullfighting pressure: "What's come over Texas, anyhow? Has the State gone sissy? A bullfight is fine, clean sport and far less cruel than a rodeo."[125] She noted that she proudly wore her eighteenth-century family heirloom lace mantilla headdress when she attended bullfights in Mexico and Spain.[126] While Zamora O'Shea spoke directly to the bullfight's masculine bravado, she also addressed a vexing question: whose history and culture would be represented at the Centennial?[127] Rodeo exhibitions, after all, generally erased the Spanish and Mexican *vaquero* origins of the cowboy in favor of representing this cultural figure as quintessentially Anglo-American.

In the combustible milieu of historical memory and mythmaking at the Centennial fairgrounds, the culturally and racially diverse bullfight challenged an Anglo-Texan vision of the past. The fair trumpeted the state's unique history as an independent republic in racially inflected terms—crafting a celebratory narrative of Protestant white settlement and civilization on the

FIGURE 6.2. The Texas Centennial celebrated the cowboy as an Anglo-American manly archetype, while simultaneously erasing his pluralistic *vaquero* origins. "Part of a carefully restored mural, one of dozens at Fair Park, site of the 1936 Texas Centennial Celebration and the Pan-American Exposition in 1937, in Dallas, Texas," Mural artist: Tom Lea, El Paso, 1936, LC-DIG-highsm-30077, the Lyda Hill Texas Collection of Photographs in Carol M. Highsmith's America Project, Library of Congress, Prints and Photographs Division, Washington, DC.

ashes of General Santa Ana and his benighted armies, as well as Quanah Parker and the bands of skilled Comanche horsemen, who posed the most serious indigenous threat to Anglo-Texan settlement after independence from Mexico was won. In "remembering the Alamo" and other dominant Euroamerican narratives in Texas history, fair organizers eclipsed the state's pluralistic identity.

Still, the bullfight controversy at the Centennial was hardly forgotten. Instead, it set the stage for the passage of state legislation (HB 76) on May 14, 1937, which authorized ordinary citizens to sue for an injunction against any form of bullfighting.[128] The *National Humane Review* hailed the new law as the "first definite anti-bullfight law in the United States" because of its singular focus. (Other states, however, included traditional bullfighting in bans against blood sports but still allowed bloodless bullfights to escape prohibition—unless explicitly part of anti-baiting legislation.)[129] The new Texas law stated that the mere announcement or advertisement of a bullfight provided sufficient grounds to sue for a court order before the attorney general or any district or county attorney, who would then decide whether the injunction and any subsequent prosecution were warranted. Nonetheless, HB 76 did not actually ban bullfighting outright in Texas because it gave individual legal authorities the power to grant (or deny) an injunction on a case-by-case basis.

A test case came just four months after the law was passed. On September 5, 1937, a bloodless bullfight was held at the Greater Texas and Pan American Exposition, at the same fairgrounds where the Centennial was held just a year before. Dallas authorities did nothing to stop it. Plans for a bloodless bullfight had been under way since the exposition opened in June. Yet in contrast to the flood of protest at the Centennial, few took notice of this latest effort to bring the bullfight to Dallas. H. B. Goodnight, president of the Dallas County Humane Society, had witnessed a bloodless bullfight elsewhere and was impressed with the skill and dexterity of its participants and its nonviolent outcome. He assured the public that "this will be high-class entertainment with no objectionable features"; additionally, the president of the Texas Humane Society, Roland Bradley of Houston, would be present to monitor the bullfight in person.[130] The presence of a humane monitor had a long history in American animal entertainments. For example, in 1866 the newly incorporated ASPCA sent its officers to monitor P. T. Barnum's American Museum because the facility used live rabbits as prey for the menagerie's boa constrictors. The surveillance ended only after naturalist Louis Agassiz defended the Museum's feeding practices as part of its obligation "to show to the public the animals, as nearly as possible, in their natural state."[131] MSPCA officers, likewise, questioned Barnum in 1873 over the use of an ankus (bull hook, or guide) on a circus elephant, but were reassured by the response of the show's treasurer, S. H. Hurd: "I have thoroughly investigated the matter, and find no marks upon the elephant. I fully appreciate the benefit arising from the humane efforts of societies such as yours."[132]

Yet in Dallas, Mrs. M. Calcote Harris remained unmoved by the Texas Humane Society's assurances of official oversight. Under the terms of the new anti-bullfighting law, Harris lodged repeated protests with exposition officials, city hall, and then the city council on the eve of the bullfighting weekend—all to no avail. The bloodless bullfight debuted at the Livestock Arena on Sunday, September 5, 1937, without incident. In a review of the event, the *Dallas Morning News* said nothing about animal cruelty. Instead, the reviewer was disappointed because the bull seemed too gentle. The Mexican matador Julian Pastor provoked the bull to charge only at the end of the fight—to the screaming delight of the crowd—before the bull retired to his stall. A clown bullfight and exhibitions of Mexican rodeo skills—trick riding and fancy roping—were also part of this show, but the real star was a cameraman dangling from a high rope to get the perfect shot just inches away from the bulls and bareback riders: "Whenever his flash bulb exploded, the crowd roared. Every time his perch teetered, scores shouted advice."[133]

What happened? Why did the bullfight receive so little protest at the Pan American Exposition in 1937 when the mere possibility of a bullfight at the Texas Centennial in 1936 triggered so much public outrage that further plans were abandoned? Why was a bloodless bullfighting exhibition at the Centennial considered "barbaric" and "cruel," while the same exhibition received a stamp of approval from the president of the Dallas County Humane Society just a year later? This disjuncture was even more perplexing because the passage of HB 76 empowered citizens to stop individual bullfights in Texas. Although both exhibitions were intended to stimulate the economy during the Great Depression, Centennial organizers were invested in a morally instructive teleological vision of Anglo-Texan progress. Once the 100th anniversary of Texas independence passed, exhibition boosters turned to the serious business of "real entertainment" during the Pan American Exposition: a statewide swing dance competition judged by Benny Goodman; a massive nightly tug-of-war at the Cotton Bowl; a "'wet' bathing revue of beauties"; rides, features, and shows galore at La Rambla, the exposition's midway; and the bullfight.[134]

The bloodless bullfight offered a virtual travel experience at the Pan American Exposition, which was billed as a "day's tour of Pan-America." The fairgrounds contained a constellation of Latin American cultural forms reconstituted into a pleasurable act of consumption.[135] Advertisements from local businesses, such as the department store A. Harris and Company, beckoned fair customers: "The Pan American spirit has swiftly spread over the entire store ... accenting fashion with splashes of daring color ... scrapes made by the Latins who weave into their designs all the passion of a tropical people ... all make you dream of mad, rhythmical rhumbas and high adventure in far-away places. In Harris' gift shops ... you'll feel you're rummaging in native, Latin American atmosphere."[136]

As part of the fair's cultural imperatives, the bullfight had been contained and transfigured into a form of ephemeral border crossing, mirroring the experience of crossing the Mexican border as a tourist and watching the corrida in Matamoros or Cuidad Juárez. Once the Centennial fairground had been shuttered and reopened as the Greater Texas and Pan American Exposition, its political significance also changed, from an edifying commemoration of Anglo-Texanness since 1836 to a pleasure-filled celebration of America's exotic "good neighbors" in Latin America. To be sure, both exhibitions were cultural products of nation and empire building, replete with paeans to free trade, technological innovation, and prosperity. Yet because the cultural field of the Pan American Exposition included the entire hemisphere, the fair decoupled any potential association between bullfighting, cruelty, and Anglo-Texan identity formation. As a "Latin" cultural production, bullfighting remained an artifact of racially exotic otherness at the fair, thereby showing that standards of cruelty were often culturally and politically contingent: the same bloodless French/Portuguese bullfight banished for its quintessential cruelty had become a harmless cultural spectacle just a year later. To this day, bloodless bullfights remain a popular legal attraction among pluralistic communities in South Texas.[137]

A resilient transnational symbol for cultural identity and civilization, the bullfight stoked incendiary political ruptures on the eve of World War II. American children's author Munro Leaf stumbled on the bullfight's volatile meanings firsthand after his book, *The Story of Ferdinand*, was published in September 1936, shortly after the outbreak of the Spanish Civil War. Leaf's friend, Robert Lawson, illustrated the text with black and white drawings of some of Spain's most recognizable corrida landmarks, such as the town of Ronda, the Andalusian birthplace of Spanish bullfighting. In *Ferdinand*, the massive, peaceable, eponymous bull preferred sunny fields, fragrant flowers, and the shade of a cork tree to the violent bullring. The book was an immediate and enduring bestseller worldwide.[138] The *National Humane Review* praised the "delightful" story of the kindly bull, who "acted with decorum, molested nobody and never went to war with his neighbors."[139] However, *Ferdinand*'s message of nonconformity was received in ways that utterly perplexed its author:

> Letters began to pour in.... [They claimed] I was deliberately corrupting children of an impressionable age. In Ferdinand people saw the laissez-faire theory of economics seconded by the bourgeois ideology of utility. Letters complained that Ferdinand was Red propaganda, others that it was Fascist propaganda, while a number protested it was subversive pacifism. On the other hand, one woman's club resolved that it was an unworthy satire of the peace movement.[140]

Leaf always insisted that he had no hidden ideological agenda in writing *Ferdinand*.[141] He recalled choosing a bull for his story because he wanted to give Lawson "an animal to draw that was not a cat, a mouse, a dog or a horse—something different in children's books."[142] Despite Leaf's neutral, nonpartisan intentions, the book was deemed politically subversive and was banned in Nazi Germany and in Spain after Franco's Nationalists defeated the Loyalist Republicans in 1939.[143] The *New York Times* observed that such bans were a gloomy omen in "an age of doctrines, tendencies and parables," in which authoritarian regimes could brand virtually any children's classic, such as the *Three Bears* or *Little Red Riding Hood*, as dangerous, "if the censors knew their business."[144] Nonetheless, *Ferdinand*'s harsh reception also implicitly acknowledged the troubled history of the bullfight—as symbol and cultural practice—and its continued combustible relevance in a world poised for war.

Conclusion

WORLD WAR II cast a grim shadow over the American animal welfare movement. M. Guy Delon, the French superintendent of the Massachusetts SPCA's American Fondouk in Fez, Morocco, was drafted into the French army in August 1939. It appeared likely that the veterinary hospital and shelter would close. Luckily, Delon's military orders stationed him in Fez, so he could work at the Fondouk part-time.[1] American humane periodicals chronicled his travails as part of their ongoing coverage of the escalating war: Ethiopian camels killed and maimed in the Italian invasion; Spanish livestock and their refugee owners struggling to flee the Civil War; London pets cowering in bombed out rubble during the Blitz; and Chinese animals starving and abandoned.[2] Susan E. Armstrong, a Congregational missionary and English teacher at Foochow (Fuzhou) College in China, recounted her harrowing escape in correspondence with the *National Humane Review*: "The Japanese bombers were calling nearly everyday." As she fled, her cat went missing, but miraculously found her nineteen days later at her new home fifteen miles away from Fuzhou: "He is now in my lap as I am writing this letter."[3]

With several nations already at war in the late 1930s, American animal protectionists redoubled their attention to military readiness. After World War I, the Red Star Animal Relief had transitioned into a peacetime disaster relief service.[4] In 1938, the American Humane Association reorganized the Red Star with an efficient new regional command system in anticipation of returning to combat zones.[5] Red Star branches donated money and supplies to war-torn China, England, and Finland, which was fighting a border war against the Soviet Union.[6] England's Royal SPCA and the National Canine Defence League advertised the Red Star's support on their ambulances, clinics, and signage as a prominent show of thanks.[7] The *National Humane Review* declared that the Red Star's work was critical to national security,

FIGURE C.1. The American Red Star Animal Relief assisted humane societies in Allied nations, such as England, to provide relief aid to animal victims of World War II. "Driver H. D. Brand of the Royal SPCA, who risked his life to rescue this cat from the debris," *National Humane Review*, September 1941, 26.

which necessitated thorough background checks for prospective volunteers: "The Red Star cannot afford to have anyone on its rolls whose loyalty to the Government or the humane cause can be doubted."[8]

The deployment of the Red Star Animal Relief reminded readers that animal labor still played a significant role in modern warfare: "Mechanized traffic can still break down. . . . And horses and mules can still move pretty freely in areas where trucks, automobiles and even tanks would be hopelessly bogged down. We've seen this in Ethiopia during the rainy season; in China when Japan was confronted by the floods of the Yellow River and the Yangtse-Kiang; and significantly in the Spanish war."[9] Humane groups urged Congress to define laboring animals as contraband to prevent the sale of horses and mules to "aggressor nations." They also advocated pasturing or euthanization for equines retiring from service in the War Department as an additional protective measure.[10]

FIGURE C.2. In the late 1930s, animal welfare organizations urged Congress to ban the sale of horses and mules to warring nations. "The Hand of Murder and the Hand of Mercy," *National Humane Review*, December 1939, 1.

Our Dumb Animals bemoaned a world that had rejected the gospel of kindness: "Never was Humane Education more needed than in the year 1940 after Christ. It is poor comfort now to observe that had this kind of education prevailed throughout the last two decades of the twentieth century we would be living in an entirely different and happier world today."[11] Just over half of the US states had passed compulsory public school humane education laws by the 1930s, many of which remained unenforced.[12] Additionally, science education itself was changing. With the rise of standardized curricula stressing the scientific method in the 1920s and 1930s, American public schools abandoned humane education and nature study.[13] Scientists also effectively appropriated the idiom of kindness to legitimize animal experimentation and to delegitimize those who opposed it. The American Red Cross supported this rhetorical fusion of science and the greater good during World War I when proclaiming its own humanitarian purposes for conducting animal experiments to find a cure for infectious diseases in Europe. The Red Cross denounced its antivivisectionist critics for "in reality giving aid and comfort to the enemy."[14]

THE FIRST SEVENTY-FIVE years of the organized animal welfare movement bore witness to a seismic change: the nation's shift from animal muscle to motor power. At its inception in 1866, the organized SPCA movement primarily protected urban laboring animals, especially the ubiquitous horse. Although the ideals of this new movement were inclusive and ecumenical, anticruelty laws invariably targeted laboring people simply because their livelihood was dependent on animal muscle in full view of the watchful community. Critics accused animal advocates of being elitist and insensitive to the economic needs of the poor.[15] While animal protectionists gladly arrested wealthy sportsmen, such defendants were politically connected and possessed effective legal representation. The poor, then as now, were more vulnerable to prosecution.

The transition from animal power to motorization gradually expanded the humane movement's agenda. Before the 1910s, animal advocates generally treated performing animals as laborers, using physical pain as a reason for intervention. Yet most activists did not question the ethics of animal performance labor wholesale.[16] In the 1910s, a gradual attitudinal sea change paralleled the slow shift to motorization. The first hint of this transformation occurred in early 1918 when the MSPCA created the Jack London Club, an organization dedicated to the abolition of animal performances in all facets of the American entertainment industry. It was named after the late author to honor his denunciation of animal acts in his posthumously published novel, *Michael, Brother of Jerry* (1917), which featured a canine protagonist who was kidnapped, tortured, and forced to perform on stage. There was only one stipulation for membership: people were required to send their names and addresses to *Our Dumb Animals*, as proof of their promise to walk out of any animal show. To underscore its seriousness of purpose, *Our Dumb Animals* evoked the hated bullfight to suggest that animals were better off dead than working in a show: "America will not sanction bullfights; they are too cruel, but she allows trained animal acts, which are far worse, for in the one performance the bull is killed and put out of its misery, but the poor suffering animal actors are tortured every day of the week."[17]

The Jack London Club, however, was a symbolic gesture. It had no formal constitution, no elected officers, no membership dues, and no planned activities. Nonetheless, it anticipated an important change. A growing number of SPCAs and humane societies viewed virtually any captive animal act to be implicitly cruel, regardless of a show's standard of care. They believed that performing animals were bored inmates tortured offstage to learn tricks. British animal advocates founded a similar organization, the Performing Animals' Defence League, in 1914 and successfully lobbied for modest regulatory legislation in 1925.[18] While American initiatives fell on deaf political ears, circus owner John Ringling sensed a business opportunity to streamline his operations and to attract media attention when he temporarily banned wild animal acts in the Ringling Brothers and Barnum & Bailey circus in 1925.[19] He personally found big cat acts logistically cumbersome and relished the opportunity to get rid of them. His prohibition, however, proved temporary because no other circus followed his lead. Market demand was too great to uphold his self-imposed ban.[20] Still, the Jack London Club exemplified the humane movement's changing worldview in an age of motorization: animal advocates increasingly believed that wild animal shows were a humiliating denaturalization of sentient, socially complex creatures, whose lives would be far better in a state of nature, separated from the built environment.

On the eve of World War II, the shift to motorization was nearly complete. While animals still labored on farms, they had all but vanished from the city.[21] Humane publications repeatedly warned their readers of the dangers of this motorized world with sobering stories of people and animals killed crossing roadways, such as "Three Killed per Mile."[22] Animal protectionists also turned to the cinema, where horse actors labored under perilous conditions. When a horse leaped to its death off a seventy-foot cliff during the production of *Jesse James* (1939), censure was swift and furious. Writing from Northfield, Minnesota, where the actual James-Younger gang was foiled during a bank robbery, L. W. Boe, the president of St. Olaf College, expressed his disgust with the film: "The Humane Association is doing a good thing in protesting inhumanity to animals.... We in Northfield naturally protest against the whole Jesse James proposition."[23]

FIGURE C.3. Humane publications cautioned their readers to protect pets from the dangers of the motorized world. "Somebody's Pal," originally published in the *Rochester [NY] Herald*, April 11, 1926, *Our Dumb Animals*, May 1926, 5.

Animal advocates responded to the mounting global crisis through the universalistic and particularistic prism of the gospel of kindness. Even though *Our Dumb Animals* loathed anti-Semitism, the magazine supported a new German humane slaughter law in 1933, which required that all warm-blooded animals be stunned before they were butchered.[24] The MSPCA's backing for the new law unintentionally blunted the organization's denunciation of the Third Reich.[25] Ultimately, these conflicting positions were of a piece. American animal advocates believed that kindness was universal in its meaning and application, a conviction that was simultaneously expansive and exclusive: if an animal was conscious during slaughter, then it suffered—irrespective of the humane ideals of the religious tradition involved. In the aftermath of the *Kristallnacht* pogrom in November 1938, *Our Dumb Animals* paraphrased Henry Fosdick and Reinhold Niebuhr to condemn Nazism, with no mention of earlier support for slaughter reform: "Christianity must fight anti-Semitism if it expects to save itself from Paganism."[26]

Humane periodicals still made religious references in the late 1930s, yet the American animal welfare movement was slowly, if imperceptibly, secularizing. On the one hand, advertisements still acknowledged "Humane Sunday" as part of "Be Kind to Animals Week." Humane periodicals still celebrated St. Francis of Assisi (patron saint of animals) and highlighted the rabbinical and ministerial endorsements they received.[27] *Our Dumb Animals* also continued to report the missionary work of Bands of Mercy in the Philippines, India, and elsewhere.[28] However, humane groups devoted less copy to "Humane Sunday" and more attention to school activities, such as poster making. The presence of religious leaders and missionaries diminished during the 1930s in favor of a growing emphasis on celebrity animal lovers like child film stars Shirley Temple and Jane Withers.

Most significantly, the allied movements that had created the gospel of kindness fractured. One break occurred as a result of the professionalization of the social sciences during the Progressive Era: child welfare organizations turned away from their original alliances with animal welfare groups in favor of a new scientific emphasis on social work.[29] Temperance politics represented another point of departure. Animal advocates lost an important partner after the Prohibition amendment was repealed in 1933 because the WCTU's political influence and membership rolls declined precipitously. Humane reportage stressed the dangers of drunk driving but rarely emphasized the causal link between drunkenness and animal cruelty.[30] The transnational missionary field of American animal advocacy and the Bands of Mercy was also in flux, especially as anticolonial liberation movements escalated.[31]

FIGURE C.4. During the 1930s, film and radio celebrities became the public face of the humane movement. "Jane Withers, Popular Screen Star of 'Young America,' and Two of Her Innumerable Pets," *Our Dumb Animals*, November 1941, 217.

Protestantism itself was starting to fissure. The rise of modernism, fundamentalism, and the growing acceptance of evolutionary theory created new schisms among liberal mainline Protestants and biblical literalists.[32] The numbers of mainline Protestant denominations most active in animal advocacy declined in the missionary field, while growing ranks of conservative missionaries had little interest in animal protectionism.[33]

Although the animal welfare movement was at a secular crossroads, its moral nexus with human rights was still strongly evident in the early 1940s. Always more outspoken on civil rights issues than the *National Humane*

Review and other mainstream animal welfare publications, *Our Dumb Animals* denounced the hollowness of patriotic paeans to American freedom in a racist society. The magazine chronicled the activity of the Ku Klux Klan, the ghastly persistence of lynching, and ongoing racial segregation in Detroit, where white housing developers responded to the migration of African Americans by building a six-foot wall to partition off the Eight Mile Wyoming neighborhood.[34] The magazine supported the Double V Campaign against racism at home and fascism abroad, and forcefully denounced the disenfranchisement of African American citizens: "That man can be sent to the frontline to be shot for the country that denies him his constitutional right to vote."[35]

Yet the MSPCA's reportage on civil rights abuses became muted after 1942 in favor of wholesale support for the war effort and America's global status as the arsenal of democracy. This silence was especially noticeable during the summer of 1943 when race riots ravaged urban centers of wartime production across the nation. In July 1943, *Our Dumb Animals* reported that uniformed African American servicemen were being denied entry into restaurants at Portland, Oregon, but mentioned nothing about race riots elsewhere.[36]

Changes in the tone and content of humane news reports during World War II and the postwar period signaled a departure from a far-ranging gospel of kindness to a more singular focus on the daily warp and woof of animal protection. The magazine's "Appeal for Syria" in 1946, for example, abandoned the rhetoric of uplift and nation building in its call to raise funds to buy a motorcycle so that N. B. Matta, the Syrian representative of the American Humane Education Society (AHES), could travel to isolated areas: "Travel is slow in his country and although he has preached the gospel of kindness to thousands of his countrymen, he is urgently in need of a motorcycle in order that he may contact the farming districts and out of the way places."[37]

While the reasons for the shift away from coverage of civil rights abuses were unstated, *Our Dumb Animals* softened its criticism of American politics more generally, like other domestic groups in a milieu of wartime consensus and subsequent suppression of dissent during the Cold War.[38] This shift was especially noticeable in light of the MSPCA's long track record as a fierce political and social critic. During World War I, *Our Dumb Animals* angrily claimed that the Espionage Act "would supplant democracy by autocracy."[39] In 1946, by contrast, the MSPCA, in carefully measured language, gently rebuked the Department of the Navy for its proposed use of animals in Operation Crossroads, the series of atomic tests at the Bikini Atoll: "The [MSPCA] ... desires to put itself on record as against the causing in any

RECEPTION COMMITTEE
A Coast Guard combat photographer caught this picture of two waifs of war. With the Japs driven back from Lingayen Gulf, a little Filipino boy and his dog came out from hiding to greet the American liberators.

FIGURE C.5. Historically, the MSPCA was a reliable critic of American foreign policy, but during World War II, the organization became a steadfast part of the wartime consensus, which endured into the Cold War. "Reception Committee," *Our Dumb Animals*, May 1945, 73.

circumstances of any unnecessary suffering to animal life."[40] The MSPCA politely confined its objections to animal experimentation; its former outspokenness likely would have led it to print a robust critique of atomic weapons and the military-industrial complex. Animal protectionists modulated their commentary and activism for fear of harassment and redbaiting. Even the most outspoken animal advocacy organizations, such as the American Anti-Vivisection Society, were subdued during the Cold War.[41]

The movement's gradual disconnection from its older interconnected gospel of animal and human kindness became especially evident when postwar civil rights activists cited animal welfare laws to demonstrate the hypocrisy of racial segregation. In 1950, veteran African American civil rights leader Mary Church Terrell and her associates were denied service at Thompson's Restaurant, a popular eatery in Washington, DC, because of their race. Terrell, who was nearly ninety years old, and her colleagues immediately filed a lawsuit, *District of Columbia v. John R. Thompson Co.*, to push for enforcement of DC's "lost laws" of 1872 and 1873, which banned racial segregation in local public facilities. In support of the plaintiffs, the DC Chapter of the National Lawyers Guild cited *Johnson v. District of Columbia* (1908), which had affirmed the legality of local animal cruelty laws as a justification for disrupting the peace:

> We think it plain that if the Legislative Assembly could prohibit mistreatment of animals, it could prohibit mistreatment of human beings. If the Assembly could legitimately conclude that the peace may be breached as a result of the indignation of a bystander who sees an animal mistreated, it could even more readily conclude that the peace may be breached as a result of the indignation of an individual who is himself mistreated and insulted by being refused service in a public place.[42]

The US Supreme Court's ruling in 1953, *District of Columbia v. John R. Thompson Co., Inc.*, affirmed the constitutionality of the "lost laws" and abolished Jim Crow in Washington, DC.[43] Earlier generations of humane activists wedded to the gospel of kindness would surely have viewed animal advocacy and African American civil rights activism as complementary, not oppositional, movements.

THE AMERICAN ANIMAL welfare movement took root and proliferated in the moral universe of nineteenth-century Protestant revivalism, social reform, war, and empire building. The Second Great Awakening and its attendant social movements—especially abolitionism and temperance—created a movement language and a theology of perfectibility that emphasized human uplift through kindness to animals. In a pluralistic society, animal kindness became a symbolic litmus test for assimilative citizenship and civilization. As an American value, the gospel of kindness was an important agent of Americanization and nation building overseas in the new empire after the

Spanish-American War. Animals were indelibly connected to the intimate, lived experiences of colonial life. As a result, human-animal interactions became a flashpoint for local nation building and anticolonial sentiment—from struggles over cockfighting in the Philippines, Cuba, and Puerto Rico, to the communalistic cow protection movement that helped define Hindu nationalism in late colonial India. Likewise, American leaders heralded bullfighting bans at home and abroad as a validation of the nation's benevolent, progressive mission of merciful empire building vis-à-vis vanquished, "barbaric" Spain.

During the first seventy-five years of the organized animal welfare movement, the cultural meanings of the animals under its protective fold changed. In 1866, a horse was the nation's primary source of muscle power; however, its affective ties to humanity, its direct participation in westward settlement, and its place in nostalgic representations of Native Americans and agrarian life made its status strongly sentimental. In 1941, urban Americans encountered the horse in the cinema, on the racetrack, in novels, and in metaphors evoking its former laboring status: "Iron Horse," "horsepower," and "horseless carriage." The horse had become a figure of speech, an image, an entertainment, and a pet in the American cultural imagination.

The dog, too, had changed. Although a beloved pet, guardian, and worker since antiquity, dogs were also feared and reviled as carriers of vermin and disease. In 1866, aggressive urban dog packs terrified local residents, but by 1941, the snarling canine "mobs" had all but disappeared, owing to the accessibility of the Pasteur vaccine, the growing (though still uncommon) practice of spaying and neutering, and the success of the sheltering movement, which mandated humane capture and housing for strays.[44] Additionally, new effective medications for parasite control were available. Infectious diseases were curable with antibacterial sulfonamides for canines and people alike.[45] While specific breeds, such as the Doberman pinscher or American Staffordshire terrier, were periodically demonized and feared, dogs were no longer deemed an automatic hazard to public health. They entered people's homes and bedrooms, where they have remained ever since. Cats benefited from the same medical technologies and humane imperatives that transformed canine and human relationships—reproductive control, parasite and disease prevention, and an ethic of proactive sheltering stewardship. In 1947, Edward Lowe met the demands of America's burgeoning indoor cat market with the introduction of his new consumer product: cat litter.

Animal advocates became even more focused on wild creatures as new threats loomed. Mass extinctions of passenger pigeons (1914) and Carolina parakeets (1920s), regional extinctions of furbearing mammals, and near extinctions of birds used in the feather trade forced Americans to confront their complicity in irrevocable wildlife destruction. Empathic representation of wildlife in film, such as Walt Disney's *Bambi* (1942), used the close-up, plaintive musical scoring, and vivid color to amplify the humane movement's goals, spurring mass audiences to recognize animal intelligence and emotional complexity.[46] Even the caged songbird, a popular pet and source of musical enjoyment in the nineteenth century, became a symbol of confinement and cruelty.

While the fragile status of wildlife became ever more visible in popular media, livestock gradually slipped out of cultural view. In 1866, urban dairies were common; livestock bound for slaughter lived (albeit briefly) in intimate physical proximity to other city dwellers after arriving by train from western grazing lands and other rural hinterlands. After World War II, livestock increasingly reached their urban consumer markets as packaged milk or meat, not living creatures. Packers transported whole or half "swinging carcasses" by refrigerated rail car or truck to supermarket chain warehouses, where butchers broke down and packaged the bodies into individual cuts for delivery to grocery stores.[47] Fewer rural Americans tended livestock because millions of country people migrated to urban centers for high-paying industrial jobs during World War II. The declining rural labor market impelled agricultural mechanization. Postwar suburbanization and highway construction consumed former grazing lands. Generating 41,000 miles of new freeways over the next twenty years, the Interstate Highway Act of 1956 enabled industrial farmers to create vast complexes far away from human habitation. They adopted automation, antibiotics, nutritional supplementation, and breed conformity on massive feedlots to maximize livestock production and profit. Most important, large-scale farmers eventually confined food animals indoors, rendering them virtually invisible.[48] This vanishing act posed special challenges to a movement whose effectiveness historically depended on bearing witness to cruelty, especially at the turn of the twenty-first century when several states passed anti-whistleblower "ag-gag" laws, which criminalized the act of recording or reporting acts of animal abuse.[49]

Livestock slaughter remained a cultural flashpoint for the nation's pluralistic religious traditions, specifically Judaism and Islam. Prior to the passage of the federal Humane Methods of Slaughter Act (HMSA) in 1958, Orthodox rabbis lobbied hard against the bill because they feared that federal mandates for stunning before slaughter and prohibitions against shackling would portend future anti-Semitism.[50] Rabbi Isaac Lewin reminded members of Congress that such legislation in Europe had accompanied the rise of Nazism just twenty-five years ago.[51] Consequently, the bill's final form exempted religious slaughter from its requirement that animals be rendered unconscious before death.[52] Further, the ASPCA helped design compact new slaughter pens that allowed the ritual slaughterer, or *shochet*, to kill an animal while it was standing, instead of being suspended, as required by Orthodox rabbis in Israel.[53]

During the 1960s and 1970s, animal advocacy separated into two overlapping strands, both of which were animal-focused and secular. The first emphasized welfare, therefore reflecting the movement's earliest objectives to prevent suffering. The second stressed rights. Influenced by contemporary social justice movements, the broader goal was the liberation of animals from industrial agriculture, hunting, fashion, entertainment, and the laboratory.[54] Disconnected from earlier religious affiliations, both strands of animal protectionism became a de facto punching bag for critics who charged that the movement cared more about animals than people.

This kind of thinking dominated the Terri Schiavo right-to-die case in 2005, when the parents of the severely brain damaged Florida woman unsuccessfully fought her husband's court order to remove her feeding tube. Headlines blared: "If Terri Schiavo Was a Dog"; "PETA Would Be Proud"; and "Give Schiavo the Same Rights as Animals."[55] For religious conservatives, the Schiavo case proved that the animal rights movement had contributed to the nation's moral ruin. They surmised that the liberal Left would have condemned Schiavo's treatment only if she had she been a dog or a cat. The online Southern Baptist Convention newswire intoned: "While the goal of animal rights lawyers is to elevate the status of animals, all they actually accomplish is the devaluing of human life. Polls repeatedly reveal that the same people who move heaven and earth to save beached whales overwhelmingly support abortion and euthanasia. If Terri Schiavo ... were a spotted owl or a kangaroo rat, she would have the support of animal rights advocates and their lawyers from sea to shining sea."[56] Not only do such views ignore the deep religious roots of animal protectionism, but they also ignore the fact that in an earlier phase of the movement, a merciful death was an essential part of the gospel of kindness.

Modern skepticism toward animal protectionism is hardly limited to political conservatives. In 2011, comedian Wyatt Cenac of the left-leaning "Daily Show with Jon Stewart" investigated a civil rights case in Turkey

Creek, Mississippi, a historically black coastal community founded after the Civil War, which had become a dumping ground for the petrochemical industry and eminent domain seizure. Despite repeated entreaties to elected officials and civil rights organizations, aggrieved residents only found redress when they teamed up with Audubon Mississippi, because the town was located on a major migration flyover for endangered birds. State officials quickly placed over 1,600 acres of land in perpetual conservation, a point of disconnection regarding human rights and animal welfare not lost on the "Daily Show."[57] Another episode, "SeaWorld of Pain," pounced on PETA in 2012 for filing a federal lawsuit on behalf of five orcas at Sea World seeking their release "from slavery" under the provisions of the Thirteenth Amendment. Cenac, who is black, interviewed Lisa Lange, the white senior vice president of communications at PETA, and playfully goaded her into saying that PETA members were "the freedom riders of the whale liberation movement." Cenac also spoke with civil rights activist and former Black Panther Party leader Elaine Brown, who denounced PETA's unsuccessful lawsuit as "a cruel racist joke."[58]

The central meaning of the gospel of kindness was rooted in human and animal salvation. Even though this message has fragmented, its definitions of inclusion, exclusion, and citizenship are still yoked to universalizing ideals of proper animal stewardship. In the early months of the second Iraq War, for example, American military officials prioritized the immediate rebuilding of the bombed-out Baghdad Zoo in 2003 as a concrete demonstration of American benevolence.[59] Cockfighters in the Philippines, Puerto Rico, and Hawaii still frame their right to fight as an essential feature of their cultural heritage. In October 2010, Puerto Rico's territorial legislature approved a resolution to protect cockfights as "an integral part of the island's folklore and patrimony."[60] That same year, Catalonian legislators voted to ban bullfighting. While corrida enthusiasts argued that the new law was akin to "throwing a Picasso painting into the garbage," its supporters cited a growing concern for animal cruelty; moreover, given the centuries-old link between bullfighting and Spanish nationalism, the ban made a potent argument for Catalan independence.[61] Indian cow protectionists, including members of the Bharatiya Janata Party (BJP), also treat animal welfare as a barometer of virtuous citizenship and belonging, which transforms beef-eating Muslims, Christians, and non-vegetarian low-caste Hindus who work with cow bodies into virtual aliens in their own country.[62] Similar arguments surfaced in the United States in 2012, as partisan critics of President Barack Obama used the president's recollections of eating dog meat as a child in Indonesia to substantiate their claims that he was a foreigner with a fake birth certificate.[63]

THE FOUNDING OF the ASPCA in New York City created an institutional blueprint for an American social movement with global reach. Roughly 150 years later, the ASPCA is at the forefront of another transformation: in late 2013 the organization transferred its policing powers to the New York Police Department in order to devote its resources to other forms of animal protection, such as canine rehabilitation.[64] This change marks a departure from the organization's original mission. Yet other direct links to the past remain. The status of the laboring horse in New York City still pits drivers and protectionists against each other. In 2013, Bill de Blasio won the mayoral election, in part because he made a campaign promise to ban the carriage horse trade in Midtown. The ASPCA and an allied organization, NYCLASS, have lobbied hard for a ban, arguing that carriage horses work in dangerous traffic conditions and receive poor care from unscrupulous drivers who cheat unsuspecting customers.[65] Drivers and their supporters emphatically disagree: they point to their safety record and compliance with sanitation and licensing regulations.[66] Actor Liam Neeson asserts that the majority of these owners are working-class immigrants demonized by elite interests: "As a result, an entire way of life and a historic industry are under threat."[67] To this day, issues of livelihood and proper animal care remain entangled with broader issues of class, race, ethnicity, and national belonging.

The ongoing battle over New York City's carriage horses represents the movement's enduring tensions between animal and human welfare. Yet another recent event bears a striking resemblance to the gospel of kindness's reconciliatory aspirations. On June 18, 2015, Pope Francis published *Laudato Si* (Praise Be to You), a sweeping papal encyclical calling for global action to combat climate change, poverty, wasteful consumerism, and environmental degradation. While the encyclical has drawn worldwide attention for its commitment to environmentalism, it also makes a strong case for animal advocacy.[68] Opening with a prayer from Saint Francis of Assisi, the encyclical proposes an "integral ecology" of global stewardship and a "culture of care." *Laudato Si* calls for Sunday rest for animals and people, denounces vivisection in all cases but those that "pertain to the necessities of human life," and castigates the consequences of modern anthropocentrism.[69] In accord with early animal protectionists, *Laudato Si* contends that the original meaning of dominion in the Book of Genesis was synonymous with benevolent stewardship.[70] Human sin, or "our presuming to take the place of God and refusing to acknowledge our creaturely limitations," ruptured gentle dominion into violent domination.[71] Denouncing rising sea levels, pollution, the privatization of public spaces, and the scarcity of potable water for the poor, Francis offers a gospel of kindness in the form of a modern environmental social justice jeremiad: "Because all creatures are connected, each must be cherished with love and respect, for all of us as living creatures are dependent on one another."[72] *Laudato Si* offers a legacy of the gospel of kindness and perhaps a guide for its future.

Notes

INTRODUCTION

1. "1935 Report of the American Fondouk Maintenance Committee, Inc.," 4, American Fondouk Annual Reports, 1929–1969, Massachusetts SPCA, Angell Memorial Hospital, Boston (hereafter cited as AMH).
2. "Mrs. Hosali's Work in North Africa," *Our Dumb Animals* (hereafter cited as *ODA*), December 1926, 112.
3. "Annual Report for 1977, Golden Anniversary, 1927–1977," American Fondouk, Fez, Morocco, USA Office: 350 S. Huntington Ave., Boston, MA, 02130, American Fondouk Golden Anniversary Reports (1927–1977) Account Book—1939, AMH.
4. "Our History," *American Fondouk*, http://www.americanfondouk.org/about/our-history.html.
5. "Annual Report for 1977, Golden Anniversary, 1927–1977," AMH.
6. "Annual Report for 1977, Golden Anniversary, 1927–1977," AMH.
7. Fashioned by local French authorities and the pasha in Fez, the medina's first anti-cruelty laws took effect in 1932; this law was followed by six Orders in Council enumerating specific violations that would lead to arrest, which invariably made impoverished drivers and peddlers more vulnerable to apprehension. "1933 Report of the American Fondouk Maintenance Committee, Inc.," American Fondouk Annual Reports, 1929–1969, AMH.
8. "Welcome to the American Fondouk," pamphlet, nd., American Fondouk Annual Reports, 1929–1969, AMH.
9. "Welcome to the American Fondouk."
10. For a succinct historical overview, see *United States Diplomatic Mission to Morocco*, "U.S. Morocco Relations—The Beginning," http://morocco.usembassy.gov/early.html.
11. "1956 Report of the American Fondouk Maintenance Committee, Inc.," American Fondouk Annual Reports, 1929–1969, AMH.

12. For an example of usage, see Marshall Saunders, *Beautiful Joe: A Dog's Own Story* (1893; repr., New York: Grosset and Dunlap, 1920), 188.
13. The "gospel of kindness" should not be confused with historian Katherine Grier's term, the "domestic ethic of kindness," which describes how the care of animals (specifically pets) in the antebellum home was intimately connected to the making of the American middle class and its gendered division of labor. See Katherine C. Grier, *Pets in America: A History* (Chapel Hill: University of North Carolina Press, 2006), chap. 3.
14. "Untitled," *ODA*, May 1917, 179.
15. Denise A. Spellberg, *Jefferson's Koran: Islam and the Founders* (New York: Knopf, 2013), 134–135.
16. Spellberg, *Jefferson's Koran*, 135.
17. Richard W. Bulliet, *Hunters, Herders, and Hamburgers: The Past and Future of Human-Animal Relationships* (New York: Columbia University Press, 2005), 3.
18. Susan Jones, *Valuing Animals: Veterinarians and Their Patients in Modern America* (Baltimore: Johns Hopkins University Press, 2002), 43.
19. "The Horseless Carriage," *New York Times* (hereafter cited as, *NYT*), September 22, 1895.
20. Edwin G. Burrows and Mike Wallace, *Gotham: A History of New York City to 1898* (New York:Oxford University Press, 1998), 786; Brett Mizelle, *Pig* (London: Reaktion Books, 2011), 56–58; Catherine McNeur, *Taming Manhattan: Environmental Battles in the Antebellum City* (Cambridge, MA: Harvard University Press).
21. "Regulations for Driving Cattle through the Streets—Important Order of Superintendent Kennedy," *NYT*, October 5, 1868.
22. "Cattle in the Streets," *NYT*, April 24, 1873.
23. Roy Rosenzweig and Elizabeth Blackmar, *The Park and the People: A History of Central Park* (Ithaca, NY: Cornell University Press), 252, 335, 454.
24. Euroamerican immigrants brought this tradition of living inside with livestock to America. Impoverished German farm laborers lived together on rural estates in a large barn-like structure called the Heuerhaus containing an open peat fire for cooking, no chimney and thus no ventilation, and livestock stalls along the walls. Up to twenty human laborers and their families slept near the choking peat fire for warmth. See Linda A. Fisher and Carolyn Bowers, *Agnes Lake Hickok: Queen of the Circus, Wife of a Legend* (Norman: University of Oklahoma Press, 2009), 14–15.
25. Burrows and Wallace, *Gotham*, 477.
26. Burrows and Wallace, *Gotham*, 744.
27. Ann Norton Greene, *Horses at Work: Harnessing Power in Industrial America* (Cambridge, MA: Harvard University Press, 2008), 174–175.
28. Sydney H. Coleman, *Humane Society Leaders in America: With a Sketch of the Early History of the Humane Movement in England* (Albany, NY: American Humane Association, 1924), 61.

29. Russia was an enduring exotic other in nineteenth- and twentieth-century American social thought and popular culture; "Darkest Russia: A Grand Romance of the Czar's Realm" debuted as a popular theatrical melodrama in 1894 and film in 1917. Reference to "Darkest Russia" courtesy of Julia Mickenberg.
30. Stephen S. Zawistowski, foreword to *The Mary Ellen Wilson Child Abuse Case and the Beginning of Children's Rights in 19th Century America*, by Eric A. Shelman and Stephen Lazoritz (Jefferson, NC: McFarland, 2005), 1; Clara Morris, "Riddle of the Nineteenth Century: Mr. Henry Bergh," *McClure's Magazine*, March 1902, 422.
31. Bergh, quoted in Coleman, *Humane Society Leaders in America*, 35–36.
32. At its inception in 1824, England's first animal protection society was called the Society for the Prevention of Cruelty to Animals. The SPCA changed its name to the Royal SPCA in 1840 when Queen Victoria granted the organization official royal sponsorship.
33. Bergh, quoted in Coleman, *Humane Society Leaders in America*, 37.
34. Coleman, *Humane Society Leaders in America*, 38; and Mark Essig, *Edison and the Electric Chair: A Story of Light and Death* (New York: Walker, 2003), 87.
35. Diane L. Beers, *For the Prevention of Cruelty: The History and Legacy of Animal Rights Activism in the United States* (Athens: Ohio University Press, 2006), 44; Bernard Oreste Unti, "'The Quality of Mercy': Organized Animal Protection in the United States, 1866–1930" (PhD diss., American University, 2002), 79.
36. NY Rev. Stat. tit. 6, sec. 26 (1829), in Animal Legal and Historical Center, https://www.animallaw.info/statute/new-york-revised-statutes-1829-title-6-section-26.
37. Coleman, *Humane Society Leaders in America*, 38.
38. "Cruelty to Animals—First Case of Punishment under the New Law," *NYT*, April 13, 1866.
39. See NY Rev. Stat. ch. 783, §§ 1–10 (1866) and NY Rev. Stat. ch. 375, §§ 1–10 (1867) in Emily Stewart Leavitt et al., *Animals and Their Legal Rights: A Survey of American Laws from 1641 to 1970* (Washington, DC: Animal Welfare Institute, 1970), 18–21.
40. C. C. Buel, "Henry Bergh and His Work," *Scribner's Monthly*, April 1879, 872–884, 872.
41. Buel, "Henry Bergh and His Work," 872; Susan J. Pearson, *The Rights of the Defenseless: Protecting Animals and Children in Gilded Age America* (Chicago: University of Chicago Press, 2011), 77; Leavitt et al., *Animals and Their Legal Rights*, 18–21.
42. Unti, "'The Quality of Mercy,'" 499–509.
43. "Cats and Old Maids 'Shot' in Pasadena," *Los Angeles Times* (hereafter cited as *LAT*), November 22, 1903, ProQuest Historical Newspapers: *Los Angeles Times* (1881–1990).
44. "Cats and Old Maids 'Shot' in Pasadena."
45. Morris, "Riddle of the Nineteenth Century," 414.
46. Coleman, *Humane Society Leaders in America*, 39.

47. Drew Gilpin Faust, *This Republic of Suffering: Death and the American Civil War* (New York: Knopf, 2008); Alan Trachtenberg, *Reading American Photographs: Images as History, Mathew Brady to Walker Evans* (New York: Hill and Wang, 1990); Franny Nudelman, *John Brown's Body: Slavery, Violence, and the Culture of War* (Chapel Hill: University of North Carolina Press, 2004).
48. E. E. Adams, "Impressions of a Visit to the Army of the Potomac," *Christian Recorder*, March 19, 1864, Accessible Archives: African American Newspapers: *Christian Recorder* (1861-1902).
49. Sharon E. Cregier, "Rarey, John Solomon," *American National Biography Online*, February 2000, http://www.anb.org.ezproxy.lib.utexas.edu/articles/20/20-00838.html.
50. Cregier, "Rarey, John Solomon"; "John Rarey: The Story of the Famous Horse Tamer and His Boyish Triumphs," *LAT*, February 11, 1899, ProQuest Historical Newspapers: *Los Angeles Times* (1881–1990).
51. Charles Francis Adams to his Mother, May 12, 1863, Camp of 1st Mass. Cavalry, Potomac Creek, in *A Cycle of Adams Letters, 1861–1865*, ed. Worthington Chauncey Ford, vol. 2 (Boston: Houghton Mifflin, 1920), 3–5. Citation courtesy of T. J. Stiles.
52. Paul D. Escott, *The Confederacy: The Slaveholders' Failed Venture* (Santa Barbara, CA: Praeger/ABC-CLIO, 2010), 137.
53. Mizelle, *Pig*, 58.
54. See George M. Frederickson, *The Inner Civil War: Northern Intellectuals and the Crisis of the Union* (1965; repr., Urbana: University of Illinois Press, 1993).
55. "Found Guilty," *LAT*, June 23, 1895, ProQuest Historical Newspapers: *Los Angeles Times* (1881–1990).
56. The defendant in the heifer starvation case successfully appealed his conviction, won a new trial, and was acquitted on a technicality. "New Trial of William Niles Ends in Acquittal," *LAT*, September 15, 1895, ProQuest Historical Newspapers: *Los Angeles Times* (1881–1990).
57. Maude Marvin, "Humane Education in an American Missionary School," *American Missionary*, July 1901, 156–157, http://ebooks.library.cornell.edu/m/moa/.
58. Pearson, *The Rights of the Defenseless*, 78–80.
59. See William Appleman Williams, *The Tragedy of American Diplomacy*, 50th anniversary ed. (New York: W.W. Norton, 2009).
60. "The Liberties of the Massachusets Collonie in New England, 1641," from *Hanover Historical Texts Project*, https://history.hanover.edu/texts/masslib.html.
61. Kathleen Kete, "Animals and Ideology: The Politics of Animal Protection in Europe," in *Representing Animals*, ed. Nigel Rothfels (Bloomington: Indiana University Press, 2002), 21, 22.
62. Rev. A. L. Riggs, "Our Indian Mission Council," *American Missionary*, July 1893, 226–227, http://ebooks.library.cornell.edu/m/moa/.

63. *Course of Study for the Indian Schools of the United States* (Washington, DC: Government Printing Office, 1901), 96.
64. On the shift from continental to international manifest destiny, see Anders Stephanson, *Manifest Destiny: American Expansionism and the Empire of Right* (New York: Hill and Wang, 1995), xii, 70–71.
65. Emily S. Rosenberg, *Spreading the American Dream: American Economic and Cultural Expansion, 1890–1945* (New York: Hill and Wang, 1982), 3.
66. On the American Red Cross, see Julia F. Irwin, *Making the World Safe: The American Red Cross and a Nation's Humanitarian Awakening* (New York: Oxford University Press, 2013); on Hoover, see Joan Hoff Wilson, *Herbert Hoover: Forgotten Progressive* (Long Grove, IL: Waveland Press, 1992); William E. Leuchtenberg, *Herbert Hoover: The American Presidents Series, the 31st President, 1929–1933* (New York: Times Books, 2009); on the Berlin Airlift and the Marshall Plan, see Michael J. Hogan, *The Marshall Plan: America, Britain, and the Reconstruction of Western Europe, 1947–1952* (New York: Cambridge University Press, 1989); Melvyn Leffler, *A Preponderance of Power: National Security, the Truman Administration, and the Cold War* (Palo Alto: Stanford University Press, 1993).
67. See Peter Singer, *Animal Liberation*, 2nd ed. (New York: New York Review of Books, 1990), 218–219, 222; Gary Francione, *Rain without Thunder: The Ideology of the Animal Rights Movement* (Philadelphia: Temple University Press, 1996); Ingrid Newkirk, *Free the Animals: The Amazing True Story of the Animal Liberation Front* (New York: Lantern Books, 2000); Matthew Scully, *Dominion: The Power of Man, the Suffering of Animals, and the Call to Mercy* (New York: St. Martin's Press, 2002), 15; Tom Regan, *The Case for Animal Rights*, updated, new preface (Berkeley: University of California Press, 2004).
68. Some humane groups have bemoaned the absence of animal concerns in contemporary churches. See Paul Berry, "Kindness Revival: Why Don't Churches Preach Compassion for Animals?" *Best Friends Magazine*, March/April 2007, 18–20.
69. See "To Mercifully Kill Horses, Dogs, and Other Animals," *ODA*, July 1887, 24; "Her Work Not Appreciated," *NYT*, October 6, 1893; "Do Not Leave Your Cat to Starve," *Starry Cross*, May 1927, 90–91.
70. James Turner's fascinating comparative intellectual history, *Reckoning with the Beast*, ties the advent of humane thought to the rise of analgesics and anesthesia in the United States and England. Because this book is principally a history of ideas, it is less concerned with the daily life of a social movement. Susan Pearson imaginatively explores the symbiotic relationship between the evolution of American liberalism, animal welfare, and child welfare in the Gilded Age; her book, *The Rights of the Defenseless*, is a major contribution to American political philosophy and intellectual history. Diane Beers's compelling narrative history, *For the Prevention of Cruelty*, recovers the vitality and passion of the early leadership to make a case for continuity between the past and present-day animal rights activism. Bernard Unti's dissertation, "'The Quality of Mercy': Organized Animal

Protection in the United States, 1866–1930," provides an extraordinarily thorough history of organized, institutional change in SPCAs across the nation. See James Turner, *Reckoning with the Beast: Animals, Pain, and Humanity in the Victorian Mind* (Baltimore: Johns Hopkins University Press, 1980); Diane L. Beers, *For the Prevention of Cruelty*; Susan Pearson, *The Rights of the Defenseless*; Unti, "'The Quality of Mercy.'" In addition, several historians have richly chronicled the omnipresence of domestic animals, particularly the laboring horse, in nineteenth-century cities. See Susan Jones, *Valuing Animals*; Clay McShane and Joel A. Tarr, *The Horse in the City: Living Machines in the Nineteenth Century* (Baltimore: Johns Hopkins University Press, 2007); Ann Norton Greene, *Horses at Work*.

71. For selected works treating the relationship between animal advocacy and empire, see, Moira Ferguson, *Animal Advocacy and Englishwomen, 1780–1900: Patriots, Nation, and Empire* (Ann Arbor: University of Michigan Press, 1998); John M. MacKenzie, *The Empire of Nature: Hunting, Conservation, and British Imperialism* (Manchester: Manchester University Press, 1988); Harriet Ritvo, *The Animal Estate: The English and Other Creatures in the Victorian Age* (Cambridge, MA: Harvard University Press, 1987); Aaron Herald Skabelund, *Empire of Dogs: Canines, Japan, and the Making of the Modern Imperial World* (Ithaca, NY: Cornell University Press, 2011); Brett L. Walker, "Meiji Modernization, Scientific Agriculture, and the Destruction of Japan's Hokkaido Wolf," *Environmental History* 9, no. 2 (April 2004): 248–274; and Walker, *The Lost Wolves of Japan*, foreword by William Cronon (Seattle: University of Washington Press, 2005). Although not topically related to the British or Japanese Empire, see also Kathleen Kete's excellent study of Parisian petkeeping, *The Beast in the Boudoir: Petkeeping in Nineteenth-Century Paris* (Berkeley: University of California Press, 1994).

72. The historian Thomas Sugrue refers to the flood of "rights" language and statist interventions in the economy as central to the World War II "rights revolution." Thomas Sugrue, *The Origins of the Urban Crisis: Race and Inequality in Postwar Detroit* (Princeton, NJ: Princeton University Press, 1996). On animal rights, see Singer, *Animal Liberation*, 6.

73. American and British women represented the largest contingent of foreign missionary women in South Asia. See Maina Chawla Singh, *Gender, Religion, and "Heathen Lands": American Missionary Women in South Asia (1860s–1940s)* (New York: Garland, 2000), 32n19.

74. Karl Marx and Friedrich Engels, *The Communist Manifesto*, ed. Samuel H. Beer (1848; repr., New York: Appleton-Century-Crofts, 1955), 40.

75. "American Society for the Prevention of Cruelty to Animals: 58th Annual Report, Year Ended December 31, 1923" (New York: ASPCA, 1924): 9.

76. See Tim Wise, "Animal Whites: PETA and the Politics of Putting Things in Perspective," August 13, 2005, originally published in *Counterpunch*, http://www.timwise.org/2005/08/animal-whites-peta-and-the-politics-of-putting-things-in-perspective/ Citation courtesy of Brett Mizelle.

CHAPTER 1

1. George T. Angell, *Autobiographical Sketches and Personal Recollections* (Boston: American Humane Education Society, 1884), 9.
2. Angell, *Autobiographical Sketches*, 12–14.
3. Bernard Oreste Unti, "'The Quality of Mercy': Organized Animal Protection in the United States, 1866–1930" (PhD diss., American University, 2002), 225.
4. Angell, *Autobiographical Sketches*, 8.
5. Angell, *Autobiographical Sketches*, 7.
6. James Turner, *Reckoning with the Beast: Animals, Pain, and Humanity in the Victorian Mind* (Baltimore: Johns Hopkins University Press, 1980), 20–22.
7. NY Rev. Stat. tit. 6, sec. 26 (1829); MA Rev. Stat. sec. 22, ch. 130 (1836); "An Act to Prevent and Punish Wanton Cruelty to Animals in the City of Philadelphia," Laws of the General Assembly of the State of Pennsylvania, no. 444, sec. 1, 1855, p. 421, quoted in Francis H. Rowley, *The Humane Idea: A Brief History of Man's Attitude toward the Other Animals, and of the Development of the Humane Spirit into Organized Societies* (1912; repr., Boston: American Humane Education Society, 1925), 36–42.
8. Susan J. Pearson, *The Rights of the Defenseless: Protecting Animals and Children in Gilded Age America* (Chicago: University of Chicago Press, 2011), 77–78.
9. See Ronald G. Walters, *American Reformers, 1815–1860* (New York: Hill and Wang, 1978); Daniel J. Czitrom, *Media and the American Mind: From Morse to McLuhan* (Chapel Hill: University of North Carolina Press, 1983).
10. Raymond Williams, *Marxism and Literature* (New York: Oxford University Press, 1977), 131.
11. Waln quoted in Unti, "'The Quality of Mercy,'" 151; and Turner, *Reckoning with the Beast*, 46.
12. Sydney E. Ahlstrom, *A Religious History of the American People*, 2nd ed. (New Haven, CT: Yale University Press, 2004), 263.
13. Robert H. Abzug, *Cosmos Crumbling: American Reform and the Religious Imagination* (New York: Oxford University Press, 1994), 35–38; Ahlstrom, *A Religious History of the American People*, 416.
14. Charles Grandison Finney, *Lectures on Revivals of Religion* (New York: Leavitt, Lord, 1835), 246–247.
15. Paul E. Johnson, *A Shopkeeper's Millennium: Society and Revivals in Rochester, New York, 1815–1837* (New York: Hill and Wang, 1978), 101–102.
16. Frances E. Willard, *Glimpses of Fifty Years: The Autobiography of an American Woman* (Chicago: Woman's Temperance Publication Association, 1889), 5.
17. Rebekah Angell to George Angell, July 2, 1833, Proctorsville, VT, Letters, R. Angell to G. Angell and Misc. Letters, 1836–1843, donated by Constance Danielson, AMH, Boston.
18. Rebekah Angell to George Angell, January 27, 1838, AMH.
19. Rebekah Angell to George Angell, February 12, 1838, AMH.

20. Angell, *Autobiographical Sketches*, 3.
21. Timothy Dwight, *Theology: Explained and Defended in a Series of Sermons*, 2nd ed., vol. 3 (New Haven, CT: S. Converse, 1823), 273–274.
22. Charles Grandison Finney, *Skeletons of a Course of Theological Lectures* (Oberlin, OH: James Steele, 1840), 194.
23. Finney, *Skeletons of a Course*, 191–192.
24. Finney, *Skeletons of a Course*, 193.
25. Dwight, *Theology*, 274–275.
26. Dwight, *Theology*, 302.
27. Dwight, *Theology*, 303–304.
28. E. P. Thompson, "Time, Work-Discipline, and Industrial Capitalism," *Past and Present* 1, no. 38 (December 1967): 58, 61.
29. Katherine C. Grier, *Pets in America: A History* (Chapel Hill: University of North Carolina Press, 2006), chap. 3.
30. See also Robert C. Allen, *Horrible Prettiness: Burlesque and American Culture* (Chapel Hill: University of North Carolina Press, 1991); Bluford Adams, *E Pluribus Barnum: The Great Showman and the Making of U.S. Popular Culture* (Minneapolis: University of Minnesota Press, 1997).
31. Harriet Beecher Stowe, *Uncle Tom's Cabin, or, Life among the Lowly* (1852; repr., New York: Signet Classic, 1998), 88.
32. Harriet Beecher Stowe, "A Talk about Birds," in *A Dog's Mission; or, the Story of the Old Avery House and Other Stories* (New York: Fords, Howard, and Hulbert, 1880), 106–107.
33. Stowe, "A Talk about Birds," 115.
34. Willard, *Glimpses of Fifty Years*, 33.
35. Willard, *Glimpses of Fifty Years*, facsimile insert between 496–497.
36. Brigette Nicole Fielder, "Animal Humanism: Race, Species, and Affective Kinship in Nineteenth-Century Abolitionism," in "Species/Race/Sex," ed. Claire Jean Kim and Carla Freccero, special issue, *American Quarterly* 65, no. 3 (September 2013): 502.
37. See, for example, American Sunday School Union, *The Sunday School Hymn Book* (Philadelphia: American Sunday School Union, 1828).
38. American Sunday School Union, *Slim Jack; or, the History of a Circus-Boy* (Philadelphia: American Sunday School Union, 1847), 50–51.
39. American Sunday School Union, *Kindness to Animals, or, the Sin of Cruelty Exposed and Rebuked* (Philadelphia: American Sunday School Union, 1845), 10–11, Shaping the Values of Youth: Sunday School Books in 19th Century America, http://digital.lib.msu.edu/projects/ssb/display.cfm?TitleID=459.
40. American Sunday School Union, *Kindness to Animals*, 12.
41. American Sunday School Union, *Kindness to Animals*, 13–14.
42. American Sunday School Union, *Kindness to Animals*, 34, 14–17.
43. Ahlstrom, *Religious History of the American People*, 642.

44. William Holmes McGuffey, *McGuffey's First Eclectic Reader*, rev. ed. (New York: John Wiley and Sons, 1879) Project Gutenberg Ebook #14640, 2005, 55, 73, 79–80, 41, 63, 56–57; http://www.gutenberg.org/files/14640/14640-pdf.pdf.

45. McGuffey, *McGuffey's Eclectic Third Reader: Containing Lessons in Prose and Poetry* (Cincinnati: Winthrop B. Smith, 1862), 23–27, 46–50, 52–54, 73–77, 89–93, 104–108, 120–123, 206–208.

46. See Myra C. Glenn, *Campaigns against Corporal Punishment: Prisoners, Sailors, Women, and Children in Antebellum America* (Albany: State University of New York Press, 1984).

47. Sharon E. Cregier, "Rarey, John Solomon," *American National Biography Online*, February 2000, http://www.anb.org.ezproxy.lib.utexas.edu/articles/20/20-00838.html.

48. "Inspection of Army Horses: The Report of Mr. Rarey," in "Report of the Committee on the Conduct of the War," *NYT*, December 24, 1862.

49. George Angell, "The Eleventh Anniversary of the Massachusetts Society for the Prevention of Cruelty to Animals," address reprinted in *ODA*, April 1879, 85, 82–85.

50. "Fountain We Erected in Custom House Square in Memory of Dorothea Dix," *ODA*, September 1900, 45; Angell, *Autobiographical Sketches*, 92.

51. Karen Halttunen, "Humanitarianism and the Pornography of Pain in Anglo-American Culture," *American Historical Review* 100, no. 2 (April 1995): 313.

52. Dorothea L. Dix, "A Memorial Soliciting Enlarged and Improved Accommodations for the Insane of the State of Tennessee" (Nashville: B. R. M'Kennie, 1847), 3, 7.

53. "Children, *The Colored American*, June 17, 1837; "A Description of the Squirrel, Squirrel Catching, &c.," *The Colored American*, May 9, 1840, both from Accessible Archives: African American Newspapers: *The Colored American* (1837-1841).

54. Elizabeth E. Clark, "'The Sacred Rights of the Weak': Pain, Sympathy, and the Culture of Individual Rights in Antebellum America," *Journal of American History* 82, no. 2 (September 1995): 476, 477.

55. Clark, "'The Sacred Rights of the Weak,'" 472, 473.

56. Clark, "'The Sacred Rights of the Weak,'" 473; Halttunen, "Humanitarianism and the Pornography of Pain in Anglo-American Culture," 310.

57. Turner, *Reckoning with the Beast*, 81–83.

58. Halttunen, "Humanitarianism and the Pornography of Pain in Anglo-American Culture," 310–311.

59. Halttunen also contends that the concurrent rise of pornography exposed the ways in which pain prevention paradoxically fetishized pain itself "as obscenely titillating precisely because the humanitarian sensibility deemed it unacceptable, taboo." Halttunen, "Humanitarianism and the Pornography of Pain in Anglo-American Culture," 305–307.

60. Halttunen, "Humanitarianism and the Pornography of Pain in Anglo-American Culture," 307.

61. Clark, "'The Sacred Rights of the Weak,'" 466, 469.
62. Philip D. Morgan, "Slaves and Livestock in Eighteenth-Century Jamaica: Vineyard Pen, 1750–1751," *The William and Mary Quarterly* 52, no. 1 (January 1995): 50. Citation courtesy of Shirley Thompson.
63. Morgan, "Slaves and Livestock in Eighteenth-Century Jamaica," 73–76.
64. Beers, *For the Prevention of Cruelty*, 132; "Foreign Intelligence—America," *The Animal's Defender and Zoophilist* (London), February 1, 1904, 210.
65. Stowe, *Uncle Tom's Cabin*, 21–22.
66. Stowe, *Uncle Tom's Cabin*, 88–89.
67. Cynthia Eagle Russett, *Sexual Science: The Victorian Construction of Womanhood* (Cambridge, MA: Harvard University Press, 1989), 26; Fielder, "Animal Humanism: Race, Species, and Affective Kinship in Nineteenth-Century Abolitionism," 492.
68. Fielder, "Animal Humanism: Race, Species, and Affective Kinship in Nineteenth-Century Abolitionism," 492.
69. Angell, *Autobiographical Sketches*, 3; "Black Beauty: The Uncle Tom's Cabin of the Horse," *ODA*, August 1890, 26.
70. Nina Moore Tiffany, *Samuel E. Sewall: A Memoir* (Boston: Houghton, Mifflin, 1898), 148.
71. Garrison, quoted in Tiffany, *Samuel E. Sewall*, 36.
72. Tiffany, *Samuel E. Sewall*, 76–79.
73. Tiffany, *Samuel E. Sewall*, 103–106.
74. Tiffany, *Samuel E. Sewall*, 127–146.
75. George Angell, quoted in Tiffany, *Samuel E. Sewall*, 93
76. William Lloyd Garrison, "The Treatment of Animals," *Liberator (1831–1865)*, March 22, 1861, 46, ProQuest: American Periodicals (1740–1940).
77. Garrison, "The Treatment of Animals."
78. Hamilton McCarthy, "Rarey, the Equine King," quoted in Sara Lowe Brown, *Rarey, the Horse's Master and Friend* (Columbus: F. J. Heer, 1916), 20.
79. Unti, "The Quality of Mercy," 153.
80. See "Lincoln at Gettysburg," June 1902, 2; "Abraham Lincoln—A Tribute," February 1926, 131; "January, 1809—Abraham Lincoln—February 1934," February 1934, 19; "Abraham Lincoln and Horses," February 1936, 21, all from *ODA*.
81. "Lincoln's Love of Animals," *ODA*, February 1936, 27.
82. "I Never Trapped an Animal in My Life—Lincoln," *National Humane Review*, March 1929, 13, excerpted from "Lincoln the Lover," *Atlantic Monthly*, December 1928, http://www.theatlantic.com/magazine/archive/1928/12/lincoln-the-lover/304444/.
83. Pearson, *The Rights of the Defenseless*, 101–102.
84. Reverend Pierpont, "Pierpont on Cruelty to Animals," *National Era*, June 17, 1847, Accessible Archives: African American Newspapers: *National Era* (1847-1860).
85. Stowe, *Uncle Tom's Cabin*, 373–374.

86. Johnson, *A Shopkeeper's Millennium*, 81.
87. Johnson, *A Shopkeeper's Millennium*, 60.
88. Dwight, *Theology*, 382, 386; Abzug, *Cosmos Crumbling*, 94–95.
89. Sydney Herbert, *The Young Volunteer Campaign Melodist* (Boston: James M. Usher, 1864), 9.
90. Herbert, *The Young Volunteer Campaign Melodist*, 17.
91. Herbert, *The Young Volunteer Campaign Melodist*, 1864, back cover.
92. "Universal Mercy Band Movement," *Christian Life: A Unitarian Journal*, March 5, 1887, 120.
93. "Signing the Pledge of the Band of Mercy," July, 1887, 1; "Report of the President," May, 1903, 155; "90,000 Bands of Mercy," March, 1914, 154; "New Bands of Mercy," November 1926, 94, all from *ODA*.
94. "Two Kinds of Armies," *ODA*, September 1888, 49.
95. Ronald Takaki, *A Different Mirror: A History of Multicultural America*, rev. ed. (New York: Back Bay Books, 2008), 134–137.
96. Takaki, *A Different Mirror*, 138–140.
97. Takaki, *A Different Mirror*, 139.
98. Tyler Anbinder, *Nativism and Slavery: The Northern Know Nothings and the Politics of the 1850s* (New York: Oxford University Press, 1992), 43–44, 309.
99. See Peter C. Mancall, *Deadly Medicine: Indians and Alcohol in Early America* (Ithaca, NY: Cornell University Press, 1997).
100. See Matthew Frye Jacobson, *Barbarian Virtues: The United States Encounters Foreign Peoples at Home and Abroad* (New York: Hill and Wang, 2000).
101. See Louise Michele Newman, *White Women's Rights: The Racial Origins of Feminism in the United States* (New York: Oxford University Press, 1999).
102. Williams, *Marxism and Literature*, 131.

CHAPTER 2

1. George T. Angell, "The Age of Woman," *ODA*, November 1887, 64.
2. Angell, "The Age of Woman," 64.
3. "Fifty Millions," and "Five Millions of Pages," *ODA*, November 1887, 64.
4. Mother Stewart (Eliza Daniel Stewart), *Memories of the Crusade, a Thrilling Account of the Great Uprising of the Women of Ohio in 1873, against the Liquor Crime*, 2nd ed. (Columbus, OH: William G. Hubbard, 1889), 457.
5. See Ruth Bordin, *Woman and Temperance: The Quest for Power and Liberty, 1873–1900* (Philadelphia: Temple University Press, 1981); Ian Tyrrell, *Woman's World/Woman's Empire: The Woman's Christian Temperance Union in International Perspective, 1880–1930* (Chapel Hill: University of North Carolina Press, 1991).
6. Alison Parker, *Purifying America: Women, Cultural Reform, and Pro-Censorship Activism, 1873–1933* (Champaign: University of Illinois Press, 1997), 5. For a

complete list of WCTU departments, see Elizabeth Putnam Gordon, *Women Torch-Bearers: The Story of the Woman's Christian Temperance Union*, 2nd ed. (Evanston, IL: National Woman's Christian Temperance Union, 1924), 296–303.

7. George T. Angell, "The Relations of Animals That Can Speak to Those That Are Dumb," *ODA* Supplement, September 1888, 52.

8. Angell, "The Relations of Animals That Can Speak to Those That Are Dumb," 49–52.

9. "Minutes of the WCTU," Temperance and Prohibition Papers, Series 3 (hereafter cited as WCTU Series), Roll 2: Annual Meeting Minutes, 1885–1888, *Minutes of the National Convention: 1887*, November 16–21, 1887, Nashville, microfilm, p.18, 19, 47.

10. Frances E. Willard, "President's Annual Address," WCTU Series, Roll 3: Annual Meeting Minutes, 1889–1892, *Minutes of the National Convention: 1889*, Chicago, November 8–13, 1889, microfilm, p. 147.

11. Born in London in 1843, Mary Frances Whitechurch moved to the United States at age five. She later married George S. Lovell, an affluent wholesale clock dealer in Philadelphia. The Lovells settled on a large estate in Bryn Mawr, where they lived until George died in 1897. Lovell moved to Jenkintown, Pennsylvania, for the rest of her life (where the AAVS still has its headquarters).

12. The AAVS magazine was known as the *Starry Cross* from 1922–1939, and today as *AV Magazine*.

13. Louise Michele Newman, *White Women's Rights: The Racial Origins of Feminism in the United States* (New York: Oxford University Press, 1999), 53.

14. See James Turner, *Reckoning with the Beast: Animals, Pain, and Humanity in the Victorian Mind* (Baltimore: Johns Hopkins University Press, 1980); Diana L. Beers, *For the Prevention of Cruelty: The History and Legacy of Animal Rights Activism in the United States* (Athens: Ohio University Press, 2006).

15. See Lovell, "Department of Mercy," WCTU Series, Roll 4: Annual Meeting Minutes, 1893–1896, *Minutes of the National Convention: 1893*, Chicago, October 18–21, 1893, microfilm, p. 371.

16. Lori D. Ginzberg, *Women and the Work of Benevolence: Morality, Politics, and Class in the Nineteenth-Century United States* (New Haven, CT: Yale University Press, 1990), 204–206.

17. "Minutes of the Eighteenth Annual Meeting of the WCTU of Minnesota," September 11–14, 1894, 70; WCTU Minnesota Collection, WCTU Minutes, box 12/6/7, vol. 3, Social Welfare History Archives, University of Minnesota, Minneapolis (hereafter cited as SWHA).

18. Mary F. Lovell, "Department of Mercy," WCTU Series, Roll 4: Annual Meeting Minutes, 1893–1896, *Minutes of the National Convention: 1894*, Cleveland, November 16–21, 1894, microfilm, p. 335.

19. Angell, "The Relations of Animals that Can Speak to Those that Are Dumb," 50.

20. See Barbara Welter, "The Cult of True Womanhood: 1820–1860," *American Quarterly* 18, no. 2, part 1 (Summer 1966): 151–174; Bordin, *Woman and Temperance*, 165, 167–168.

21. Bordin, *Woman and Temperance*, 61.
22. See Gayatri Chakravorty Spivak, "Subaltern Studies: Deconstructing Historiography," in *The Spivak Reader: Selected Works of Gayatri Chakravorty Spivak*, ed. Donna Landry and Gerald MacLean (New York: Routledge, 1995): 203–236.
23. Caroline Earle White to Henry Bergh, March 23, 1867, quoted in Bernard Oreste Unti, "'The Quality of Mercy': Organized Animal Protection in the United States, 1866–1930" (PhD diss., American University, 2002), 153, 155.
24. "How Animals Have Been Saved from Cruelty," *NYT*, February 13, 1875.
25. Unti, "'The Quality of Mercy,'" 174–178.
26. Unti, "'The Quality of Mercy,'" 168–170.
27. See Moira Ferguson, *Animal Advocacy and Englishwomen, 1780–1900: Patriots, Nation, and Empire* (Ann Arbor: University of Michigan Press, 1998); Hilda Kean, *Animal Rights: Political and Social Change in Britain since 1800* (London: Reaktion Books, 1998), chap. 4, "Bringing Light into Dark Places: Antivivisection and the Animals of the Home," 96–112.
28. Bernard Unti, "The Foremother to American Animal Advocacy," *AV Magazine*, Spring 2008, 6–9, 8, www.aavs.org/.
29. Sydney H. Coleman, *Humane Society Leaders in America: With a Sketch of the Early History of the Humane Movement in England* (Albany, NY: American Humane Association, 1924), 205–206; Unti, "The Foremother to American Animal Advocacy," 6–9.
30. The six states included Massachusetts (1894, 1902); Oklahoma (1908); Illinois (1910); South Dakota (1903); Washington (1897, 1903); and Pennsylvania (1905). Beers, *For the Prevention of Cruelty*, 139.
31. Jennifer Price, *Flight Maps: Adventures with Nature in Modern America* (New York: Basic Books, 1998), 64.
32. Lovell, "Department of Mercy," WCTU Series, Roll 4: Annual Meeting Minutes, 1893–1896, *Minutes of the National Convention: 1894*, Cleveland, November 16–21, 1894, microfilm, p. 338.
33. "Points Way to End Slaughter of Birds," *NYT*, January 2, 1911.
34. Lovell, "Department of Mercy," WCTU Series, Roll 5: Annual Meeting Minutes, 1897–1900, *Minutes of the National Convention: 1897*, Buffalo, October 29–November 3, 1897, microfilm, p. 434.
35. William Williams Keen, *Animal Experimentation and Medical Progress* (Boston: Houghton Mifflin, 1914), 234–235.
36. Keen, *Animal Experimentation and Medical Progress*, 243n1.
37. Lovell, "Department of Mercy," WCTU Series, Roll 4: Annual Meeting Minutes, 1893–1896, *Minutes of the National Convention: 1893*, Chicago, October 18–21, 1893, microfilm, p. 372.
38. Lovell, "Department of Mercy," *Minutes of the National Convention: 1897*, 430–432.
39. Dean Wilson Kuykendall, "The History of Humane Education" (master's thesis, University of Texas, 1935), 86–90.

40. The Reverend Charles Scanlon, "The Presbyterian Church and Humane Education," *National Humane Review* (hereafter cited as *NHR*), March 1921, 46.
41. The most common denominations in the WCTU were Methodist, Baptist, Presbyterian, and Congregationalist. Bordin, *Woman and Temperance*, 164, 168–169.
42. Anderson H. Wimbish, "The Broader Catechism," undated, 14, Anderson H. Wimbish Papers, 1836–1906, Manuscript Notebooks, #A/.W757, box 1, Correspondence and Miscellaneous Papers, Minnesota Historical Society (hereafter cited as MHS).
43. See, for example, "News of the Week: States and Territories," *Christian Recorder*, August 15, 1868; "Book Table," *Christian Recorder*, April 20, 1876; both from Accessible Archives: African American Newspapers: *Christian Recorder* (1861–1902); and "'The Journal of Zoöphily,' Philadelphia, Pa.," *Golden Age: An Inspirational Weekly for the Home and the Citizen*, June 28, 1906, 12.
44. In 1907, the Mercy superintendent for California reported that *Christ among the Cattle* was "being specially circulated among ministers." Lovell, "Mercy," WCTU Series, Roll 7: Annual Meeting Minutes, 1906–1910, *Minutes of the National Convention: 1907*, Nashville, November 8–13, 1907, microfilm, p. 317.
45. Frederic Rowland Marvin, *Christ among the Cattle: A Sermon*, 6th ed. (Boston: Sherman, French, 1912), 1–2.
46. "Table of Contents 1—no Title," or "The World's News in Today's Times," *LAT*, October 26, 1914, ProQuest Historical Newspapers: *Los Angeles Times* (1881–1990); "'Humane Sunday' to Be Observed in Pittsburgh Soon," *Pittsburgh Press*, August 9, 1914.
47. Roswell McCrea writes that the American Humane Association (AHA) initiated the Mercy Sunday movement in 1908; other historians, however, note that the AHA formalized the practice of Mercy Sunday as part of its annual "Be Kind to Animals Week," starting in 1915. See Roswell C. McCrea, *The Humane Movement: A Descriptive Survey* (New York: Columbia University Press, 1910), 106–107; Kuykendall, "The History of Humane Education," 151; Unti, "'The Quality of Mercy,'" 590–594.
48. "Worship Service for Humane Sunday," *NHR*, April 1930, 22.
49. Walter Rauschenbusch, "For This World," *Prayers of the Social Awakening* (Boston: Pilgrim Press, 1909), 47–48. Citation courtesy of Paul Brandeis Raushenbush.
50. Kuykendall, "The History of Humane Education," 86–88.
51. "Minutes of the 22nd Annual Meeting of the WCTU of the State of Minnesota" (St. Paul: W. J. Woodbury, 1898), 5–6, 24, WCTU Minutes, vol. 3 (1893–1899), WCTU Minnesota Collection, box 12/6/7, SWHA.
52. "Minutes of the 22nd Annual Meeting of the WCTU of the State of Minnesota—Report of the Department of Mercy," 1898, 97.
53. Nina Halvey, "As She Passed along Our Way," "Memorial Number, Commemorative of Mary F. Lovell," *Starry Cross*, July 1932, 102.

54. S. Parkes Cadman, "Man and Beast: A Humane Sermon," *NHR*, February 1926, 6–7; Kuykendall, "The History of Humane Education," 86.
55. "Cameras for Humane Society," *LAT*, May 10, 1901, ProQuest Historical Newspapers: *Los Angeles Times* (1881–1990).
56. "Monthly Meeting Minutes," December 4, 1923, St. Paul Society for the Prevention of Cruelty to Animals Records, P1546, Minutes, 1917–1920, file 2, MHS.
57. Marvin, *Christ among the Cattle*, 26–28.
58. See Hal Herzog, *Some We Love, Some We Hate, Some We Eat: Why It's So Hard to Think Straight about Animals* (New York: Harper, 2010), 29–34.
59. G. Stanley Hall, quoted in Louis N. Wilson, *G. Stanley Hall: A Sketch* (New York: G. E. Stechert, 1914), 20–21.
60. Lovell, "Mercy," WCTU Series, Roll 7: Annual Meeting Minutes, 1906–1910, *Minutes of the National Convention: 1906*, Hartford, CT, October 26–31, 1906, microfilm, p. 305.
61. Susan E. Lederer, *Subjected to Science: Human Experimentation in America before the Second World War* (Baltimore: Johns Hopkins University Press, 1995), 41.
62. "The Twenty-first Annual Report of the American Anti-Vivisection Society for the Year 1903" (Philadelphia: AAVS, 1904): 24.
63. In 1900, the percentage of fourteen- to seventeen-year-olds enrolled in school compared to the total population in that age group was 10.6 percent. In 1920, 35 percent of all fourteen- to seventeen-year-olds in the United States were enrolled in school. "No. HS-20. Educational Summary—Enrollment, 1900 to 2000, and Projections, 2001," *2003 Statistical Abstract: Mini-Historical Statistics*, 33–34, United States Census Bureau, http://www2.census.gov/library/publications/2004/compendia/statab/123ed/hist/hs-20.pdf.
64. Lovell, "Mercy," WCTU Series, Roll 8: Annual Meeting Minutes, 1911–1912, *National Meeting Minutes: 1912*, Portland, OR, October 19–25, 1912, microfilm, p. 310.
65. Unti, " 'The Quality of Mercy,' " 582.
66. "Swing Wide Mercy's Side," *LAT*, January 12, 1905, ProQuest Historical Newspapers: *Los Angeles Times* (1881–1990).
67. Lovell, "Mercy," WCTU Series, Roll 7: Annual Meeting Minutes, 1906–1910, *Minutes of the National Convention: 1906*, Hartford, CT, October 26–31, 1906, microfilm, p. 305.
68. Ferguson, *Animal Advocacy and Englishwomen*, 75–78.
69. "Margaret Marshall Saunders—The Storyteller and a Woman ahead of her Time," Beautiful Joe Heritage Society, http://www.beautifuljoe.org/all-about-joe/the-story-teller; Marshall Saunders, *Beautiful Joe: A Dog's Own Story* (1893; repr., New York: Grosset and Dunlap, 1920), dedication page; "Black Beauty: The Uncle Tom's Cabin of the Horse," *ODA*, August 1890, 26.
70. Anna Sewell, *Black Beauty* (1877; repr., New York: Signet Classic, 2002), 164.
71. Saunders, *Beautiful Joe*, 4.
72. Susan Pearson, *The Rights of the Defenseless: Protecting Animals and Children in Gilded Age America* (Chicago: University of Chicago Press, 2011), 90–91.

73. Saunders, *Beautiful Joe*, 25.
74. Sewell, *Black Beauty*, 103, 184.
75. Saunders, *Beautiful Joe*, 27.
76. Saunders, *Beautiful Joe*, 175, 170–188.
77. *Black Beauty* is reportedly the sixth most popular book of all time in the English language. By the 1930s, *Beautiful Joe*'s worldwide sales topped 7 million copies. Ferguson, *Animal Advocacy and Englishwomen*, 76; "Margaret Marshall Saunders—The Storyteller and a Woman ahead of her Time," http://www.beautifuljoe.org/all-about-joe/the-story-teller.
78. "Minutes of the Seventeenth Annual Convention of the WCTU of Minnesota," September 12, 1893, 50; WCTU Minnesota Collection, WCTU Minutes, box 12/6/7, vol. 3, SWHA.
79. "Minutes of the Seventeenth Annual Convention of the WCTU of Minnesota," 69.
80. "Mr. Bergh Enlarging His Sphere of Usefulness," *NYT*, April 10, 1874.
81. Coleman, *Humane Society Leaders in America*, 72; Linda Gordon, *Heroes of Their Own Lives: The Politics and History of Family Violence* (New York: Penguin Books, 1988), 33–34; Pearson, *The Rights of the Defenseless*, 1–20.
82. "The Mission of Humanity," *NYT*, April 11, 1874.
83. "Waifs and Strays," *NYT*, April 11, 1874.
84. Coleman, *Humane Society Leaders in America*, 257.
85. "Constitution" (Article 1), St. Paul Society for the Prevention of Cruelty, adopted March 4, 1899, St. Paul Society for the Prevention of Cruelty to Animals Records, P1546, Minutes, 1917–1920, file 1, MHS.
86. In accord with the right to privacy of the people involved, all parties to abuse cases (with the exception of SPCA and humane officers) are unnamed here, although they are identified in the records themselves. Case Numbers 44, 45, 48 (May 14, May 16, May 17, 1892), St. Paul Society for the Prevention of Cruelty to Animals Records, P1546, Humane Society Complaint Records, vol. 2, MHS.
87. Case Number 78, July 6, 1892, St. Paul Society for the Prevention of Cruelty to Animals Records, P1546, Humane Society Complaint Records, vol. 2, MHS.
88. Case Number 66, May 7, 1917, St. Paul Society for the Prevention of Cruelty to Animals Records, P1546, Miscellaneous Papers, Record Books, vol. 4, 1917, MHS.
89. Correspondence, June 16, [no year], St. Paul Society for the Prevention of Cruelty to Animals, P1546, Reports of Cases, 1905–1908, MHS.
90. "Minutes of the Nineteenth Annual Meeting of the WCTU of the State of Minnesota," (Minneapolis: Harrison and Smith, 1895), 17–18, WCTU Minutes, vol. 3 (1893–1899), WCTU Minnesota Collection, box 12/6/7, SWHA.
91. See "Maudlin Sentiment in Parallel Case," April 28, 1895; "Maria Barberi Is Guilty," July 16, 1895; "Maria Barberi's Father in Poverty," July 17, 1895; "Maria Barberi Breaks Down," July 18, 1895; "Maria Barbella to Die," July 19, 1895; "Meeting in Behalf of Maria Barberi," August 8, 1895; "A 'New Journalist's' Plan," February 7, 1897, all from *NYT*.

92. Owing to a groundswell of protest, Maria Barberi was retried and acquitted in December 1896, after spending over a year at Sing-Sing. "Minutes of the Twentieth Annual Meeting of the State of the WCTU of the State of Minnesota," Minneapolis, September 29–October 2, 1896 (Austin, MN: Register Printers, 1896), 32, WCTU Minutes, vol. 3 (1893–1899), WCTU Minnesota Collection, box 12/6/7, SWHA.

93. See Nancy F. Cott on the history and historiography of "social feminism," "What's in a Name? The Limits of 'Social Feminism;' or, Expanding the Vocabulary of Women's History," *Journal of American History* 76, no. 3 (December 1989): 809–829.

94. Lovell, "Mercy," WCTU Series, Roll 8: Annual Meeting Minutes, 1911–1915, *Minutes of the 38th Annual Convention: 1911*, Milwaukee, October 28–November 2, 1911, microfilm, p. 332.

95. Lovell, "Mercy," WCTU Series, Roll 6: Annual Meeting Minutes, 1901–1905, *Minutes of the National Convention: 1904*, Philadelphia, November 29–December 4, 1904, microfilm, p. 287.

96. Lovell, "Department of Mercy," WCTU Series, Roll 4: Annual Meeting Minutes, 1893–1896, *Meeting of the National Convention: 1895*, Baltimore, October 18–23, 1895, microfilm, p. 293.

97. Lovell, "Department of Mercy," WCTU Series, Roll 4: Annual Meeting Minutes, 1893–1896, *Minutes of the National Convention: 1896*, St. Louis, November 13–18, 1896, microfilm, p. 346.

98. Lovell, "Mercy," WCTU Series, Roll 8: Annual Meeting Minutes, 1911–1915, *Minutes of the 38th Annual Convention: 1911*, Milwaukee, October 28–November 2, 1911, microfilm, p. 335.

99. The Department of Mercy's work in prisons had historical legs. Today there are multiple programs across the nation in which prisoners train selected shelter dogs to assist people with disabilities: from national groups like Pathways to Hope Prison Dog Project, to state organizations like New York's Puppies behind Bars.

100. "Funeral for Nationally Known Humane Worker Held Tuesday," in "Memorial Number, Commemorative of Mary F. Lovell," *Starry Cross*, 108.

101. Bordin, *Women and Temperance*, 82–83.

102. Bordin, *Woman and Temperance*, 76–79.

103. Bruce A. Glasrud, "Time of Transition for Black Women in Early Twentieth-Century Texas, 1900–1930," in *Black Women in Texas History*, ed. Glasrud and Merline Pitre (College Station: Texas A&M University Press, 2008), 111.

104. Newman, *White Women's Rights*, 68–69.

105. Glasrud, "Time of Transition for Black Women in Early Twentieth-Century Texas, 1900–1930," 111.

106. Lovell, "Mercy," WCTU Series, Roll 7: Annual Meeting Minutes, 1906–1910, *Minutes of the National Convention: 1907*, Nashville, November 8–13, 1907, microfilm, p. 316.

107. Lovell, "Mercy," *Minutes of the National Convention: 1904*, 289; Ruth Bordin, *Woman and Temperance*, 84.
108. "Mercy," WCTU Series, Roll 6: Annual Meeting Minutes, 1901–1905, *Minutes of the National Convention: 1905*, Los Angeles, October 27–November 1, 1905, microfilm, p. 325.
109. Lovell, *Minutes of the National Convention: 1907*, 316.
110. Lovell, WCTU Series, Roll 7: Annual Meeting Minutes, 1906–1910, *Minutes of the National Convention: 1909*, Omaha, October 22–27, 1909, microfilm, p. 317.
111. Lovell, "Humane Education," WCTU Series, Roll 8, Annual Meeting Minutes, 1911–1915, *Minutes of the National Convention: 1915*, Seattle, October 9–14, 1915, microfilm, p. 275.
112. Lovell, "Humane Education," WCTU Series, Roll 9: Annual Meeting Minutes, 1916–1917, 1919, 1921–1924, *Meeting of the National Convention: 1916*, Indianapolis, November 17–22, 1916, microfilm, p. 293.
113. Lovell, "Department of Mercy," WCTU Series, Roll 5: Annual Meetings Minutes, 1897–1900, *Minutes of the National Convention: 1899*, Seattle, October 20–25, 1899, microfilm, p. 273.
114. Lovell, "Department of Mercy," WCTU Series, Roll 6: Annual Meetings and Minutes, 1901–1905, *Minutes of the National Convention: 1903*, Cincinnati, November 13–18, 1903, microfilm, p. 289.
115. Cynthia M. Fairchild, "Caught in His Own Trap—A Steel Trap," in *Pleadings of Mercy for the Animal World and All Other Defenseless Creatures* (Chicago: Albert W. Landon, 1883), 41.
116. Fairchild, "Caught in His Own Trap—A Steel Trap," 37–45.
117. Steven Hahn, "Hunting, Fishing, and Foraging: Common Rights and Class Relations in the Postbellum South," *Radical History Review* 26, no. 26 (October 1982): 36–64.
118. Hahn, "Hunting, Fishing, and Foraging," 52.
119. Booker T. Washington to James Fowle Baldwin Marshall, November 4, 1883, in *The Booker T. Washington Papers*, vol. 2, 1860–1889, ed. Louis R. Harlan (Urbana: University of Illinois Press, 1972), 242–243; Lovell, WCTU Series, Roll 5: Annual Meeting Minutes, 1897–1900, *Minutes of the National Convention: 1900*, Washington, DC, November 30–December 7, 1900, microfilm, p. 297.
120. "Where Kindness Is the Rule," *ODA*, April 1919, 173.
121. Lovell, *Minutes of the National Convention: 1899*, 273–274.
122. The Southern Methodist Episcopal Church, also known as the Methodist Episcopal Church, South, was a branch of the Methodist Church that broke away in 1844 because many of its members supported slavery. Lovell, *Minutes of the National Convention: 1915*, 273–274.
123. On the social and political implications of "talking back," see Harriet Ritvo, *The Animal Estate: The English and Other Creatures in the Victorian Age* (Cambridge,

MA: Harvard University Press, 1987); and Aaron Herald Skabelund, *Empire of Dogs: Canines, Japan, and the Making of the Modern Imperial World* (Ithaca, NY: Cornell University Press, 2011), 15.

124. Lovell, "Mercy," *Minutes of the 38th Annual Convention: 1911*, 332, 334–335.
125. Lovell, *Minutes of the National Convention: 1912*, 311–312.
126. Lovell, *Minutes of the National Convention: 1909*, 317.
127. Lovell, WCTU Series, Roll 7: Annual Meeting Minutes, 1906–1910, *Minutes of the National Convention: 1910*, Baltimore, November 12–17, 1910, microfilm, p. 332.
128. Horatio Alger, *Ragged Dick and Struggling Upward* (1868; repr., New York: Penguin Books, 1985).
129. Saunders, *Beautiful Joe*, 81.
130. Saunders, *Beautiful Joe*, 137.
131. See Lovell, "Mercy," *Minutes of the National Convention: 1907*, 318; Lovell, "Mercy," WCTU Series, Roll 8: Annual Meeting Minutes, 1911–1915, *National Meeting Minutes: 1913*, Ashbury Park, NJ, October 31–November 5, 1913.
132. Lovell, "Mercy," *Minutes of the National Convention: 1896*, 344; *Minutes of the National Convention: 1897*, 433; Lovell, WCTU Series, Roll 6: Annual Meeting Minutes, 1901–1905, *Minutes of the National Convention: 1902*, Portland, ME, October 17–22, 1902, microfilm, p. 316.
133. Angell, "The Relations of Animals that Can Speak to Those that Are Dumb," 52.
134. See Edward J. Blum, *Reforging the White Republic: Race, Religion, and American Nationalism, 1865–1898* (Baton Rouge: Louisiana State University Press, 2007); Richard W. Leeman, *"Do Everything" Reform: The Oratory of Frances E. Willard* (New York: Greenwood Press, 1992); Gordon, *Heroes of Their Own Lives*, 142–144.
135. Frances E. Willard, "Tenth Annual Address, 1889," quoted in Leeman, *"Do Everything" Reform*, 147.
136. Amos Judson Bailey, "For Preventing Strikes," *ODA*, November 1903, 66–68.
137. Bailey, "For Preventing Strikes," 68.
138. "The Crime of the Strikers," *ODA*, September 1934, 136.
139. Karl Marx and Friedrich Engels, *The Communist Manifesto*, ed. Samuel H. Beer (1848; repr., New York: Appleton-Century-Crofts, 1955), 40.
140. Upton Sinclair, *The Jungle* (1906; repr., New York: Bantam Dell, 2003), 37.
141. Gordon, *Women Torch-Bearers*, 299.
142. In addition to her leadership role in the AAVS, Lovell served as a member of the Board of Directors of the American Humane Association starting in 1903; she was also corresponding secretary of the Women's Pennsylvania SPCA and served as its honorary president. Nicole Perry, "Mary Frances Lovell: Writing the Wrongs of Animals," *AV Magazine*, Spring 2008, 15; "Memorial Number, Commemorative of Mary F. Lovell," *Starry Cross*, 99–109.
143. "The Fundamental Need," Radio Address given by Mrs. Mary F. Lovell, May 24, 1932, in "Memorial Number, Commemorative of Mary F. Lovell," *Starry Cross*, 108.

144. "The Fundamental Need," 109; see also J. M. Grange, "Effective Vaccination against Tuberculosis—A New Ray of Hope," *Clinical and Experimental Immunology: The Journal of Translational Immunology* 120, no. 2 (May 2000): 232–234, http://www.ncbi.nlm.nih.gov/pmc/articles/PMC1905635/; see also Jeannette Vaught, "'Materia Medica': Technology, Vaccination, and Antivivisection in Jazz Age Philadelphia," in "Species/Race/Sex," ed. Claire Jean Kim and Carla Freccero, special issue, *American Quarterly* 65, no. 3 (September 2013): 575–595.
145. Susan McHugh, *Dog* (London: Reaktion Books, 2004), 137–139; for a thorough treatment, see Coral Lansbury, *The Old Brown Dog: Women, Workers, and Vivisection in Edwardian England* (Madison: University of Wisconsin Press, 1985).
146. "Illustrations of Human Vivisection" (Chicago: Vivisection Reform Society, 1906).
147. Beers, *For the Prevention of Cruelty*, 139–142.
148. "The Fundamental Need," 109.
149. Brigette Nicole Fielder, "Animal Humanism: Race, Species, and Affective Kinship in Nineteenth-Century Abolitionism," in "Species/Race/Sex," ed. Claire Jean Kim and Carla Freccero, special issue, *American Quarterly* 65, no. 3 (September 2013): 502.

CHAPTER 3

1. "Igorrotes Saying Good-By," *LAT*, May 12, 1906, ProQuest Historical Newspapers: *Los Angeles Times* (1881–1990).
2. "'Nigs Get 'Em?' See Pound Man," *LAT*, March 9, 1906, ProQuest Historical Newspapers: *Los Angeles Times* (1881–1990), quoted in Janet M. Davis, "The Dog Ate My Birth Certificate," *NYT*, May 7, 2012, http://www.nytimes.com/2012/05/08/opinion/the-dog-ate-my-birth-certificate.html?_r=1&ref=opinion.
3. This article states that the Igorots opened their exhibition at Chutes Park on December 15, 1905, but others place the starting date in January 1906. "Igorrotes Saying Good-By"; "The Right to Eat Dog," December 17, 1905, and "'Nigs Get 'Em?' See Pound Man," March 9, 1906, both from *LAT*, ProQuest Historical Newspapers: *Los Angeles Times* (1881–1990).
4. Lovell, "Mercy," WCTU Series, Roll 7: Annual Meeting Minutes, 1906–1910, *Minutes of the National Convention: 1906*, Hartford, CT, October 26–31, 1906, 306.
5. "Igorrotes Saying Good-By."
6. José D. Fermin, *1904 World's Fair; The Filipino Experience* (West Conshohocken, PA: Infinity, 2004), 17–20; Sharra L. Vostral, "Imperialism on Display: The Philippine Exhibition at the 1904 World's Fair," *Gateway Heritage* 13, no. 4 (Spring 1993), http://collections.mohistory.org/media/CDM/gateway/85.pdf.

7. Fermin, *1904 World's Fair; The Filipino Experience*, 20, 27.
8. Animals were consistently used to construct representations of irreconcilable racial and ethnic difference. See Claire Jean Kim, *Dangerous Crossings: Race, Species, and Nature in a Multicultural Age* (New York: Cambridge University Press, 2015); other classic treatments of animalized racial representations include David Roediger, *The Wages of Whiteness: Race and the Making of the American Working Class* (New York: Verso 2007 [1991]); Matthew Frye Jacobson, *Barbarian Virtues: The United States Encounters Foreign Peoples at Home and Abroad, 1876-1917* (New York: Hill and Wang, 2000); Matthew Frye Jacobson, *Whiteness of a Different Color: European Immigrants and the Alchemy of Race* (Cambridge, MA: Harvard University Press, 1999); and Robert G. Lee, *Orientals: Asian Americans in Popular Culture* (Philadelphia: Temple University Press, 1999).
9. In using the terminology "in" and "out" groups, I owe a debt to the French historian Kathleen Kete, who argues that the history of European animal welfare is not inevitably tied to the history of social liberation. Kathleen Kete, "Animals and Ideology: The Politics of Animal Protection in Europe," in *Representing Animals*, ed. Nigel Rothfels (Bloomington: Indiana University Press, 2002), 20.
10. "Southern California News," *LAT*, October 25, 1894, ProQuest Historical Newspapers: *Los Angeles Times* (1881-1990).
11. See, for example: "Peddler Is Mobbed as Heat Fells Pony," June 25, 1923; "More Cars and Stages Stopped by Order of Mr. Bergh," July 1, 1871; "Woman Blocks City Traffic in Pity for Mail Wagon Horse," July 12, 1927; "Say Milkman Stabbed Horse," June 12, 1904; "Worked a $2.50 Horse: Woman Has the Owner of a Decrepit Animal Arrested," October 22, 1905, all from *NYT*.
12. "The Horse," *Nation*, June 20, 1895, 476, quoted in Clay McShane and Joel A. Tarr, *The Horse in the City: Living Machines in the Nineteenth Century* (Baltimore: Johns Hopkins University Press, 2007), 46; for an overview of carters and teamsters, see 36-46.
13. "Henry Bergh and His Work," *Scribner's Monthly*, April 1879, 872.
14. It should be noted, however, that some local SPCAs did not provide official uniforms for their officers owing to limited budgets. In St. Paul, Minnesota, for one, local SPCA leaders worried that their animal agents dressed in street clothes received little credit for their good work because the organization could not afford uniforms. See "Report and Recommendations—Committee on Agents," May 1, 1917, St. Paul Society for the Prevention of Cruelty to Animals Records, P1546, Minutes, 1917-1920, File 1, Minnesota Historical Society.
15. McShane and Tarr, *The Horse in the City*, 51.
16. "Starving Horse," April 25, 1903; "Bronco 'Busting,'" April 30, 1903; "John Rarey: The Story of the Famous Horse Tamer and His Boyish Triumphs," February 11, 1899, all from *LAT*, ProQuest Historical Newspapers: *Los Angeles Times* (1881-1990).

17. David Favre and Vivien Tsang, "The Development of Anti-Cruelty Laws during the 1800's," *Detroit College of Law Review* 1 (Spring 1993): 29.
18. McShane and Tarr, *The Horse in the City*, 49.
19. "Convicted of Vicious Abuse of Horses," *LAT*, April 3, 1903, ProQuest Historical Newspapers: *Los Angeles Times* (1881–1990).
20. "Find Mules Sorry Lot," *LAT*, July 29, 1904, ProQuest Historical Newspapers: *Los Angeles Times* (1881–1990).
21. "Find Mules Sorry Lot."
22. "Los Angeles County—Its Cities and Towns: Inhuman Was Their Cruelty," May 20, 1905; "Might Take Bit in Teeth," July 18, 1911; "Over a Million Is Paid for Mercantile Place," November 14, 1919; "Lacy Property Is Sold Again," December 2, 1922; "Millions for New Theaters," August 12, 1924, all from *LAT*, ProQuest Historical Newspapers: *Los Angeles Times* (1881–1990); Jules Tygiel, *The Great Los Angeles Swindle: Oil, Stocks, and Scandal during the Roaring Twenties* (Berkeley: University of California Press, 1994), 157–159.
23. "A Horse Starved to Death," *LAT*, October 2, 1894, ProQuest Historical Newspapers: *Los Angeles Times* (1881–1990).
24. "All Along the Line," April 15, 1900; "The City in Brief: Where Is the Owner? Starving Chinaman, Suffering Horse Killed," July 24, 1900; "The City in Brief: Horse Shot," August 1, 1900, all from *LAT*, ProQuest Historical Newspapers: *Los Angeles Times* (1881–1990).
25. "'Goo Goo Eyes' under Arrest," *LAT*, June 13, 1904, ProQuest Historical Newspapers: *Los Angeles Times* (1881–1990).
26. "Woes of an Old Horse," *LAT*, October 6, 1903, ProQuest Historical Newspapers: *Los Angeles Times* (1881–1990).
27. McShane and Tar, *The Horse in the City*, 27, 51.
28. M. B. McMullan, "The Day the Dogs Died in London," *London Journal* 23, no. 1 (May 1998): 35–36.
29. McMullan, "The Day the Dogs Died in London," 33.
30. McMullan, "The Day the Dogs Died in London," 39.
31. Tracy Wuster, "'The Most Popular Humorist Who Ever Lived': Mark Twain and the Transformation of American Culture" (PhD diss., University of Texas at Austin, 2011).
32. "Kicked Her Dog," *New York Herald*, September 23, 1866, 8.
33. "Irate Negress Prays for Him: Humane Officer Condemns Her Horse to Die," *LAT*, October 28, 1905, ProQuest Historical Newspapers: *Los Angeles Times* (1881–1990).
34. "Mr. Bergh and the Mayor: Cruelty to Car-Horses—Reply to Mayor Hall's Letter," *NYT*, July 14, 1871.
35. See "For Humanity's Sake," *LAT*, November 14, 1903, ProQuest Historical Newspapers: *Los Angeles Times* (1881–1990).

36. "The East Side Pests," *NYT*, January 27, 1885.
37. "Healthy Meat the Object," *LAT*, April 7, 1907, ProQuest Historical Newspapers: *Los Angeles Times* (1881–1990).
38. "Healthy Meat the Object."
39. Jacobson, *Barbarian Virtues*, 160–163; 190–201.
40. James C. Mohr, *Plague and Fire: Battling Black Death and the 1900 Burning of Honolulu's Chinatown* (New York: Oxford University Press, 2005); Robert Sullivan, *Rats: Observations on the History and Habitat of the City's Most Unwanted Inhabitants* (New York: Bloomsbury, 2004), 154–155.
41. "The Control of Rabies," *Monthly Bulletin of the Department of Health of the City of New York*, September 1911, 202, 203.
42. Katherine C. Grier, *Pets in America: A History* (Chapel Hill: University of North Carolina Press, 2006), 90.
43. See "Enforcement of the Dog Law," June 18, 1867; "A Plea for the Dogs," July 19, 1903; "Unmuzzled Dogs Now Shot on Sight," July 30, 1908; "Dr. Goldwater Aims to End Dog Dangers," July 24, 1914, all from *NYT*.
44. Harriet Ritvo, *The Animal Estate: The English and Other Creatures in the Victorian Age* (Cambridge, MA: Harvard University Press, 1987), 174; Bernard Oreste Unti, "'The Quality of Mercy': Organized Animal Protection in the United States, 1866–1930" (PhD diss., American University, 2002), 161–163.
45. "Dog Bites Nine Persons: Big Newfoundland Spreads Terror Down Town," February 19, 1903; "Rabies Raging in Chicago," April 20, 1903, both from *NYT*.
46. "Department Notes," *Monthly Bulletin of the Department of Health of the City of New York*, September 1911, 208.
47. "Department Notes," 208.
48. See, for example, "Opening the Dog Pound," June 24, 1879; "Dogs in the City," March 29, 1903, both from *NYT*.
49. "The Pleasures of the Chase," April 13, 1873; "Mr. Bergh on the Dog Ordinance," June 29, 1875, both from *NYT*.
50. "A Violent Deputy Dogcatcher," *NYT*, August 2, 1877.
51. "A Day of Many Crimes," August 11, 1882; "The Murder by a Dog-Catcher," August 18, 1882, both from *NYT*.
52. "Dog Catchers Defeated," *NYT*, July 15, 1886.
53. See "Another Dog-Catcher in Trouble," August 8, 1877; "A Dog-Catcher Convicted," August 9, 1878; "A Warning to Dog-Catchers," August 3, 1881; "Dog-Catcher Culley in Trouble," August 3, 1883; "Dog Catchers Too Zealous," September 12, 1884, all from *NYT*.
54. "Dog Catchers Complained Of," *NYT*, December 25, 1889.
55. "A Warning to the Dogs," *NYT*, June 2, 1883.
56. "A Warning to the Dogs."
57. Unti, "'The Quality of Mercy,'" 165–175.

58. "Hydrophobia," April 14, 1874; "Mr. Bergh and the Dogs," September 25, 1868; "The Dog Snatchers," February 6, 1887, all from *NYT*; Unti, "'The Quality of Mercy,'" 471–475.
59. "Department Notes," 208–209; "Summary of Vital Statistics for the Year 1911," *Monthly Bulletin of the Department of Health of the City of New York*, January 1912, 27.
60. "Homeless Cats and Dogs Cared For," *NYT*, March 1, 1896; Unti, "'The Quality of Mercy,'" 475.
61. Unti, "'The Quality of Mercy,'" 478–486.
62. "Round-Up for Ki-Yi Reform," *LAT*, August 9, 1908, ProQuest Historical Newspapers: *Los Angeles Times* (1881–1990).
63. "Old Dog Tray Sees New Day," *LAT*, November 8, 1908, ProQuest Historical Newspapers: *Los Angeles Times* (1881–1990).
64. "Old Dog Tray Sees New Day."
65. Robin W. Doughty, *Feather Fashions and Bird Preservation: A Study in Nature Protection* (Berkeley: University of California Press, 1975), 59.
66. "Topics of the Times: Bird Shooting in the Parks," *NYT*, May 15, 1905.
67. "To Stop Songbird Killing," *NYT*, April 22, 1907.
68. Doughty, *Feather Fashions and Bird Preservation*, 59.
69. Unti, "'The Quality of Mercy,'" 111–113.
70. *The Hebrew Standard*, reprinted as "One of Many," *ODA*, June 1914, 8.
71. Francis H. Rowley, "Slaughter-House Reform in the United States and the Opposing Forces" (Boston: Massachusetts Society for the Prevention of Cruelty to Animals, 1913): 11, Dr. Francis H. Rowley, News Clippings and Writings, 1900–1927, AMH.
72. Rowley, "Slaughter-House Reform," 10–11.
73. Rowley, "Slaughter-House Reform," 9–10.
74. "Rabbi Max Samfield," obituary, September 29, 1915; "Rabbi Abram Simon Is Dead in Capital," December 25, 1938, both from *NYT*.
75. "Dumb Slaves," *Brooklyn Eagle*, March 22, 1880.
76. George Angell, "The Poor Jews," *ODA*, December 1905, 95.
77. Jonathan Burt, "Conflicts around Slaughter in Modernity," in Animal Studies Group, *Killing Animals* (Champaign: University of Illinois Press, 2006), 126.
78. "$15,000 Prizes for Better Methods of Humane Slaughter in Abattoirs," *NYT*, December 31, 1922.
79. Burt, "Conflicts around Slaughter in Modernity," 125.
80. Maureen Ogle, *In Meat We Trust: An Unexpected History of Carnivore America* (Boston: Houghton Mifflin Harcourt, 2013), 20–25.
81. W. Joseph Grand, *The Illustrated History of the Union Stockyards, Chicago, Ill.: With Humorous Stories* (1896; repr., Chicago: Thos. Knapp, 1901), 15.
82. Grand, *Illustrated History*, 146.
83. Grand, *Illustrated History*, 244–245.

84. "Sermon of the Rev. Thomas Van Ness," *ODA*, April 1909, 170.
85. Upton Sinclair, *The Jungle* (1906; repr., New York: Bantam Dell, 2003), 38, 39.
86. "Yellow Dogs Safe on Tehama Street: Children Pledged to Protect Animals from Hoodlums," *San Francisco Call*, May 31, 1896, Chronicling America: Historic American Newspapers, http://chroniclingamerica.loc.gov/lccn/sn85066387/1896-05-31/ed-1/seq-18/.
87. "Yellow Dogs Safe on Tehama Street."
88. "Yellow Dogs Safe on Tehama Street."
89. On African American ideologies of racial uplift and self-help in relation to the uses of early cinema, see Cara Caddo, "'Put Together to Please a Colored Audience': Black Churches, Motion Pictures, and Migration at the Turn of the Twentieth Century," *Journal of American History* 101, no. 3 (December 2014): 778–803.
90. "Our Slides in Texas Theatres," April 1917, 170; "One Month's Work," June 1917, 10; "Humane Sermons in Austin," July 1917, 26; "In South Carolina," October 1917, 74; "Bird-House Contest in Texas," May 1919, 185; "The American Humane Education Society," May 1919, 188, all from *ODA*.
91. "Who's Who in the Humane Field?" *National Humane Review*, June 1921, 112; R. T. Tatum, ed., "Department of Health Education," *Texas Standard*, October 1937, 5–6, http://texashistory.unt.edu/ark:/67531/metapth193741/m1/7/.
92. "Humane Standard-Bearers, VI. Reverend John W. Lemon," *ODA*, July 1927, 106.
93. "Humane Standard-Bearers, VI. Reverend John W. Lemon."
94. "Humane Standard-Bearers, VI. Reverend John W. Lemon."
95. "Seymour Carroll Succumbs after Protracted Illness," *Palmetto Leader*, March 20, 1943, http://emilyevaughn.com/palmeto.htm; "Our Work in the South," *ODA*, December 1913, 107.
96. "Humane Standard-Bearers: VII. Seymour Carroll," *ODA*, September, 1927, 138; Robert M. Muth and Wesley V. Jamison, "On the Destiny of Deer Camps and Duck Blinds: The Rise of the Animal Rights Movement and the Future of Wildlife Conservation," *Wildlife Society Bulletin* 28, no. 4 (Winter 2000): 841–851, 843.
97. "All in the Month's Work," *ODA*, May 1926, 188.
98. "Seymour Carroll School Speaker," *Spartanburg Herald*, February 12, 1932.
99. "Negroes for Preparedness," [Sumter, SC] *Watchman and Southron*, April 4, 1917, Chronicling America: Historic American Newspapers, http://chroniclingamerica.loc.gov/lccn/sn93067846/1917-04-04/ed-1/seq-5/.
100. "Humane Standard-Bearers: VII. Seymour Carroll."
101. "Our Lynching Record for 1926," *ODA*, May, 1927, 72.
102. "Our Disgrace," *ODA*, September 1917, 51.
103. "Our Disgrace"; see also, "Were They Men or Were They Devils?" *ODA*, April 1918, 168.

104. "Race Prejudice," *ODA*, November 1936, 163.
105. "Race Prejudice," *ODA*, June 1915, 8.
106. "Summary Texas Justice," *Christian Recorder*, May 19, 1887, Accessible Archives: African American Newspapers: *Christian Recorder* (1861-1902).
107. "Anti-Vivisection in California," *LAT*, June 4, 1915, ProQuest Historical Newspapers: *Los Angeles Times* (1881–1990).
108. "The 'Right' to Take Life," editorial, *LAT*, November 23, 1906, ProQuest Historical Newspapers: *Los Angeles Times* (1881–1990).
109. "Barbarians and Murderesses," *LAT*, November 17, 1906, ProQuest Historical Newspapers: *Los Angeles Times* (1881–1990).
110. "Club Women Bar Aigrette," *LAT*, April 7, 1907, ProQuest Historical Newspapers: *Los Angeles Times* (1881–1990).
111. Jennifer Price, *Flight Maps: Adventures with Nature in Modern America* (New York: Basic Books, 1998), 79–80.
112. William T. Hornaday, *Our Vanishing Wild Life: Its Extermination and Preservation* (New York: New York Zoological Society, 1913), 125.
113. "Woman, Spare that Bird," *LAT*, June 11, 1899, ProQuest Historical Newspapers: *Los Angeles Times* (1881–1990).
114. Hornaday, *Our Vanishing Wild Life*, 117.
115. "Jews and Birds," Editorial in *Die Wahrheit*, April 3, 1911, repr. in *Forest and Stream*, April 22, 1911, 614.
116. "Points Way to End Slaughter of Birds," *NYT*, January 2, 1911.
117. Sarah Abrevaya Stein, *Plumes: Ostrich Feathers, Jews, and a Lost World of Global Commerce* (New Haven, CT: Yale University Press, 2008), 116.
118. Stein, *Plumes*, 117.
119. Stein, *Plumes*, 114–115.
120. Stein, *Plumes*, 112–116.
121. "Kind to Our Ostriches," January 10, 1906; "Humane Society: Ostrich Feather Plucking Said to Be Not Cruel," January 15, 1896, both from *LAT*, ProQuest Historical Newspapers: *Los Angeles Times* (1881–1990); Stein, *Plumes*, 125.
122. For a concise overview, see "Overview of the Lacey Act of 1900 (16 U.S.C. §§ 3371–3378), in Animal Legal and Historical Center, http://www.animallaw.info/articles/ovuslaceyact.htm.
123. "Notes and Gleanings," January 12, 1913; "Dinner to Aaron J. Levy," November 17, 1913, both from *NYT*.
124. "Jews and Birds," 614.
125. Channing Severance, "Hell Is Not Hot Enough," letter to the editor, *LAT*, April 3, 1903, ProQuest Historical Newspapers: *Los Angeles Times* (1881–1990).
126. M. Horace Hayes, *Veterinary Notes for Horse Owners: A Manual of Horse Medicine and Surgery, Written in Popular Language* (London: Hurst and Blackett, 1906), 677.
127. Unti, "'The Quality of Mercy,'" 346.

128. Hayes, *Veterinary Notes for Horse Owner*, 674–675.
129. "Untitled," *Zoöphily*, May 1901, 83; Frank Greaves, "Curtin's Curtail," *LAT*, February 11, 1907, ProQuest Historical Newspapers: *Los Angeles Times* (1881–1990).
130. "Tail-Docking Prohibited," *NYT*, July 1, 1894.
131. "Docking Tails of Horses," and "Registration of Docked Horses," enacted March 15, 1907, California Penal Code, §597a[2] and §597b[2], in *Statutes of California and Amendments to the Code Adopted at the Special Session, 1906, and the Regular Session, 1907*, arr. and annot. by James M. Kerr (San Francisco: Bender-Chaquette, 1907), 530–531.
132. Anna Sewell, *Black Beauty* (1877; repr., New York: Signet Classics, 2002), 37.
133. Moira Ferguson, *Animal Advocacy and Englishwomen, 1780–1900: Patriots, Nation, and Empire* (Ann Arbor: University of Michigan Press, 1998), 77–78.
134. "The Polo Club's Triumph," *NYT*, June 20, 1878.
135. "The Polo Club's Triumph."
136. John Dimon, *American Horses and Horse Breeding* (Hartford, CT: John Dimon, 1895), 334; "Pasadena: What the Humane Society Proposes to Do," January 7, 1895; "Cruelty to Horses," December 19, 1898, both from *LAT*, ProQuest Historical Newspapers: *Los Angeles Times* (1881–1990).
137. "War on Docking Tails," *NYT*, December 24, 1903; see also, "The President's Humane Example," *LAT*, February 4, 1902, ProQuest Historical Newspapers: *Los Angeles Times* (1881–1990).
138. Diana L. Beers, *For the Prevention of Cruelty: The History and Legacy of Animal Rights Activism in the United States* (Athens: Ohio University Press, 2006), 112.
139. "Untitled," *ODA*, February 1921, 131.
140. "The Cruel Steel Trap," *ODA*, March 1921, 150.
141. Muth and Jamison, "On the Destiny of Deer Camps and Duck Blinds," 843.
142. Alice Jean Cleator, "Fur and the Steel Trap: What the Women Say," *ODA*, January 1921, 119, 128.
143. Sydney H. Coleman, "Shall American Boys Be Taught to Torture and Kill?" *National Humane Review*, February 1920, 23.
144. "Dog Fighting: Human Brutes in New York Amuse Themselves," *Daily Memphis Avalanche*, October 16, 1866, NewsBank: America's Historical Newspapers.
145. Martin and Herbert J. Kaufman, "Henry Bergh, Kit Burns, and the Sportsmen of New York," *New York Folklore Quarterly* 28, no. 1 (March 1972): 15–29, 16, 18.
146. Anyone charging admission or aiding the arrangements of said fight could be convicted of a misdemeanor. "New York Revised Statutes 1867: An Act for the More Effectual Prevention of Cruelty to Animals," ch. 375, §§ 1–10, in Animal Legal and Historical Center, http://www.animallaw.info/historical/statutes/sthusny1867.htm.
147. "Funeral of 'Kit Burns,'" *NYT*, December 24, 1870.

148. "Dog Fighting: Human Brutes in New York Amuse Themselves."
149. Other blood sport enthusiasts like the cocker Mike Reynolds, made similar arguments regarding chickens. Nonetheless, the ASPCA's continued surveillance eventually drove them to the perimeter of the city. Kaufmans, "Henry Bergh, Kit Burns, and the Sportsmen of New York," 20–21.
150. "The Water Street Revival," *New York Herald*, September 27, 1868.
151. "Vaudeville Bills in New York City," *Dallas Morning News*, July 28, 1918, NewsBank: *Dallas Morning News* Archive (1885–1984); "As Seen in Vaudeville," *NYT*, January 14, 1903; James Turner, *Reckoning with the Beast: Animals, Pain, and Humanity in the Victorian Mind* (Baltimore: Johns Hopkins University Press, 1980), 63, 70.
152. "Pity the Poor Horses," *LAT*, February 11, 1905, ProQuest Historical Newspapers: *Los Angeles Times* (1881–1990).
153. "Bilderrain in Trouble," March 18, 1900; "Bilderrain Goes Free after All," January 24, 1901; "New Humane Society," March 2, 1901, all from *LAT*, ProQuest Historical Newspapers: *Los Angeles Times* (1881–1990).
154. "Bilderrain Saw Nothin,'" *LAT*, May 4, 1904, ProQuest Historical Newspapers: *Los Angeles Times* (1881–1990).
155. "Killed by an Officer in Raid on a Cock Fight," May 2, 1904; "Says Shots Confused Him," May 3, 1904; "Swing Wide Mercy's Side," January 12, 1905; "Widow Sues Humane Men," April 29, 1905, all from *LAT*, ProQuest Historical Newspapers: *Los Angeles Times* (1881–1990).
156. "Swing Wide Mercy's Side."
157. "Swing Wide Mercy's Side."
158. "Henry Bergh on Fox-Hunting," *NYT*, November 27, 1875; "Mr. Bergh's Views of Fox-Hunting," *NYT*, October 10, 1877, and Beers, *For the Prevention of Cruelty*, 9, 58, 77.
159. Unti, 322–329; "Will Fight Pigeon Law," *NYT*, March 19, 1902; see also Simon Bronner, *Killing Tradition: Inside Hunting and Animal Rights Controversies* (Lexington: University Press of Kentucky, 2008).
160. "Cruelty in Moving Pictures," September 1914, 58; "The Moving Picture Industry," June 1926, 195, both from *ODA*.
161. Jonathan Burt, *Animals in Film* (London: Reaktion Books, 2002), 153.
162. For a classic treatment, see C. Vann Woodward, *The Strange Career of Jim Crow* (New York: Oxford University Press, 1955); see also Elizabeth Abel, "Double Take: Photography, Cinema, and the Segregated Theater," in *Signs of the Times: The Visual Politics of Jim Crow*, ed. Abel (Berkeley: University of California Press, 2010), 195–216.
163. *The Battle at Elderbush Gulch*, directed by D. W. Griffith (Biograph, 1913), video, https://www.youtube.com/watch?v=k92jpf0eBAs.
164. *Rules for Indian Schools with Course of Study* (Washington, DC: Government Printing Office, 1892), 39 [emphasis mine].

165. Mabel Hill, *The Teaching of Civics* (Boston: Houghton Mifflin, 1913), 92, 93.
166. Henry Noble Sherwood, *Civics and Citizenship* (Indianapolis: Bobbs-Merrill, 1934), 425.
167. Sherwood, *Civics and Citizenship*, 160.
168. Waldo H. Sherman, *Civics: Studies in American Citizenship* (New York: Macmillan, 1905), 292.
169. "The Way to Carry Chickens," *LAT*, July 9, 1899, ProQuest Historical Newspapers: *Los Angeles Times* (1881–1990).

CHAPTER 4

1. George Angell, "The Present War Craze," *ODA*, April 1898, 134.
2. Angell, "The Present War Craze," 133–134 [emphasis in original].
3. George Angell, "Our Naval Folly," *ODA*, June 1903, 2 [emphasis in original].
4. In 1902, thirty-four out of fifty-one towns in the province of Iloilo alone reported to Governor Taft that 35,000 carabao had died. In March that same year, a cholera epidemic swept across the Islands, killing 109,461 people over the next twenty-three months. Reynaldo C. Ileto, "Cholera and the Origins of the American Sanitary Order in the Philippines," in David Arnold, ed., *Imperial Medicine and Indigenous Societies* (Manchester, UK: Manchester University Press, 1988), 127, 131; Arthur Judson Brown, *The New Era in the Philippines* (New York: Fleming H. Revell, 1903), 231–232.
5. Julian Go, *American Empire and the Politics of Meaning: Elite Political Cultures in the Philippines and Puerto Rico during U.S. Colonialism* (Durham, NC: Duke University Press, 2008), 6; Paul A. Kramer, *The Blood of Government: Race, Empire, the United States, and the Philippines* (Chapel Hill: University of North Carolina Press, 2007), 157.
6. Bertrand Shadwell, "Malevolent Assimilation," and "To the Filipino," quoted in *ODA*, June 1902, 2.
7. George Angell, "Shooting Boys in the Philippines," *ODA*, June 1902, 2 [emphasis in original].
8. "Untitled," *ODA*, August 1917, 35; for Rowley's condemnation of the Philippine-American War, see "Clergymen Protest against the Philippine Policy," *Congregationalist and Christian World*, May 31, 1902, 796.
9. "United States Army Animals on the Border," *National Humane Review*, November 1916, 248; Bernard Oreste Unti, "'The Quality of Mercy': Organized Animal Protection in the United States, 1866–1930" (PhD diss., American University, 2002), 460–462.
10. F. W. Fitzsimons, "Our Sub-Human Army," *ODA*, July 1917, 21.
11. "A Fifty Thousand Dollar Peace Endowment," *ODA*, February 1919, 144.
12. "We Helped You Win—Now Help Us to Freedom from Abuse," photo caption, *ODA*, March 1919, 151.

13. "Humane Educator Criticizes Roosevelt and Taft," *Wilmar* [Minnesota] *Tribune*, October 14, 1908, Chronicling America: Historic American Newspapers, http://chroniclingamerica.loc.gov/lccn/sn89081022/1908-10-14/ed-1/seq-3/.
14. "Angell Attacks Roosevelt," *Washington Post*, June 14, 1907, 6, ProQuest Historical Newspapers: *Washington Post* (1877–1997).
15. "William Howard Taft, President of the United States," *ODA*, March 1909, 147.
16. On other key transnational American moral reform activities, including temperance and missionary work, see Ian Tyrrell, *Reforming the World: The Creation of America's Moral Empire* (Princeton, NJ: Princeton University Press, 2010). Tyrrell's introduction contains a concise overview of select keywords in American diplomatic history, such as "cultural imperialism," "transnationalism," and "humanitarianism."
17. "Humane Educator Criticizes Roosevelt and Taft."
18. I use 1899 as the starting date for the American Occupation of the Philippines because the American Senate officially ratified the Treaty of Paris on February 6, 1899 (with a razor-thin margin of a single vote beyond the required two-thirds majority). Moreover, the civilian US government was established on the Islands in 1899. Although Spain formally ceded the Philippines to the United States in the Treaty of Paris for $20 million on December 10, 1898, President McKinley sought Senate ratification to make the treaty official. Some historians, however, use 1898 as the starting date for the Occupation because American soldiers occupied the Islands during the Spanish-American War, and Secretary of State John Hay signed the Treaty of Paris in December.
19. On bees, see (Bees) File Marker 17648, Box 790, General Records, 1898–1914, Entry 5, Record Group 350, Stack Area 150, Row, 56, Compartment 20, Shelf 4 (hereafter cited as 350:150:56:20:4); on livestock imports, see (Mules, Goats, Cows, Horses, Etc., for P.I.) File Marker 10865, Box 625, General Records, 1898–1914, Entry 5, 350:150:56:17:1; on efforts to introduce American wood to the Philippines, see (Ants, white) File Marker 7641, Box 504, General Records, 1898–1914, 350:150:56:14:5, all from Record Group 350—Records of the Bureau of Insular Affairs, 1868–1945 (hereafter cited as RG 350), National Archives and Records Administration, College Park, MD (hereafter cited as NARA II).
20. On livestock diseases, see (Diseases of Cattle, Cuba) File Marker 802, Box 106, General Records, 1898–1914, Entry 5, 350:150:56:6:4; and (Diseases, animals) File Marker 2298, Box 266, General Records, 1898–1914, Entry 5, 350:150:56:9:6, all from RG 350, NARA II.
21. Elizabeth Stuart Phelps Ward to President Theodore Roosevelt, February 5, 1904 (Animals, Cruelty to—Philippines) File Marker 10795, Box 622, General Classified Files 5A (1898–1913), 350:150:56:17:1, RG 350, NARA II.
22. Chapter 24, "Animal Cruelty," *Message from the President of the United States transmitting the report of the Hawaiian Commission: appointed in pursuance of the "Joint resolution to provide for annexing the Hawaiian Islands to the United States,"*

approved July 7, 1898: together with a copy of the civil and penal laws of Hawaii (Washington, DC: Government Printing Office, 1898), 345–346, (hereafter cited as *Laws of Hawaii*).

23. The society was divided into local "juntas," which were required to keep monthly accounts chronicling the number of arrests for cruelty to animals and the amount fined; these were submitted to the president of the organization based in San Juan, who in turn submitted these reports to the civil secretary of the governor general of Puerto Rico. "General Orders No. 122," San Juan, Puerto Rico, August 17, 1899 (Animal Cruelty, Puerto Rico) File Marker 971, Box 151, General Classified Files, Entry 5A (1899–1913), 350:150:56:7:3, RG 350, NARA II.

24. Acting Secretary of Porto Rico (unsigned/unnamed) to W. O. Stillman, San Juan, July 11, 1910; and Ella E. Payne to Bureau of Insular Affairs, Mayagüez, Porto Rico, August 12, 1913, both from (Animal Cruelty, Puerto Rico) File Marker 971, Box 151, General Classified Files, Entry 5A (1898–1913), 350:150:56:7:3, RG 350, NARA II.

25. "General Orders No. 165," Havana, Cuba, April 19, 1900 (Cockfighting Prohibition, Cuba) File Marker 1660, Box 213, General Classified Files, Entry 5A (1898–1913), 350:150:56:8:6, RG 350, NARA II.

26. Taft to E. B. McCagg, April 16, 1900, quoted in Peter W. Stanley, *A Nation in the Making: The Philippines and the United States, 1899–1921* (Cambridge, MA: Harvard University Press, 1974), 64.

27. Here is the law in its entirety: "Section 1: No person shall overload, overwork, cruelly beat, torture, torment, mutilate, or cruelly kill any animal; or carry, drive or lead any animal in an unnecessary cruel manner; or abandon or cruelly work any old, maimed, infirm, sick or disabled animal; or cause or knowingly allow any of the same to be done. Section 2: No person shall fail to provide any animal in his charge or custody, as owner or otherwise, with proper food, drink and shelter. Section 3: No person shall give or permit, or aid, abet or encourage, by his presence at an exhibition or otherwise, the giving or permitting of any exhibition of bull fighting, dog fighting, cock fighting or fighting of any animals." "Ordinance for the Prevention of Cruelty to Animals," Ordinances City of Manila (Manila: Bureau of Printing, 1902), 115, vol. 376, 112.150 Philippine Materials Collection, Entry 95, 350:150, 58:20:2, RG 350, NARA II.

28. See Law No. 1285, Act of Incorporation for Society for the Prevention of Cruelty to Animals in the Philippines, January 19, 1905; Second Philippine Legislature, Law No. 2101, "An Act to Prohibit Certain Cruel Practices on Horses, and for Other Purposes," January 24, 1912; Section 40 (i), Philippine Commission, *Municipal Code and the Provincial Government Act, as Amended by the Acts of the Philippine Commission Down to and Including May 31, 1905* (Manila: Bureau of Public Printing, 1905), 112:135, vol. 352, Entry 95, Library Materials, Philippines— Miscellaneous, 350:150:57:20:1; No. 55, "An Act to Provide for Wholesome Food Supplies and to Prevent Cruelty to Animals in Transportation," *Public Laws*

Passed by the Philippine Commission, September 1, 1900–August 31, 1902, vol. 266 (Manila: Bureau of Printing, 1902), 73–74; Section 969, "Examination; Condemnation of Milch Animals," 520, in George A. Malcolm, ed., *The Charter of the City of Manila and the Revised Ordinances City of Manila* (Manila: Bureau of Printing, 1927), vol. 379, 112.150 Philippine Materials Collection, Entry 95, 350:150:58:20:2; Section 781, "Unlawful Acts in Parks," 330, in Malcolm, ed., *The Charter of the City of Manila and the Revised Ordinances of the City of Manila* (Manila: Bureau of Printing, 1917), vol. 378, 112.150 Philippine Materials Collection, Entry 95, 350:150:58:20:2; No. 1537, "Horse Races Act, amended" 142, in Malcolm, ed., *The Municipal Code and the Provincial Government Act Compiled and Annotated Being Acts Nos. 82 and 83, as Amended by Acts of the Philippine Commission and Legislature Down to February 3, 1911* (Manila: Bureau of Printing, 1911), vol. 354, 112:135 Entry 95, 350:150:58:19:6, all from RG 350, NARA II.

29. The terms of Act 1285 granted the SPCA the power to hire a maximum of only five paid deputized agents in Manila, and two in each province. Although these numbers were later expanded to ten agents in Manila and an agent in each provincial municipality, the dependency of this private organization on public money and labor was significant. "No. 1285, An Act authorizing the incorporation of the Society for the Prevention of Cruelty to Animals in the Philippine Islands," in *A General Act for the Organization of Provincial Governments in the Philippine Islands as Amended by the Acts of the Philippine Commission ... May 31, 1905* (Manila: Bureau of Public Printing, 1905), 56, 112:135, vol. 352, Library Materials, Philippines—Miscellaneous, Entry 95, 350: 150:57:20:1; "Commonwealth Act No. 148—An Act to amend section four of Act No. 1285," *Public Laws of the Commonwealth enacted by the National Assembly, December 21, 1935–March 9, 1937*, vol. 1, Acts Nos., 1–232 (Manila: Bureau of Printing, 1939), 706, vol. 308, Philippine Materials Collection, Entry 95, Library Materials, Philippines—Misc., 112.111 Public Laws; 350:150:58:19:5, both from RG 350, NARA II.

30. Ornithologist Richard McGregor reported in 1909 that American scientists had already collected approximately 8,000 Philippine bird specimens (with roughly 150 others yet to be captured) during a series of expeditions across the Islands for the Occupation Government's Bureau of Science. Richard C. McGregor, *A Manual of Philippine Birds, Part One: Galliformes to Eurylaemiformes* (Manila: Bureau of Printing, 1909), 2.

31. Chief of Bureau of Insular Affairs to American Ornithologists' Union, Committee on Foreign Relations, February 9, 1903; William Dutcher, Chair of the Commission on Foreign Relations of the American Ornithologists' Union to Clarence R. Edwards, Chief of the Bureau of Insular Affairs, February 11, 1903; Acting Executive Secretary to Clarence R. Edwards, March 26, 1903 (Ornithology, Philippines) File Marker 5817, Box 429, General Classified Files, Entry 5A (1898–1913), 350:150:56:13:1, RG 350, NARA II.

32. Section 3497–3498, *A Compilation of the Acts of the Philippine Commission* (Manila: Bureau of Printing, 1908), 1050, vols. 263–280, Philippine Materials Collection, Entry 95, 111.54 Executive Orders and Proclamations, and Public Laws, 350:150:58:19:3–5, RG 350, NARA II.
33. "Price and Exchange List of Philippine Bird Skins in the Collection of the Bureau of Science, Manila, Philippines, Effective 1911," 1–2 (Ornithology, Philippines) File Marker 5817, Box 429, General Classified Files, Entry 5A (1898–1913), 350:150:56:13:1, RG 350, NARA II.
34. Specifically, Act 2590 declared it unlawful to kill, wound, or sell any protected bird, mammal, or bird's nest or eggs, to include "insect-eating birds, song birds, game birds and generally all wild birds," with the exception of those proving to be "injurious" to one's property. Act No. 2590, "An Act for the Protection of Game and Fish," Enacted February 4, 1916, Philippine Laws, Statutes and Codes, Chan Robles Virtual Law Library, http://www.chanrobles.com/acts/actsno2590.html.
35. Act No. 2590, "An Act for the Protection of Game and Fish."
36. Kramer, *The Blood of Government*, 155.
37. "New Rules and Regulations," *Philippine Public Schools, a Monthly Magazine for Teachers*, November 1931, 406, vol. 677, 121.195 Philippine Materials Collection 350:150, 58:22:5–6, RG 350, NARA II.
38. See Andrew J. Rotter, "Empires of the Senses: How Seeing, Hearing, Smelling, Tasting, and Touching Shaped Imperial Encounters, *Diplomatic History* 35, no. 1 (January 2011): 3–19.
39. *Laws of Hawaii*, 364.
40. See "The Situation in Cuba," and "Mrs. Jeannette Ryder," *ODA*, March 1911, 152; "The Button in Cuba," *ODA*, March 1914, 154; "Jeannette Ryder, the Humane Heroine of Cuba," *ODA*, August 1920, 43; " 'Band of Mercy' Is Making Havana Paradise for Animals," [Ogden City, UT] *Evening Standard*, December 28, 1912, http://chroniclingamerica.loc.gov/lccn/sn85058397/1912-12-28/ed-1/seq-13/; see also "Suppressing Cock Fighting," *Washington* [DC] *Times*, September 11, 1909, http://chroniclingamerica.loc.gov/lccn/sn84026749/1909-09-11/ed-1/seq-7/; "Untitled," [Honolulu, HI] *Pacific Commercial Advertiser*, December 18, 1909, http://chroniclingamerica.loc.gov/lccn/sn85047084/1909-12-18/ed-1/seq-11/, all from Chronicling America: Historic American Newspapers.
41. " 'Band of Mercy' Is Making Havana Paradise for Animals."
42. " 'Band of Mercy' Is Making Havana Paradise for Animals."
43. " 'Band of Mercy' Iis Making Havana Paradise for Animals."
44. "A Blessed Martyr," *ODA*, October 1910, 75; " 'Band of Mercy' Is Making Havana Paradise for Animals."
45. Ordinance No. 13 contained meticulous rules for canine licensing: "Section 1: Every person who owns or keeps a dog over three months old shall obtain a license therefor, and shall provide a leather or metal collar to which the license tag hereinafter provided for shall be securely fastened. He shall also muzzle the dog,

if so ordered, as hereinafter provided. Failure to comply with any of the provisions of this section shall subject the owner or keeper to a fine of $5.00." "Ordinance No. 13, An Ordinance Regulating the Keeping and Licensing of Dogs," *Report of Lieutenant General Commanding the Army*, April 6, 1901, 260–261, Ordinances City of Manila, Nos. 265–740, 112.150, Philippine Materials Collection, vol. 375, Entry 95, 350:150, 58:20:2, RG 350, NARA II.

46. "Ordinance No. 13, An Ordinance Regulating the Keeping and Licensing of Dogs," sec. 1–14, 260–261.
47. "Ordinance No. 13, An Ordinance Regulating the Keeping and Licensing of Dogs," sec. 9, 261.
48. W. Cameron Forbes, Newton W. Gilbert, et al., *Report of the Philippine Commission to the Secretary of War, 1911* (Washington, DC: Government Printing Office, 1912), 63, 85.
49. "Chapter Four: Dogs and Other Animals," in George A. Malcolm, *The Charter of the City of Manila and the Revised Ordinances City of Manila* (Manila: Bureau of Printing, 1927), 183, vol. 379, 112.150 Philippine Materials Collection, Entry 95, 350:150:58:20:2, RG 350, NARA II.
50. Harriet Ritvo, *The Animal Estate: The English and Other Creatures in the Victorian Age* (Cambridge, MA: Harvard University Press, 1987), 188.
51. Ritvo, *The Animal Estate*, 190–192.
52. Ritvo, *The Animal Estate*, 192–193.
53. "Know Your Laws: CrPC, Section 144, 'Prohibition of Assembly,'" *India Update*, January 3, 2013, http://shovonc.wordpress.com/2013/01/03/know-your-laws-crpc-section-144-prohibition-of-assembly/.
54. Krishnadas Rajagopal, "Stray Dogs, a 120-Year-Old Problem," *The Hindu*, December 8, 2012, http://www.thehindu.com/todays-paper/tp-national/tp-kerala/stray-dogs-a-120yearold-problem/article4177232.ece.
55. Aaron Herald Skabelund, *Empire of Dogs: Canines, Japan, and the Making of the Modern Imperial World* (Ithaca, NY: Cornell University Press, 2011), 71–73, 81–82.
56. Skabelund, *Empire of Dogs*, 73.
57. Skabelund, *Empire of Dogs*, 46–49.
58. Skabelund, *Empire of Dogs*, 66, 65–69.
59. "Section 477. Dogs' Sale Prohibited; Penalty," in George A. Malcolm, ed., *The Charter of the City of Baguio and the Revised Ordinances of the City of Baguio* (Manila: Bureau of Printing, 1934), 261–262, vol. 380, 112.151 Philippine Materials Collection, Entry 95, 350:150:58:20:2, RG 350, NARA II.
60. Rick Baldoz, *The Third Asiatic Invasion: Empire and Migration in Filipino America, 1898–1946* (New York: New York University Press, 2011), 39–43.
61. See, for example, R. F. Barton, *The Half-Way Sun: Life among the Headhunters of the Philippines* (New York: Brewer and Warren, 1930); Albert Ernest Jenks, *The Bontoc Igorot*, Department of Interior, Ethnological Survey Publications, vol. 1 (Manila: Bureau of Public Printing, 1905); Bruce L. Kershner, *The Head*

Hunter and Other Stories of the Philippines (Cincinnati, OH: Powell and White, 1921); and Dean C. Worcester, "Headhunters under the Stars and Stripes: The Evolution of a Constabulary Sergeant from an Igorot Headhunter," *NYT*, October 25, 1908; Worcester, *The Philippines Past and Present* (1914; repr., New York: Macmillan, 1930).

62. Barton, *The Half-Way Sun,* 16, 13; José D. Fermin, *1904 World's Fair: The Filipino Experience* (West Conshohocken, PA: Infinity, 2004), 17–20.
63. W. M. Morrill, "Dog Trafficking with the Igorrotes," *ODA*, August 1920, 39.
64. "No. 2101, An Act to Prohibit Certain Cruel Practices on Horses, and for Other Purposes," January 24, 1912 (Animals, Cruelty to, Philippines) File Marker 10,795, Box 622, General Classified Files, Entry 5A (1898–1913), 350:150:56:17:1; Edward Bowditch (Private Secretary to Governor-General Forbes) to Brigadier General Clarence R. Edwards, Chief of the Bureau of Insular Affairs, January 29, 1912, Manila (Animals, Cruelty to, Philippines) File Marker 10,795, Box 622, RG 350, NARA II.
65. "Offenses against Public Morals," in George A. Malcolm, *The Manila Charter as Amended and the Revised Ordinances of the City of Manila* (Manila: Bureau of Printing, 1908), 229–239; vol. 377, 112.150 Philippine Materials Collection, Entry 95, 350:150, 58:20:2; Ordinance No. 267, *Ordinances City of Manila* (1916), Nos. 265–740, 1–2; vol. 375, 112.150 Philippine Materials Collection, Entry 95, 350:150, 58:20:2, all at RG 350, NARA II.
66. *Minutes of the Twenty-fourth Annual Meeting of the Woman's Christian Temperance Union of the State of Minnesota*, August 28–31, 1900, Mankato (St. Paul: W. J. Woodbury, 1900), 21, WCTU Minnesota Collection, vol. 4 (1900–1906), WCTU MN Collection, Box 12/6/7, Social Welfare History Archives, University of Minnesota, Minneapolis.
67. *Minutes of the Twenty-fourth Annual Meeting of the Woman's Christian Temperance Union of the State of Minnesota*, August 28–31, 1900, 21.
68. Mercer G. Johnston, "Statement of Facts in re. Carnival Cockpit," 1908, 4 (Cockfighting, Philippines) File Marker 6633, Box 454, General Classified Files, Entry 5A (1898–1913), 350:150: 56:13:5, RG 350, NARA II.
69. "Telegram," Secretary of War Elihu Root to William Howard Taft, Washington, DC, January 15, 1901; "Telegram," Taft to Root, Manila, January 17, 1901, Correspondence of the Philippine Taft Commission, Entry 34, Box 1, 350:150:58:4:6, RG 350, NARA II; see also Paul A. Kramer, "Colonial Crossings: Prostitution, Disease, and the Boundaries of Empire during the Philippine-American War," in *Body and Nation: The Global Realm of U. S. Body Politics in the Twentieth Century*, ed. Emily S. Rosenberg and Shanon Fitzpatrick (Durham, NC: Duke University Press, 2014), 17–41.
70. "Telegram," Taft to Root, Manila, January 17, 1901.
71. "Cockfighting Ban Dates by State," *Animal Protection of New Mexico*, http://www.apnm.org/campaigns/cockfighting/ban_dates.html.

72. Angel J. Lansang, *Cockfighting in the Philippines (Our Genuine National Sport)* Baguio City, Philippines: Catholic School Press, 1966), 140.
73. John Noble Wilford, "First Chickens in Americas Were Brought from Polynesia," *NYT,* June 5, 2007, www.nytimes.com/2007/06/05/science/05chic.html; Tim Pridgen, *Courage: The Story of Modern Cockfighting* (Boston: Little, Brown, 1938), 72–85.
74. Brigadier General J. Franklin Bell, "Telegraphic Circular No. 19," *Telegraphic Circulars and General Orders* (Bantangas: Headquarters, Third Separate Brigade, 1902), 17–18.
75. "An Ordinance for the Prevention of Cruelty to Animals," [Ordinance No. 20], Ordinances City of Manila (Manila: Bureau of Printing, 1902), 115, vol. 376, 112.150 Philippine Materials Collection, Entry 95, 350:150:58:20:2, RG 350, NARA II.
76. José Rizal, *Nole Me Tangere* (Touch Me Not), trans. Harold Augenbraum (1887; repr., New York: Penguin Classics, 2006), 307–308.
77. Lansang, *Cockfighting in the Philippines*, 20.
78. Rizal, *Nole Me Tangere*, 302.
79. Emilio Aguinaldo, quoted in Mercer Green Johnston, "A Covenant with Death, an Agreement with Hell: A Sermon Preached in the Cathedral of St. Mary and St. John, Manila," February 23, 1908 (Cockfighting, Philippines) File Marker 6633, Box 454, General Classified Files, Entry 5A (1898–1913), 350:150:56:13:5, RG 350, NARA II.
80. See, for example, Johnston, "A Covenant with Death, an Agreement with Hell."
81. Such views were widespread among Americans in the Philippines. For example, the writer Frederick Chamberlin posited that the Tagalogs were fatalistic as a result of their devotion to cockfighting: "The prevailing vice was gaming, and with the utmost nonchalance they would risk everything they possessed upon the turn of a single card or the outcome of some cockfight." Arthur Judson Brown, *The New Era in the Philippines* (New York: Fleming H. Revell, 1903), 72–73; Frederick Chamberlin, *The Philippine Problem, 1898–1913* (Boston: Little, Brown, 1913), 41.
82. Worcester, *The Philippines Past and Present*, 408–409.
83. Worcester, *The Philippines Past and Present*. 408–409.
84. For a thorough discussion of Philippine cockfighting during the Spanish colonial era, see Scott Guggenheim, "Cock or Bull: Cockfighting, Social Structure, and Political Commentary in the Philippines," in *The Cockfight: A Casebook*, ed. Alan Dundas (Madison: University of Wisconsin Press, 1994), 136–139.
85. Charles W. Briggs, *The Progressing Philippines* (Philadelphia: Griffith and Rowland Press, nd), 101.
86. Bruce L. Kershner, *The Head Hunter and Other Stories of the Philippines* (Cincinnati: Powell and White, 1921), 68–69.
87. See Ussama Makdisi, *Artillery of Heaven: American Missionaries and the Failed Conversion of the Middle East* (Ithaca, NY: Cornell University Press, 2008).

88. New municipal laws specifically designated the time (festival days), location (registered cockpits), and rules (no municipal official could run a cockpit; cockers had to have time-sensitive permits; each fight was taxed and [ostensibly] alcohol free). See, for example, "An Act Amending Section 40 of Act #82 Entitled 'A General Act for the Organization of Municipal Governments in the Philippine Islands,'" No. 364, Enacted February 20, 1902 (Cockfighting, Philippines) File Marker 6633, Box 454, General Classified Files, Entry 5A (1898–1913), 350:150:56:13:5, RG 350, NARA II.
89. "Section 40 (j) 3., Present Character of Cockfights," in George A. Malcolm, ed., *The Municipal Code and the Provincial Government Act* (Manila: Bureau of Printing, 1911), 138; 112:135, vol. 354, Entry 95, 350:150:58:19:6, RG 350, NARA II.
90. Guggenheim, "Cock or Bull," 136–139.
91. "The Government and Gambling in the Philippines," nd, np (Cockfighting, Philippines) File Marker 6633, Box 454, General Classified Files, Entry 5A (1898–1913), 350:150:56:13:5, RG 350, NARA II.
92. Telegram from the Evangelical Union to President Roosevelt, February 25, 1908 (Cockfighting, Philippines) File Marker 6633, Box 454, General Classified Files, Entry 5A (1898–1913), 350:150:56:13:5, RG 350, NARA II.
93. Johnston, "A Covenant with Death, an Agreement with Hell," 5.
94. Johnston, "A Covenant with Death, an Agreement with Hell," 9.
95. "Protestantism in the Philippines," *Silliman Truth*, Dumaguete, Negros Oriental (Philippines), July 1, 1911, (Missionary Work of Protestants) File Marker 1158, Box 170, Entry 5, General Records, 1898–1914, 350:150:56:7:6, RG 350, NARA II.
96. Clarence Edwards to William Howard Taft, Secretary of War, February 24, 1908, Washington, DC (Cockfighting, Philippines) File Marker 6633, Box 454, General Classified Files, Entry 5A (1898–1913), 350:150:56:13:5, RG 350, NARA II.
97. Lansang, *Cockfighting in the Philippines*, 54.
98. Louis Pérez, *On Becoming Cuban: Identity, Nationality, and Culture* (Chapel Hill: University of North Carolina Press, 1999), 22.
99. "Military Order No. 165," April 19, 1900, Havana; Charles E. Magoon to William Howard Taft, Habana, February 25, 1907, 2, both from (Cockfighting prohibition, Cuba) File Marker 1660, Box 213, General Classified Files, Entry 5A (1898–1913), 350:150:56:8:6, RG 350, NARA II.
100. "President Palma Message to Congress on January 6, 1904," quoted in Magoon to Taft, February 25, 1907, 12–13.
101. Magoon to Taft, February 25, 1907, 1.
102. Magoon to Taft, February 25, 1907, 3.
103. Magoon to Taft, February 25, 1907, 8.
104. Antonio Ruiz, "Manifest to the Public in General," January 20, 1907, (Cockfighting prohibition, Cuba) File Marker 1660, Box 213, General Classified Files, Entry 5A (1898–1913), 350:150:56:8:6, RG 350, NARA II.

105. Narciso Lopez Quintana, et al. to Charles E. Magoon, Havana, February 24, 1907, (Cockfighting prohibition, Cuba) File Marker 1660, Box 213, General Classified Files, Entry 5A (1898–1913), 350:150:56:8:6, RG 350, NARA II.
106. Narciso Lopez Quintana, et al. to Charles E. Magoon, Havana, February 24, 1907.
107. D. M. Pearcy, et al. to Charles E. Magoon, Nueva Gerona, February 17, 1907, (Cockfighting prohibition, Cuba) File Marker 1660, Box 213, General Classified Files, Entry 5A (1898–1913), 350:150:56:8:6, RG 350, NARA II.
108. George Angell to Charles E. Magoon, Boston, February 12, 1907, (Cockfighting prohibition, Cuba) File Marker 1660, Box 213, General Classified Files, Entry 5A (1898–1913), 350:150:56:8:6, RG 350, NARA II.
109. John L. Shortall to Charles E. Magoon, Chicago, February 16, 1907, (Cockfighting prohibition, Cuba) File Marker 1660, Box 213, General Classified Files, Entry 5A (1898–1913), 350:150:56:8:6, RG 350, NARA II.
110. Alfred Wagstaff to Governor Magoon, February 18, 1907, (Cockfighting prohibition, Cuba) File Marker 1660, Box 213, General Classified Files, Entry 5A (1898–1913), 350:150:56:8:6, RG 350, NARA II.
111. Magdalena Peñarredonda to Charles E. Magoon, Yagaujay, Cuba, February 16, 1907, (Cockfighting prohibition, Cuba) File Marker 1660, Box 213, General Classified Files, Entry 5A (1898–1913), 350:150:56:8:6, RG 350, NARA II.
112. Although planters pushed to preserve the ban, they were willing to support a modest repeal that would limit cockfights to legal holidays and periods outside the growing season. Edwin F. Atkins to Charles E. Magoon, Cienfuegos, Cuba, March 2, 1907, (Cockfighting prohibition, Cuba) File Marker 1660, Box 213, General Classified Files, Entry 5A (1898–1913), 350:150:56:8:6, RG 350, NARA II.
113. Magoon to Taft, Habana, February 25, 1907, 7–8.
114. Magoon to Taft, Habana, February 25, 1907, 11–12.
115. Magoon to Taft, Habana, February 25, 1907, 11–12.
116. Telegram from Charles E. Magoon to William Howard Taft, Havana, April 23, 1907, (Cockfighting prohibition, Cuba) File Marker 1660, Box 213, General Classified Files, Entry 5A (1898–1913), 350:150:56:8:6, RG 350, NARA II.
117. Colonel Frank E. McIntyre to Gus J. Karger, Washington, DC, May 23, 1910, (Cockfighting prohibition, Cuba) File Marker 1660, Box 213, General Classified Files, Entry 5A (1898–1913), 350:150:56:8:6, RG 350, NARA II.
118. Magoon to Taft, February 25, 1907, 11–12; "Inclosure to Dispatch No. 992: An Act Legalizing Cock-Fighting," trans. from the Official Gazette, July 3, 1909, (Cockfighting prohibition, Cuba) File Marker 1660, Box 213, General Classified Files, Entry 5A (1898–1913), 350:150:56:8:6, RG 350, NARA II.
119. Colonel Frank E. McIntyre to Gus J. Karger, Washington, DC, May 23, 1910.
120. No. 33: "An Act to Amend Section 5 of an Act Entitled 'An Act to Prevent Cruelty to Animals,' [Originally] Approved March 10, 1904," Approved, May

4, 1933, (Cockfighting, Puerto Rico) File Marker 26484, Box 1074, General Classified Files, Entry 5B (1914–1945), 350:150:57:11:2, RG 350, NARA II.

121. William Dinwiddie, *Puerto Rico: Its Conditions and Possibilities* (New York: Harper and Brothers, 1899), 179.

122. Go, *American Empire and the Politics of Meaning*, 84–90.

123. "Bill to Legalize Cock Fighting Vetoed by Governor H. M. Towner," *San Juan* [Puerto Rico] *Times*, May 16, 1928, 1, (Cockfighting, Puerto Rico) File Marker 26484, Box 1074, General Classified Files, Entry 5B (1914–1945), 350:150:57:11:2, RG 350, NARA II.

124. Dinwiddie, *Puerto Rico: Its Conditions and Possibilities*, 179.

125. Puerto Rico's own political, geographical, and cultural history shaped the tenor of local protests against the cockfighting law, as in other colonial settings. Puerto Rico became a US territory fairly peacefully in 1898; the majority of the Island's elites supported eventual US statehood with autonomous internal governance, or strong advantageous trade (coffee and sugar) and tax privileges as a territory, rather than outright independence. See Go, *American Empire and the Politics of Meaning*.

126. Manuel Jiménez Santa to U.S. Secretary of State Bainbridge Colby, Rio Piedras, June 18, 1920; see also Santa to Colby, Rio Piedras, June 8, 1920; Santa to Antonio R. Barceló, Presidente del Senado, Rio Piedras, June 8, 1920, (Cockfighting, Puerto Rico) File Marker 26484, Box 1074, General Classified Files, Entry 5B (1914–1945), 350:150:57:11:2, RG 350, NARA II.

127. Santa to Colby, June 18, 1920.

128. "Cock of the Walk No More," [Manila] *Philippines Herald*, September 16, 1928, (Cockfighting, Puerto Rico) File Marker 26484, Box 1074, General Classified Files, Entry 5B (1914–1945), 350:150:57:11:2, RG 350, NARA II.

129. Harwood Hull, Cockfighting Bill Fails in Porto Rico," *NYT*, June 3, 1928; "Bill to Legalize Cock Fighting Vetoed by Governor H. M. Towner," *San Juan* [Puerto Rico] *Times*, May 16, 1928.

130. "Cock of the Walk No More."

131. *Indianapolis News*, June 11, 1928, (Cockfighting, Puerto Rico) File Marker 26484, Box 1074, General Classified Files, Entry 5B (1914–1945), 350:150:57:11:2, RG 350, NARA II.

132. No. 33, "An Act to Amend Section 5 of an Act Entitled 'An Act to Prevent Cruelty to Animals,'" First Special Session of the Thirteenth Legislature, Puerto Rico, May 4, 1933, (Cockfighting, Puerto Rico) File Marker 26484, Box 1074, General Classified Files, Entry 5B (1914–1945), 350:150:57:11:2, RG 350, NARA II.

133. Robert H. Gore quoted in Martín Travieso, "Puerto Rico Cockfighting," *New York Herald Tribune*, October 22, 1933, (Cockfighting, Puerto Rico) File Marker 26484, Box 1074, General Classified Files, Entry 5B (1914–1945), 350:150:57:11:2, RG 350, NARA II.

134. Travieso, "Puerto Rico Cockfighting."
135. N. J. Walker to K. F. Baldwin, Albany New York, June 13, 1933, (Cockfighting, Puerto Rico) File Marker 26484, Box 1074, General Classified Files, Entry 5B (1914–1945), 350:150:57:11:2, RG 350, NARA II.
136. See Dennis Merrill, *Negotiating Paradise: U.S. Tourism and Empire in Twentieth-Century Latin America* (Chapel Hill: University of North Carolina Press, 2009).
137. Encarnacion Alzona, *A History of Education in the Philippines, 1565–1930* (Manila: University of the Philippines Press, 1932), 189–190.
138. Alzona, *A History of Education in the Philippines*, 208.
139. Kramer, *The Blood of Government*, 203–204.
140. For more information on Protestant and Catholic concerns over the Occupation Government's secular education policy, see (Missionary Work of Protestants) File Marker 1158, Box 170, Entry 5, General Records, 1898–1914, 350:150:56:7:6; and (Education, inquiries, suggestions, criticisms, and complaints) File Marker 3140, Box 322, Entry 5, General Records, 1898–1914, 350: 150:56:10:7, all from RG 350, NARA II.
141. At the start of the Occupation, it was rumored that powerful Catholic friars had colluded with General Otis, a Catholic, to ban the sale of Protestant Bibles in the Philippines and to influence public education. Simultaneously, Catholic periodicals characterized Occupied public schools as "Godless" institutions, whose teachers and administrators were "full of anti-Catholic and distinctly Protestant notions." J. G. Junkin to President McKinley, Wyandot, Ohio, August 8, 1899, and Iring W. Street to John A. Johnston (Assistant Adjutant General), Lima, Ohio, December 19, 1899; "Catholic Education in the Philippines," *London Tablet*, May 10, 1913, (Missionary Work of Protestants) File Marker 1158, Box 170, Entry 5, General Records, 1898–1914, 350:150:56:7:6, RG 350, NARA II.
142. Alzona, *A History of Education in the Philippines*, 210–212.
143. Gilbert S. Perez, *From the Transport Thomas to Sto. Tomas: The History of the American Teachers in the Philippines* (Manila: Bureau of Public Schools, nd), 7.
144. "The Filipino Teachers," in *Report of the Secretary of Public Instruction of the Philippine Islands for the Year Ending October 15, 1902* (Manila: Bureau of Printing, 1902), 873, vol. 680, Reports Secretary of Public Instruction and Director of Education, etc., 1900–1910, Philippine Materials Collection, Entry 95, 350:150:58:22:7, RG 350, NARA II.
145. John A. Staunton, quoted in "The Filipino Teachers," 947.
146. See, for example, Harriet Beecher Stowe, "A Talk about Birds," in *A Dog's Mission; or, The Story of the Old Avery House and Other Stories* (New York: Fords, Howard, and Hulbert, 1880), 106–107.
147. Sally Gregory Kohlstedt, *Teaching Children Science: Hands-On Nature Study in North America, 1890–1930* (Chicago: University of Chicago Press, 2010), 133, 137–138

148. See, "For the Teacher's Home Library," *Philippine Public Schools: A Monthly Magazine for Teachers*, March 1928, 146–147, *Philippine Public Schools*, (January–December, 1928), vol. 675, 121.195 Philippine Materials Collection 350:150:58:22:5–6, RG 350, NARA II.

149. One can see the influence of progressive pedagogy in the monthly column, "Helpful Lesson Plans," in *Philippine Public Schools*. See *Philippine Public Schools, a Monthly Magazine for Teachers*, March 1930, 127; *Philippine Public Schools* (January–December, 1930–1931), vol. 677, 121.195 Philippine Materials Collection, 350:150:58:22:5–6, RG 350, NARA II.

150. "Nature," *Course of Study in Drawing for Normal Schools—Bureau of Education* (Manila: Bureau of Printing, 1929), 16, 25, 121.143 Courses of Study, Philippines Materials Collection, Entry 95, vol. 654, 350:150:58:22:5, RG 350, NARA II.

151. "Nature," *Course of Study in Drawing for Normal Schools—Bureau of Education* (Manila: Bureau of Printing, 1929), 25.

152. "Little Patriots of the Air," *ODA*, July 1917, 29.

153. *Drawing Course of Study for Primary Grades* (Manila: Bureau of Printing, 1926), 23, 121.143 Courses of Study, Philippines Materials Collection, Entry 95, vol. 654, 350:150:58:22:5, RG 350, NARA II.

154. *Philippine Public Schools*, July 1931, 197–198, *Philippine Public Schools* (January–December, 1930–1931), vol. 677, 121.195 Philippine Materials Collection, 350:150:58:22:5–6, RG 350, NARA II.

155. "Exercise 29: Change Present-Tense Forms to Past-Tense Forms," *A Workbook in Language for Grade VII*, vol. 1 (Manila: Bureau of Printing, 1935), 55, vols. 654–655, 121.143 Courses of Study and Textbooks: English, Philippine Materials Collection, Entry 95, 350:150:58:22:5, RG 350, NARA II.

156. "Lesson for Fourth-Year English," *Philippine Public Schools*, September 1929, 265, *Philippine Public Schools* (January–December, 1929), vol. 676, 121.195 Philippine Materials Collection, 350:150:58:22:5–6, RG 350, NARA II.

157. "Memorandum for General McIntyre from G. A. Briggs (Director of Education, Philippines)," Manila, May 21, 1913, (Education, inquiries, suggestions, criticisms, and complaints) File Marker 3140, Box 322, Entry 5, General Records, 1898–1914, 350:150:56:10:7, RG 350, NARA II.

158. "Thomas Jefferson," *A Work Book in Language*, vol. 2 (Manila: Bureau of Printing, 1935), 46, vols. 654–655, 657–658, Courses of Study and Text Books 121.143 and 121.16 Philippine Materials Collection, Entry 95, 350:150:58:22:5, RG 350, NARA II.

159. "Pupil's Home Improvement Card," *Philippine Public Schools*, October 1931, 202–203, *Philippine Public Schools* (January–December, 1930–1931), vol. 677, 121.195 Philippine Materials Collection, 350:150:58:22:5–6, RG 350, NARA II.

160. *Drawing Course of Study for Primary Grades* (Manila: Bureau of Printing, 1926); *Course of Study in Drawing for Normal Schools—Bureau of Education*

(Manila: Bureau of Printing, 1929), 23, vol. 654, 121.143 Courses of Study, Philippine Materials Collection, Entry 95, 350:150:58:22:5, RG 350, NARA II.

161. *Manual of Directions for the Philippine Educational Achievement Tests* (Manila: Bureau of Printing, 1926), 23, 29, vol. 654, 121.143 Courses of Study, Philippine Materials Collection, Entry 95, 350:150:58:22:5, RG 350, NARA II.

162. Antonio Nera, *Nature Study Readers, Book Four* (Rizal, PI: Oriental Commercial Co., 1933), vol. 658, 121.16 Catalogue—Course of Study and Textbooks, 121.144, Philippine Materials Collection, Entry 95, 350:150:58:22:5, RG 350, NARA II.

163. Frank L. Crone (Acting Director of Education, Philippines) to Barksdale Hamlett (Superintendent of Schools, Frankfort, Kentucky), Manila, December 27, 1912, 1 (Education, inquiries, suggestions, criticisms, and complaints) File Marker 3140, Box 322, Entry 5, General Records, 1898–1914, 350:150:56:10:7, RG 350, NARA II.

164. "Commonwealth Act No. 148," Public Laws of the Commonwealth enacted by the National Assembly, December 21, 1935, to March 9, 1937, vol. 1, Acts Nos., 1–232 (Manila: Bureau of Printing, 1939), 706, 112.111 Public Laws, vol. 308, Philippine Materials Collection, Entry 95, 350:150:58:19:5, RG 350, NARA II.

CHAPTER 5

1. "For the Starving in India," *ODA*, July 1900, 15.
2. Stanley Wolpert, *A New History of India*, 3rd ed. (New York: Oxford University Press, 1989), 267–268.
3. "Delhi, India," *ODA*, February 1903, 106 [emphasis in original].
4. Edward Said, *Orientalism* (New York: Pantheon, 1978).
5. See Susan S. Bean, *Yankee India: American Commercial and Cultural Encounters with India in the Age of Sail, 1784–1860* (Salem, MA: Peabody Essex Museum, 2001); Kirin Narayan, "Refractions of the Field at Home: American Representations of Hindu Holy Men in the 19th and 20th Centuries," *Cultural Anthropology* 8, no. 4 (November 1993): 476–509.
6. Andrew J. Rotter, "Empires of the Senses: How Seeing, Hearing, Smelling, Tasting, and Touching Shaped Imperial Encounters," *Diplomatic History* 35, no. 1 (January 2011): 7.
7. Maina Chawla Singh, *Gender, Religion, and "Heathen Lands": American Missionary Women in South Asia (1860s–1940s)* (New York: Garland, 2000), 5, 32n19.
8. Humanitarian animal welfare conferences also brought humane advocates together from around the globe. See, for example, American reportage of the Second Humanitarian Conference in Broach, India; "For Animals and Birds in India," *ODA*, March 1919, 157.
9. Despite the popularity of South Asia as an American mission field, conversion of South Asians to Christianity remained uncommon. Although a few high-caste

Hindus like the Bengali writer Michael Sudhan Datta became Christians, the majority of Hindu converts were lower caste. Hindus and Muslims as a whole were unreceptive to proselytizing. Missionaries found better reception among India's peripatetic hill tribal communities, particularly in the isolated northeastern regions of current-day Assam, Nagaland, Manipur, and Mizoram—places where there was no centralized state or religious apparatus in place. (Missionary efforts there were so successful that Nagaland, for example, has a Christian majority today.) Accordingly, American evangelicals maintained an active presence among northeastern hill tribal communities. Percival Spear, *A History of India: From the Sixteenth Century to the Twentieth Century*, vol. 2 (London: Penguin Books, 1978), 163–164.

10. Guy Richardson, "The Story of 'Black Beauty,'" *ODA*, September 1910, 60.
11. Bernard Oreste Unti, "'The Quality of Mercy': Organized Animal Protection in the United States, 1866–1930" (PhD diss., American University, 2002), 213.
12. "Signing the Pledge of the Band of Mercy," *ODA*, July, 1887, 1.
13. "Universal Mercy Band Movement," *Christian Life: A Unitarian Journal*, March 5, 1887, 120.
14. The Universal Mercy Band contained 107,000 members in 500 Bands throughout the empire in 1887. The American Band, by comparison, was even larger because of its initial rapid growth within the United States and then overseas. In just five years, the Band sprouted 5,703 branches with approximately 400,000 members; it grew to 53,642 branches in 1903, 90,000 branches (containing over 3 million signers) in 1914, and 157,057 branches in 1926. "Signing the Pledge of the Band of Mercy," *ODA*, July, 1887, 1; "Report of the President," *ODA*, May, 1903, 155; "90,000 Bands of Mercy," *ODA*, March, 1914, 154; "New Bands of Mercy," *ODA*, November 1926, 94; Harriet Ritvo, *The Animal Estate: The English and Other Creatures in the Victorian Age* (Cambridge, MA: Harvard University Press, 1987), 5.
15. "Increasing Our Army," *ODA*, August 1901, 27.
16. James M. Thoburn, *The Christian Conquest of India* (Cincinnati, OH: Foreign Christian Mission Society, 1906), 52–53.
17. " Band of Mercy in India," *ODA*, April 1914, 170.
18. George A. Raeth, "Boys and Birds in Milwaukee," *ODA*, October 1910, 67.
19. "For Kindness in India," *ODA*, August 1914, 45.
20. See "Sandwich Islands: Statements Relative to the Population and Progress of the Mission," *Missionary Herald*, August 1836, 305–309; "Letter from Mr. Smith, Dated November 5, 1833," *Missionary Herald*, May 1835, 187–189, 188; Marshall Saunders, *Beautiful Joe: A Dog's Own Story* (1893; repr., New York: Grosset and Dunlap, 1920), 4.
21. "Letter from Mr. Lyons, at Waimea on Hawaii, September 18, 1837," *Missionary Herald*, July 1838, 255–259, 256; "Sandwich Islands: Statements Relative to the Population and Progress of the Mission," *Missionary Herald*, 305.

22. Thoburn, *The Christian Conquest of India*, 95.
23. See "Domestic Animals and Pets of India," *Heathen Woman's Friend*, September 1889, 80–82.
24. Eugenia Gibson, "Holy Cows," *Heathen Woman's Friend*, May 1889, 300–301.
25. Frederick B. Price, ed., *India Mission Jubilee of the Methodist Episcopal Church in Southern Asia* (Calcutta: Methodist Publishing House, 1907), 143.
26. T. J. Scott, "Our Dumb Fellow Creatures," *Methodist Review*, July 1918, 557–569, 557.
27. Matt Kinnell, "E. Stanley Jones," Asbury University Archives and Special Collections: Biographies, https://www.asbury.edu/offices/library/archives/biographies/e-stanley-jones; "Eli Stanley Jones," United Christian Ashrams, http://vaxxine.com/eves/jones.htm.
28. "India: Pundita Ramabai Request for Subscriptions to *Our Dumb Animals*," *ODA*, November 1887, 65; Ian Tyrrell, *Woman's World, Woman's Empire: The Woman's Christian Temperance Union in International Perspective, 1880–1930* (Chapel Hill: University of North Carolina Press, 1991), 142.
29. Clementina Butler, *Pandita Ramabai Sarasvati: Pioneer in the Movement for the Education of the Child-Widow of India* (New York: Fleming H. Revell, 1922), 4.
30. "Pundita Ramabai Humane Pamphlet," quoted in Pandita Ramabai Sarasvati, *Pandita Ramabai's American Encounter: The Peoples of the United States (1889)*, ed. and trans. Meera Kosambi (Bloomington: Indiana University Press, 2003), 26.
31. "Let Every Lover of Birds," *ODA*, May 1888, 147.
32. The Sharada Sadan initially opened in Bombay in 1889, moved to less expensive Pune a year later, and then finally to Kedgaon, Maharashtra, in the late 1890s to escape a bubonic plague epidemic.
33. Ramabai, quoted in Kosambi, *Pandita Ramabai's American Encounter*, 250n48.
34. Kosambi, *Pandita Ramabai's American Encounter*, 39.
35. Ramabai, quoted in Kosambi, *Pandita Ramabai's American Encounter*, 133; see also 250n48.
36. According to the Laws of Manu, high-caste Hindu widows were supposed to shave their heads, wear coarse white saris without jewelry, and eat only one meal every twenty-four hours in obedience to their marginalized place in society as shamed, inauspicious figures. European orientalist scholars such as Max Müller asserted that the Laws of Manu were a degraded, corrupted form of Hinduism; in its "purer" ancient Vedic form, Hinduism respected women, and traditions like sati [widow self-immolation] did not exist. Butler, *Pandita Ramabai Sarasvati*, 23, 40–41.
37. "Report of the Annual Meeting of the American Ramabai Association, Held on March 11, 1891" (Boston: Lend a Hand, 1891), 21.
38. Pandita Ramabai, quoted in Helen S. Dyer, *Pandita Ramabai: The Story of Her Life* (New York: Fleming H. Revell, 1900), 103.
39. "Report of the Annual Meeting of the American Ramabai Association (1891)," 33.

40. See Antoinette Burton, *Burdens of History: British Feminists, Indian Women, and Imperial Culture, 1865–1915* (Chapel Hill: University of North Carolina Press, 1994); Vijay Prasad, *The Karma of Brown Folk* (Minneapolis: University of Minnesota Press, 2001), 25–26; Lila Abu-Lughod, *Do Muslim Women Need Saving?* (Cambridge, MA: Harvard University Press, 2013).
41. "Report of the First Annual Meeting of the American Ramabai Association, Held March 24, 1899" (Boston: Geo. H. Ellis, 1899), 27–28.
42. "Annual Report of the Calcutta SPCA," quoted in *ODA*, October 1887, 52; by contrast, in 1885, the ASPCA investigated 2,846 cases of suspected animal cruelty in New York City, out of which 722 were prosecuted in the courts. Published reports did not list the numbers actually convicted. "Henry Bergh's Society," *NYT*, January 7, 1886.
43. "C.S.P.C.A.," *Amrita Bazar Patrika*, June 29, 1933, Prevention of Cruelty to Animals in India, Meetings of I.O. Officials and RSPCA, 2076, 1933, IOR/L/PJ/7/531, Public and Judicial Departmental Papers: Annual Files, India Office Records (hereafter cited as IOR), British Library (hereafter cited as BL).
44. HAR (abbreviated signature), Notes on Calcutta SPCA, 27 July, 1933, Prevention of Cruelty to Animals in India, Meetings of I.O. Officials and RSPCA, 2076, 1933, IOR/L/PJ/7/531, Public and Judicial Departmental Papers: Annual Files, IOR, BL.
45. Tanika Sarkar, *Bengal, 1924–1934: The Politics of Protest* (Delhi: Oxford University Press, 1987),101.
46. "C.S.P.C.A.," *Amrita Bazar Patrika*.
47. HAR, Notes on Calcutta SPCA; on earlier clashes, see "The Strikes at Calcutta," June 17, 1901; "Cruel Treatment of Bullocks," October 13, 1911; "The Calcutta S.P.C.A.: Grave Allegations," May 20, 1925, all from *Times of India*, ProQuest Historical Newspapers: *Times of India* (1861—current).
48. Sarkar, *Bengal, 1928–1934*, 104; "C.S.P.C.A.," *Amrita Bazar Patrika*.
49. Newly outlawed acts of cruelty included "setting on or urging any dog or other animal to attack, worry or put in fear any person, horse or any other, or, cruelly beating, or torturing any animal." Ministry of Food and Agriculture, *Report of the Committee for the Prevention of Cruelty to Animals* (New Delhi: Government of India, 1957), 15–16, Shelfmarks V14599, IOR, BL.
50. Local and regional precedents included the Madras Police Act of 1888, which made owners financially liable for the costs of caring for an infirm animal seized by the police. Furthermore, the India-wide Code of Criminal Procedure of 1882 defined the legal parameters of the search warrant. Section 11 of the Gambling Act II of 1867 in Bengal made public bird baiting a punishable crime.
51. Local officials could "opt-out" of specific sections of the PCA Act, as long as they documented their reasons in the official regional Gazette.
52. The PCA Act was the product of two months of dialogue between far-flung officials across the subcontinent. Its final form created an exceptionally rigorous framework

for surveillance and enforcement, "opting out" notwithstanding. Any documented act of beating, overdriving, overloading, binding, mutilating, starving, killing in an "unnecessarily cruel manner," or carrying an animal in a position that caused suffering in a street was punishable by a fine of 100 rupees, three months' imprisonment, or both. The practice of *phuka* (designed to increase milk production) was also banned under the law. Any owner who worked an infirm animal that was subsequently seized by the authorities and placed in a hospital (pinjrapole), was liable for the cost of treatment, room, and board. Owners who allowed any animal infected with a contagious disease to wander in the street were liable for a 100-rupee fine. The law authorized any magistrate, commissioner of police, or district superintendent of police to destroy any animal "if in his opinion its sufferings are such as to render such a direction proper." While the law required police officers to possess a written search warrant to enter a private residence, it also authorized high-ranking officials to grant themselves a warrant if they had written information regarding any act of cruelty that "is being or is about to be or has been committed in any place." The PCA Act also established a three-month statute of limitations for prosecution. Prevention of Cruelty to Animals Act, Act No. XI of 1890, 1 April 1890, L/PJ/6/275, File 698, Public and Judicial Departmental Papers: Annual Files; No. 801, Dated Calcutta, February 6, 1890. J. Lambert, Esq. CIE, Commissioner of Police, Calcutta, to Chief Secretary to the Government of Bengal, Papers relative to Prevention of Cruelty to Animals Bill, February 25, 1890, L/PJ/6/272, File 473, Public and Judicial Departmental Papers: Annual Files; Prevention of Cruelty to Animals Act, Act No. XI of 1890, all from IOR, BL.
53. Prevention of Cruelty to Animals Act, Act No. XI of 1890.
54. E. N. Baker, Esq. Deputy Commissioner of Manbhoom, to the Chief Secretary to the Government of Bengal, No. A, February 7, 1890, Papers relative to Prevention of Cruelty to Animals Bill, February 25, 1890, L/PJ/6/272, File 473, Public and Judicial Departmental Papers: Annual Files, IOR, BL.
55. Prevention of Cruelty to Animals Act, Act No. XI of 1890.
56. Based on the legal precedent of the Madras City Police Act of 1888, the PCA Act vested police with the power to "direct the immediate destruction of the animal if in his opinion its sufferings are such as to render such a direction proper." Prevention of Cruelty to Animals Act, Act No. XI of 1890.
57. Major C. P. G. Griffin (Commander, Aden Troops), to First-Assistant Resident, Aden, September 18, 1908, 101, Prevention of Cruelty to Animals, 1907–1936, File 99/1 of 1907 I, IOR/R/20/A/2416, Public and Judicial Departmental Papers: Annual Files, IOR, BL.
58. The PCA Act of 1890 allowed pinjrapoles to sell infirm animals whose owners abandoned them. Prevention of Cruelty to Animals, 823; (Bombay Amendment) Act 1933, February 20, 1933, to April 27, 1933, IOR/L/PJ/7/497, Public and Judicial Departmental Papers: Annual Files, IOR, BL.
59. Sarkar, *Bengal, 1924–1934*, 6.

60. This annual list was also known as the "Report on the Destruction of Wild Animals and Venomous Snakes."
61. See Julie E. Hughes, "From Tiger Domains to Sandgrouse Realms: Sovereignty, Status, and Shooting Grounds in Princely India, 1880s–1930s" (PhD diss., University of Texas at Austin, 2010); and Julie E. Hughes, *Animal Kingdoms: Hunting, the Environment, and Power in the Indian Princely States* (Cambridge, MA: Harvard University Press, 2013).
62. "Mission in Ceylon: Mr. Meigs's Journal Kept at Batticotta," *Missionary Herald*, October 1821, 316–317.
63. *Big Game Hunting in India and the Game Animals of India* (New Delhi: Government of India, 1948), 163, India, Big Game Hunting, 1948, IOR/V/27/560/142, IOR, BL.
64. Saunders, *Beautiful Joe*, 149.
65. "Royal Sport: Its Pains and Perils," *ODA*, June 1909, 4.
66. "Out of Thine Own Mouth," *ODA*, September 1910, 54.
67. Labhshankar Laxmidas, "The Sufferings of Animals in India, An Address to the Humanitarian League" (London: Humanitarian League, 1907), 10, Shelfmarks: Tr. 766(i), IOR, BL.
68. According to Section 11: "Nothing in this Act shall render it an offence to kill any animal in a manner required by the religion or religious rites and usages of any race, sect, tribe or class." Prevention of Cruelty to Animals Act, Act No. XI of 1890.
69. J. Lockwood Kipling, *Beast and Man in India: A Popular Sketch of Indian Animals in Their Relations with the People* (London: Macmillan, 1891), 8.
70. Critics of religious slaughter frequently targeted the festival of Moharam [Muharram], for example, in which indigent Muslims and Hindus temporarily smashed the human/animal divide by transforming themselves into tigers, prowling the streets for alms, biting sheep and goats in the throat, and then shaking the animals to death. See Mr. Allen, "Mahrattas: Journal of Mr. Allen," *Missionary Herald*, August 1841, 342–344.
71. Laxmidas, "The Sufferings of Animals in India."
72. Orders, Demi-official, from Sir Herbert Risley, Secretary to the Government of India, Home Department, to the Honorable Mr. H. Bradley, Chief Secretary to the Government of Madras (No. 57, February 19, 1907), Religious Sacrifices in India, Cruelty to Animals Madras Government Bulletin [Including Village Deities of Southern India], November 25, 1907, to February 6, 1908, IOR/L/PJ/6/838, File 4100, Public and Judicial Departmental Papers: Annual Files, IOR, BL.
73. See, for example, R. Ramachandra Rao, District Magistrate of Kurnool (9), to Chief Secretary to the Government of Madras, April 22, 1907, Religious Sacrifices in India, Cruelty to Animals Madras Government Bulletin [Including Village Deities of Southern India], November 25, 1907 to February 6, 1908, IOR/L/PJ/6/838, File 4100, Public and Judicial Departmental Papers: Annual Files, IOR, BL.

74. See Peter van der Veer, *Imperial Encounters: Religion and Modernity in India and Britain* (Princeton, NJ: Princeton University Press, 2001); see also Wendy Doniger, *The Hindus: An Alternative History* (New York: Viking Press, 2009).
75. See "Lecture by Swanei [sic] Vivekananda," May 3, 1894; "Vivekananda Will Lecture Monday," February 24, 1895, both from *NYT*.
76. "Editorial Paragraphs," July 1894, 273; "The Hindu Monk Vivekananda," May 1897, 172, both from *Missionary Herald*.
77. Adam D. Shprintzen, *The Vegetarian Crusade: The Rise of an American Reform Movement, 1817–1921* (Chapel Hill: University of North Carolina Press, 2013), 156.
78. "Had No Meats at the Dinner," *NYT*, May 2, 1894.
79. Thomas A. Tweed, *The American Encounter with Buddhism, 1844–1912: Victorian Culture and the Limits of Dissent* (Chapel Hill: University of North Carolina Press, 1992), 81; Shprintzen, *The Vegetarian Crusade*, chap. 1.
80. Shprintzen, *The Vegetarian Crusade*, 21–22; Robert H. Abzug, *Cosmos Crumbling: American Reform and the Religious Imagination* (New York: Oxford University Press, 1994), 166.
81. Abzug, *Cosmos Crumbling*, chap. 4; Shprintzen, *The Vegetarian Crusade*, 33.
82. Harvey Green, *Fit for America: Health, Fitness, Sport and American Society* (Baltimore: Johns Hopkins University Press, 1986), 48, 135; Shprintzen, *The Vegetarian Crusade*, chap. 5.
83. Labhshankar Laxmidas, "As Others See Us," *Vegetarian Magazine*, June 15, 1900, 11.
84. Maureen Ogle, *In Meat We Trust: An Unexpected History of Carnivore America* (Boston: Houghton Mifflin Harcourt, 2013), 56–62; Upton Sinclair, *The Jungle* (1906; repr., New York: Bantam Dell, 2003).
85. Shprintzen, *The Vegetarian Crusade*, 154–182.
86. Laxmidas, "As Others See Us."
87. Ogle, *In Meat We Trust*, 11.
88. Ogle, *In Meat We Trust*, 20–25.
89. "Cruelty to Animals—First Case of Punishment under the New Law," *NYT*, April 13, 1866.
90. Unti, "'The Quality of Mercy,'" 203.
91. "Western Dressed Beef," *NYT*, March 24, 1884.
92. Emily Stewart Leavitt, et al., *Animals and Their Legal Rights: A Survey of American Laws from 1641 to 1970* (Washington, DC: Animal Welfare Institute, 1970), 30–32.
93. "A Word from India," September 1927, 132; "Funeral for Nationally Known Humane Worker Held Tuesday, in "Memorial Number, Commemorative of Mary F. Lovell," July 1932, 108; "The Folly and Cruelty of Meat Eating," February 1927, 20; all from *Starry Cross*.
94. Sinclair, *The Jungle*, 367.
95. W. Joseph Grand, *The Illustrated History of the Union Stockyards, Chicago, Ill.: With Humorous Stories* (1896; repr., Chicago: Thos. Knapp, 1901), 130.

96. "A Country Rich in Cattle," *ODA*, September 1914, 50.
97. George Hendrick, *Henry Salt, Humanitarian Reformer and Man of Letters* (Champaign: University of Illinois Press, 1977), 7, 143, 166; Henry S. Salt, *Animals' Rights Considered in Relation to Social Progress* (New York: Macmillan, 1892), 96, 108–109, 113; Salt, *The Logic of Vegetarianism: Essays and Dialogues* (London: George Bell and Sons, 1906), 14.
98. Henry S. Salt, *Life of Henry David Thoreau* (London: Walter Scott, 1896), 95.
99. Salt, *Life of Thoreau*, 100–101.
100. Salt, *Life of Thoreau*, 166–167.
101. Salt, *The Logic of Vegetarianism*, 30.
102. Tweed, *The American Encounter with Buddhism, 1844–1912*, 55–56.
103. Van der Veer, *Imperial Encounters*, 55–57; Carol Hanbery MacKay, "Confounding or Amazing? The Multiple Deconversions of Annie Besant," *Quest: Journal of the Theosophical Society in America* 90, vol. 2 (March–April 2002): 50–56; Thomas D. Clark, "Annie Besant's Lecture Tour of San Diego," *Journal of San Diego History* 23, no. 2 (Spring 1977), http://www.sandiegohistory.org/journal/77spring/besant.htm.
104. Anna Kingsford, *The Best Food for Man* (Bombay: International Book House), 5, 11, 16–17.
105. On Tingley, see Rebecca D'Orsogna, "Yoga in America: History, Community Formation, and Consumerism" (PhD diss., University of Texas at Austin, 2013).
106. "To Spread Theosophy," *Greenville* [OH] *Journal*, October 3, 1907, Chronicling America: Historic American Newspapers, http://chroniclingamerica.loc.gov/lccn/sn83035565/1907-10-03/ed-1/seq-6/.
107. "Theosophists Pray against Vivisection," *ODA*, April 1904, 140.
108. Marshall Lewis, letter to the editor, "Great Kindness of the Jains," *ODA*, June 1909, 25.
109. "Sermon of the Rev. Thomas Van Ness," *ODA*, April 1909, 170.
110. Sandria B. Freitag, *Collective Action and Community: Public Arenas and the Emergence of Communalism in North India* (Berkeley: University of California Press, 1989), 150.
111. Freitag, *Collective Action and Community*, 152–153.
112. Chief Secretary to Government, North-Western Provinces and Oudh to the Secretary to the Government of India, Home Department, January 23, 1894, Allahabad, Case of Hanuman Tewari and others and the punishment of Hindu officials for having subscribed or supported cow protection societies, IOR/L/PJ/6/370, File 557, Public and Judicial Departmental Papers: Annual Files, IOR, BL.
113. Freitag, *Collective Action and Community*, 150–153.
114. J. D. La Touche, Chief Secretary to Government North-Western Provinces and Oudh, undated notes, in Case of Hanuman Tewari and others and the punishment of Hindu officials for having subscribed or supported cow protection societies, IOR/L/PJ/6/370, File 557, Public and Judicial Departmental Papers: Annual Files, IOR, BL.

115. Freitag, *Collective Action and Community*, 169–170.
116. "When Mussulman and Hindu Fight," *NYT*, September 17, 1893; "England, India, and the Stick," *NYT*, October 1, 1893.
117. M. K. Gandhi, "Cow Protection," *Young India*, October 6, 1921, in *How to Serve the Cow*, ed. Bharatan Kumarappa (Ahmedabad: Navajivan, 1954), 3–4.
118. M. K. Gandhi, "Mother Cow," *Harijan*, September 15, 1940, in *How to Serve the Cow*, 4.
119. M. K. Gandhi, "Cow Protection," *Young India*, November 11, 1926, in *How to Serve the Cow*, 5.
120. Although Gandhi often used the term "cow protection," he preferred "cow service." The cow protection movement ratcheted communal tensions when it targeted Islamic sacrifice, whereas a commitment to "service" conveyed a more neutral emphasis on overall bovine welfare and scientific breeding programs. See M. K. Gandhi, "Service, Not Protection," *Young India*, August 2, 1928, 258–259.
121. M. K. Gandhi, "Befriend Musalmans," *Young India*, May 29, 1924; "Cow Slaughter," *Harijan*, September 15, 1946, in *How to Serve the Cow*, 15, 25.
122. M. K. Gandhi, "Cow Protection," *Young India*, May 18, 1921, in *How to Serve the Cow*, 13.
123. Gandhi, "Cow Protection."
124. Gandhi also urged the state to purchase pastureland; run model farms to promote agricultural education and new cattle breeds; buy all available cattle in the open market; and run all tanneries. Gandhi posited that these ventures would simultaneously protect the cow and provide the state with critical revenue. M. K. Gandhi, "States and Cow Slaughter," *Young India*, July 7, 1927, in *How to Protect the Cow*, 20–21.
125. Gandhi, "States and Cow Slaughter," 21.
126. See Katherine Mayo, *Justice for All: The Story of the Pennsylvania State Police* (Boston: Houghton Mifflin, 1920); and *The Isles of Fear: The Truth about the Philippines* (New York: Harcourt, Brace, 1924).
127. Katherine Mayo, *Mother India* (1927; repr., New Delhi: Anmol, 1986), 20; Mrinalini Sinha, "Refashioning Mother India: Feminism and Nationalism in Late-Colonial India," *Feminist Studies* 26, no. 3 (Autumn 2000): 623–644.
128. See Mrinalini Sinha, *Specters of Mother India: The Global Restructuring of an Empire* (Durham, NC: Duke University Press, 2006); Nupur Chaudhuri and Margaret Strobel, ed., *Western Women and Imperialism: Complicity and Resistance* (Bloomington: Indiana University Press, 1992); Tony Ballantyne and Antoinette Burton, ed., *Bodies in Contact: Rethinking Colonial Encounters in World History* (Durham, NC: Duke University Press, 2005).
129. Mayo, *Mother India*, 202.
130. Mayo, *Mother India*, 239.
131. Mayo, *Mother India*, 225.
132. Mayo, *Mother India*, 221, 227, 234–235.

133. Mayo, *Mother India*, 235.
134. Mayo, *Mother India*, 242.
135. Mayo, *Mother India*, 235.
136. M. K. Gandhi, "Drain Inspector's Report," *Young India*, September 15, 1927, 310.
137. Gandhi, "Drain Inspector's Report," 308.
138. Gandhi, "Drain Inspector's Report," 310.
139. Lala Lajpat Rai, *Unhappy India* (Calcutta: Banna, 1928), 298; 291–292.
140. Tagore observed that Hindu priests only rarely used dung in expiatory rituals and never as food. Tagore, quoted in Rai, *Unhappy India*, 489.
141. Tagore, quoted in Rai, *Unhappy India*, 488.
142. C. F. Andrews, "The Facts about India, a Reply to Miss Mayo," pt. 9, *Young India*, July 12, 1928, 234.
143. Andrews, "The Facts about India, a Reply to Miss Mayo," 235. On racism, see C. F. Andrews, "The Facts about India, a Reply to Miss Mayo," pt. 8, *Young India*, July 5, 1928, 227.
144. Ministry of Food and Agriculture, *Report of the Committee for the Prevention of Cruelty to Animals*, 1.

CHAPTER 6

1. See Bullfighting Correspondence, June 1936, Texas Centennial Series 1935–1937, Records of James V. Allred, Texas Office of the Governor (1935–1939), Archives and Information Services Division, Texas State Library and Archives Commission (hereafter cited as TSLAC), Austin, Texas.
2. Mrs. Ella M. Megginson to Governor James V. Allred, June 20, 1936, Bullfighting Correspondence, June 1936, Texas Centennial Series 1935–1937, Records of James V. Allred, Texas Office of the Governor (1935–1939), TSLAC.
3. Christine Stevens, "Fighting and Baiting," in *Animals and Their Legal Rights*, ed. Emily Stewart Leavitt et al. (Washington, DC: Animal Welfare Institute, 1970), 110–127; Cities and Towns, chap. 10, tit. 17, art. 398, *The Revised Statutes of Texas* (Galveston: A. H. Belo, 1879), 69.
4. "From the Texas Centennial Commission," Dallas, October 8, 1935, Press Releases on Centennial Topics, Centennial of Texas Records, 1935–1939, Folder—Releases on Centennial, October 1936, Box 2C439, Dolph Briscoe Center for American History (hereafter cited as CAH), University of Texas at Austin. [Please note that selected documents from 1935 are located in files dated 1936.]
5. See Robert W. Rydell, *All the World's a Fair: Visions of Empire at American International Expositions, 1876–1916* (Chicago: University of Chicago Press, 1984); and Robert W. Rydell, *World of Fairs: The Century-of-Progress Expositions* (Chicago: University of Chicago Press, 1993).
6. "What Ben Beverly Saw at the Great Exposition, by a Chicago Lawyer" (Chicago: Moses Warren, 1877), 244, 247; "A Curious Show," *St. Louis*

Globe-Democrat, August 1, 1876; "Centennial Display of the Society for the Prevention of Cruelty to Animals," *Frank Leslie's Illustrated Newspaper*, January 13, 1877, 314; "The Work of Mr. Bergh's Society," *NYT*, April 13, 1876.

7. Burton Benedict, *The Anthropology of World's Fairs: San Francisco's Panama Pacific International Exposition of 1915* (London: Scolar Press, 1983), 50; Mim Eichler Rivas, *Beautiful Jim Key: The Lost History of a Horse and a Man Who Changed the World* (New York: William Morrow, 2005).
8. George Angell, frontispiece, Albert R. Rogers, *The Story of Beautiful Jim Key: The Most Wonderful Horse in All the World* (New York: A. R. Rogers, 1905).
9. Diane L. Beers, *For the Prevention of Cruelty: The History and Legacy of Animal Rights Activism in the United States* (Athens: Ohio University Press, 2006), 132; "Foreign Intelligence—America," *The Animal's Defender and Zoophilist* [London], February 1, 1904, 210.
10. National Commission from the United States of Mexico to the Pan-American Exposition, "Official Catalogue of the Mexican Exhibits at the Pan-American Exposition" (Buffalo: White-Evans-Penfold, 1901), 164.
11. Walter G. Cooper, "Cotton States and International Exposition and South, Illustrated" (Atlanta: Illustrator, 1896), 90.
12. See Press Releases on Centennial Topics, Centennial of Texas Records, 1935–1939, Box 2C438 and Box 2C439, CAH.
13. "Introduction," in *Rereading the Black Legend: The Discourses of Religious and Racial Difference in the Renaissance Empires*, ed. Margaret R. Greer, Walter D. Mignolo, and Maureen Quilligan (Chicago: University of Chicago Press, 2008), 14.
14. "Introduction," *Rereading the Black Legend*, 5–6.
15. "Introduction," *Rereading the Black Legend*, 1–2.
16. "Table 359. U.S.-Canada and U.S.-Mexico Border Lengths," US Census Bureau, Statistical Abstract of the United States: 2011, http://www2.census.gov/library/publications/2010/compendia/statab/130ed/tables/11s0359.pdf.
17. See John McKiernan-González, *Fevered Measures: Public Health and Race at the Texas-Mexico Border, 1848–1942* (Durham, NC: Duke University Press, 2012).
18. Richard Wright, *Pagan Spain* (New York: Harper and Bros., 1957), 1–2.
19. "Introduction," 8–9; and Barbara Fuchs, "The Spanish Race," 88–98, both in *Rereading the Black Legend*.
20. Alexander Jardine, *Letters from Barbary, France, Spain, Portugal, &c. By an English Officer. In Two Volumes*, vol. 2 (Dublin, 1789), 89, Gale Eighteenth Century Collections Online.
21. "Bull-fighting in Spain," *Ballou's Dollar Monthly Magazine*, December 1855, 596, ProQuest: American Periodicals.
22. Ernest Hemingway, *Death in the Afternoon* (New York: Charles Scribner's Sons, 1932), 21.
23. Wright, *Pagan Spain*, 109, and 88–114.

24. Carrie B. Douglass, *Bulls, Bullfighting, and Spanish Identities* (Tucson: University of Arizona Press, 1997), 33–36.
25. See Timothy Mitchell, *Blood Sport: A Social History of Spanish Bullfighting* (Philadelphia: University of Pennsylvania Press, 1991).
26. Major W. W. Hastings, "Sport in Spain," *Forest and Stream: A Journal of Outdoor Life, Travel, Nature Study, Shooting, Fishing, Yachting*, May 7, 1898, 363, ProQuest: American Periodicals.
27. Thomas Ewing Moore, *In the Heart of Spain* (New York: Universal Knowledge Foundation, 1927), 104.
28. Hemingway, *Death in the Afternoon*, 20.
29. George E. Vincent, "Memories of Spain," *The Chautauquan: A Weekly Newsmagazine*, August 1892, 529, ProQuest: American Periodicals.
30. John Hay, *Castilian Days* (1871; repr. Boston: Houghton Mifflin, 1913), 100–101.
31. Moore, *In the Heart of Spain*, 99–100.
32. Moore, *In the Heart of Spain*, 124–125.
33. "Cardinal Merry del Val Calls Prizefights 'Almost as Objectionable' as Bullfights," *NYT*, December 4, 1927.
34. "Letters and the Arts: Bullfighting Brutalized," *The Living Age*, September 1930, 93, ProQuest: American Periodicals; Hemingway, *Death in the Afternoon*, 7–8; Mitchell, *Blood Sport*, 90.
35. Ernest Hemingway described the picador horses as disembodied birdlike creatures, whose death in the ring was surreal, even comic, reminding him of the Fratellinis, a French family clown troupe that burlesqued such deadly scenes with fake horses and viscera made of sausages and bandages. Hemingway, *Death in the Afternoon*, 6.
36. Christa Weil, "We Eat Horses, Don't We?" *NYT*, March 5, 2007, http://www.nytimes.com/2007/03/05/opinion/05weil.html?_r=0.
37. See "To Run without Horses," *NYT*, November 10, 1895; "The Passing of the Horse," *NYT*, February 13, 1896.
38. See Father John Walsh, "A Priest at a Bullfight: The Brutal Spectacle Disgusts an American Visitor," *NYT*, June 16, 1896; Stewart Beach, ed., "What the World Is Doing," *Independent*, March 5, 1927, 274, ProQuest: American Periodicals; "Bullfighting Brutalized," *The Living Age*, 93.
39. Cesare Lombroso, "Crime in Spain and Its History," *Independent*, December 9, 1909, 1292–1293, ProQuest: American Periodicals.
40. Hay, *Castilian Days*, 76–77; "Philip II," Catholic Encyclopedia, New Advent, http://www.newadvent.org/cathen/12002a.htm.
41. Kadra Maysi, *ODA*, January, 1933, 11.
42. Hay, *Castilian Days*, 105–106.
43. "Twilight in the Plaza de Toros," repr. from the *Christian Science Monitor* in *ODA*, February 1933, 20.
44. Frank L. Kluckhohn, "Twilight of the Bullfight in Spain," *NYT*, February 26, 1933.

45. Hemingway, *Death in the Afternoon*, 22.
46. Mitchell, *Blood Sport*, 57; Carrie B. Douglass, *Bulls, Bullfighting, and Spanish Identities*, 102–104; "Spain's Brutal Bullfights," *The* [Shreveport, LA] *Progress*. September 17, 1898, Chronicling America: Historic American Newspapers, http://chroniclingamerica.loc.gov/lccn/sn88064460/1898-09-17/ed-1/seq-2/.
47. Mitchell, *Blood Sport*, 68.
48. Mitchell, *Blood Sport*, 57–87.
49. Mitchell, *Blood Sport*, 147.
50. Katharine Lee Bates, "The Carnival in Spain: In Spite of the Result of the War, the People Romped as Usual," *NYT*, March 19, 1899.
51. "Cuba as Proctor Saw It," *NYT*, March 18, 1898.
52. "Cuba as Proctor Saw It."
53. "The Spirit of Progress," *Cleveland Gazette*, January 7, 1899, America's Historical Newspapers: NewsBank.
54. "Festivities by Cubans," *NYT*, May 19, 1902; "A Foul Aspersion," *Outlook (1893–1924)*, June 10, 1899, 331, ProQuest: American Periodicals.
55. José Martí, quoted in Louis Pérez, *On Becoming Cuban: Identity, Nationality, and Culture* (Chapel Hill: University of North Carolina Press, 1999), 78.
56. Pérez, *On Becoming Cuban*, 51–60, 75–82.
57. See Nan Boyd, *Wide Open Town: A History of Queer San Francisco* (Berkeley: University of California Press, 2005).
58. John Richard Betts, *American Sporting Heritage* (Reading, MA: Addison-Wesley, 1974), 25; Matthew McCurrie, "How Animals on the Pacific Coast Are Cared for by the San Francisco SPCA," *ODA*, June 1909, 7.
59. See California Statutes of 1900: §§597–599c, Historical: Related Statutes, Animal Legal and Historical Center, http://www.animallaw.info/historical/statutes/table_hist_stat.htm.
60. "On Bull-Fighting," *Los Angeles Times* (hereafter cited as *LAT*), December 17, 1891, in ProQuest Historical Newspapers: *Los Angeles Times* (1881–1990).
61. M. D. Lummis, "Letters to the Times: The Fight of Los Toros," *LAT*, December 18, 1891, ProQuest Historical Newspapers: *Los Angeles Times* (1881–1990).
62. F. Morse Hubbard, *II. Prevention of Cruelty to Animals in the States of Illinois, Colorado and California*, 309–310, in *Proceedings of the Academy of Political Science*, ed. Henry Raymond Mussey and William L. Ransom, vol. 6 (New York: Academy of Political Science, 1916).
63. "Bergh on Bullfights," *NYT*, July 20, 1884.
64. "Bergh on Bullfights."
65. "Aftermath of the Bullfights: The Promoter of the Sport Arrested with the Mexicans," *LAT*, August 28, 1895, ProQuest Historical Newspapers: *Los Angeles Times* (1881–1990).
66. "Humane Society: A Disposition to Censure the Colorado Secretary," *LAT*, September 26, 1895, ProQuest Historical Newspapers: *Los Angeles Times* (1881–1990).

67. As film began to displace the popularity of bullfighting in Spain, bullfighters introduced the charlotada as a way to mock cinema's biggest star. Miguel-Anxo Murado, "Catalonia Has Sounded the Death Knell for Bullfighting," *Guardian*, July 29, 2010, http://www.theguardian.com/commentisfree/2010/jul/29/catalonia-bullfighting-death-knell.
68. "Law Seizes Bull Fight Promoters," *LAT*, August 19, 1924, ProQuest Historical Newspapers: *Los Angeles Times* (1881–1990).
69. "Bullfight Staged in Newark; 6 Held," August 18, 1924; "More 'Bull Fights' and More Arrests," August 19, 1924, both from *NYT*.
70. See Stevens, "Fighting and Baiting," in Leavitt et al., *Animals and Their Legal Rights*, 110–112.
71. "Legion Drops Bullfight," *NYT*, February 18, 1922.
72. "Mrs. Fiske Asks Yale Protest on Bull Fight; Appeals to 'Chivalry' to Stop Newark 'Invasion,'" *NYT*, November 20, 1930.
73. "Dr. Hibben Protests Newark Bullfight," November 21, 1930; "Newark Official Bans Franklin Bull Fight," November 22, 1930, both from *NYT*.
74. Captain C. H. Wilson, U. S. V., "Through Mexico in a Private Car," *Frank Leslie's Popular Monthly*, April 1899, 12, ProQuest: American Periodicals.
75. Dallas E. Wood, "Vivid Picture of a Bullfight in Mexico," *NHR*, April 1937, 7.
76. "Among the Aztecs," *The Old Guard*, October 1870, 741, ProQuest: American Periodicals; "Free Lecture: Mexico and the Customs of the People," *Washington D.C. Bee*, November 19, 1904, NewsBank: America's Historical Newspapers.
77. Wood, "Vivid Picture of a Bullfight in Mexico."
78. "Mexican Tradition Broken: First Recorded Plea for Mercy to Bull-Ring Horse Published by Leading Journal of Mexico," *LAT*, December 13, 1925, ProQuest Historical Newspapers: *Los Angeles Times* (1881–1990).
79. Gwendolen Overton, "The Bull-Fight of Fact," *LAT*, April 16, 1899, ProQuest Historical Newspapers: *Los Angeles Times* (1881–1990).
80. "Fight between a Bull and a Lion," *ODA*, December 1903, 92.
81. "State Humane Body Convenes," *LAT*, February 27, 1924, ProQuest Historical Newspapers: *Los Angeles Times* (1881–1990).
82. "The Danger from Mexico," June 1914, 8; see also, "Untitled," October 1915, 65, all from *ODA*.
83. Felix J. Koch, "Dumb Friends in Turbulent Mexico," *ODA*, July 1914, 19–20.
84. Edward Eccleston, "The Mexican Bull-fight," *ODA*, June 1915, 2.
85. Eccleston, "The Mexican Bull-fight."
86. The Magonistas, followers of Ricardo and Enrique Flores Magón, leaders of the progressive revolutionary Partido Liberal Mexicano movement, were highly critical of the bullfight and the Diaz regime. David Dorado Romo, *Ringside Seat to a Revolution: An Underground Cultural History of El Paso and Juárez: 1893–1923* (El Paso: Cinco Puntos Press, 2005), 184. Citation courtesy of Cary Cordova.
87. "'Black Beauty' in Spanish: Missionaries of Kindness to Animals at Work," *LAT*, January 3, 1904, ProQuest Historical Newspapers: *Los Angeles Times* (1881–1990).

88. Romo, *Ringside Seat to a Revolution*, 188–189.
89. Romo, *Ringside Seat to a Revolution*, 189.
90. "The Rough Rider Regiment's Horses," *ODA*, May 1905, 163.
91. "Bull-fight Opposed in Manila," *ODA*, July 1926, 20.
92. "Untitled," *ODA*, April 1921, 163.
93. "A Roosevelt and the Spanish Bull-fight," *ODA*, October 1933, 147.
94. "Caffery Issues a Denial," *NYT*, September 3, 1934.
95. "No. 33, An Act to Amend Section 5 of an Act Entitled 'An Act to Prevent Cruelty to Animals,'" First Special Session of the Thirteenth Legislature, Puerto Rico, May 4, 1933; Record Group 350, General Classified Files, Entry 5B (1914–1945), Cockfighting (Puerto Rico), Box 1074, File Marker 26484, 350:150:57:11:2, National Archives and Records Administration, College Park, MD.
96. "Caffery Issues a Denial"; "Caffrey Denies He Favored Cuba Bull Ring Return," *Washington Post*, September 3, 1934, ProQuest Historical Newspapers: *Washington Post* (1877–1997); "Cuba and Bull-fighting," *ODA*, October 1934, 153.
97. Rosalie Schwartz, *Pleasure Island: Tourism and Temptation in Cuba* (Lincoln: University of Nebraska Press, 1997), 98.
98. Sidney Franklin, *Bullfighter from Brooklyn: The Amazing Autobiography of Sidney Franklin* (New York: Prentice-Hall, 1952), 213–215.
99. "Against Bullfights," NHR, May 1937, 6.
100. "Against Bullfights," 6; Michael Fakhri, "The 1937 International Sugar Agreement: Neo-Colonial Cuba and Economic Aspects of the League of Nations," *Leiden Journal of International Law* 24, no. 4 (2011): 899–922; 917, http://law.uoregon.edu/assets/facultydocs/mfakhri/cubaarticle.pdf.
101. "Bullfight Propaganda for Tourist Trade," *NHR*, July 1937, 9.
102. Schwartz, *Pleasure Island*, 98; Pérez, *On Becoming Cuban*, 75–82.
103. Spanish toreros apparently sought the ban because they were losing audiences to the showy, crowd-pleasing Mexican bullfighters on tour. "Spanish Bullfighters Are Forced into Ring with Mexican Rivals," *Dallas Morning News* (hereafter cited as *DMN*), May 26, 1936, NewsBank: *Dallas Morning News* Archive (1885–1984).
104. "Record Crowd Is to See American in Bullfight Sunday," May 17, 1936; Hal Eustace, "The Sports Spade," May 19, 1936, both from *Heraldo de Brownsville*, NewsBank: America's Historical Newspapers (Hispanic Newspapers); "Bull Ring Bars Franklin," *NYT*, May 19, 1936.
105. "Bullfight Is Opposed by Church Group," *Heraldo de Brownsville*, May 13, 1936, NewsBank: America's Historical Newspapers (Hispanic Newspapers).
106. "Bullfight Is Opposed by Church Group."
107. "Ministers Protest Bullfight Set at Brownsville Fete," *DMN*, May 10, 1936, NewsBank: *Dallas Morning News* Archive (1885–1984).
108. "Texas Centennial Exposition, Hearings before the Committee on Foreign Affairs," House of Representatives, May 23, 1935, 12, http://hdl.handle.net/2027/mdp.39015067196587.

109. "From the Texas Centennial Commission," March 1935, Press Releases on Centennial Topics, January–March 1936, Centennial of Texas Records, 1935–1939, Box 2C438, Folder—Releases on Centennial March 1936, CAH.
110. "From the Texas Centennial Commission," April 4, 1936, Press Releases on Centennial Topics, January–March 1936, Centennial of Texas Records, 1935–1939, Folder—Releases on Centennial April 1936; "Texas Centennial Exposition—Dallas," May 1936, and "Texas Centennial Exposition—Dallas," September 1936, all from Box 2C439, Press releases on Centennial Topics, January–March 1936, CAH.
111. Kevin Mooney, "Texas Centennial 1936: African-American Texans and the Third National Folk Festival," *Journal of Texas Music History* 1, no. 1 (2001), https://digital.library.txstate.edu/handle/10877/2654.
112. Rydell, *World of Fairs*, 176–179.
113. J. T. Tanner to Governor James V. Allred, June 20, 1936, Shreveport, Louisiana, Bullfighting Correspondence, June 1936, Texas Centennial Series 1935–1937, Records of James V. Allred, Texas Office of the Governor (1935–1939), TSLAC.
114. "Humane Forces Attack Plans for a Bullfight," *DMN*, May 22, 1936, NewsBank: *Dallas Morning News* Archive (1885–1984).
115. "Humane Forces Attack Plans for a Bullfight."
116. "Texas Centennial Exposition, Dallas," Press Releases on Centennial Topics, January–March 1936, Centennial of Texas Records, 1935–1939, Folder—Releases on Centennial May 1936, Box 2C439, CAH.
117. For anti-rodeo articles, see, for example, "In the Rodeo's Wake," *ODA*, September 1934, 141; "Rodeo Cruelties," *NHR*, December 1937, 8.
118. Oscar W. Hooper, "And Now the Bullfight," letter to the editor, *DMN*, May 28, 1936, NewsBank: *Dallas Morning News* Archive (1885–1984).
119. "Just Bull, That's All," *DMN*, June 18, 1936, NewsBank: *Dallas Morning News* Archive (1885–1984).
120. "Bullfight Plans Renewed under way to Satisfy Law," *DMN*, May 27, 1936, NewsBank: *Dallas Morning News* Archive (1885–1984).
121. "Bloodless French Bullfights Urged for Fair by American Matador, Veteran of Arena," *DMN*, May 31, 1936, NewsBank: *Dallas Morning News* Archive (1885–1984).
122. John Rosenfield Jr., "Death Takes a Holiday in the Afternoon; or a Visit from a Matador," August 12, 1936; "Plans Centennial Bullfight," August 14, 1936, both from *DMN*, NewsBank: *Dallas Morning News* Archive (1885–1984); "Centennial World of Sports," Press Releases on Centennial Topics, January–March 1936, Centennial of Texas Records, 1935–1939, Texas Centennial Exposition—Dallas, undated, Box No. 2C439, Folder—Releases on Centennial, August, 1936, CAH.
123. Rosenfield, "Death Takes a Holiday in the Afternoon."
124. "Protesting the Bull-fight," *ODA*, August 1936, 120; "Fair Nearing 800,000 Mark in Attendance," June 21, 1936; "Fair at Pittsburg to Open Thursday,"

October 29, 1936, both from *DMN*, NewsBank: *Dallas Morning News* Archive (1885–1984).
125. "'Texas Gone Sissy?' Asks Bullfight Fan of Old Texas Family," *DMN*, June 23, 1936, NewsBank: *Dallas Morning News* Archive (1885–1984).
126. "'Texas Gone Sissy?'"
127. On Maria Elena Zamora O'Shea, see John Morán González, *Border Renaissance: The Texas Centennial and the Emergence of Mexican American Literature* (Austin: University of Texas Press, 2009), chap. 2.
128. William M. Thornton, "More than 500 Bills Passed by Legislature at Late Session," *DMN*, May 23, 1937, NewsBank: *Dallas Morning News* Archive (1885–1984); "Bullfighting Ban Passed by Senate, *Heraldo de Brownsville*, May 16, 1937, NewsBank: America's Historical Newspapers (Hispanic Newspapers).
129. "Texas Law Bans Bullfighting," *NHR*, July 1937, 6.
130. "Fair's Officials Make Plans to Greet Notables," August 31, 1937; "Big Week End Is Scheduled at Exposition," September 5, 1937, both from *DMN*, NewsBank: *Dallas Morning News* Archive (1885–1984).
131. Henry Bergh (ASPCA) to the Managers of Barnum's Museum, December 11, 1866; Louis Agassiz to P. T. Barnum, included in P. T. Barnum's reply to Henry Bergh, February 28, 1867, The Lost Museum, http://chnmn.gmu.edu/lostmuseum/lm/192/.
132. "Barnum's Positive Orders," *ODA*, June 1873, 5.
133. "Pacifist Bull at Bloodless Bullfight Provides Matador Little Chance to Show Skill," *DMN*, September 6, 1937, NewsBank: *Dallas Morning News* Archive (1885–1984).
134. "Noted Matador to Be Greeted at Exposition," *DMN*, August 23, 1937, NewsBank: *Dallas Morning News* Archive (1885–1984); "Dallas Exposition Is Swinging into Its Autumn Stride," *Victoria* [Texas] *Advocate*, September 1, 1937, http://news.google.com/newspapers?nid=861&dat=19370901&id=uzZSAAAAIBAJ&sjid=RjYNAAAAIBAJ&pg=5011,3925771.
135. "Noted Matador to Be Greeted at Exposition."
136. "Good Neighbors Get Together," advertisement for A. Harris & Co., *DMN*, June 6, 1937, NewsBank: *Dallas Morning News* Archive (1885–1984).
137. Katy Vine, "Bloodless Sport," *Texas Monthly*, June 2014, http://www.texasmonthly.com/the-culture/bloodless-sport/.
138. "The Best-Selling Books," *NYT*, November 7, 1937.
139. "Ain't We Got Fun!" *NHR*, November 1938, 8.
140. "Ferdinand," *NYT*, November 20, 1937.
141. Philip Nel, "Ferdinand at 75," *Nine Kinds of Pie: Philip Nel's Blog*, http://www.philnel.com/2011/09/17/ferdinand/.
142. Ben A. Franklin, "Munro Leaf, Author, Dead at 71; Creator of Ferdinand the Bull," *NYT*, December 22, 1976.
143. Nel, "Ferdinand at 75."
144. "Ferdinand," *NYT*, November 20, 1937.

CONCLUSION

1. Because of American hostilities with Vichy France, operational funds from MSPCA benefactors could not reach Fez until 1943; nonetheless, Delon continued the Fondouk's bare-bones operations with local loans. "The Fondouk in Fez," *NHR*, December 1939, back inside cover; "Fez Fondouk," *ODA*, April 1940, 58, 64; "What's New in Morocco?" *NHR*, July 1943, 10–11.
2. "Animals in the China War Zone," May 1938, back inside cover; Charles Hoppe, "Animals in War," May 1939, 5–6; "Animals of Spanish Refugees," July 1939, 26; "The War in China," September 1939, 22; "Aid to Britain," December 1941, 26, all from *NHR*.
3. "Rastus, a Foochow Cat," *NHR*, September 1939, 26.
4. "Disaster Strikes: Look to the Red Star," American Humane Association, *Protecting Children & Animals*, 43–46, http://www.americanhumane.org/assets/pdfs/animals/pa-aes-redstar.pdf.
5. "Animal Red Star Relief," February 1942, 4–5; "The Red Star," August 1940, 14, both from *NHR*.
6. "Help for China," March 1938, 21; "Foreign War Animal Relief," July 1940, 14, both from *NHR*.
7. "Red Star in England," *NHR*, August 1941, 26.
8. "Red Star Workers," *NHR*, December 1940, 14.
9. "Animals in War," 6.
10. "Selling Horses into Slavery," *NHR*, May 1938, 9.
11. "The American Humane Education Society," *ODA*, March 1941, 55.
12. Wyoming, for one, had a state humane education law but no active humane societies to create and implement new curricula. Dean Wilson Kuykendall, "The History of Humane Education" (master's thesis, University of Texas at Austin, 1935), 114, 146.
13. Bernard Oreste Unti, "'The Quality of Mercy': Organized Animal Protection in the United States, 1866–1930" (PhD diss., American University, 2002), 575, 610; Sally Gregory Kohlstedt, *Teaching Children Science: Hands-on Nature Study in North America, 1890–1930* (Chicago: University of Chicago Press, 2010); Rebecca Onion, "The Science of Childhood: Modernity, Discovery, and the National Investment in Scientific Learning, 1890–1960" (PhD diss., University of Texas at Austin, 2012).
14. Grayson Murphy to H. P. Davidson, quoted in Julia F. Irwin, *Making the World Safe: The American Red Cross and a Nation's Humanitarian Awakening* (New York: Oxford University Press, 2013), 94.
15. See "A Strange Affair," *NYT*, February 6, 1875.
16. See Brett Mizelle, "Horses and Cat Acts in the Early American Circus," in *The American Circus*, ed. Susan Weber, Kenneth L. Ames, and Matthew Wittmann (New York and New Haven: Bard Graduate Center and Yale University Press, 2012), 251–275; Susan Nance, *Entertaining Elephants: Animal Agency and the Business of the American Circus* (Baltimore: Johns Hopkins University Press, 2013).
17. "The Jack London Club's Rapid Growth," *ODA*, May 1919, 180.

18. The Performing Animals (Regulation) Act of 1925 stipulated that all persons training and/or exhibiting animals had to register in their home district under the terms of this act. Moreover, all said persons had to abide by specific animal welfare standards or be subject to prosecution. For a complete overview, see Performing Animals (Regulation) Act 1925, 1925 chap. 38 15 and 16 Geo 5 (United Kingdom), in Official Home of UK Legislation, 1267–Present, http://www.legislation.gov.uk/ukpga/Geo5/15-16/38.
19. "Circus Beasts Roar for Radio Audience," *NYT*, April 5, 1925.
20. See LaVahn G. Hoh and William H. Rough, *Step Right Up! The Adventure of Circus in America* (Blue Ash, OH: Betterway Books, 1990).
21. Urban laboring animals, of course, did not completely disappear. To this day, several cities maintain a mounted police force. Carriage horses remain in Central Park in New York City and in Austin, Texas, among other places, while some fresh produce vendors, most notably Baltimore's Arabbers, travel by horse-cart, a tradition dating back to Reconstruction. African American men comprise the majority of the Arabbers, many of whom have clashed with local authorities over animal welfare and safety regulations. Jessica Anderson, "City Officials Remove 14 Horses from Arabber Stable," *Baltimore Sun*, January 16, 2015, http://www.baltimoresun.com/news/maryland/baltimore-city/bs-md-ci-arabbers-20150116-story.html.
22. "Three Killed per Mile," *NHR*, May 1938, 14.
23. "Verdict of the Colleges," March 1939, 22; Irvin John Scully, "Cruelty to Animals in Filming 'Jesse James,'" February 1939, 3–6, both from *NHR*.
24. "In the Name of Humanity," *ODA*, August 1933, 115; "Untitled," *ODA*, September 1933, 131.
25. See Boria Sax, *Animals in the Third Reich: Pets, Scapegoats, and the Holocaust* (New York: Continuum, 2002); Kathleen Kete, "Animals and Ideology: The Politics of Animal Protection in Europe," in *Representing Animals*, ed. Nigel Rothfels (Bloomington: Indiana University Press, 2002).
26. "To Be a Jew in Germany," *ODA*, November 1940, 170.
27. See, for example, "Rabbi Lauds Society," March 1938, 16; " Making the Most of Kindness Week," April 1938, 3–4, back cover; "When the Devil Came to Church," June 1938; "St. Francis of Assisi," October 1938, 18; Cover, November 1939; "Christmas, Mercy for Wild Creatures," December 1939, 18–19, all from *NHR*.
28. See "The Great Band of Mercy," August 1940, 120; "Humane Education in India: An Extraordinary Band of Mercy," November 1940, 170, both from *ODA*.
29. See Susan J. Pearson, *The Rights of the Defenseless: Protecting Animals and Children in Gilded Age America* (Chicago: University of Chicago Press, 2011).
30. "Drink and Cruelty," *NHR*, September 1938, 14.
31. Maina Chawla Singh, *Gender Religion and "Heathen Lands": American Missionary Women in South Asia (1860s–1940s)* (New York: Garland, 2000), 330; Dana L. Robert, *Christian Mission: How Christianity Became a World Religion*

(West Sussex, UK: Wiley-Blackwell, 2009), 68; Sarah E. Ruble, *The Gospel of Freedom and Power: Protestant Missionaries in American Culture after World War II* (Chapel Hill: University of North Carolina Press, 2012): 27–33.

32. See Lawrence W. Levine, *Defender of the Faith: William Jennings Bryan, the Last Decade, 1915–1925* (New York: Oxford University Press, 1965); and George M. Marsden, *Fundamentalism and American Culture*, 2nd ed. (1980; repr., New York: Oxford University Press, 2006).

33. In 1953, so-called Mainliners represented more than 50 percent of the American career missionary force; in 1985, they constituted only 11.5 percent of the total field, a drop that reflected shrinking mainline church membership and the growth of conservative evangelical churches. Ruble, *The Gospel of Freedom and Power*, 20, 49.

34. "Still the Ku Klux Klan," March 1940, 40; "The Land of Lynchers," March 1941, 50; "And This Happened in Detroit," October 1941, 190, all from *ODA*.

35. "Untitled," *ODA*, September 1942, 163.

36. "Is This Democracy?" *ODA*, July 1943, 130.

37. "Appeal for Syria," *ODA*, September 1946, 174.

38. The Federal Bureau of Investigation kept no files on the MSPCA or Francis H. Rowley from 1939 to 1946; David M. Hardy, Section Chief, Records/Information Dissemination Section, Records Management Division, Federal Bureau of Investigation, US Department of Justice, to Janet M. Davis, July 24, 2013.

39. "Free Speech," *ODA*, June 1917, 3.

40. "Atomic Bomb," *ODA*, April 1946, 78.

41. Diane L. Beers, *For the Prevention of Cruelty: The History and Legacy of Animal Rights Activism in the United States* (Athens, OH: Swallow Press, 2006), 155.

42. *Brief of the District of Columbia Chapter of the National Lawyers Guild as Amicus Curiae*, p. 3, District of Columbia v. John R. Thompson Co., Inc., No. 99150 (Municipal Court for the District of Columbia, Criminal Division, May 24, 1951), Coordinating Committee for the Enforcement of the DC Anti-Discrimination Laws Records, 1949–1954, Historical Society of Washington, DC, citation courtesy of Audrey Russek.

43. Abraham L. Davis and Barbara Luck Graham, *The Supreme Court, Race, and Civil Rights: From Marshall to Rehnquist* (Thousand Oaks, CA: Sage, 1995), 83–84.

44. Unti, "'The Quality of Mercy,'" 165–175; 475–486.

45. Katherine C. Grier, *Pets in America: A History* (Chapel Hill: University of North Carolina Press, 2006), 85–90.

46. See Paula Marantz Cohen, *Silent Film and the Triumph of the American Myth* (New York: Oxford University Press, 2001); and Jonathan Burt, *Animals in Film* (London: Reaktion Books, 2002), 12.

47. Maureen Ogle, *In Meat We Trust: An Unexpected History of Carnivore America* (Boston: Houghton Mifflin Harcourt, 2013), 157; Jonathan Burt, "Conflicts

around Slaughter in Modernity," in *Killing Animals*, ed. Animal Studies Group (Urbana: University of Illinois Press, 2006), 120–144.
48. Ogle, *In Meat We Trust*, 136–147; Jonathan Safran Foer, *Eating Animals* (New York: Back Bay Books, 2009), 104–107.
49. "Ag-gag Laws," SourceWatch, http://www.sourcewatch.org/index.php/Ag-gag_laws.
50. William M. Blair, "Humane Appeals Swamp Congress," *NYT*, May 4, 1958.
51. Blair, "Humane Appeals Swamp Congress."
52. Jeff Welty, "Humane Slaughter Laws," *Law and Contemporary Problems* 70, no. 1, "Animal Law and Policy" (Winter 2007): 175–206, 189, http://www.jstor.org/stable/27592169.
53. In 2004, an undercover PETA member working at a major Orthodox kosher slaughterhouse in Postville, Iowa, secretly videotaped graphic scenes of conscious steers suspended upside down bellowing in pain after the ritual cut. In response to the video and reports of repeated labor violations at the plant in 2008, rabbis in the United Synagogue of Conservative Judaism created the *Hekhsher Tzedek* campaign, or "justice certification" in Hebrew, which would certify that kosher food had been produced with the highest ritual and ethical standards for the treatment of plant workers and animals—a movement that Orthodox rabbis deemed unnecessary at Postville. In the summer of 2008, the Postville plant, owned by AgriProcessors, Inc., went into bankruptcy after 389 undocumented workers were arrested and the company's owners subsequently convicted of fraud. The plant is still a kosher facility and is now owned by Agri Star Meat and Poultry. Donald G. McNeil Jr., "Videos Cited in Calling Kosher Slaughter Inhumane," *NYT*, December 1, 2004; Julia Preston, "Rabbis Debate Kosher Ethics at Meat Plant," *NYT*, August 23, 2008; Jean Caspers-Simmet, "Agri Stars Promises Big Economic Effect in Postville," *Agri News*, April 29, 2010, http://www.agrinews.com/agri/star/promises/big/economic/effect/in/postville/story-2369.html.
54. Peter Singer, *Animal Liberation*, 2nd ed. (1975; repr., New York: New York Review of Books, 1990), chap. 1; Beers, *For the Prevention of Cruelty*, chap. 7, 147–196; see also Gary Francione, *Rain without Thunder: The Ideology of the Animal Rights Movement* (Philadelphia: Temple University Press, 1996); Ingrid Newkirk, *Free the Animals: The Amazing True Story of the Animal Liberation Front* (New York: Lantern Books, 2000); Matthew Scully, *Dominion: The Power of Man, the Suffering of Animals, and the Call to Mercy* (New York: St. Martin's Press, 2002), 15; Tom Regan, *The Case for Animal Rights*, updated, new preface (Berkeley: University of California Press, 2004); Steven Wise, *Rattling the Cage: Toward Legal Rights for Animals* (New York: Da Capo Press, 2000).
55. Kelly Boggs, "First-Person: If Terri Schiavo Was a Dog," Baptist Press, March 18, 2005, www.bpnews.net; Diane Alden, "Futile Care: The Terri Schiavo Case," Newsmax, October 16, 2003, www.newsmax.com; Becky Perry, "Give Schiavo the Same Rights as Animals," *Daily Texan*, March 24, 2005.

56. Boggs, "First-Person."
57. "Bird like Me," episode on *The Daily Show with Jon Stewart*, aired January 24, 2011, on Comedy Central, http://thedailyshow.cc.com/videos/rqgnz4/bird-like-me.
58. "SeaWorld of Pain," episode on *The Daily Show with Jon Stewart*, aired on February 15, 2012, on Comedy Central, http://thedailyshow.cc.com/videos/g144yr/seaworld-of-pain.
59. Kelly Milner Halls and Major William Sumner, *Saving the Baghdad Zoo: A True Story of Hope and Heroes* (New York: Green Willow Books, 2010), 10; Ian Fisher, "'Zookeepers' New Task: Getting Animals Back," *NYT*, May 6, 2003.
60. Danica Coto, "Puerto Rico Cockfighting: Legal Cockfights in Danger in U.S. Territory," *Huffington Post*, July 24, 2012, http://www.huffingtonpost.com/2012/07/22/puerto-rico-cockfighting_n_1693362.html.
61. "Bullfighting in Barcelona Ends with Catalonia Ban," BBC *News Europe*, September 25, 2011, http://www.bbc.co.uk/news/world-europe-15050706.
62. Max Bearak, "Indian Beef Workers Fight to Bring Back the Bull Market," *NYT*, June 28, 2015; Nida Najar, "Rumors of Cow Killings in India Deepen Rift between Hindus and Muslims," *NYT*, October 15, 2014.
63. Janet M. Davis, "The Dog Ate My Birth Certificate," *NYT*, May 7, 2012, http://www.nytimes.com/2012/05/08/opinion/the-dog-ate-my-birth-certificate.html?_r=1&ref=opinion.
64. Merritt Clifton, "New York Police Department Eclipses ASPCA Humane Law Stats in First Full Year on the Beat," *Animals 24–7*, February 9, 2015, http://www.animals24-7.org/2015/02/09/new-york-police-department-eclipses-aspca-humane-law-enforcement-stats-in-first-full-year-on-the-beat/; Corey Kilgannon, "Dogs Hurting the Most Have a Special Place to Heal," *NYT*, October 1, 2015.
65. See "NYCLASS: We Love Animals and We Vote!," http://www.nyclass.org.
66. Lee Siegel, "Clomping toward Oblivion," *New York Magazine*, January 24, 2014, http://nymag.com/news/features/carriage-horses-2014-2/index3.html#print.
67. Liam Neeson, "Carriages Belong in Central Park," NYT, April 15, 2015.
68. Jim Yardley and Laurie Goodstein, "Pope Francis, in Sweeping Encyclical, Calls for Swift Action on Climate Change," *NYT*, June 19, 2015.
69. Pope Francis, *Encyclical Letter Laudato Si, of the Holy Father Francis, on Care for Our Common Home* (Vatican: Vatican Press, 2015), 51, 86, 97, 167, 173.
70. Pope Francis, *Laudato Si*, 48.
71. Pope Francis, *Laudato Si*, 48.
72. Pope Francis, *Laudato Si*, 30.

Index

Adams, Charles Francis, 15
Affective kinship, 41, 235n59
African Methodist Episcopal (AME) Church, 73
Agassiz, Louis, 42
Aguinaldo, Emilio, 131
Ahimsa (nonviolence), 152, 155–57, 160, 170–78
American Anti-Vivisection Society, 51, 55, 59, 62, 80–83, 82f, 180, 218, 245n142. *see also* Antivivisection movement
American exceptionalism, 17–19, 22–23
American Fondouk, 1–4, 3f, 209, 227n7, 285n1
American Humane Association, 59, 62–63, 68, 83, 104–5, 113, 213, 217, 240n47
American Humane Education Society, 74, 102, 142
American Missionary Association, 16, 18
American Museum, 205–6
American Ornithological Union, 96, 121
American Red Cross, 19, 212
American Relief Administration, 19
American Society for the Prevention of Cruelty to Animals. *see* ASPCA
American Sunday-School Union, 35
American Temperance Society, 46
"Amos Hunt and His Steel Trap," 73–74, 109

"An Act for the More Effectual Prevention of Cruelty to Animals," 11, 28
Analgesics, anesthesia, 40–41
Andrews, Charles Freer, 177
Angell, George Thorndike, 26–27, 30–31, 38, 42–44, 48, 50–52, 62–63, 77–78, 99–101, 116–18, 151, 154, 157, 172, 197
Angell, Rebekah, 30–31
Animal fights as entertainment, 110–15, 213, 253n146, 254n149, 286n18. *see also* bloodsports; bullfighting; Dogs, fighting; cockfighting; ratbaiting
Animalized racial representations, 42, 48, 91–92, 110–11, 111f, 247n8
Animal protectionism. *see also* Cuba; India; Philippines; Puerto Rico
activities of, 12–14, 18, 75, 118–19, 151–52, 209–14, 210–11f, 285n1
American aid organizations, humanitarian programs, 18–19
animal fights as entertainment, 110–15, 253n146, 254n149
asylum reformers in, 38, 43
birth of, 5–6, 26–9
bourgeoisie social order and, 24
changing values of, 19–22, 20f, 24–25, 231n68, 232n72
in Cuba, 122–24, 190–91

Animal protectionism (Cont.)
    enforcement, 113 (see also
        enforcement of anticruelty laws)
    global dimensions of, 21, 231n70
    limitations of, 23–24, 77–78
    sense of mission in, 18
    skepticism towards, 222–23
    social justice focus, 99–104, 219, 222–23
    state legislation, 77
Animal welfare movement
    celebrity endorsement of, 215, 216f
    fractures within, 215–17, 287n33
    legacy of, 219–25
    women's networks, 53, 55–56
Animal World, The, 27
Anticruelty laws
    animals as property, 16, 28
    anti-trapping legislation, 109–10
    cultural specificity in, 4
    enforcement of (see
        enforcement of anticruelty laws)
    humane slaughter, 96–98, 215, 221–2
    imperilment of animals by, 89–90
    in India, 160–67, 162f, 165f, 271nn49–52, 273n68, 273n70
    laboring animal cruelty cases, 88–89
    legislative history of, 28
    Massachusetts Body of Liberties, 17
    in Morocco, 2, 227n7
    in New York, 8–11, 14, 16, 28, 229n29, 229n32
    in Philippines, 120–24, 128, 257n23, 257n27, 258nn29–30, 259n34
    in United States, 12
Anti-immigrant ideologies, 48, 90–91
Antipoverty activism, 75–77
Anti-Semitism, 215, 222
Anti-Steel Trap Law of 1928, 102
Anti-Steel Trap League, 109
Antivivisection movement. *see also*
        American Anti-Vivisection Society
    activities, 56–57, 119

animal experimentation, 55–56, 80–83, 82f, 119, 180
    animal welfare activists in, 12, 55, 70
    legacy, 80–83, 245n142
"Appeal for Syria," 217
Appeal in Favor of that Class of Americans called Africans, An (Child), 41
Appleton, Emily, 26
Arabbers, 286n21
Armstrong, Susan E., 209
ASPCA
    activities of, 137, 180, 192–93, 205
    changing agenda of, 19–21, 20f, 83, 212
    founding of, 8–10, 229n29, 229n32
    legacy of, 224–25
    legal blueprint created by, 12
    policing authority, 9–11, 15–16, 224
    sheltering of animals by, 95
    uniforms, 9–11, 15, 24, 86–87, 160, 247n14
Assimilation, 17–18, 85–86, 91, 96, 97f, 111, 114–115, 118, 126, 139, 141, 143, 147, 181, 190, 194. *see also* citizenship
Asylum reforms, 38, 43
Audubon Mississippi, 223
Audubon Society, 56

Bailey, Amos Judson, 78
Band of Hope, 46–47, 51, 61–62
Bands of Mercy
    in Cuba, 123–24, 137
    in India, 153–55, 269n14
    in Philippines, 142f
    in United States, 48, 51, 61–64, 63f, 71–75, 100
Barbarism, etymology and racial history, 4–5
Barberi, Maria, 70, 243n92
Barnum, P. T., 205–206
Barnwell, F. Rivers, 100–101, 101f
Barton, R. F., 127
Baseball, 131–32, 197

Battle at Elderbush Gulch, The, 113–14
Battle Creek Sanitarium, 168
Beal, A. H., 191–92
Beautiful Joe (Saunders), 64–67, 76–77, 164, 242n77
Beef Trust, 168–69
Be Kind to Animals Week, 59, 59f, 214f, 215, 240n47
Bell, J. F., 130
"Benevolent Assimilation" (McKinley), 181
Ben-Hur: A Tale of the Christ, 113
Bergh, Henry, 8–11, 10f, 14–16, 22, 67, 68, 86–87, 90–91, 95–98, 192, 229n29, 229n32, 247n14
Bergh, Katherine Matilda Taylor, 8
Berlin Airlift, 19
Bharatiya Janata Party (BJP), 223
Bibb, Henry, 41
Biblical dominion, stewardship, 32–37, 66
Bilderrain, Ignacio, 111–12
Bird conservation movement
  domestic, 56, 62, 96–97, 97f, 220–23
  global, 121–22, 143–50, 144f, 148–49f, 259n34
Birth of a Nation, The, 103, 114
Black Beauty (Sewell), 42, 64–67, 76–77, 108, 153, 187, 242n77
Blavatsky, Helena, 171–72
Blood sports, 16, 17, 110–15, 164, 191, 195, 253n146, 254n149. *see also* bullfighting; cockfighting; hunting, trapping
Bontoc Igorots, 84–85, 126, 127, 246n3
Bowlby, Harry L., 194
Brown, John, 43
Brown Dog Riots, 81
Bubonic plague, 92
Buffalo's Pan American Exposition, 1901, 180
Bullfighting
  American tradition, 191–99, 281n67, 281n86
  bans on, 186, 196–200, 205–6, 223, 282n103

Black Legend, 23, 182, 188
Brownsville Port Celebration, 200
Catholic policies towards, 188–91
charlotada, 193, 281n67
in Cuba, 190, 198–99
cultural status of, 181–82
enforcement of anticruelty laws, 193
humane education and eradication of, 196, 207–8, 281n86
Magonistas, 281n86
mock (bloodless), 193–94, 203, 206
as moral temptation, 192–98, 202–3
overview, 23, 179–82
Pan American Exposition, 204f, 205–7
in Philippines, 197–98
picador horses, 184–87 279n35
procedure, 183–84, 185f
public opinions of, 181, 184–87, 190–91
racialization of, 192–94, 201, 281n67
Spanish tradition, 183–96, 279n35
Texas Centennial, 179, 181, 199–206, 204f, 282n103
tourism, 194–99, 281n86
Bulliet, Richard, 6
Burns, Anthony, 43
Burns, Kit (Christopher Keyburn), 110, 111f

Cadman, S. Parkes, 61
Caffery, Jefferson, 198
Calcutta SPCA, 160–63. *see also* India
Calhoun, John C., 45
Cameras, photography, 14, 61
Carpenter, C. F., 112
Carriage horse trade, 224
Carrillo, John F., 88
Carroll, Richard, 102
Carroll, Seymour, 100, 102–3, 109–10
Catholic Church, 130, 132–33, 188–91, 194
Cats, 12–13, 13f, 220. *see also* stray animals
Cat ladies, 13
Central Centennial Exposition (1936). see Texas Centennial (1936)

Chaffee, Adna R., 120
Chamberlin, Frederick, 262n81
Checkrein, 11f, 12, 53f, 65, 107–8
Child, Lydia Maria, 41
Child protection
  combined animal and child protection societies, 67–70, 69f, 242n86, 243n92
  in India, 158–59, 159f, 166–67
Christ among the Cattle (Marvin), 58, 61, 240n44
Christian Commission, 14–15
Chutes Park, 84, 246n3
Citizenship
  animal advocacy in claims to, 5, 17–18, 49
  animal kindness as pathway to, 113–15, 120
  assimilation, 17–18
  military enlistment as claim to, 102–3
  for Native Americans, 113–14
  and Philippines, 147
  and Puerto Rico, 139–40
Civilization, concept of,
  birds and, 145
  bullfighting and, 179, 181–3, 191, 194, 198, 207
  children and, 33, 37, 61, 64, 71, 74, 147
  cockfighting and, 135, 137
  humane slaughter and, 143
  hunting of predators, 164
  India and, 152, 177–8
  medical vs. humane education, 80, 83
  normative ideologies of, 23, 204–5
  in opposition to barbarism, 4–5, 17, 48, 113–14, 154
  Second Great Awakening and, 21, 49, 219
  temperance movement and, 48–9, 51, 128
  vegetarianism and, 171–2
Civil rights movement, 99–104, 217, 219, 222–23
Civil War, 14–16, 45, 74
Clark, Elizabeth, 40
Cobbe, Frances Power, 55

Cockfighting
  arguments in favor of, 130, 254n149
  banning of, 12, 17, 130, 134–41
  in Cuba, 120, 134–38, 138f, 264n112
  in Philippines, 129–34, 223, 262n81, 263n88
  portrayal of, 111–12
  in Puerto Rico, 139–41, 223, 265n125
Cock-throwing, 17
Cold War, 217–18, 287n38
Commons ideal, 74
Connolly, Mary, 67–68
Cooper, Ashley, 40
Cooper, Bessie Dean, 1, 6
Cornell, Ezra, 9
Cotton States and International Exposition, 1895, 181
Crone, Frank L., 147
Cruelty narrative, 40–41
Cruelty to Animals Act (Great Britain, 1876), 55
Cuba
  animal protectionism in, 122–24, 190–91
  atrocities committed in, 116, 190
  Bands of Mercy in, 123–24
  bullfighting in, 190, 198–99
  child protection in, 123–24
  cockfighting in, 120, 134–38, 138f, 264n112
  enforcement of anticruelty laws, 120, 123, 134–35
  Order 165, 120, 134
  reconcentrado, 116, 190
  Rural Guard, 135, 137–38
Cultural practice as animal cruelty, 96–99
Curtis, Evelyn A., 75

"Daily Show with Jon Stewart," 222–23
Datta, Michael Sudhan, 268n9
Davis, George W., 120
Deardorff, E. M., 62, 64, 84–85
De Blasio, Bill, 224

"Declaration of the Rights of Animals," 9
Delon, M. Guy, 209
Department of Humane Education, 80. *see also* Woman's Christian Temperance Union (WCTU)
Department of Mercy, 22, 51–53, 56–58, 60, 67, 71, 75–78, 243n99
Department of Penal and Reformatory Work, 71–72, 243n99
District of Columbia v. John R. Thompson Co., 219
Dix, Dorothea, 38, 39f
Dogcatchers, 92–96
Dogs
   Beautiful Joe (Saunders), 64–67, 76–77, 164, 242n77
   bounties on, 7, 93
   changed status of, 220
   ear cropping, 107–9
   eating, 84–85, 113–14, 126–27, 246n3
   euthanasia, 94–95
   fighting, 110–11, 111f, 253n146
   in McGuffey *Readers*, 37
   summer stray roundup, 92–96
Domestic violence, 70
Double V Campaign, 217
"Drain inspector's report," 175–77, 277n140
Drummond, William H., 44
Dwight, Timothy, 30, 31, 33–35, 46

Earle, John Milton, 44
Eccleston, Edward, 196
Eclectic Readers, 37
Edward VII, 151
Egan, William J., 194
Enforcement of anticruelty laws
   bullfighting, 193
   Cuba, 120, 123, 134–35
   Hawaii, 122
   India, 160–63, 271n52
   overview, 68, 89
   Philippines, 120–22, 125, 145–46, 150, 257n27, 258nn29–30, 259n34
   Puerto Rico, 120, 139–41
Engels, Friedrich, 24
Episcopal Church, 58
Ethical sentimentalism, 40
Ex-slave narratives, 40, 41

Feast of Dogs, 113–14
Fielder, Bridgette, 42
Film industry, 112–14, 213
Finney, Charles Grandison, 30–33, 40
Fiske, Minnie Maddern, 194
Folger, Charles, 9
"For this World" prayer (Rauschenbusch), 60
Franklin, Sydney, 194, 198–201, 203–4
Frey, C. David, 112
Fugitive Slave Law of 1850, 42, 43
Fur, feather trades, 104–10, 121–22, 259n34

Gandhi, Mahatma, 161, 171, 174, 176, 276n120
Garrison, William Lloyd, 43, 44
General Federation of Women's Clubs, 105
Gerry, Elbridge, 55, 68
Gómez, José Miguel, 135, 138
Gore, Robert H., 140
Gospel of kindness
   animals, Sunday Sabbath application to, 31–32
   biblical dominion and stewardship, 32–37, 66
   children, moral development in, 33–37
   domestic ethic of kindness vs., 34, 228n13
   expansion of, 13–14
   free moral agency, 31, 40–41
   global justice ideal, 18–19
   kinship and belonging, 35
   legacy of, 219–25
   as moral imperative, 4, 9, 14–15, 23
   origins of for George Angell, 27–28
   principles of, 4–5, 14, 18, 223

Gospel of kindness (*Cont.*)
   racial uplift, 72–73
   theological and social foundations of, 29–38, 39f
   vegetarianism, 167–75
Grand, W. Joseph, 98–99, 170
Greater Texas and Pan American Exposition. *see* Pan American Exposition (1937)
Grier, Katherine, 34, 228n13
Griffin, C. P. G., 163
Griffith, D. W., 113–14
Grinnell, Fordyce, 13
Grinnell, George Bird, 56

Hall, G. Stanley, 62
Halttunen, Karen, 41, 235n59
Hampton Institute, 74
Harris, M. Calcote, 206
Hawaii, 122, 155, 223
Hay, John, 188
Hayes, Rutherford B., 169
Heifer starvation case, 15–16, 230n56
Hekhsher Tzedek (justice certification) campaign, 288n53
Hemingway, Ernest, 183, 184, 186, 198–99, 279n35
Hogs. *see* pigs
Hornaday, William T., 105
Horses
   advocacy for, 53f, 211, 211f
   American relationship with, 186–87, 220
   animal cruelty cases, 88–89
   Beautiful Jim Key, 180
   Black Beauty (Sewell), 42, 64–67, 76–77, 108, 153, 187, 242n77
   checkrein, 11f, 12, 53f, 65, 107–8
   in film industry, 113, 213
   gentle taming of, 15, 37–38, 44, 88, 180
   picador horses, 184–87 279n35
   sentimental status of, 220
   tail docking, 107–9, 127–28

   treatment of generally, 6, 9, 11, 11f, 15
Humane education programs
   African American children, 72–75, 100–102
   anti-trapping curricula, 109–10
   Be Kind to Animals Week, 59, 59f, 215, 240n47
   bullfighting, eradication of, 196, 207–8, 281n86
   child development, 61–67, 63f, 241n63, 242n77
   child protection, 67–70, 69f, 242n86, 243n92
   children enrolled in, 63–64, 241n63
   civics textbooks, 114–15
   civil rights movement, 99–104, 217, 219, 222–23
   enforcement of participation, 64
   as highest form of social reform, 71–80, 243n99, 244n122
   Humane (Mercy) Sunday, 59–60, 214f, 215, 240n47
   in India, 153–59, 159f, 268nn8–9, 269n14, 270n32, 270n36
   Native Americans, 17–18, 114
   overview, 23, 24
   in Philippines, 141–50, 142f, 144f, 148–49f, 266n141
   post-WWII, 212, 285n12
   in Wyoming, 285n12
Humane Methods of Slaughter Act (HMSA) of 1958, 221–22
Humane movement
   abuse case reports, 69–70, 242n86
   belonging and exclusion in, 85–86, 247n8
   Christian pastors involvement in, 58–61, 73, 78, 100–103, 240n44, 240n47
   journalistic narratives of, 86, 89–90
   municipal stray reform, 94–96
   publications, 59–60, 214f, 215 (*see also specific publications*)
   Social Gospel, 60

tactics, 88–90, 113
teamsters, confrontations with, 85–88, 87f, 246n3, 247n8, 247n14
women's leadership in, 54–56
Humane (Mercy) Sunday, 59–60, 214f, 215, 240n47
Humphrey, Richard Burton, 201–2
Hunting, trapping, 62, 73–74, 164, 165f

Illinois Humane Society, 61
Immigration Restriction League, 92
India
  ahimsa (nonviolence), 152, 155–57, 160, 170–78
  animal protection activism in, 151–52
  anticruelty laws in, 160–67, 162f, 165f, 271nn49–52, 273n68, 273n70
  Bands of Mercy in, 153–55, 269n14
  bird baiting, 271n50
  Calcutta SPCA, 160–63
  Carters' Strike, 160–61, 163
  child protection activism in, 158–59, 159f, 166–67
  child-widows in, 158–59, 159f, 270n36
  Christian converts in, 153, 268n9
  Code of Criminal Procedure of 1882, 271n50
  cow protection movement, 173–75, 223, 276n120, 276n124
  cow worship in, 155, 168, 173
  dog management in, 125–26
  "drain inspector's report," 175–77, 277n140
  dung in expiatory rituals, 277n140
  enforcement of anticruelty laws, 160–63, 271n52
  Gambling Act II of 1867, 271n50
  humane education programs in, 153–59, 159f, 268nn8–9, 269n14, 270n32, 270n36
  human rights activism in, 158–59, 159f, 166–67

Laws of Manu, 270n36
Madras Police Act of 1888, 271n50
missionary work in, 153–59, 268nn8–9, 269n14, 270n32, 270n36
overview, 23, 177–78
Prevention of Cruelty to Animals Act of 1890, 161–66, 271nn51–52, 273n68
religious slaughter, 166–67, 173–74, 273n68, 273n70
search warrants requirements, 271n50
Sepoy Rebellion (1857), 161, 166, 174
Sharada Sadan, 157–59, 159f, 270n32
Universal Mercy Band, 269n14
vegetarianism in, 167–75
wild animal destruction in, 163–64
Industrial Courts, 78
Irish Catholics, 48, 110
Islam, 173–75, 183, 221–22, 276n120

Jack London Club, 212–13
Japan, 126
Jarvis Christian Institute, 74
Jefferson School, 99–100
Jesse James, 113
Johnson, Charles, 89
Johnson v. District of Columbia, 219
Johnston, Mercer, 133–34
Jones, Eli Stanley, 156
Jones, Susan, 6
Judaism, 96–98, 106–7, 221–22
Jungle, The (Sinclair), 80, 99, 169, 170
Justice certification *(Hekhsher Tzedek)* campaign, 288n53

Keen, William W., 57
Kellogg, John Harvey, 168
Kershner, Bruce Lesher, 132
Kete, Kathleen, 17
Key, William "Doc," 180
Kindness to Animals, Or, The Sin of Cruelty Exposed and Rebuked, 35–37
King's Declaration of Sports, 17

Kingsford, Anna, 172
Kipling, Lockwood, 166
Kosher slaughter *(shechita)*, 96–98, 166, 288n53
Kyle, Mollie A., 76

Labor radicalism, 77–80, 79*f*
Labor strikes, 78, 106
Ladies' Health Protective Association, 91
Laudato Si (Praise Be to You), 224–25
Law enforcement. *see* anticruelty laws; ASPCA; enforcement of anticruelty laws; MSPCA
Laxmidas, Labhshankar, 164, 166, 168–70
Leaf, Munro, 207–8
Lemon, John W., 100–102
Lewin, Isaac, 222
Liberator, 43, 44
Lincoln, Abraham, 45
Livestock
  acts of kindness towards, 69*f*
  changed status of, 221
  depiction of by temperance movement, 66–67
  driving, 7–8
  Hawaii, street obstruction laws in, 122
  heifer starvation case, 15–16, 230n56
  laboring animals, urban, 286n21
  labor strike effects on, 78
  living arrangements for, 228n24
  railroad transport of, 169–70
  slaughterhouses, 90, 98–99, 169–70, 288n53
  starvation of, 15–16, 230n56
  28-Hour Law, 68, 169–70
Lopez Quintana, Narciso, 136
Los Angeles SPCA, 85, 88–89, 95–96, 112, 192
Los Angeles Times, 16, 88, 90, 91, 105, 111, 112, 115, 191–92, 194–95
"Lost laws," 219
Louisiana Purchase Exposition, 1904, 180

Lovell, George S., 238n11
Lovell, Mary Frances (Whitechurch), 51, 55, 57–58, 61, 63, 72, 80–83, 106, 170, 238n11, 245n142
Loyal Temperance Legions, 51, 61–62
Lynching, 103, 104

Magoon, Charles E., 135–38
Marital property rights, 43
Marshall Plan, 19
Marvin, Frederic Rowland, 58–59, 61
Marx, Karl, 24
Massachusetts Body of Liberties, 17
Massachusetts Society for the Prevention of Cruelty to Animals (MSPCA). *see* MSPCA
Matta, N. B., 217
Mayo, Katherine, 175–78
Maysi, Kadra, 188
McCarthy, Hamilton, 44
McCrea, Roswell, 240n47
McGuffey, William H., 37
McKinley, William, 181, 256n18
McMahon, John, 94
Media technologies, 60–61
Medical experimentation on animals, 55–56, 80–83, 82*f*, 119, 180
Mercy Sunday movement, 59–60, 240n47. *see also* Humane Sunday
Metropolitan Police Act of 1839, 90
Mexican Revolution, 195–96
Mexican War, 182
Mexico. *see* bullfighting
Mexico SPCA, 196
Minnesota WCTU, 60, 67, 70, 128
Missionaries, 18, 23, 287n33. *see also specific organizations*
Modern Art of Taming Wild Horses, The (Rarey), 15, 37–38
Moore, J. Howard, 104–5
Moore, Thomas Ewing, 184, 186
Morales, William, 89

Moral suasion, as gendered tactic, 52–53, 65–66
Morton, Samuel, 42
Mother India (Mayo), 175–78
MSPCA
    activities of, 24, 53, 78, 80, 142, 151, 206, 215, 217–18, 218*f*, 287n38
    American Fondouk, 1–4, 3*f*, 209, 227n7, 285n1
    antiwar views of, 116–118, 217–218
    boycotts, 103
    founding of, 26–27
    Jack London Club, 212–13
    masthead, seal, 53, 54*f*
    peace endowment sponsorship, 117
    sheltering of animals by, 95
Murphy, M. M., 99–100
My Friend Flicka (O'Hara), 187

NAACP, 103
Narrative of the Life and Adventures of Henry Bibb, an American Slave, Written by Himself (Bibb), 41
National Association of Colored Women, 73
National Era, 45
National Humane Review, 44, 45, 59, 166, 199, 202, 205, 208, 209, 211, 216–17
Nativist exclusion, 48
Nazism, 215, 222
New York City
    animal fight bans, 110, 253n146
    city pound, dog treatment in, 92–96
    sanitation problems, 6–8, 7*f*, 228n24
New York Society for the Prevention of Cruelty to Children (NYSPCC), 68–69
Nonviolence *(ahimsa)*, 152, 155–57, 160, 170–78
Nott, Josiah, 42

Oberlin College, 40
Olcott, Henry Steel, 171–72

Olmsted, Frederick Law, 8
Ostrich feathers, 106–7
Our Dumb Animals, 4, 19, 27, 38, 44, 48, 51, 75, 78, 100, 103, 116–18, 151, 160, 164, 170, 172, 188, 195–97, 212, 213, 215, 217

Pagan Spain (Wright), 183
Pain control, 40–41
Palma, Tomás Estrada, 135
Pan American Exposition, 1937, 205–7
Pasteur, Louis, 92, 125
Pearson, Susan, 16, 45, 231n70
Peñarredonda, Magdalena, 137
Pennsylvania SPCA, 51, 53, 61
People v. Tisdale, 88
Performing Animals (Regulation) Act of 1925, 286n18
Performing Animals' Defence League, 213, 286n18
PETA, 223, 288n53
Pet population control, 19–21, 20*f*
Philadelphia Bible-Christian Church, 168
Philadelphia Centennial International Exhibition, 1876, 179–80
Philippine-American War, 116–17, 255n4
Philippines
    Act 1285, 258n29
    Act 2590, 121–22, 259n34
    American Occupation of, 119, 256n18
    An Act for the Protection of Game and Fish of 1916, 121–22, 259n34
    animal protectionists activism in, 116–18
    anticruelty laws in, 120–24, 128, 257n23, 257n27, 258nn29–30, 259n34
    baseball in, 131–32
    Bird and Arbor Day, 143–44, 144*f*
    bird conservation movement, 121–22, 143–50, 144*f*, 148–49*f*, 259n34
    bird specimen collecting, 258n30
    bullfighting in, 197–98
    citizenship for, 147

Philippines (*Cont.*)
  cockfighting in, 129–34, 223, 262n81, 263n88
  disease epidemics, animals dying in, 116, 255n4
  dog management in, 124–27, 259n45
  dog muzzling laws, 124–25
  domestic hygiene education, 147, 148*f*
  enforcement of anticruelty laws, 120–22, 125, 145–46, 150, 257n27, 258nn29–30, 259n34
  fur, feather trades in, 121–22, 259n34
  humane education programs in, 141–50, 142*f*, 144*f*, 148–49*f*, 266n141
  juntas, 257n23
  medical experimentation in, 119
  Ordinance 13, 124–25, 259n45
  Ordinance for the Prevention of Cruelty to Animals, 120, 257n27
  Organic School Act, 141–42
  Tagalogs, 131, 262n81
  vice laws in, 128–29
Philippines SPCA, 121, 150, 197
Picador horses, 184–87 279n35
Pigeon shooting bans, 112
Pigs
  Civil War slaughter of, 15
  cholera epidemic, 1849, 7
  confiscation of, 8, 228n24
  urban conditions of, 6–8, 170
Pius V, 188–89
Plumb, Mina D., 71
Pneumonia, 95
Policing powers. *see* enforcement of anticruelty laws
Polygenesis theory, 42
Pornography, 67, 235n59
Presbyterian Church, 58, 60
Prison reform, 71–73, 243n99
Proctor, Redfield, 190, 197
Protestantism, 23, 59, 117, 133–34, 201, 215–16. *see also* Second Great Awakening

Puerto Rico
  American citizenship, 139–40
  cockfighting in, 139–41, 223, 265n125
  General Order No. 122, 120
  Protectora de los Animales, 120, 257n23
Puritans, 17

Quakers, 40–41

Rabies, 92–95, 125
Race rioting, 103, 217
Racial segregation, 219
Racism, 72, 81, 86, 90–93, 99–100, 101*f*, 102–106, 110–115, 217
Radical Reconstruction, 74
Radio, 61
Ragged Dick (Alger), 76
Rai, Lala Lajpat, 177
Raja-Yoga Academy, 172
Ramabai Sarasvati, Pandita, 156–59, 270n32
Ramish and Marsh, 89
Rarey, John Solomon, 15, 37–38, 44, 88
Rat baiting, 110–11, 111*f*
Rauschenbusch, Walter, 60
Reckoning with the Beast (Turner), 231n70
Reconstruction, 16, 45
Red Star Animal Relief, 209–11, 210*f*
Reynolds, Mike, 254n149
Richards, John Gardiner, 102
Ringling, John, 213
Ringling Brothers and Barnum & Bailey circus, 213
Rizal, José, 130–31, 143
Robert Sherer & Company, 88–89
Rodeo, 181, 202, 204, 206
Roosevelt, Theodore, 109, 117–18, 164, 198
Rowley, Francis, 97–98, 100–101, 117, 198
Royal Society for the Prevention of Cruelty to Animals, 9, 27, 229n32
Ruiz, Antonio, 136
Ryder, Jeannette, 122–24

Sacramento SPCA, 98
Salt, Henry, 170–71
Samfield, Max, 98
Santa, Manuel Jiménez, 139–40
Saunders, Margaret Marshall, 65
Scanlon, Charles, 58
Schiavo, Terri, 222
Scott, T. J., 156
Second Great Awakening
    abolitionism, 39–45, 235n59
    anticruelty reforms of, 14, 21, 22, 27–29
    revival experience, 29–31
    Sunday school movement, 35–37
    temperance movement, 45–49, 235n59
Sewall, Samuel E., 43–44
Sewell, Anna, 65, 108
Shechita (kosher slaughter), 96–98, 166, 288n53
Sheltering movement, 55, 94–96
Shortall, John G., 61, 137
Simon, Abram, 98
Sims, Thomas, 43
Sinclair, Upton, 80, 99, 170
Sixth Commandment, 32–33
Skeletons of a Course of Theological Lectures (Finney), 32
Slaughterhouses, 90, 98–99, 169–70, 288n53
Slim Jack, or the History of a Circus-Boy, 35
Social purity activism, 60
Southern Methodist Episcopal Church, 75, 244n122
Spain. *see* bullfighting
Spanish-American War, 22–23, 117, 168–69, 182, 189–91, 219–20, 256n18
Spectatorial sympathy, 41, 235n59
St. Paul SPCA, 61, 69, 70, 247n14
Starry Cross, 19, 170
Stein, Gertrude, 183
Stewardship, 32–37, 66
Stewart, Eliza Daniel, 50
Story of Ferdinand, The (Leaf), 207–8

Stowe, Harriet Beecher, 34, 35, 42
Strategic essentialism, 53
Stray animals
    bounties on, 7, 93–95
    humane capture of, 55, 94
    humane euthanasia, 12, 19–21, 20f
    summer roundup, 92–96
Strong, Josiah, 18
Student Volunteer Movement for Foreign Missions, 18
Stuntz, Homer C., 133
Sugrue, Thomas, 232n78

Taft, William Howard, 118, 120, 128–29
Tagore, Rabindranath, 177
Tail docking, 107–9, 127–28
"Taking the pledge," 46
Talmage, T. DeWitt, 157
Temperance movement, 46–48, 47f, 50–52, 66–67, 72. *see also* Woman's Christian Temperance Union (WCTU)
Tennessee SPCA, 98
Terrell, Mary Church, 219
Texas Centennial, 179, 181, 199–206, 204f, 282n103
Theosophy, 171–72
"The Silent Appeal," 47, 47f
Thoburn, James, 154, 155
Thoreau, Henry David, 152, 171
Thurman, Lucy, 72–75, 109–10
Thurman WCTUs, 72–73
Timmins, Thomas, 48, 153
Towner, H. M., 139, 140
Travieso, Martín, 141
Turkey Creek case, 222–23
Turner, James, 40, 231n70
Tuskegee Institute, 74
28-Hour Law, 68, 169–70

Uncle Tom's Cabin (Stowe), 42, 45
Union Stock Yards, 78, 98–99 170
Unitarianism, 40–41

United Synagogue of Conservative Judaism, 288n53
Universal Mercy Band Movement, 153–54
USS *Maine*, 116, 197

Vaccines, 80–83, 82f, 92, 119
Vaux, Calvert, 8
Vegetarianism, 167–75
Vivekananda, Swami, 167–68

Waln, Samuel Morris, 29, 55
Washington, Booker T., 74, 102
Washington Temperance Society, 46
Wheeler, Etta Angell, 67–68
White, Caroline Earle, 44, 53, 55, 122
Willard, Frances, 30, 34–35, 51, 63, 72, 78, 157–59
Williams, S. F., 73
Wilson, Mary Ellen, 67–68, 158
Wilson, Woodrow, 18
Wimbish, Anderson H., 58
Withers, Jane, 215, 216f
Women's Branch. *see* Women's PSPCA
Woman's Christian Temperance Union (WCTU)
  activities, 56–57, 60, 70, 75–76
  animal advocacy networks, 51–52, 238n11
  antipoverty activism, 75–77
  Department of Humane Education, 80
  Department of Mercy, 22, 51–53, 56–58, 60, 67, 71, 75–78, 243n99
  Department of Penal and Reformatory Work, 71–72, 243n99
  "Do Everything" policy, 51, 52
  labor radicalism views of, 77–80, 79f
  moral suasion tactic, 52–53, 65–66
  overview, 22, 50–51
  racial segregation of, 72
  social purity activism, 60
  tactics, 52–53, 61
  white ribbon gospel, 51–52
Women's PSPCA, 55, 94–95
Wong Si Sue, 89
Worcester, Dean, 131–32
World War I, 103, 117, 209, 212, 217
World War II, 21–22, 207, 209–10, 217–18, 218f, 232n72, 285n1
Wright, Richard, 183

Young Defenders' Leagues, 64

Zamora O'Shea, Maria Elena, 204
Zoöphily, 56–57

www.ingramcontent.com/pod-product-compliance
Ingram Content Group UK Ltd.
Pitfield, Milton Keynes, MK11 3LW, UK
UKHW041307180426
11947UKWH00009B/736